*An official publication of*

**THE AMERICAN SOCIOLOGICAL ASSOCIATION**

N. J. DEMERATH III, *Executive Officer*

# SOCIOLOGICAL
# METHODOLOGY
## 1971

# Herbert L. Costner
### EDITOR

# SOCIOLOGICAL
# METHODOLOGY
## 1971

 Jossey-Bass Inc., Publishers
San Francisco · Washington · London · 1971

SOCIOLOGICAL METHODOLOGY 1971
Herbert L. Costner, *Editor*

**Library of Congress Catalogue Card Number LC 73-170211**

**International Standard Book Number ISBN 0-87589-115-2**

Manufactured in the United States of America

JACKET DESIGN BY WILLI BAUM

FIRST EDITION

*Code 7135*

# SOCIOLOGICAL
# METHODOLOGY
# 1971

EDITOR    Herbert L. Costner

ADVISORY EDITORS    Hubert M. Blalock, Jr.*

Edgar F. Borgatta***

Otis Dudley Duncan**

Herbert Hyman***

Robert McGinnis*

Peter H. Rossi**

\* Term ends with 1971 volume
\*\* Term ends with 1972 volume
\*\*\* Term ends with 1973 volume

# CONSULTANTS

# PROLOGUE

When John Stuart Mill sought a "larger logic, which embraces all the general conditions of the ascertainment of truth,"[1] he proceeded largely by systematizing the methodological strategies of his day—or at least "the best ideas which have been promulgated . . . or conformed to by accurate thinkers in their scientific inquiries." (p. 3) Methodological development still proceeds in much the same way—from practice to principle—although principles made explicit can then serve to inform practice. Methodological principles thus developed carry with them, not the imperative of logical necessity, but the very considerable weight of prior successful applications.

Detailed scrutiny of John Stuart Mill's work suggests that he was able to abstract from the practices of his day the basic ideas that still dominate methodological thinking, even though these basic ideas have

---

[1] John Stuart Mill, *An Examination of Sir William Hamilton's Philosophy.* London, 1867, p. 461. Quoted in Ernest Nagel's editorial introduction to *John Stuart Mill's Philosophy of Scientific Method.* New York: Hafner Publishing Company, 1950, pp. xxxi–ii. All subsequent quotations from Mill are from the edited and abridged text of Mill's *A System of Logic* presented in that volume and are identified simply by page number.

ix

been elaborated in ways that Mill did not foresee. Mill was evidently aware of what would currently be called the problem of internal validity, and although he formulated no general concept of that problem, it constitutes one of the principal themes of his work. Although his first and second canons seem initially to suggest otherwise, Mill presented quite sophisticated conceptions of multiple causation, and he recognized the "intermixture of effects" (pp. 238 ff) as a practical difficulty in the application of his simpler methods. In discussing his "method of concomitant variation," Mill explicitly refers to the possibility of a spurious correlation in terms that sound quite current; that is, concomitant variation "may and indeed must happen supposing [the two phenomena] to be two different effects of a common cause." (p. 227) Although Mill had no conception of the statistical control of extraneous variables, his "method of residues" (pp. 221 ff) quite clearly suggests it, and his assertion that "the effect produced, in social phenomena, by any complex set of circumstances amounts precisely to the sum of the effects of the circumstances taken singly" (p. 332) comes very close to being a verbal statement of a multiple-regression equation. In his programmatic plan for social science (which, Mill remarked, "by a convenient barbarism, has been termed sociology" p. 332), he suggested the necessity for building what would currently be called models of complex social phenomena and their "verification"; that is, "The ground of confidence . . . is not the a priori reasoning itself but the accordance between its results and those of observation a posteriori." (p. 333)

But if the roots of much of contemporary sociological methodology can be found in Mill's *System of Logic* (first published in 1843), the implication is not that research methodology has been at a standstill for more than a century. On the contrary, although Mill was able to formulate a seminal set of problems and sketch the outlines of potential solutions, the detailed solutions are not to be found in Mill, and the past century has witnessed rather remarkable developments in the direction of technical solutions to the problems that he sketched. But, the major thrust of methodological effort in sociology has remained concentrated on Mill's basic concern, that is, how to draw valid conclusions from data, while the problem of how to produce the data to be thus utilized has remained a neglected stepchild in sociological methodology. This is not to disparage efforts to improve the quality of sociological data, but simply to note that the problem of data production has always been less systematically treated than has the problem of drawing conclusions from data. The great diversity in the kinds of information that can be considered sociologically relevant, the absence of institutional mechanisms for producing sociologically useful records (with notable exceptions in

economic and demographic data), and the apparent difficulty of formulating many data-production problems in general logical or mathematical
terms have undoubtedly hampered the development of a sophisticated
methodology of data production in sociology. However, the development
of a systematic methodology of data production seems also to have been
retarded by the absence of any effort of the kind and scope undertaken
by John Stuart Mill in regard to drawing conclusions from data; that is,
no one has yet done the work of systematizing "the best ideas which have
been promulgated . . . or conformed to by accurate thinkers in their
scientific inquiries" with particular reference to the production of sociological data. Although we know something of observer bias, Hawthorne
effects, measurement and classification errors, although we have some
rather highly developed models for scaling and sampling, and although
we have a considerable body of accumulated wisdom in regard to observation, interviewing, and questionnaire construction, our methodological
knowledge in regard to data production remains to be systematized.
Such a systematization would, we may presume, provide a major impetus
toward improving the quality of social data in much the same way that
Mill's early effort provided the foundation for subsequent developments
in the methodology of drawing conclusions from data.

   This volume, the third in a continuing series sponsored by the
American Sociological Association, includes chapters that are so contemporary that much of their content will be new and informative even
to newly minted Ph.D.'s. But the general methodological questions that
motivate these chapters spring from the continuing methodological tradition that John Stuart Mill sought to systematize. The questions are,
fortunately, no longer phrased in the same way that Mill and his con-
temporaries posed them; the questions have been sharpened and shaped
by a growing body of experience in social research.

   In describing his general strategy for social science, Mill was not
optimistic about the potential for developing this science by "simple
observation" (p. 320) alone, but observation was of such paramount importance to Mill's conception of knowledge that his discussion never
wanders far away from it. Sociology has come to be heavily dependent for
its systematic data on what people report about themselves and the
events in which they participate—second hand observations. This dependence is so commonly assumed that a false dilemma is sometimes posed
between survey and demographtic data on the one hand and unsystematic, impressionistic first-hand observation on the other. In his chapter
"On Systematic Observation of Natural Social Phenomena," Albert J.
Reiss, Jr. effectively argues that this is, indeed, a false dilemma. Although systematic observation evidently requires more detailed planning

than the more casual kinds of observation that have, in the past, provided more insights than systematic data, and although organizing a systematic observation effort entails some kinds of problems not ordinarily encountered in the more familiar survey operation, the systematic observation of natural social phenomena is, as Professor Reiss points out, a feasible way of generating sociological data not available by other means with comparable accuracy.

Much current sociological thinking is based, implicitly or explicitly, on presumptions about the perceptual distinctions that people can and do make in the social world around them—distinctions between political candidates, between social class or ethnic groupings, between ideologies, and so on. Although we sometimes assume that the distinctions made by sociologists are mirrored in the distinctions made by the people that sociologists study, this is probably a gross oversimplification. Darrell K. Adams and Z. J. Ulehla, in their chapter on "Detection Theory and Problems of Psychosocial Discrimination," discuss procedures for producing data on the "discriminability" between social stimuli. If different societal groupings show different degrees of ability to discriminate between alternatives of sociological interest, such data may provide clues to differential learning experiences and biases, and to different bases for social action.

Observation for scientific purposes clearly requires discriminability and the classification of that which is observed into the categories to be utilized in the analysis. Mill wrote at some length on the subtle philosophical and psychological problems entailed in devising classifications for scientific purposes (pp. 35 ff), but he seems to have been unconcerned with the problems of placing observations into the classes thus devised, or what is commonly called coding in survey research. Mill's assumption that coding is unproblematic is, of course, contrary to the experience of contemporary social investigators. In their chapter on "Coding the Responses to Open-ended Questions," Kenneth C. W. Kammeyer and Julius A. Roth focus, not on the usual problem of intercoder reliability, but on the question of agreement between the respondent as coder of his own responses and the coding provided by another. Their findings suggest that codings by an objective coder may differ in persistent ways from the codings by the respondent as coder, suggesting subtle problems in coding not yet completely illuminated by empirical inquiry. While it may be naive to assume that the respondent himself will provide the most valid coding of his own responses, it is nonetheless troublesome to find that the respondent perceives his own responses in a different way than others do.

Coding problems are, in slightly different guise, measurement problems, and just as Mill considered coding unproblematic, he also disregarded problems of measurement error. Sociologists have traditionally been almost as unconcerned as Mill. Even though we have long been aware of measurement and classification errors in sociological data, this awareness has rarely manifest itself in any very thorough examination of the impact of such errors on the outcomes of data analysis. Largely through the efforts of people working in other disciplines, there is now a rather well-developed body of literature on measurement error, and this literature has achieved a high level of mathematical sophistication. Robert M. Hauser and Arthur S. Goldberger, writing on "The Treatment of Unobservable Variables in Path Analysis," take sociologists (including the editor of the present volume) to task for failing to avail themselves of these developments. Hauser and Goldberger seek to bring to the attention of sociologists a set of procedures for incorporating into their data analyses assumptions about measurement error, or more generally, about unobservable variables about which inferences are made only by using measured surrogates.

Measurement error is also one of the major foci in the chapter "On Robustness in Regression Analysis," by George W. Bohrnstedt and T. Michael Carter. Their chapter explores circumstances that may distort estimates of regression parameters, and they conclude that random measurement error may produce serious distortions. They also note that specification errors may systematically distort the estimates of regression parameters, which is another way of saying that the parameter estimates may be misleading if the substantive assumptions about causal structure are incorrect. The utility of regression analysis (and of its close relative, path analysis) is thus conditioned by the adequacy of the substantive knowledge base that serves as its foundation.

Measurement in sociology is sometimes crude, and crude data may mean not only a high degree of random measurement error and the use of surrogate measures imperfectly correlated with the dimensions of theoretical interest but a number of other things as well, including coarse grouping and even coarse grouping into intervals of unknown and possibly unequal width. In early work with correlation analysis, the consequences of coarse grouping came to be recognized, and techniques for correcting regression and correlation coefficients for coarse grouping were developed. But data in coarse and unequal intervals (that is, the usual kind of "ordinal" data in sociology) present special problems, and simple corrections are not feasible without introducing a priori assumptions about interval width. Among the interesting attempts to deal with ordinal data that have been explored in recent years, the procedure of devising effect-proportional rescalings through the use of dummy variable analysis seems to be of special interest because it accords well with current interest in regression and path analysis. In his chapter on

"Techniques for Using Ordinal Measures in Regression and Path Analysis," Morgan Lyons examines this procedure in some detail.

Since John Stuart Mill was suspicious of both a priori reasoning and empirical generalization, he suggested the necessity of working with both: "The conclusions of theory cannot be trusted unless confirmed by observation; nor those of observation unless they can be affiliated to theory by deducing them from the laws of human nature and from a close analysis of the circumstances of the particular situation." (p. 324) For Mill, general and abstract theories were a necessity in social science, and he therefore proposed, as the most promising way of developing social-science knowledge, the "inverse deductive method" (pp. 342 ff), by which he seems to have meant something very similar to what is currently called retroduction, that is, one devises a general theory to fit the specific facts in hand but from which other facts not yet observed may also be deduced. But such an indirect (or inverse) strategy for arriving at basic principles requires special care in specifying what constitutes a fit between theory and fact, that is, in how the conclusions "of observation . . . can be affiliated to theory by deducing them." Formal and mathematical theories would seem to offer some clear advantages in this respect. As Kenneth C. Land notes in the opening paragraph of his chapter on "Formal Theory in Sociology: A Survey of the Methodology of Mathematical Sociology," formalized sociological theories are a relatively recent development, and the paraphernalia of formal theory construction may be less than clear to many sociologists. Land has attempted in this chapter to clarify the interplay of formal theorizing with traditional theorizing and data collection.

As attempts are made to incorporate subtle and complex reasoning about social events into formalized theories, it becomes evident that drawing even seemingly simple implications about matters of fact from such theories is not readily accomplished by simple logic. Special problems arise, for example, in formulations that entail causal loops instead of the simpler step-by-step series of effects that is commonly assumed in path analysis. Phillip Bonacich and Kenneth Bailey have addressed a special class of such problems in their chapter on "Key Variables: When Static Theories Fail." In this chapter the authors explore the difficulties in drawing ostensibly simple implications when system effects may counteract the apparent implications of ostensibly simple postulates.

Although causal models provide a useful format for theory construction, other types of formal models have also proved useful in sociology. Among these are a number of social-process models developed by James Coleman. In his chapter entitled "Coleman's Process Approach: An Expository Analysis," Martin Jaeckel has explored these models and presented an assessment of their nature, relevance, and scope. Jaeckel's characterization of these models as synthesizing, that is, as consisting of "the exploration of what selected assumptions . . . together imply" is reminiscent of Mill's discussion of "compounding several tendencies together and computing the aggregate result of many coexistent causes" (p. 333). Mill, with his incomplete conception of how to represent his "coexistent causes" in mathematical form, was somewhat perplexed by the difficulties entailed in such an attempt: ". . . we attempt a task to proceed far in which surpasses the compass of the human faculties." (p. 333) Jaeckel's discussion suggests that "the compass of the human faculties" has been much extended by models of the kind developed by Coleman.

But if Mill was inclined to emphasize the necessity for some rather complex theories in social science, he was no less emphatic about the necessity for examining the empirical adequacy of those theories: "To prove, in short, that our science and our knowledge of the particular case render us competent to predict the future, we must show that they would have enabled us to predict the present and the past." (p. 341) Fully aware of the intermixture of effects and the complications thus introduced (but apparently insensitive to measurement and classification errors and the inaccuracies in prediction that they imply), Mill was concerned about prediction errors—"a residual phenomenon, requiring further study . . ." (p. 341). A similar concern (not always coupled, unfortunately, with the admonition that it requires further study) is manifest in current statistical thinking in the form of measures of the relative improvement in predictive accuracy made possible by the association between variables. Robert K. Leik and Walter R. Gove, in their chapter on "An Integrated Approach to Measuring Association," discuss various measures of improvement in predictive accuracy and a general logic of which each such measure is a special case. Utilizing a general perspective based on a comparison of pairs of cases, Leik and Gove show that the usual measures of association have the same basic form.

Attempts to predict social phenomena are the subject of Karl Schuessler's chapter on "Continuities in Social Prediction." After examining several examples of social prediction, Schuessler notes that efforts at social prediction have been "somewhat episodic and at times no more than faddish," apparently because of the uncertainty among sociologists about their goals and priorities. Mill, in contrast, seemed to have his goals and priorities well formulated:

> "It is no disparagement, therefore, to the science of human nature that those of its general propositions which descend sufficiently into detail to serve as a foundation for predicting

phenomena in the concrete are for the most part only approximately true. But in order to give a genuinely scientific character to the study, it is indispensable that these approximate generalizations, which in themselves would amount only to the lowest kind of empirical laws, should be connected deductively with the laws of nature from which they result, should be resolved into the properties of the causes on which the phenomena depend." (p. 313)

As Schuessler suggests in his comments on modelling, certain prediction attempts in sociology do incorporate theoretical reasoning, and he suggests further that if such attempts reach "their goal of specifying and identifying all of the factors producing a given effect," then the attainment of predictive knowledge may be facilitated.

The chapters so briefly mentioned in the comments above cover a broad range of methodological thinking in current sociology, but not the whole range. In a single volume it is not possible to cover in any detail the range of methodological strategies and procedures employed by sociologists in their research. The present volume can, at best, serve only to provide a sampling of recent developments and thinking about sociological methodology, and we leave to subsequent volumes the task of extending the scope and representativeness of the sample.

Discussions of research methodology, with attention to hazards and possible pitfalls, seem to stimulate in some readers a kind of defeatism that paralyzes research through the fear of doing something wrong. For others, discussions of research methodology, especially of relatively new methodological developments, seem to excite a kind of euphoric dream of dramatic breakthroughs that is poor preparation for the frequent disappointments that real research entails. The chapters in this volume will undoubtedly be misread if viewed in either of these ways. They will serve their purpose adequately if viewed simply as sketching possible, but imperfect, ways of approaching and resolving research problems that will probably be either discarded or improved after continued use. This, I believe, is the spirit in which John Stuart Mill viewed methodology, and in that, we would do well to emulate him.

*Seattle*                                                    HERBERT L. COSTNER
*September 1971*

# CONTENTS

# SOCIOLOGICAL
# METHODOLOGY
## 1971

PART ONE

STRATEGIES OF
DATA PRODUCTION

# ❦ 1 ❦

# SYSTEMATIC OBSERVATION OF
# NATURAL SOCIAL PHENOMENA

*Albert J. Reiss, Jr.*

YALE UNIVERSITY

Much argument about the merits of various methods and techniques of social investigation is based on misconceptions of how data are gathered and analyzed. At the core of most of the argument is a faulty definition of observation. Observation is fundamental to all forms of data collection. The forms differ primarily in how techniques of investigation are organized, how observations are made and recorded, and in their own validity and reliability (Reiss, 1968a).

The object of much observation in social science is to capture events for later measurement and analysis. Some data are gathered by having the subject make observations about himself or others. This is commonly the case with interviews and standardized tests. Most records of organizations are evidence of observations. Oral interviews quickly become records, and it is these records that are observed and analyzed by the investigator and his staff. Unfortunately, precise measurement by *direct* observation and recording of events as they occur is seldom done by sociologists. Systematic social observation of natural social phenomena is one procedure for doing so.

In writing about what I have come to regard as systematic social observation, I risk contributing to further misunderstanding about methods and techniques of social investigation since the terms may suggest more, and less, than is intended. By systematic observation, I mean only that observation and recording are done according to explicit procedures which permit replication and that rules are followed which permit the use of the logic of scientific inference. The means of observation and recording, whether a person or some form of technology, must be independent of that which is observed and the effects of observing and measuring must be measurable. By natural social phenomena, I mean that events and their consequences, including properties of organization, can be observed more or less as they occur.

Any data gathering procedure organizes a number of techniques that are used in other procedures as well. Sampling, for example, can be used to select events for observation, and subjects in an experiment can be interviewed. For that reason, systematic social observation shares many technical problems with other procedures of social investigation (Reiss, 1968a). The main procedures incorporated into a systematic social observation actually are homologous to those of survey research. They include selection of problems for investigation, preliminary investigation by direct observation (optional), definition of the universe to be observed, sampling for observation, development of instruments to collect and to record observations systematically, provision for measuring error, pretesting instruments, organization for direct field observations, processing observations, and quantitative analysis.

Given what is already known about the techniques usually organized into systematic social observation, what follows focuses primarily on three matters: the organized procedure of systematic observation of natural social phenomena, special features of that organization, and special problems that arise when some common techniques of investigation are employed in systematic social observation. Some attention is also given to the effects of systematization on direct observation in field settings.

Although my discussion is restricted to field phenomena, much of it applies to systematic observation in laboratory experiments with human subjects. Whether or not an investigator intervenes in social processes is less material than whether or not the effects of any intervention (including effects of observation) can be measured. Measurement of these effects may be easier for experiments than for participant observations in the field, but, as I shall try to show, some effects of participation and observation can also be measured.

## DESIGNING THE STUDY

### Selecting a Problem

Many field studies have no clearly formulated problem for investigation at the outset. They frequently lack precise specification of what shall be observed and recorded (and what ignored). This is particularly true for investigations where the observer is also a participant. Such studies commonly assume that something new or unusual will be discovered with participation in social life. Less value is attached to the precision with which it is known.

As partisans of survey research have been quick to point out, many surveys have discovered new knowledge, overturning both common belief and observation (Lazarsfeld, 1949, p. 379). Contending claims about the role of methods in discovery fail to make clear what is meant by discovery. Observation of and in itself does not lead to discovery, as many participant observation studies in sociology bear eloquent testimony. Moreover, all men by nature and socialization not only observe but also treat many observations as requiring explanation. What is necessary to discovery is that what is observed be problematic in some important sense, thus requiring a theory or explanation.

Indeed, making an observation problematic often does not explain it, as studies of reports of unidentified flying objects make abundantly clear (Condon, 1969; Vallee, 1965). The study by Bernard Barber and Renee Fox of two scientists who separately observed that papain injected into rabbits results in their ears flopping is another case in point (Barber and Fox, 1958). Initial attempts by both scientists at scientific explanation proved unprofitable. A successful explanation of the effects of papain on ear cartilage came by chance when the experiment was used as a classroom demonstration, not from any attempt at systematic observation and experimentation. But science patently rests on systematic endeavor as well as chance. All investigators observe in anticipation of discovery. The precise manipulation of variables in a controlled experiment or by statistical methods, the inclusion of open-ended questions in questionnaires, and systematic observation are also ways of discovery.

Elsewhere I have pointed out that something more seems to underlie the contention that participation and observation in natural settings is a superior technique of discovery (Reiss, 1968a, pp. 352–353).

Whatever the arguments may be, and there are many, the case rests on the assumed importance of direct observation through participation. The systematization of such observation and the precision with which observation is made need not be at issue. Claims to the superiority of direct observation as a mode of discovery should not be confused with the precision of observation.

Some kinds of problems or explanations apparently require systematic social observation. One of the continuing arguments in sociology is about the relationship between words and deeds or between attitudes and behavior (Deutscher, 1966). If one is interested in the relationship between prejudice and discrimination, for example, one must not only systematically investigate prejudice but also systematically observe behavior in situations.

Systematic observation also can be used to evaluate any other technique of social observation or social reporting about social life. The Langs' study of bias and selection in television coverage of the MacArthur Day parade in Chicago is a case in point (Lang and Lang, 1953). The reliability of official statistical systems can be assessed not only by sample surveys but also by systematic social observation.

More important, perhaps, many aspects of social life can be measured only through systematic social observation. This is true of much of the ebb and flow of life in time and space. To be sure, not all such observation must be done by participant observers or by mere presence. Many organizations are programmed to systematically record observations of events, whether they be transactions, such as sales or bank deposits, or events, such as trial proceedings. One can argue that in the long run the success of social investigation depends upon convincing organizations to systematically observe and record events. Most of modern economics rests on that foundation (Johnson, 1968, pp. 76–77).

In any case, there is no inherent contradiction between what is often called exploratory research and systematic-observation research. A period of exploratory research prior to systematic social observation in the field often is necessary for one or more reasons. Some of the common ones are these. Exploratory observations often turn up important explanatory variables that can be systematically investigated. Experience in direct observation is helpful in learning what can be observed and what empirical distinctions can be made through observation. For example, in our studies of the police we found that tape recorders could not be utilized to record information in the field, that we could not distinguish reliably between a search of the person and a frisk, and that it was difficult to record all of the sequential changes in the behavior of officers and citizens. The latter observation led us to select certain common points in *all* transactions for observation and recording so that we could make comparisons systematically (Reiss, 1967). Finally, exploratory observation teaches us much about how to organize the observation process and train observers for large-scale collection of data.

## Amenability of Social Phenomena to Observation

One can readily think of factors that affect the ease with which one can penetrate social life to observe it. The accessibility of social life to direct observation and recording is circumscribed by institutions and organizations. Institutions of secrecy and privacy restrict the accessibility of events to observation. The more secret or private is the behavior, the less amenable to direct observation. One should not confuse the privacy of behavior with the privacy of places, however. Some very private behavior, such as homosexual acts between consenting adults, is amenable to systematic observation when it occurs in public settings, such as a public restroom (Humphreys, 1970).

Parenthetically, we note that the invasion of privacy is no more acceptable when procedures are unsystematic. Systematic social observation often forces the investigator to confront issues of secrecy and the invasion of privacy as elements of design. In the long run, the success of sociology as an observational science depends upon our capacity to legitimate intervention and observation.

The frequency and predictability of the occurrence of events affects how systematically one can sample and observe them. Nonetheless, rare events and those that are not predictable may be effectively studied by systematic observation. So far as we know, acts of police brutality, for example, are infrequent events for most police officers and their occurrence in time and space cannot be forecast for individual officers. Therefore, it is difficult for a solo participant observer to gather much information on police brutality. Yet systematic observation of transactions between police and citizens by 36 observers assigned daily to eight-hour tours of duty resulted in the observation of 37 encounters in two months in which police used force unduly (Reiss, 1968b).

The degree to which any activity is organized affects its amenability to systematic observation. The more formally organized is the activity or process, the more open to systematic observation. The rise in popularity of participant observation can probably be accounted for by its success in investigating informal organizations. Yet, there seems no inherent reason why many aspects of informal organization cannot be systematically observed and recorded as Barker and Wright's studies of child behavior amply demonstrate (Barker and Wright, 1955; Wright, 1967).

It is no simple matter to conclude that an event is not amenable
to systematic observation, provided it is not demonstrably "nonobserv-
able." One can easily become convinced that a theoretically observable
event is not amenable because the design precludes observation. No-
where is this more apparent than when questions are raised about past
behavior in relation to present behavior. Clearly one cannot observe the
past.

Yet, it is by no means clear why many investigators continue to
rely upon recall of past behavior when so often a comparison of observed behavior with recall of it demonstrates such high unreliability.
This has often been demonstrated in the field of child development where
as early as the thirties such evidence of its unreliability was available.
Marjorie Pyles and her coworkers, for example, in an early report of the
Berkeley longitudinal study of child development found that by the
time an infant was 21 months of age, the mother's reports of pregnancy
and delivery were so unreliable they had to be disregarded (Pyles, Stolz,
and MacFarlane, 1935). The reports by Marian Yarrow (Yarrow, 1963;
Yarrow, Campbell, and Burton, 1964) at the National Institute of
Mental Health comparing observations of mother-child interaction with
recall of it showed a consistency as low as 50 per cent. In our attempts to
use surveys to estimate victimization from crime and mobilization of the
police, we observed police and citizen transactions and then within three
months interviewed citizens about their experience. Our studies show
that almost four in ten citizens either did not recall their transactions
with the police or reported the event that gave rise to it but denied having had any contact with the police.

The recall of events recorded by official systems of observing and
recording also often show high unreliability. There is considerable under-
reporting of hospitalization and visits to doctors, for example, in the
National Health Survey. One study of visits to doctors during a two-
week period prior to the week of reporting showed that 30 per cent of the
known visits to doctors were not reported to survey interviewers; 23 per
cent remained unreported after three special probe questions were asked
(Cannell and Fowler, 1963, p. 8).

It would be a mistake to conclude that many such studies amply
demonstrate the unreliability of recall of behavior and, therefore, demonstrate the superiority of observation. They do not. What they show is
that the modes of investigation we use in recall studies generally show
substantial unreliability when compared with observation of the behavior. We may find more reliable ways to investigate recall, but in doing
so, it will be necessary to observe as well to assess the reliability of the
mode of recall. The studies, however, indicate that it behooves investiga-

tors to consider whether, by avoiding observation of a kind of behavior in the present for some means of gathering data about the past, the amount of error introduced does not invalidate many of the findings.

The systematic social-observation study generally must be more restricted in the units that can be investigated in a single study as compared with the survey or field-observation study, at least as commonly practiced. The restriction is partly due to practical consideration as to what can be efficiently investigated in a single study and partly due to other factors such as the accessibility of all elements to direct observation or the necessity to complete some observations and to analyze them before others can be undertaken. These differences among types of investigations are perhaps more of degree than of kind. Often it will prove worthwhile to combine several types of data gathering, such as questionnaires and interviews, with observation.

In any case, it should be incumbent upon investigators, having defined a problem, to raise the question of whether the problem can be investigated by direct observation and, if so, in what ways. The systematic-observation design should be one of those considered where now it is ruled out.

## Sampling Elements

Most sampling principles and practices that are applicable to the design of survey samples are also applicable to sampling for systematic social observation. According to Kish (1965, p. 4) "The survey objectives should determine the sample design; but the determination is actually a two-way process, because the problems of sample design often influence and change the survey objectives." Among the major survey objectives Kish considers are the definition of the variables and statements of the methods of measurement, analysis, and desired precision.

To design a systematic observation sample the major variables and units of observation and measurement must be defined before one can choose a sampling frame. The availability of sampling frames in turn may force a reconsideration of variables and modes of measurement. The problems in selecting a sampling frame are much like those in survey research (Kish, 1965, pp. 384–438). Perfect sampling frames, where each element to be selected appears only once, are rare. In practice, therefore, one tries to remedy deficiencies in one or more frames. An example may make clear some of the problems involved in selecting a sampling frame for an observation study. In one of our observation studies we were interested in transactions between police and citizens. No single frame of such transactions existed in the police jurisdictions selected for study. Transactions were recorded separately for different divisions of the police department, and no official record was kept for many of them. At the outset we decided to limit our search for a satisfactory frame to patrol divisions where the largest volume of transactions with the public occurred. Although the police department recorded all calls for police service from citizens, it would have been impractical to sample them at the time received and to dispatch an observer to be present when the transaction took place. Moreover, that sampling frame would have excluded all transactions the police developed on their own initiative, and no sampling frame existed for them. The fact that the men working on beat patrol accounted for all of both types of transactions dictated our choice of the sampling frame. The foot and car beats in precincts were chosen as the sampling frame.

When it is difficult to locate a satisfactory sampling frame for the variables under investigation, time often is a useful sampling frame. Either socially organized units of time (work shifts, for example) or segments of the clock and calendar can constitute the sampling frame. When time is the sampling frame to observe events or behavior, it should be apparent that short segments of time, unless they occur quite frequently, are uneconomical as too many segments do not include the desired event or characteristic. Moreover, short segments of time increase the likelihood that one will begin the observation with an event in progress.

Area sampling frames, lists of events, organizations, situations, and activities are among the common sampling frames that can be used in designing samples for observation studies. Standard listing and selection procedures of survey sampling can be used to obtain desired sampling units for observation.

When events are relatively rare, it does not necessarily follow that sampling frames cannot be established. Procedures of snowball sampling where one begins with known elements often provide a way to select the units to be observed. Kish's discussion of selection techniques for rare traits in population surveys is largely applicable to studies of systematic social observation. Controlled selection, disproportionate stratified sampling, double and multiphase sampling, and batch processing are among the ways to select rare elements for observation (Kish, 1965, pp. 404–414).

One cannot always produce economical sampling designs in observation studies any more than one can do so in sample surveys. This is particularly true if the event is rare or if the event is a rare outcome from a sequence of events that must be observed. Were one interested, for example, in observing how trial proceedings result in hung juries (an outcome that is a rare event) the design would be necessarily uneconomical compared with a design to study these outcomes by survey research (Kalven and Zeisel, 1966). The observation-study design requires that one observe a large number of jury trials to obtain the rare outcome, and far more of the non-rare outcomes would be observed than would be necessary to provide an adequate number for comparison.

## DESIGNING THE INSTRUMENTS

For the most part, the instruments designed for systematic social-observation studies do not differ materially from those designed for laboratory experiments or interviewers in survey research. My own experience with various types of observation instruments has led me to conclude that the question and answer format of the typical survey interview usually brings high reliability in recording. The observer is essentially asked the questions by the instrument and records the response. The format depends in part upon whether the recording is done during the observation or at some time after it is completed. In our police observation study, where recording followed observation of the transaction, questions were asked in the past tense. The following sequence adopted from our dispatched-mobilization form in that study illustrates this format.

32.    Was a personal and/or property *search* attempted or conducted by the police? (1) yes (go to 32a); (2) no (go to 33).

32a.    What kind of search was attempted or conducted? (1) personal ("frisk") (go to 32b); (2) property (e.g., auto or house) (go to 32c); (3) both personal and property (continue with 32b *and* 32c).

32b.    If "personal":

32b-1.    Would observer say this "frisk" was necessary for the protection of the officer(s)? (1) yes; (2) no; (9) don't know.

32b-2.    Did the police ask the possible offenders permission before this "frisk" was conducted? (1) yes; (2) no; (9) don't know.

32b-3.    Did the possible offender(s) *object* to being "frisked"? (1) yes (go to 32b-3a); (2) no (go to 32b-4).

    32b-3a.    What was said by each of the offender(s)?

    32b-3b.    What was said by each of the officers?

    32b-3c.    Was the "frisk" conducted after objection? (1) yes; (2) no.

32b-4.    Was a weapon or other possible evidence found? (Check all that apply.) (1) gun; (2) knife; (3) other weapon (Specify); (4) narcotics evidence (Specify); (5) stolen property (Specify); (6) other evidence (Specify); (7) none found; (9) don't know.

32c.    If property:

32c-1.  Was this search attempted or made prior to an arrest? (1) yes; (2) no; (9) don't know.

32c-2.  How did the police attempt or manage to gain entrance? (1) simply entered without asking permission; (2) asked and were granted permission; (3) asked permission and were refused, did not enter; (4) asked permission and were refused, entered anyway; (5) gained entrance with search warrant; (6) other (Specify); (9) don't know.

32c-3.  Were there any objections to the attempt to gain entry? (1) yes; (2) no; (9) don't know.

      32c-3a.  What was said by the parties objecting? (Specify for each party.)

      32c-3b.  What was said by each officer?

32c-4.  Were there any objections to the search? (1) yes; (2) no; (9) don't know.

32c-5.  Was a weapon or other possible evidence found? (1) gun; (2) knife; (3) other weapon (Specify); (4) narcotics evidence (Specify); (5) stolen property (Specify); (6) other evidence (Specify); (7) none found; (9) don't know.

32c-6.  Was a property search of a *vehicle* attempted or conducted? (1) yes (go to 32c-6a; (2) no; (9) don't know.

      32c-6a.  Was the vehicle search attempted or conducted at or near the scene of a possible crime? (1) yes; (2) no; (9) don't know.

            32c-6a1.  Where was it conducted? (1) street or alley away from traffic or public view; (2) moved to parking area or yard away from public view; (3) moved to police station; (4) other moved (Specify).

      32c-6b.  Did the police look closely at the vehicle's interior without actually reaching or climbing into it? (1) yes; (2) no; (9) don't know.

      32c-6c.  Did the police enter the vehicle and search it at any time? (1) yes; (2) no; (9) don't know.

      32c-6d.  Was any weapon or other possible evidence found in the search? (1) gun; (2) knife; (3) other weapon (Specify); (4) narcotics evidence (Specify); (5) stolen property (Specify); (6) other evidence (Specify); (7) none found; (9) don't know.

When relations or transactions among persons are to be recorded, there are simple ways of doing so provided that observers are trained in systems of codification. Bales' work on recording characteristics of inter-action (Bales; 1950) and Wright's observation forms for recording the behavior of children in field settings (Wright; 1967) provide useful models. A simple two-dimensional block design where blocks represent a space for coding relationships among persons or events often is useful.

Generally, observational instruments should be structured to record sequences of events and behavior as they occur during the time interval of observation, whether or not the observations are recorded immediately. Memory is facilitated by recalling sequences. Recording may also be facilitated by developing a number of different observational instruments, each adapted to a particular set or order of events. In our studies of the police we found it necessary to employ five different ob-servational and reporting forms. Four of these were quite similar, but each was adapted to the episode or stimulus that produced the encounter being observed. We had separate instruments for recording encounters to which the officer was dispatched, those arising from his own initiative, those initiated by citizens in field settings, and those that arose within the precinct station. A separate instrument was completed for each en-counter, with 5,360 encounters recorded. In addition, we had a general observational form that recorded information on the behavior of officers apart from transactions, their verbal behavior on various subjects during the tour of duty, and self-observations of the observer. In a current study of the discretion of public prosecutors with respect to criminal charges, recording was facilitated by developing separate forms for the warrant recommendation and the pretrial recommendation of the prosecutor, though in many ways the two forms are identical.

Nothing in the systematic-observation study precludes the inclu-sion of verbal description in response to open-ended questions. What applies to the use of verbal description in interviews or survey question-naires applies *mutatis mutandis* to observational instruments. Rossi's observations (1955; p. 127) about reasons analysis apply as well to al-most all open-ended questions and observational descriptions. Unless one establishes an a priori frame of reference outlining the kinds of data necessary to analysis and unless the categories are established in ad-vance, barring the inconceivable total description by recording, one will miss essential classifications. When one uses such open-ended or descrip-tive recordings, they should be restricted to special ends of the investiga-tion. We have used description as a means of determining the reliability of observer categorization of some events. For example, in our police-observation studies we had observers write out a description of the matter brought to the attention of the police by the complainant as a means of checking the observers' coding of it. We also sought descrip-tion when our interest lay in categorizing stereotypes. We asked for police stereotypes of race, social class, categories of offenders, and others with whom they engaged in transactions. To be sure, many times we may lack information to provide mutually exclusive-exhaustive code categories in advance of observation, but a partial list with provision for recording other observations seems preferable to leaving it entirely to the observer to record as he sees fit.

## Recording

Systematic social-observation studies place heavy reliance upon paper and pencil forms for recording observations. Observers are trained to record observations in code categories of the observational instruments while in the field setting. The reliability of observation can then be assessed only by using more than one observer for the same events. The study design should plan for testing reliability of observation in this way.

Surprisingly little use is made of technological aids to observation and recording, such as film and sound tape, despite great gains in reliability. Although there are normative, technological, and situational limitations on their use in many situations, failure to use them often lies in lack of consideration rather than in such limitations. One need only reflect on how well television crews record events that can readily be coded by social scientists to recognize the potential of technological aids for systematic observation.

The reader may test some of the problems that arise in the use of still and motion-picture photography by examining the highly interesting, if not always definitive, set of pictures assembled by the President's Commission on Campus Unrest to depict violence at Kent State University (1970; pp. 291–410). The absence of any study design, the sheer unpredictability of events, and the dangers inherent in the situation once violence erupted limited data collection and analyses. Yet, the Commission was able to assemble 58 photographs depicting the main sequence of events and cast of characters in the situations by utilizing the work of at least 15 different photographers who were in one observational role or another. Despite obvious difficulties in the use of the photographs, investigators were able to document more reliably the roles and events than was possible from separate observer accounts.

To record variables in events, special consideration must be given to the position observers can occupy in situations. Such matters as the freedom of the observer to move about and the effects of a fixed observational position must be considered. When observers must assume fixed positions in a situation, it often will be necessary to place several observers at different points if one is to record what is of interest. It also may be necessary to program a division of labor among observers, each being given a special recording task, particularly when the tasks are complex.

Whether or not the recording takes place at the time of observation or afterward depends in large part on the social acceptability of recording within a situation and on the effects that situational recording has on what is observed. When in doubt as to whether recording should be done at the time of observation, it may be necessary to pretest various modes of recording to determine not only their feasibility but their reliability. Despite some experience and advice that one should not record in the presence of the police, in our police-observation studies pretesting disclosed that observers could keep an incident log during the period of observation. The log recorded the major events, their time and duration of occurrence, and a description of the salient features and participants in them. It was possible to do so because not uncommonly officers perform similar tasks in the field.

One should bear in mind that the observer must always legitimate his position as observer in situations. One form of legitimation is to provide visible evidence that one is working. Our incident log was such evidence. By telling officers that such a record was being made and showing them, if necessary, what was being done, observers could legitimate their presence by stating that this was *their job*. A do-nothing observer role can be as unsettling as a limited recording role in many situations that are seemingly inimical to recording at the time of the observation. Similarly, Buckner found that his fellow officers were suspicious of his note-taking even though he was a fellow reserve officer and the department legitimated note-taking by officers as a part of their job. By showing officers what he was recording, he was able to allay their suspicion (Buckner, 1967, pp. 477–478). Needless to say, there are great gains in reliability when some recording can be done in situations. To cite but one example, the sequence and duration of events have a high reliability in our police-observation study, because they were recorded at the time of occurrence.

The usual issues of protecting the rights and integrity of individuals in investigations are posed in recording observations in systematic social-observation studies. The problems are especially acute when what is observed and recorded is potentially damaging to individuals or organizations. Decisions must be made as to whether or not guarantees protecting anonymity will be given. The systematic social-observation investigation poses special problems of implementing such guarantees as compared with solo observation.

Guarantees of anonymity and protection of rights depend upon organizational and legal means to implement them. It is difficult to implement such guarantees within a research organization. How does one insure that each observer will respect the rights of others? When the legality of behavior is at issue, how does one deal with subpoenas to secure information from observer employees? May one ethically bind observers to the guarantees given an organization or individuals when one lacks the legitimacy of legal institutions to withhold information?

Such questions are not easily answered. My own experience in observation studies convinces me that one should not extend such guarantees where the legality of behavior is at issue. The main reasons for this are twofold. One cannot be certain that one's observers will fulfill the guarantees given, and lacking the professional privilege of confidentiality of information, one cannot protect one's employees against legal sanctions.

This is not to say that one must simply inform organizations that no such guarantees can be given. Several alternatives are available to the principal investigator. For example, he can inform the organization or individuals of the steps he has taken to insure that rights are protected, making explicit that no such guarantees are given where legality is at issue. Moreover, the risk can, and perhaps should, be shared with organizations when they are studied. I have shared with the chief prosecutor the right to screen and reject all observers in my current observational studies of prosecutorial discretion, recognizing that rejection of observers poses problems for the design.

### Sponsorship and License

Much systematic social observation occurs in essentially public contexts where license to observe is not required. Much will not, however. Just as in the typical survey, it is necessary to design and standardize the way that observers enter and participate in situations, particularly where there is feedback within the system about the behavior of different observers.

When working with organizations that grant and may withdraw the license to observe, one must reach agreement on such matters as the roles of participant observers, the treatment of privileged information, and feedback within and outside the organization. We have found it useful, following verbal agreement on such matters, to exchange letters of agreement. It is important also to provide clear lines for authoritatively handling any matters of disagreement or dissatisfaction. This necessitates reaching agreement on how matters are to be channeled within the organization studied and on how the organizations are to proceed with any grievances or problems that arise concerning the observers. The lines of authority should be clear on both sides. Any complex participant-observation study will create many problems in the field setting that cannot and should not be decided by individual observers. The observers must regard their role, and their roles must be regarded, as employees who have access to channels for handling field problems, a matter we shall consider later in the organization of the observational team.

## Determining Roles

The discussion of observer roles in social observation is obscured by distinguishing between participant-observer and the nonparticipant-observer roles in observation. I suspect that the way participant and observer are defined in these distinctions cloaks the major issues. Elsewhere I have pointed out that the question of who does the observation and how it is done are important primarily in terms of the effect on what is measured (Reiss, 1968a; pp. 359–360). One may also be concerned with the effect on maintaining relations with the system observed or on attempts to change it. Similarly, the issues in participation are matters of the effect participation has on what is observed and on the observer, who in turn affects the observations.

The major concern then in designing the roles that observers are to take in systematic observation is resolved if one can define the variables under investigation and devise ways to measure the effects of participation and observation on them. It should be evident that in measuring such effects we are concerned with the measurable effect on the data to be *analyzed*. Interviewer-effect studies have shown that the effects generally are joint ones of variables characterizing interviewers and respondents with the variables investigated. There can be no laws of interviewer effect without taking into account characteristics of the respondent and information requested. The same should apply, if we make the necessary changes, to observer and participant effects in systematic social observation.

It should be evident that the systematic social-observation study, using multiple observers, possesses a power to measure such effects not available in the solo-observation study precisely because one can measure whether or not there is covariation between observer characteristics and what is observed. Indeed, one can design the study to vary characteristics among the observers and measure the effect on the quantity and quality of observations. In our police-observation studies we selected three major types of observers, for example, 12 with law training, 12 with police training, and 12 with social-science training. We did so for two reasons. Since the study included variables where the expertise of each of these groups might have a measurable effect on what was observed, we wished to be able to assess such effects. Would observers with training in the law, for example, classify fewer arrests as bona fide than those with a police background? They didn't. Or, would observers trained in social science more frequently assess the social class of participants in police and citizen encounters than did those with a police background? They did.[1] We also recognized that our capacity to measure the effects of differences according to the background of observers had other potential effects for our study. It would help to legitimate the study while the observation was taking place and to legitimate the "facts" when the study was completed. The solo-participant observer is at a disadvantage in these respects.

The problem of socialization of observers in observational settings is common to all social observation, solo or systematic. While the problem is commonly stated as one of oversocialization, it is apparent that observers may shift in any direction, if direction is measurable. Systematic social-observation studies can make some provision for quantitatively measuring the effects of socialization. By testing observers prior to their entry into the observational setting and by testing for effects on observation, one can make some assessment of effect (Lang and Lang, 1953, p. 4).

Testing our observers before, during, and after their work in the police-observation study, we found a substantial shift toward the pro-police end of a scale by the conclusion of the study (Reiss, 1968; pp. 364–66). The shift was related to the background of the observer. Law-trained observers shifted from a mild antiofficer position (those with strong antipositions were excluded by design) to a pro-officer, antisystem position. Perhaps the written word of one law-trained observer may convey this more eloquently to the reader used to language rather than statistical expression. The exit report of one such observer contains the following passage:

> I have been asked a lot what I thought of the police in Boston. Before I answer that question I always have to be careful to distinguish between my estimate of the job that these men are doing and my feeling of friendship for many of the men. All in all, the police in Roxbury were very good to us. They were extraordinarily candid in many situations, and they trusted us with information that could have ruined these men on the

[1] Parenthetically, one might note that this finding suggests something about the sensitivity of persons with police training to the social-class origins of citizens in encounters and the relevance it may have for their dealing with them. The police might even behave more universalistically toward citizens in this respect than would sociologists!

force. They were not brutal, antagonistic men. They were not looking for trouble. For the most part they were men with very middle-class values. They had families, which occupied their conversation far more than any other subject, and cars and houses. Most were seriously religious and extremely publicly patriotic. They accepted me as one of them, and they talked to me in their language about their things. After watching these men for almost 6 weeks, I cannot be convinced that they are not good men. I was constantly amazed that people who had worked in Roxbury as long as some of these men could be still so sensitive toward the problems of other human beings with a skin colored differently than their own. Their job, to quote a tired authority, is a tough one. The police in Roxbury cannot be more than a worn band-aid which is slapped over the worst of the problems that emerge in that society. There is no time to be pretty or clean or thorough or to do what the book says to do. They are dealing, first of all, with a culture for which no book on police procedure or practice has been written. If they clean up the mess a little, keep the societal ball from unraveling completely, they are doing an excellent job. They could do their job better only by being on the job more of the time, by taking the calls as they come in. But it is not surprising that the police in Roxbury are not eager to respond to the calls they get. They know that they are entering a situation where something has gone amiss, and more often than not, the problem is at least partially caused by the established system of power of which they are the most obvious, if not the most deserving, representatives. If Negroes do hate the police, and I am not sure that they do in Boston, they hate not only the immediate authority of the badge, but also that secondary more awesome authority of a government (and I include the voters here) primarily white.

Testing for the effects of socialization is important in assessing error in measurement. One's object, however, may be to control in the design and execution of a study the effects of socialization on the variables observed. Experience suggests several ways this may be done in designing the role of observers in systematic social observation and by control imposed during its execution.

The solo observer typically performs all roles in an investigation from designer of the study through data collector to analyzer. While he typically can decide all questions then as they arise, the flexibility of a division of labor is lost. In the systematic social-observation study, observers are allocated the role of data collector. We have found that the socialization of the observer in this role can be controlled to some extent by emphasizing the qualities of an employer-employee relationship. The observer is trained to perceive his role as that of an employee in an organization, and he can be taught to use that role of employee in his own socialization. We taught our observers of the police, for example, to utilize their employee relationship to handle attempts by police officers to co-opt them in situations ("If I did that, I could be fired, and I need the money"). The employee role was particularly useful in handling relations with the organization as well. Problems with the organization can be shifted to the employer who is in charge of such problems. Furthermore, by relating all employees to a field supervisor, we were able to exercise supervision over the socialization process. We provided for every other day debriefings of each observer in a conference with the supervisor. While the solo can devise ways to consult with others to accomplish some of the same ends, short of duplicity, he cannot use the employee relationship effectively.

In designing observer roles, we found it particularly important to provide ways that observers can handle their relations with others so that the relations are not only manageable but also as free as possible from manipulation that others will undertake in the situation. Often it may be necessary to have observers remind others that they are employees and that their employer will measure them in these terms. In this respect it is important to remember that the more one can demonstrate an observer output to others, the greater the advantage in using an employee role. How one's observers can show evidence of work as an employee of an organization is a question deserving careful consideration.

To be sure, natural social environments do not admit of preprogramming, and depending upon what is observed, some situations are less amenable to the application of strict rules than others. At the end of an evening tour, one of our police observers reported, for example:

> Both officers were very grateful to have this observer along in an on-view incident. A fight ensued in #3 incident where both officers lost control of the offender and this observer had to restrain him, until the officers could handle the offender. Officer #1 stated he was glad the observer was along because they really needed him. I might add that in the process of the fight either I was bitten by the offender or my hand scraped against his mouth, because I have two lovely abrasions on my hand.

Of course it is difficult to assess in this situation whether he should have followed our rule prohibiting intervention in any law-enforcement process, a rule that was imposed on all our observers. Obviously this observer did not ask himself, as we had trained him to ask: What would have happened if I were not present? It also is apparent he got "brownie points" for what he did.

This simple incident also poses interesting questions about some things one cannot measure well because of the presence of an observer. We found it impossible to adequately assess the difference between one and two officers working together because the presence of an observer made every situation either a two- or three-man situation in some respects.

## Reliability

Sociologists unfortunately make little attempt to measure the reliability of their observations, particularly errors of measurement. Yet, the conclusions reached depend upon the reliability of the observations.

Schuessler (1971; pp. 348–381) calls our attention to the fact that techniques for assessing errors of measurement are more developed than those for measuring errors of classification. Measurement errors occur whenever there is a difference between an object's true value and its measured value, a matter of magnitude; whereas classification errors occur whenever an object is misplaced in a class. In survey research and observation studies more attention has been given to errors of classification than to errors of measurement, partly owing to the lack of systematization and precision in measurement. It does not appear that systematic social observation poses any special problems in assessing errors in measurement, but problems of measuring errors in classification must be considered as a matter of design.

The recording of observation almost necessarily results in some classification of observations in the field setting, thereby raising questions of the reliability of such classification. In designing the study, we must give much attention to considering how much of the observation shall be classified in the field setting and how reliability of the observation can be assessed. Since almost by definition an event in a natural setting is not repeatable, some method of determining the reliability of classification in field settings must be built into the design. Apart from recording events both in narrative and in classes, thereby permitting one check on the reliability of classification, the major means available is to use more than one observer for the same event.

Experience shows that reliability in classification in field settings is largely a function of the precision with which classes are defined and the extent to which observers are trained in their application. Substantial increase in observer reliability for classification of objects and events in the field is often obtained by filming prototypical events and presenting them to observers in practice sessions prior to their going into the field. This also allows for the calculation of observer errors in classification.

In designing the observational instrument, we are mistaken if we assume that the observer can operate without analytically classifying objects and events in field settings, because the observer cannot record everything and, therefore, must be sensitized to record some objects or events and not others. Yet there is an enormous difference in the kind of observational instruments and recording developed by Wright (1967), where detailed description of behavior is recorded, and the kind of instruments developed by Reiss and his co-workers (1967) or by Mileski (1971a and 1971b). The difference depends upon how much of the analytical classification will be done in the field setting and whether or not one requires that evidence be recorded for the class selected. Some of our observational instruments have checked the reliability of classification by requiring the observer to record evidence for the classification. In our police-observation study, for example, we asked the observer to write out a description of the situation when the police arrived at the setting as a means of checking the reliability of their classification of that event. We did so because our code provided for 70 classes of events, a condition that could easily lead to low reliability in classification.

Errors in measurement arise in systematic social observation whenever an observer fails to record an event when it actually occurs. This kind of error can be investigated by using multiple observers in situations, but it is difficult to know whether the difference among observers is an error in classification or one of measurement. To be sure, the larger the number of observers used, the more one has presumptive evidence for errors of measurement. One way we have attempted to assess errors in nonreporting of events that occur is by examining differences among observers in their production of a particular item of information, making assumptions about the occurrence of that event over a large number of observations.

During our police-observation study, we required observers to report all instances of deviance on the part of officers. Observers were given instructions as to what constituted deviance but were required to provide a behavioral description of all events they considered falling within the deviance categories, rather than to simply code the event. Thirty-nine per cent of all tours of duty produced a report of deviance by at least one officer during the tour of duty, giving a probability, all other things being equal, that two in five tours should provide a report of deviance. There was a considerable variation among the observers, however, in reporting deviance, suggesting that our data underestimated the extent of deviance on the part of the officers. Yet, it is difficult to estimate precisely the extent, although the usual procedures of estimating such error on different assumptions can be followed. One can, for example, assume that each observer should produce evidence of deviance in at least two in five tours of duty and correct accordingly.

Unless one can provide some explanation for the variation in observer reporting of an object or event, one may have reason to doubt whether error in measurement has occurred. Examining the reporting of deviance by whether the observer came from law, police, or social-science training produced no significant difference in the report of deviance. We had thought that the degree of rapport an observer achieved with officers would affect the reporting of deviance, particularly if one assumes that officers will behave with higher conformity if observer rapport is only fair or poor. We asked the observer to rate his rapport with the officer. There was a fair amount of variation in observer self-ratings of rapport with officers; for example, four observers never rated their rapport as excellent, and 22 of the 36 never rated their rapport as poor. No relationship was found, however, between the observer's report of rapport with officers and their report of deviance, as Table 1 shows. Other variables

Table 1
Percentage of Tours with Deviance of Officers Reported by Self-Reports of
Observer Rapport with Officers

| Deviance on Tours | Rapport Rate as: | | | | |
|---|---|---|---|---|---|
|  | Excellent | Good | Fair | Poor | Total |
| Deviance reported | 30 | 48 | 18 | 4 | 100 |
| All tours | 28 | 48 | 18 | 6 | 100 |

were tested, but none systematically explained observer variation in the report of deviance. Our failure to do so can be a failure in design; yet, it does cast doubt on assumptions that we have errors in measurment because of considerable variation among the observers in the report of deviance by officers.

It behooves the investigator in systematic social-observation studies to examine carefully and, if possible, to design ways to assess the effects of observer presence and participation on the observations. Sociologists are inclined to assume that such effects exist. In our police-observation study we were well aware that the occurrence of deviance on the part of officers could readily be affected by the presence of the observer and made attempts to investigate such possible effects. Since interviewer-effect studies have shown that the race of the participants and the observers can affect response (Hyman and others, 1954; Table 31), we hypothesized that race of observer should have an effect on the behavior of observed officers and participants according to their race. Unfortunately, we were able to employ only one Negro observer for the study, and therefore, no reliable estimates could be obtained. Nonetheless, in my examination of the undue use of force by the police (Reiss, 1968b) I was confronted with the fact that the report of undue force on the part of black officers was disproportionally accounted for by the single black observer.

Just as in interviewer-effect studies it has been shown that effects depend substantially on what is being investigated, so in observation studies care should be exercised not to assume there is a uniform effect, even for a category of behavior such as deviance.

In considering the possible effects that the presence and participation of an observer may have on events as they occur, I have found it useful to develop hypotheses about possible effects on given kinds of observation. It is particularly important to bear in mind that it is sociologically naive to assume that for many events the presence or participation of the observer is more controlling than other factors in the situation. For example, in my study of undue use of force by police officers, I try to show that often the use of force by the police is situationally determined by other participants in the situation and by the officers' involvement in it, to such a degree that one must conclude the observer's presence had no effect (Reiss, 1967b). I need only remind my readers that many teachers who are rated as poor discussion leaders by their students have similar difficulties in leading a discussion when a master teacher is present. Often the only one in a situation who is convinced that he is "putting on" for others is the one who "puts on."

Indeed, our use of the interview as a major data-gathering tool may have misled us into overestimating the effect of investigators in altering behavior. It probably is the case that the maximum degree of alteration in the behavior of the observed occurs in an interview setting, since what is at stake is verbal response to verbal stimulus. Altering behavior in real-life situations where the observed is responding to others provides far less opportunity for alternation in the presence of investigators.

## Problems in Natural Settings

Legal liability attaches to organizations that permit observers to enter their domain and to organizations such as universities when they employ or sponsor observers. Almost no attention has been given to this matter despite its potential importance in any investigation or, for that matter, in the typical methods of field training.

Typically, public organizations have dealt with problems of legal liability by requiring persons who are not employees to waive their right to hold the organization liable if they observe as participants in the organization with its permission. At law such waivers by no means govern all possible liability situations. Were an observer, for example, to be injured in an accident while riding a police car driven by an officer found guilty of intoxication while operating the vehicle, the typical waiver probably would not suffice. At law a public employer generally will be held liable for injury resulting from gross negligence of an employee. For this reason, public organizations may be reluctant to allow observation where there is a risk of injury or exposure to litigation.

The principal investigator should also give close attention to what constitutes his liberty to civil suit and what protection he has from civil damages, including protection provided by his employing organization. Most public universities regard all research personnel as public employees eligible for the usual insurance provisions of public acts. Such provisions often are inadequate by other standards of compensation for injury, and the principal investigator will want to consider purchasing insurance to cover litigation and claims. At private universities it is necessary to investigate the forms of coverage provided and the nature of liability and awards. Many universities, for example, will not pay for the cost of litigation should a principal investigator be sued for damages. Historically, these matters have not been considered important, though civil suits against investigators are not unknown. The growth of training in field research, of action-research investigation, and of systematic social observation may make suits more common events.

It is advisable that a principal investigator attempt to reach agreements with observers on matters of privileged information. The problem is especially vexing since it is not clear whether one can legally bind the observer employee to maintain confidentiality of information. The problem can be a more complex one for many reasons. The observer is, after all, the principal witness to an event; and in all likelihood, in matters of controversy, it is the observer who will be subpoenaed. While the university or research organization may seek to protect the identity of its employees with respect to information, it cannot usually guarantee that protection. Moreover, what provision is made for the protection of the observer is crucial, particularly whether provision is made for legal counsel should it be required.

Observers should be advised of the potential risks and the protection provided. Parenthetically, I might add that perhaps such procedures should be followed for students who take field-research roles whether in survey research or systematic social observation in natural settings.

These concerns with risk of injury and civil suit and confidentiality of information raise policy issues for principal investigators, their sponsoring organizations, and universities. Even though one can advise students or observer employees of the risks and they agree to assume them, should one proceed on that basis? Is it not an obligation of the university or the sponsoring organization to provide protection, at least minimally, in the form of legal counsel and insurance?

## Training

How much training must be given to observers depends upon the scale of the observational organization. Madge (1939) apparently used the same observers in many of his mass-observation studies in England. Nonetheless, observers must be trained to administer a particular observational instrument, regardless of the scale of organization. It is this training that will be discussed briefly.

Where possible, part of the training should include audio-visual materials since they expose all observers to a common situation. Frequently the principal investigator will not have to prepare the audio-visual materials, since there exists a large library of films and television materials that provide natural situations that can be used in such training. Even when prototypes are not available for training, analogues may readily be found.

When both formal bureaucratic and informal rules apply in a setting, observers must not only be aware of both, but also be instructed in how they are to behave when there are conflicting expectations. Observers are particularly subject to pressures to breach the formal rules and to follow the informal rules of those observed. To conduct the observation, it may be necessary to follow many of the informal rules, but this should not be made a matter of discretion for each individual observer. The design of the study and the training, therefore, must emphasize how discretion is to be exercised. We found, for example, it useful to follow a rule that observers follow informal rules only when clearly invited to do so. Even that is not enough since one may decide that some formal rules are never to be breached for obvious reasons of risk or responsibility. In our police-observation study we had to decide for many situations whether or not the observer was to follow the informal rule, under what conditions, and we had to communicate these specific guidelines in formal training sessions. Just as police officers are trained to a manual of procedure, so it was necessary to train observers to a manual of procedure. Should observers drink on duty when it is formally prohibited by the department (except in connection with special assignments)? Should observers accept free meals? Are they permitted to participate in an arrest situation? Should they accept confiscated liquor or other material? How should they respond to an officer's invitation to line-up some "good sex"? Should they remind the officer of the formal rules to be followed in a situation? Should they file a report for the officer? Should they take up the officer's invitation to "goof-off." There must be answers to such questions, and observers must be trained in how to handle them.

I do not mean to suggest that all such questions can be anticipated in advance of field observation. This means that provision must be made for continuing education of the field staff. As situations arise and rules of behavior are developed for observers, the rules must be communicated to all workers. To maintain such continuing education requires continuing feedback from observers, reporting such problems and how they were handled without previous guidelines.

### Rapport

The problems of establishing and maintaining rapport in systematic social observation of natural phenomena are basically the same as those in solo observation. Special problems arise, however, when two or more observers are part of the same feedback system under observation. The rapport of each depends in part upon the rapport established by others.

When several observers are within the same setting, those being observed may make problematic the relations among observers. Suspicion may arise that there is a hidden agenda for the observation. This is especially true when one is observing situations where the participants are vulnerable to secret investigation. Nevertheless, when one has a hierarchical structure and observation occurs below the top, those observed can become suspicious that the observer is feeding information to his superiors. The behavior of the observers in their relations with one another can easily lead into such suspicions, particularly if their behavior suggests a close or closed group.

Such suspicions are more easily allayed if two simple rules are followed. Observers should behave toward one another as workers, and they should avoid situations where they are seen together except in the presence of persons being observed. Put another way, if observers continually mix with those being observed and systematically avoid being alone as a group in the presence of others, they are less likely to arouse suspicion. In our police study, for example, generally our observers did not arrive or leave together, nor were they permitted to congregate together unless with a group of officers.

It is not uncommon for participant observers to report they are tested by persons they observe. Such tests take many forms. Where multiple observers are involved in the same feedback system, the tests often take the form of an individual trying to learn what other observers may have reported about him or others who have been observed. Often these tests are designed to see how circumspect the observer is in giving out information and to learn what evaluation is placed on information. Since we could not easily know what assessment was made of such reports by observers, we followed the rules that information flow should be limited to indications of satisfaction with ones work and ones previous experi-

ences and that the observer must be nonevaluative, even when it seemed
obvious that some evaluation was called for and might enhance the observer's position. Above all, one should avoid passing information where
any person can be identified.

It is useful also to attempt to gain some measure of the rapport
that observers achieve with those they are observing. Ordinarily, unless
multiple observers are used in the same situation, so that each observer
may rate the rapport achieved by others, or unless some provision can
be made for measuring rapport independent of the observer, one must
rely upon self-observation of observers on the rapport achieved. These
measures can in turn be related to variation in the observed phenomena.
In our police-observation study each observer at the close of a tour of
duty responded to the question: "Did you have any reason to think that
the officers were behaving in an 'unnatural' or 'put-on' fashion as a result
of your presence? If 'yes,' specify."

In 14 per cent of all tours of duty, one or more officers was seen as
behaving "unnaturally," for at least part of the tour, most commonly the
early part of the tour. One in ten observers never reported that an officer
behaved unnaturally during a tour of duty. Yet one in five observers
rated either three or four of every ten tours they observed as having an
officer behaving unnaturally. There were no significant differences among
observer ratings in terms of their educational training, however, though
we had expected those with police experience and training might more
often see officers as behaving unnaturally in the presence of an observer.

During the eight-hour observation period, observers were expected not only to report on all transactions between officers and citizens
but also to informally interview the officers on a variety of matters including their attitudes toward Negroes, ethnic groups, the civil-rights
movement, protest, the courts, and various aspects of police work and
organization. Examining what observers specified as the basis for their
perception that an officer behaved unnaturally in the observer's presence,
we found that observers far more often mentioned the verbal responses
of officers to such inquiries than what the officer did in transactions with
citizens. It was most common to report that officers did not speak freely
on matters involving the department's organization and operation, particularly its supervision system, and matters involving race relations
and civil rights. The second major way that officers were perceived as
behaving unnaturally was in behavior during the tour that did not
involve transactions with citizens. There were reports, for example, that
officers attempted to hide the fact that they were not paying for their
meals or that they received a discount.

The fact that, when observers were unable to report information from the informal interview, they were more likely to report the officer behaved unnaturally, of course, does not prove that the latter is the cause of the former. Nonetheless, the finding is consistent with a more general explanation of the alteration of behavior in the presence of observers. It seems reasonable to expect that people are more able to alter their behavior when questioned by an observer or when they are in settings that involve only their behavior and not that of others than when they are in transactions with others. They should be least able to alter their behavior in transactions with others, particularly when the behavior of the others is a major element in determining their response. Such a conception seems useful, for example, in explaining why officers will exercise undue force in the presence of an observer (Reiss, 1968b).

In slightly more than one in five instances where observers reported that officers behaved unnaturally in their presence, the observer did not respond to the qualifying phrase, "as a result of your presence." Rather, he reported on the unnatural behavior of the officer as a result of other persons in the situation. The most common reason given was the presence of some other officer. This was particularly the case in one of our cities where the patrol cars were being racially integrated during the period of our observation. Observers reported that black and white officers behaved unnaturally in the presence of one another, a matter they usually made apparent to the observer when the other was absent. They similarly reported that officers changed their behavior in the presence of supervisors who rode with the officers or when they encountered supervisors in the course of duty.

Of the 14 per cent of all tours where one or more officers were perceived as behaving unnaturally, in only roughly one in three were they regarded as behaving unnaturally during the entire tour of duty. Typically, what an observer reported was that the officers behaved unnaturally only during the initial part of the tour of duty, a not unexpected result given the fact that the observer and the officer begin as strangers. Only after an initial period of testing will officers come to behave in a routine fashion. Thus, it was not uncommon for an observer to say as this one did: "The officers' language was too clean and too good for about the first two hours. By the end of the evening they were talking in the usual police language. Perhaps the degree of vulgarity in language is a good indication of ones success with officers." Or, "At first they were worried that I was an investigator (they told me later), but then they discovered that I was a baseball fan, and we were going to the Sox baseball game when the tour is over."

To be sure, all such observer ratings of rapport and of how the officer behaved also may tell us something about real variation among observers in their capacity to make it with officers. A small number of observers usually reported that they did not achieve very good rapport with officers and that officers often behaved unnaturally in their presence. Their observation forms confirm that officers typically behaved stereotypically in their presence. Two of our observers in Washington, D.C., and one in Boston displayed this pattern. We are inclined to conclude that these three observers rather consistently affected officer behavior in their presence.

Where a number of observers are in the same situation over a period of time, as is often the case, the testing of observers declines, and there is evidence of general acceptance of the observers. The feedback system of the observed clearly carries with it messages of their being accepted. In our police-observation study the observers were increasingly made part of the life of the station and conversations continued, rather than stopped, on their approach. Moreover, the observers came increasingly to report that officers were friendly. At times they reported a feeling and belief that there was a sharing despite tacit understanding that they did not view the world alike. Initially officers made attempts to imbue the observers with their point of view, giving clear evidence that observers were outsiders and like all outsiders they must be converted to the officers' point of view if observers were to make it with the officers. Reports of such attempts declined markedly with time. One observer made particular note of this: "I've been with one of these officers before. He doesn't try to convert me. One often feels that we are brothers in the spirit; both, as Jonathan Edwards would say, 'sinners in the hands of an Angry God.' "

At times in the history of an observation team, there may be events that signal a high degree of mutual acceptance. One such event stood out in our police-observation study. Our observers in the Roxbury District of Boston, the lowest prestige police precinct, decided that on their last night in the district they wished to show the officers some measure of appreciation. They hit upon the idea of presenting the officers with several boxes of cigars at the time of the last roll call. Following the presentation, and to the observers' surprise, one of the officers stepped forward and presented each of the observers with a certificate making them honorary police officers of the Roxbury District. While such ceremonies may raise questions of oversocialization of observers, their reports of transactions do not show evidence of such effects.

Observers in a systematic social-observation study are not simply employees since it is they who have had the experiences and who have shared events with those observed. It is the observers who make and sever the relationships with particular individuals, and it is they who assume the legal status of witness to events. The supervisors and principal investigators are stripped of these relationships and of the status of witness, though the principal investigators hold the written record of evidence. The latter record, by the way, implicates both observer and observed.

Where the legality of observed behavior is at issue, as it was in our police-observation study, the positions of the observer, as witness, and of the principal investigator, who holds the evidence, are consequential. What protection is offered and can be guaranteed depends in part on maintaining the allegiance of observers when the study is completed. When one wishes to maintain such protection after the study is completed, attention must be given to the problem. The incorporation of observers into a continuing relationship is in part simplified by the employer relationship. Most of our observers came to list us as references. A few became loyal alumni. All of the law-trained utilized us as character references in applications for admission to the bar. With few exceptions, both in their exit reports and in subsequent correspondence, each reported gratitude for their experience. A viable social science based on systematic social observation inevitably must pay attention to the relationships established with the observers as well as the observed.

## CONCLUDING REMARKS

The foregoing is no manual of procedure on how to do systematic social observation. Indeed, the basic point of view is that most of the elements in systematic social observation of natural social phenomena are common to other modes of investigation. Moreover, many of the problems of observation are common to solo as well as team observation. I have tried to call attention to the way that some of these problems take a special form in systematic social observation and to suggest some elements for dealing with them. Hopefully, a body of literature will grow on systematic social observation of social phenomena that is akin to that on solo observation. More important to the writer is the hope that sociologists will adopt systematic practice in the observation of natural phenomena, that the day is not far off when systematic social observation is as common as sample surveys.

## REFERENCES

BALES, R. F.
    1950  *Interaction Process Analysis: A Method for the Study of Small Groups.* Cambridge, Mass.: Addison-Wesley.

BARBER, B. AND FOX, R.
    1958   "The case of the floppy eared rabbits: an instance of seren-
           dipity gained and serendipity lost." *American Journal of
           Sociology* 64: 128–136.
BARKER, R. G. AND WRIGHT, H. F.
    1955   *Midwest and its Children.* New York: Harper and Row.
BUCKNER, H. T.
    1967   "The police: the culture of a social control agency." Uni-
           versity of California (unpublished doctoral dissertation).
CANNELL, C. F. AND FOWLER, F. J.
    1963   "A study of the reporting of visits to doctors in the National
           Health Survey." Ann Arbor: Survey Research Center,
           University of Michigan.
CONDON, E. U.
    1969   *Study of Unidentified Flying Objects.* New York: Dutton.
DEUTSCHER, I.
    1966   "Words and deeds: Social science and social policy." *Social
           Problems* 13: 235–254.
HUMPHREYS, L.
    1970   *Tearoom Trade: Impersonal Sex in Public Places.* Chicago:
           Aldine.
HYMAN, H. H. AND OTHERS
    1954   *Interviewing in Social Research.* Chicago: University of
           Chicago Press.
JOHNSON, H. G.
    1968   "The economic approach to social questions." *Public
           Interest* 4: 68–79.
KALVEN, H. JR. AND ZEISEL, H.
    1966   *The American Jury.* Boston: Little, Brown.
KISH, L.
    1965   *Survey Sampling.* New York: Wiley.
LANG, K. AND LANG, G.
    1953   "The unique perspective of television and its effect: A
           pilot study." *American Sociological Review* 18: 3–12.
LAZARSFELD, P. F.
    1949   "The American soldier—an expository review." *Public
           Opinion Quarterly* 13: 377–404.
MADGE, C.
    1939   *Britain by Mass Observation.* Hammondsworth: Penguin.
MILESKI, M.
    1971a  "Policing slum landlords: An observation study of adminis-

trative control." Yale University (unpublished doctoral dissertation).

1971b  "Courtroom encounters: An observation study of a lower criminal court." *Law and Society Review*, in press.

PRESIDENT'S COMMISSION ON CAMPUS UNREST
1970  *Campus Unrest*. Washington, D.C.: Government Printing Office.

PYLES, M. K., STOLZ, H. R., AND MACFARLANE, J.
1935  "The accuracy of mothers' reports on birth and developmental data." *Child Development* 6: 372–392.

REISS, A. J., JR.
1967  *Studies in Crime and Law Enforcement in Major Metropolitan Areas*, Field Studies III, Vol. II, Section I. Washington, D.C.: Government Printing Office.

1968a  "Stuff and nonsense about social surveys and observation." Pp. 351–367 in H. Becker, *et al.* (Eds.), *Institutions and the Person*. Chicago: Aldine.

1968b  "Police brutality—answer to key questions." *Trans-action* 5: 10–19.

ROSSI, P. H.
1955  *Why Families Move: A Study in the Social Psychology of Urban Residential Mobility*. New York: Free Press.

SCHUESSLER, K.
1971  *Analyzing Social Data*. Boston: Houghton Mifflin.

VALLEE, J.
1965  *Anatomy of a Phenomenon: The Detailed and Unbiased Report of U.F.O.'s*. New York: Regnery.

WRIGHT, H. F.
1960  "Observational child study." Pp. 71–139 in P. H. Mussen (Ed.), *Handbook of Research Methods in Childhood Development*. New York: Wiley.

1967  *Recording and Analyzing Child Behavior*. New York: Harper and Row.

YARROW, M. R.
1963  "Problems of methods in parent-child research." *Child Development* 34: 215–226.

YARROW, M. R., CAMPBELL, J. D., AND BURTON, R. G.
1964  "Reliability of maternal retrospection: A preliminary report." *Family Process* 3: 207–218.

# 2

# DETECTION THEORY AND PROBLEMS OF PSYCHOSOCIAL DISCRIMINATION

*Darrell K. Adams*

UNIVERSITY OF DENVER

*Z. Joseph Ulehla*

UNIVERSITY OF DENVER

*The major portion of the work reported here was supported by grant number GB-3081 from the National Science Foundation awarded to the second author.*

A pervasive concern with analyses of the impact of distal variables upon the functioning organism has characterized both theory and research in the behavioral sciences. Distal variables that make a difference are those that are discriminable, that is, where different values of the variable are, or can be, accompanied by different probabilities of behavior.

The process of discrimination has played a central role in experimental psychology in the analysis of stimulus effects on psychological experience. In such analyses the discrimination process has not been found to be an all-or-nothing matter; it occurs in degrees and may be obscured by a subject's bias toward one or another of the available stimulus alternatives. Over the last two decades a quantitative theory of discrimination—the theory of signal detection, or *detection theory* for short—has found wide application in the study of both magnitude and bias aspects of discrimination; its concepts and measures have become consensually accepted means of evaluating the discrimination process. In particular, mutually independent measures of the degree of discrimination and of bias or response preference have been developed. The purpose of this chapter is to extend that theory and its associated methods and measures to variables of concern to sociologists. Fortunately, detection theory appears to be as applicable to stimuli and behavior at the psychosocial level as at the level of psychophysics.

## *PERCEPTUAL VERSUS PERFORMANCE DISCRIMINATION*—CAN *VERSUS* DO

A special case of discrimination of particular interest to experimental psychologists involves the explicit differentiation between, or identification of, stimulus alternatives. We term this perceptual discrimination because the interest is in how well someone can (that is, is able to) discriminate between the stimulus alternatives and, thus, to assess the subject's capacity for discrimination. A perceptual-indicator response is employed, this response being one that is expected to be as sensitive to the stimulus difference as any response the subject can make. With adult humans a stimulus-labelling response is often used (high versus low, warm versus cold, and so on). In perceptual discrimination research is oriented toward the perceptual abilities of the subject, toward discovering what discriminations he can make if instructed or programmed to do so. In contrast, the performance-discrimination, or *do*, problem involves discovering the stimulus or situational alternatives to which the person responds differentially in the context of psychosocially significant behavior. Here the behavior itself is of importance; it is the focus of the researcher's interest and is not used merely as an indicator of perceptual ability, of the subject's capacity to discriminate. We may thus term discrimination in the do context performance discrimination.

Some examples here may illustrate the distinction. The extent to which an apartment-house superintendent can judge which prospective residents are Jewish or non-Jewish relates to the can problem—perceptual discrimination. Traditionally, one would assess this ability by using a labelling response; the superintendent would be asked to label each prospective resident Jewish or not Jewish. The relationship between the superintendent's judgments and some criterial identification of the Jews among the prospective tenants would indicate how well he can perceive Jewishness—a kind of perceptual ability. Of greater intrinsic interest in an equalitarian society, however, is the matter of differential awarding of apartments. The relationship between the awarding of apartments and the criterial identification of Jewishness would constitute a kind of performance discrimination; the behavior has importance in its own right rather than as a perceptual indicator. The researcher, in this situation, would be concerned with the contingency of the superintendent's performance (accepting residents) upon his discrimination of the ethnic variable.

In another kind of situation people attempting to learn new roles confront the problem of discriminating role-appropriate from role-inappropriate behaviors. The researcher might, of course, be interested in a wide variety of problems in this context. From the can orientation he might ask to what extent is the person able to discriminate between the two classes of behavior? From the do orientation he might want to assess how much discrimination is actually evidenced in the person's performance. As a quantitative model for discrimination processes, detection theory may provide the researcher with tools that will facilitate answering such questions.

More generally, it is the purpose of this chapter to offer the sociological researcher an extension of detection theory, an extension that will add to his repertoire concepts and methods well-suited for problems of psychosocial discrimination. In psychology detection theory has been most widely used in the can context—in what we have termed perceptual discrimination. In light of this, detection theory will be explained and extended to psychosocial applications in the can context first; then, use of detection theory in the do context will be discussed. In addition, it should be noted that the basic concepts of detection theory bear strong similarity to Thurstonian scaling theory (compare Thurstone, 1927a, 1927b; Saffir, 1937; Lee, 1969). Even though this procedure is not typical, detection theory will be discussed here using Thurstone's terms whenever they are applicable because of their greater familiarity to sociological readers.

## DETECTION THEORY

### Basic Model

Detection theory treats man as a rational organism reflectively choosing between alternative responses on the basis of their expected payoff. Its view of man, therefore, is compatible with prevailing psychosocial or sociocultural views of man. Detection theory applies to perceptual discrimination conceptions similar to those developed by Thurstone (1927a, 1927b) as a basis for scaling techniques. In detection theory discrimination is partitioned into two components, an informing process and a decision process. Two types of events are involved, the observable physical stimuli and the unobservable domain of a subject's reactions to the stimuli. The unobservable reactions were termed "discriminal processes" by Thurstone. The discriminal process of a subject (or of a specified population of subjects) to a specified class of stimuli will vary from trial to trial yielding a discriminal distribution (Figure 1). The discriminal distribution is normal in form, and its midpoint is called the modal-discriminal process. In general, different stimulus classes yield different discriminal distributions and different modal-discriminal processes. The distance between the modal-discriminal processes in standard-deviation units is the difference in Thurstonian-scale value for the alternative stimulus classes. For detection theory this distance serves as an index of detectability or discriminability between the alternative stimulus classes. If the distance between the modal-discriminal processes of two stimulus alternatives is not great, the discriminal distributions will overlap; thus, some discriminal processes can result from either stimulus alternative. In this case, because the discriminal processes are a subject's source of information as to which response should be made, he cannot reliably make a unique response to each stimulus alternative. The degree of unreliability in a subject's response to alternative-stimulus classes provides an empirical basis for estimating the distance between the modal-discriminal processes.

The decision process is the strategy adopted by a subject in his use of the information provided by the discriminal process to guide his response. Detection theory provides for a variety of decision processes, depending upon the type of response demanded of a subject. Four of these will be mentioned in this chapter: dichotomous judgments of stimuli presented singly, ratings of stimuli presented singly, two-alternative forced choice, and four-alternative forced choice. Only minor reference will be made to the forced-choice conditions.

In the dichotomous-decision case the subject's task is to indicate which of two stimulus alternatives was presented in each trial. It is theorized that he establishes a criterion value for the discriminal process such that any stimulus presentation which yields a discriminal process greater than the criterion will elicit one response (for example, response $R_b$) and any stimulus presentation that yields a discriminal process that falls short of the criterion will elicit the alternative (for example, $R_a$). Thus, the discriminal-process continuum serves as a decision axis.

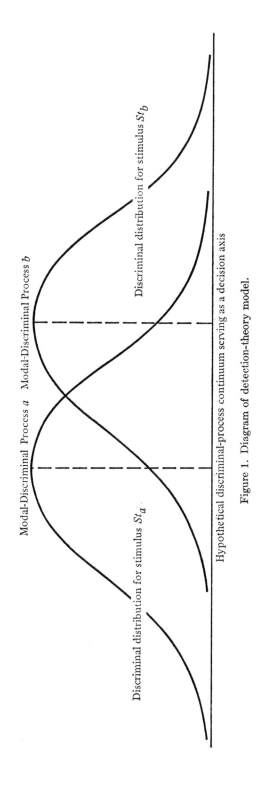

Modal-Discriminal Process $a$    Modal-Discriminal Process $b$

Discriminal distribution for stimulus $St_a$

Discriminal distribution for stimulus $St_b$

Hypothetical discriminal-process continuum serving as a decision axis

Figure 1.  Diagram of detection-theory model.

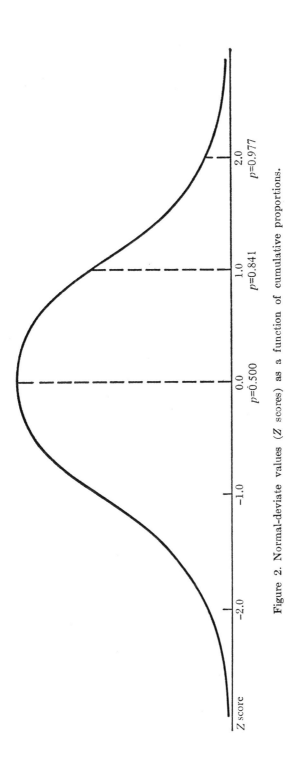

Figure 2. Normal-deviate values (Z scores) as a function of cumulative proportions.

0.0
p=0.500

1.0
p=0.841

2.0
p=0.977

Z score

-1.0

-2.0

The location of the criterion upon a discriminal distribution can be inferred from the response rates to the stimulus. For example, an $R_b$ response rate of 0.5 to stimulus $St_a$ (symbolized as $p$ $(R_b/St_a) = 0.50$) would imply that the criterion was placed at the median of the distribution.

In almost all applications detection theory postulates that the discriminal distributions of the alternative stimuli are normal in form. This postulate implies that normal-deviate values of a given discriminal distribution will provide a means of scaling the decision axis. For example, as illustrated in Figure 2, a decision criterion yielding an $R_a$ response probability of 0.500 would be associated with a normal-deviate value of 0. This criterion would be as far on the decision axis from a second criterion which yielded an $R_a$ response probability of 0.841 (thus having a normal deviate of 1.0) as the second criterion would be from a third criterion which yielded an $R_a$ response probability of 0.977 (with a normal deviate of 2.0). Thus, the normal deviates of the cumulative-response probabilities to each stimulus alternative yield a scale for the decision axis with ratio-scale level of measurement. The scales imposed upon the decision axis by the alternative discriminal distributions will have equal-sized units if the two distributions are assumed to have equal variance. As will be shown later, the assumption of equal variance is testable.

A plot of the criterion projections upon the two normal-deviate scales is termed an operating characteristic. Various detection-theory measures and assumptions can be referred to features of the operating characteristic, as will be discussed later.

## Measures

If we assume equal variance, the scales yielded by the normal deviates of the cumulative-response probabilities provide two measures important in detection theory. These measures are shown graphically in Figure 3. First, the difference between the normal deviates associated with the two alternative stimuli for a single decision criterion provides a measure of the distance between the modal-discriminal processes (symbolized as $d'$) and, thus, serves as a measure of discriminability between the alternative stimuli. For example, let the $R_b$ response rate to $St_b$ stimuli be 0.841, and the $R_b$ response rate to $St_a$ stimuli be 0.159. The normal deviate for the $St_b$ discriminal distribution ($Z_b''$ for criterion $X_2$ in Figure 3) would be $-1.0$, and the normal deviate for the $St_a$ discriminal distribution ($Z_a$ for criterion $X_2$ in Figure 3) would be $+1.0$, thus yielding a $d'$ of 2.0.

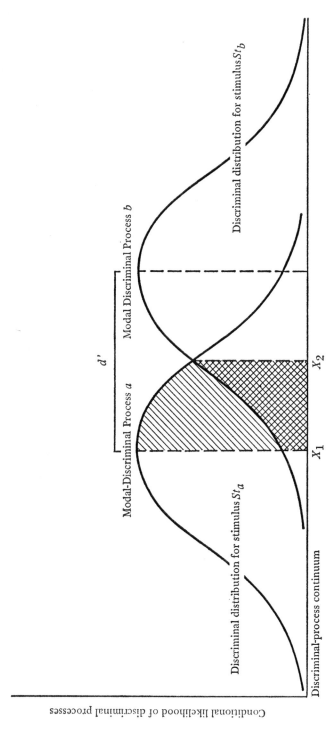

Conditional likelihood of discriminal processes

Discriminal-process continuum

Figure 3. Detection theory with the normal-distribution and equal-variance assumptions, showing the discriminal-process continuum, discriminal dispersions, and modal-discriminal processes. For decision criterion at $X_1$: $p(R_b/St_a) = 0.500$; $p(R_b/St_b) = 0.977$; $Z_a = 0.0$; $Z_b = -2.0$; $B = [0 + (-2.0)/2] = -1.0$; $d' = 0 - (-2.0) = 2.0$. For decision criterion at $X_2$: $p(R_b/St_a) = 0.159$; $p(R_b/St_b) = 0.841$; $Z_a = 1.0$; $Z_b = -1.0$; $B = [1.0 + (-1.0)/2] = 0.0$; $d' = 1.0 - (-1.0) = 2.0$.

The second important measure derived from the normal-deviate scales is the mean of the two normal deviates yielded by the alternative stimuli. This measure, which we can symbolize with $B$ for bias, locates the decision criterion in terms of its distance from the midpoint between the modal-discriminal processes. Any departure of the criterion from the midpoint between the modal-discriminal processes favors one response alternative at the expense of the other and can thus serve as a measure of response bias. For example, if the criterion is placed away from the midpoint in the direction of the $St_a$ distribution midpoint, the $R_b$ response rate will be augmented at the expense of the $R_a$ response rate. To simplify discussion of $B$, assume that $R_a$ is the correct response to $St_a$, and $R_b$ is the correct response to $St_b$. If the stimulus probabilities are equal, the gain in correct responses to $St_b$ would be less than the loss in correct responses to $St_a$, implying that a response bias leads to an increase in incorrect decisions when stimulus probabilities are equal. For an example, let us again refer to Figure 3. Adopting criterion $X_1$ rather than $X_2$ would reduce the rate of correct responses to $St_a$ stimuli by the lined and crosshatched area of the $a$ curve. However, the gain in correct responses to $St_b$ stimuli would only be that indicated by the crosshatched area under the $b$ curve.

A more common representation of criterion placement than the $B$ value is the likelihood ratio. This expresses the ratio of the probability densities of the two discriminal distributions at the point where the criterion is located. The original psychological applications of detection theory presumed that a subject placed his criterion at the optimal point, that is, the point that would maximize his expected monetary payoff. The likelihood ratio is appropriate when optimality of criterion location is under consideration and is highly useful in normative applications of detection theory. For most descriptive applications, however, the likelihood ratio appears to offer no advantage over $B$ because real subjects do not follow the optimal model for criterion placement (Ulehla, 1966). The $B$ measure is simpler and possesses the same scale unit as $d'$.

## EVALUATION OF ASSUMPTIONS

### Normality Assumption

The validity of the normal-deviate scales, and thus of the $d'$ and $B$ measures derived from them, rests upon the tenability of the normality and equal-variance assumptions. If several decision criteria are available, these assumptions can be evaluated. The use of a rating-scale response provides multiple criteria for analysis. A $k$-category ordered rating scale can be considered to yield $k - 1$ decision criteria, each criterion located between adjacent rating categories (see Figure 4). Each criterion partitions both discriminal distributions. The proportion of the $St_a$ discriminal distribution that exceeds a given criterion (for example, the criterion located between categories 5 and 6 in Figure 4) determines the proportion of $St_a$ stimuli which elicit rating categories above that criterion. For example, the crosshatched area under the $St_a$ curve of Figure 4 would determine the proportion of $St_a$ stimuli receiving ratings of 5, 6 or 7. The equivalent-response proportion for $St_b$ would reflect the lined and crosshatched areas under the $St_b$ discriminal distribution. Thus, within the limit of sampling variation, any criterion can be located on a discriminal distribution by using the proportion of the stimuli that elicits rating categories beyond the criterion as an estimate of the proportion of the distribution that falls beyond the criterion. When response proportions are cumulated over the rating categories taken in order, an additional criterion is located when each response proportion is added to the cumulation.

The set of equivalent-response proportions for the two discriminal distributions, when plotted against one another, defines an operating characteristic. Analogous to the operating characteristic of a statistical test, it describes the set of success rates and error rates that would accompany any choice of a decision criterion. The way in which these rates covary depends upon the shape of the discriminal distributions and determines the form of the operating characteristic. Thus, the form of the operating characteristic provides a means of assessing some characteristics of the discriminal distributions, in particular, the normality and equal-variance assumptions. As noted above, only when the normality assumption is valid for the discriminal distribution will normal-deviate transforms of the cumulative-response probabilities yield ratio scales. Each of the $k - 1$ decision criteria would intersect the normal-deviate ratio scale derived from each stimulus alternative. Over the several criteria the corresponding normal deviates would be characterized by a linear relationship. Thus, a linear relationship between the normal deviates of the two cumulative-response distributions is implied by the normality assumption. At least three criteria, and thus four ratio categories, are necessary to assess linearity. A nonzero $d'$ is also required; for, two equal nonlinear scales would bear a linear relation if they possessed identical location.

Linearity of the operating characteristic can be evaluated by visual inspection of a normal-normal plot or by a variety of statistical procedures, for example, a product-moment correlation coefficient computed between the two sets of normal transforms.

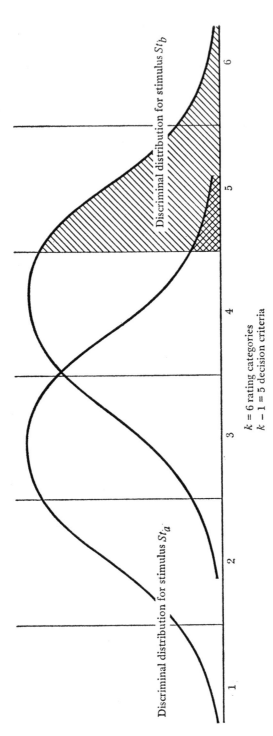

Discriminal distribution for stimulus $St_a$

Discriminal distribution for stimulus $St_b$

$k = 6$ rating categories
$k - 1 = 5$ decision criteria

Figure 4. Rating-scale decision process, showing areas under the discriminal distributions corresponding to certain cumulative-response proportions.

When we evaluate the distribution assumptions, the important issue is whether they are accurate enough to make the measures meaningful. Perhaps more to the point, the assumptions should be accurate enough to make the $d'$ and $B$ measures more meaningful than the alternatives available to the investigator—be they detection-theory measures based on other distribution assumptions or measures based on another theoretical scheme. No formulae or automatic-decision rules appear available for comparison between detection theory and other approaches to discrimination. However, a comparison of different shape assumptions within the detection-theory approach can be based upon the comparative linearity of operating characteristics obtained with the different shape assumptions. The heart of this measurement approach is the scaling of the decision axis through the use of an appropriate transformation of response proportions. The normality assumption makes normal-deviate transformation appropriate. A different shape assumption would make a different transformation appropriate. The accomplishment of linear scaling of the decision axis is supported when, after the appropriate transformation, two substantially different sets of response proportions (as yielded by two discriminable stimuli) bear a linear relation to one another. Since the rationale of the measures is based upon the same assumptions as is the prediction of operating-characteristic linearity, it would appear that an operating-characteristic plot that looks linear justifies the use of detection-theory measures and that, if a choice is to be made between two different shape assumptions, the assumption that yields the closer approximation to linearity is to be preferred.

If an alternative to the normality assumption should appear tenable, measures consistent with the logic of detection theory could be developed ad hoc for the substituted distribution. Although unusual in most data, the rectangular assumption would be particularly amenable in that the measures could be the same except that the normal deviate would be replaced, as the scale unit for $d'$ and $B$, by the standard deviation. The rectangular assumption would be supported by a linear relationship between the untransformed cumulative-response proportions; this linear relationship can be evaluated by computing a correlation coefficient between the untransformed cumulative-response proportions. Incidentally a linear operating characteristic with untransformed response proportions is also predicted by the traditional threshold theory which underlies much of psychometrics as well as threshold measures in psychophysics (Green and Swets, 1966; Hohle, 1965). It should be noted that both the normal deviate and the untransformed $r$'s may approximate 1.0 if the $d'$ value is low. The distribution assumption can only be meaningfully tested if $d'$ is substantial.

Most psychophysical studies using detection theory have relied on large data sets to minimize sampling variability and have treated the resultant sample data as sufficiently precise to make statistical estimation procedures unnecessary. With its extension to more complex phenomena where large data sets are more difficult to obtain, estimation procedures for detection-theory parameters are being developed (see Dorfman and Alf, 1969).

## Equal-Variance Assumption

The assumption of equal variance of the two discriminal distributions implies equal scale units for the two normal-deviate scales. Equality of scale unit implies a slope of 1.0 for the operating characteristic. Slope values substantially different from 1.0 would make the equal-variance assumption inapplicable. In this case the conceptual model must be altered to provide for different scale units to be obtained from the normal deviates yielded by the alternative stimuli. The $d'$ measure, operationally defined as the difference in normal deviates, will no longer be independent of bias but will vary according to where on the decision axis the criterion is placed. A form of $d'$ can still be used to index discrimination, but it must possess a specified location on the decision axis. Two alternative locations have been proposed by detection theorists, the midpoint of one distribution (the noise-alone distribution in a signal-detection task) and the point of zero bias, where the likelihood ratio is 1. The latter, which can be symbolized as $d_s$, seems, in general, appropriate for discrimination tasks where neither distribution provides a more meaningful frame of reference than the other.

Estimation of $d_s$ will ordinarily require fitting a straight line to the operating-characteristic points and computing the distance between that line and the line of chance performance (the positive diagonal) along the line of zero bias (the negative diagonal). Of course, at least two operating-characteristic points and, thus, three response categories are needed to obtain the straight-line function.

Although a multicategory response scale is needed to specify the operating characteristic and to assure computability of $d_s$, a two-alternative scale will suffice if the single criterion is located at the point of zero bias. If the discrimination task is symmetric in terms of stimulus probability as well as explicit and implicit payoffs, criterion placement is likely to show little bias. Reasonable measurement of discrimination with a binary response is often feasible for such tasks.

Without the equal variance assumption the point of zero bias can still be defined as the point where the likelihood ratio is one. A reasonable unit for the bias scale would appear to be the mean of the scale units yielded by the alternative discriminal distributions. If conceptualized this way, the operational definition of the bias measure, $B$, remains the mean of the two normal deviates.

## EXPLORATORY EXPERIMENTS

In order to apply detection theory to psychosocial dimensions, discrimination tasks were required in which many stimuli drawn from two well-defined, alternative stimulus sources could be presented to the subject. The verbal production of each of two identified sources served as the stimulus alternatives; small random samples of the verbal material comprised the set of stimulus items. The task for the subject was to judge which source produced each stimulus item. This general paradigm was used in several exploratory studies tapping a variety of psychosocial-stimulus dimensions.

An initial effort involving political alternatives capitalized on the interest in the 1964 presidential campaign. It seemed that sentences drawn from the campaign speeches of Senator Goldwater and President Johnson could be presented to subjects in random order and that their judgments as to which presidential candidate uttered each sentence could then be subjected to detection-theory analyses.

Two experiments were conducted, each testing a different prediction drawn from the detection theory. The first prediction concerned the operating characteristic yielded by rating-scale judgments. A four-point rating scale was used. The rating categories were: Goldwater—confident, Goldwater—not confident, Johnson—not confident, and Johnson—confident. Seventy-two subjects rated the source—Goldwater or Johnson—of 40 sentences, 20 of which were taken from the speeches of each candidate. From the resulting 1440 ratings, three points of the group operating characteristic were estimated. The data plot approximates the straight line of unit slope predicted by theory (see Figure 5).

The second prediction tested was a prediction of proportion correct in a two-alternative, forced-choice task based on performance in judging single sentences. The theory states that the same discrimination process underlies forced-choice behavior as underlies judgments of single items. To test this prediction, one may estimate the acuity of the discrimination process ($d'$) from the single-item performance and then use this $d'$ value to predict how well subjects should do on the forced-choice task. Tables for converting response proportions to $d'$ values, and vice versa, are available if equal variance of the two discriminal distributions is assumed (Elliott, 1964).

In the experiment one half of the students in each of two political-

DARRELL K. ADAMS AND Z. JOSEPH ULEHLA

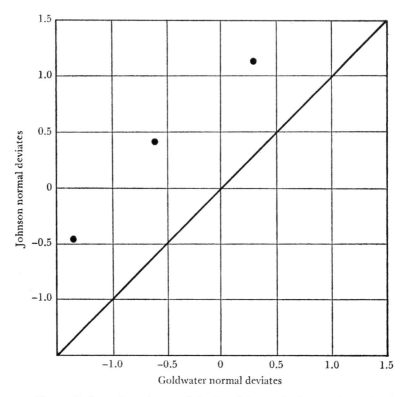

Figure 5. Operating characteristic for Johnson-Goldwater discrimination task.

science classes attempted to identify the source—Goldwater or Johnson—of each of 40 sentences presented singly. The other half of the students received 20 pairs of sentences, one member of each pair drawn from Johnson, the other from Goldwater. Their task was to state which member of each pair was produced by Goldwater and which by Johnson. The data of each class were analyzed separately. First, $d'$ values based upon the single-sentence judgment data were computed. These $d'$ values permitted prediction of the proportion correct yielded by the students who performed the forced-choice task. One class performed quite closely to theory; the predicted proportion correct of 0.83 was close to the obtained value of 0.81. The results for the second class were somewhat weaker: the prediction was 0.84, but the obtained success rate was 0.77.

On the whole, the results of these studies of the discriminability of politically oriented psychosocial alternatives were encouraging. This method may be used to ascertain the discriminability of any pair of political figures for any subject group of interest. Is the "old" Nixon really different from the "new" Nixon in the eyes of the American public? Is Agnew more different from Wallace than from Nixon? To what extent does the discriminability of such comparisons depend on the subject groups' own political preferences? Other examples of interesting comparisons will occur to the reader. The point is, any such combination of pairwise comparisons can be studied quantitatively using the present applications of the detection-theory model.

The most precise tests of the theory involve within-subjects analyses which require a large number of stimulus presentations to each subject. Thus, it was desirable to develop a psychosocial-discrimination task which could simultaneously yield a large number of stimulus items and maintain the subject's interest. To this end, two different magazines were selected as stimulus sources; several issues of each comprised the verbal material from which stimuli were sampled. Included were a "male" magazine, emphasizing adventure and sex, and a "female" magazine, which featured first-person accounts of romantic and family involvements. The specific stimuli were sets of randomly selected sequences of four (in most cases) consecutive words. In general, the subject's task was to judge whether a given stimulus item (that is, a four-word sequence) came from the male or the female magazine.

In order to test the fit of detection theory with the normality assumption to these data, operating characteristics based on within-subjects analyses were evaluated. Two interrelated predictions regarding $r$'s were tested: (1) The $r$'s between the normal-deviate transforms of the cumulative-response probabilities yielded by the two stimulus alternatives would exceed the $r$'s computed between the untransformed cumulative-response probabilities. This would hold if the normality assumption were superior to the comparison assumption of rectilinear discriminal distributions. (2) The $r$'s between the normal-deviate transforms would approximate unity if detection theory with the normality assumption were valid.

Operating-characteristic data bearing on the above predictions were obtained in two earlier studies. In one study (Ulehla, Canges, and Wackwitz, 1967) the operating characteristics were based on a six-category rating scale and 400 trials of two-word and 400 trials of four-word stimuli per subject. In the case of the four-word stimuli, both predictions were confirmed for five of the six subjects; the normal-deviate $r$'s were at least 0.99 and exceeded the untransformed $r$'s. The two-word stimuli, on the other hand, yielded ambiguous results. The $d'$ values were lower, and as noted earlier, low $d'$ values weaken tests of theory based on operating-characteristic analyses. A second study

(Ulehla, Little, and Weyl, 1967) employed a larger data set. In that study 19 subjects used a 12-category rating scale to evaluate 1,000 four-word stimulus items. For all 19 subjects the normal-deviate $r$'s exceeded the untransformed $r$'s; for 17 of the 19 subjects the normal-deviate $r$'s were at least 0.99. Thus, these studies provided substantial evidence supporting the fit of detection theory with the normality assumption to ratings of stimuli drawn from male-oriented versus female-oriented literature.

A different kind of test of detection theory can be made by examining what happens to $d'$ values when they are derived from different response conditions—that is, two-alternative, and four-alternative, forced-choice conditions as well as the rating-scale response condition described above. According to detection theory, for a given subject exposed to a particular set of stimulus sources, equivalent estimates of $d'$ should result from all three response modes. The Ulehla, Canges, and Wackwitz study (1967) included all three response conditions, and additionally, within each condition the data were divided into arbitrary halves. Estimates of $d'$ were computed for each half of each condition, and the discrepancies between the various estimates were calculated. The average discrepancy between $d'$ estimates derived from different response conditions in this study did not exceed the average discrepancy between $d'$ estimates obtained by using a single-response condition.

All of the discrepancies were deemed due to sampling error, and it was concluded that the different response conditions provided equivalent estimates of $d'$—as predicted by the theory. One of the important implications of this finding is that detection theory provides convergent measurement of a subject's ability to discriminate psychosocial, as well as physical, alternatives, in that $d'$ is not tied to a specific response mode but can be convergently estimated from different types of behavior.

The cues involved in the masculine-feminine magazine discrimination task are difficult to determine—probably involving sex-associated differences in both style and content. In view of the subtle nature of the cues, most subjects initially doubted that they would discriminate at all but then proceeded to discriminate very well. To the investigators' surprise sentence-sized units proved too discriminable for optimal testing of detection theory, which led to the use of two-word and four-word samples. It is possible that stimulus sources in the sociocultural environment that differ only in subtle ways may, with the use of this model, prove highly discriminable.

A final exploratory study focused on a very different aspect of variables in the stimulus source—their affective or emotive character, rather than their ideological nature. The stimuli were taken from a novel.

First, the experimenter selected portions of the discourse in which the speaker was clearly hostile toward the listener and other portions in which the speaker clearly was not. Then, individual four-word sequences were nonsystematically drawn from each portion, thus providing stimulus items which could be characterized as hostile or nonhostile. Taking each item in turn, the subject was to judge whether the item was drawn from the hostile or nonhostile pool. These discrimination judgments, when combined with three degrees of expressed confidence in the discrimination judgment, yielded a six-category rating scale. The operating characteristic shown in Figure 6 reflects the ratings of 100 stimuli by 12 subjects. The departure from linearity was not great; these results encourage the further application of detection theory to stimulus variables of an affective nature.

In the foregoing experiment the psychologically-defined stimulus variable involved hostility or threat. Persons termed paranoid are often characterized by a propensity to attribute threat to stimulus events. De-

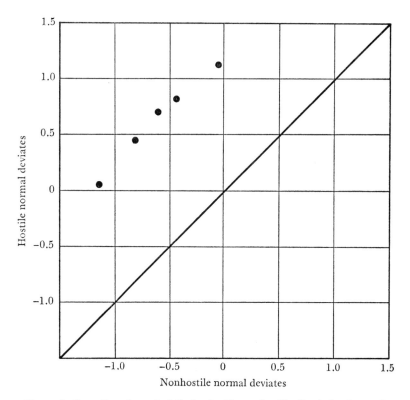

Figure 6. Operating characteristic for hostile-nonhostile discrimination task.

tection theory leads one to consider two alternative determinants, inability to discriminate threating from nonthreatening events versus a bias toward the attribution of threat. The two detection-theory measures, $d'$ and $B$, can be used to provide independent, quantitative indices of these two determinants. The research paradigm embodied in the above experiment could be adapted to more realistic stimuli and responses. Each subject would be presented with a large number of stimulus events, including both events defined as threatening and events defined as non-threatening by some criterial authority. Some dichotomous response indicator of threat would be elicited from the subject following each stimulus presentation. The $2 \times 2$, stimulus $\times$ response, matrix could then be subjected to detection-theory analysis to yield both $d'$ and $B$. Subject groups of particular concern (for example, paranoid patients) could be compared with normal controls.

## DISCRIMINATION IN THE DO CONTEXT

The foregoing experiments were designed to explore the applicability of detection theory to sociocultural discrimination in the perceptual, or can, context, the context inherent in almost all detection theory applications to date. As noted previously, Thurstonian scaling theory, especially in the version presented by Saffir (1937) utilizes much the same conceptual model as detection theory. Many applications of Thurstone's approach would fit one criterion for discrimination in the do context in that the behavior is not used as a perceptual indicator and yields weaker discrimination than a perceptual indicator would. For example, in Thurstone's research on the palatability of foods, the response was an indication of taste preference and probably yielded poorer discrimination than food-labelling response would have. The reader may have noted that Thurstonian scaling is ordinarily applied to stimulus sets that include more than two alternatives; whereas detection theory is usually applied to two-alternative stimulus sets. This is because detection theorists have defined the decision axis in terms of the stimulus alternatives, or likelihood ratios yielded by them, since the subject is ordinarily asked to judge which stimulus was presented. For a stimulus-labelling response multiple stimulus alternatives would require a multidimensional decision space, and the simple model described above would be invalid. In contrast, Thurstone has defined the decision axis in reference to the attribute being scaled (for example, palatability); this permits any number of stimulus alternatives to be used. In general, if an attribute rating is substituted for the stimulus-labelling response, if multiple stimuli are used, and if scale values are substituted for the detection-theory measures, detection theory becomes virtually identical with Thurstonian scaling theory, especially in the form presented by Saffir (1937).

In addition to its demonstrated utility for perceptual discrimination, this theory might prove applicable to performance discrimination—the dependence of behavior of intrinsic interest upon stimulus or situational alternatives. The dependence of the awarding of an apartment upon the ethnic status of the prospective rentor and the dependence of salary upon ethnic status or sex constitute examples of performance discriminations for which detection theory might be appropriate. For the theory to be applied, several conditions must obtain: the set of behavioral alternatives used must be binary or unidimensional; the rate of occurrence of each response to each stimulus must be ascertainable; in general, these rates must not equal or closely approximate either zero or one. (Sometimes adjacent response categories can be combined to avoid zero rates.) If these conditions obtain, the analytic procedures and measures of detection theory could be used. The decision axis would not be defined in terms of choice between stimulus alternatives but would be defined in terms of the behavioral alternatives. For example, awarding versus not awarding an apartment presumably reflects an underlying continuum such as perceived desirability of the applicant as a tenant. Presumably, individuals drawn from a given ethnic group would vary in their desirability in the eyes of the manager, and this variability would generate a discriminal distribution for that ethnic group. The difference between the modal-discriminal processes for two ethnic groups, as indexed by the $d'$ measure, would indicate the difference between the ethnic groups in the underlying attribute (for example, perceived desirability as a tenant) in relation to the variability that characterizes individuals within each ethnic group.

As in the case of Thurstonian scaling, more than two stimuli could be used because the stimulus alternatives do not define the poles of the decision axis. The $d'$ between any two stimuli would index their difference on the underlying continuum or decision axis. If the stimulus lowest on the scale $(St_a)$ is given a scale value of zero, the next lowest $(St_b)$ is given a value equal to the $d'$ between $St_a$ and $St_b$, the third lowest $(St_c)$ is assigned a scale value equal to the $d'$ between $St_a$ and $St_b$ plus the $d'$ between $St_b$ and $St_c$, and so forth, the result would, in essence, be a Thurstonian scaling of the stimuli on the decision axis which underlies the overt behavior under study.

The foregoing scheme sets the zero point at the stimulus lowest on the decision axis. Perhaps a more useful measurement scheme can be found in a generalization of the detection-theory measure explained for two stimulus variables earlier in this chapter. The bias measure, $B$, which locates a given decision criterion in reference to the discriminal distributions, can still be the mean normal deviate over the alternative stimuli and would continue to index the overall propensity to favor the response(s) whose response region(s) fall(s) on a given side of the criterion. For example, the rentor of the earlier hypothetical examples might much more frequently accept than reject applicants; the degree to which he does this could be indexed by the $B$ measure regardless of the number of stimulus alternatives. The difference in acceptance between any two ethnic groups could be expressed in terms of a $d'$. When only two groups are involved, $d'$ can be thought of as the effect of the stimulus person being in one group as opposed to the other. If this total effect $(d')$ is partitioned equally between the two stimulus groups, each stimulus alternative would exercise an effect equal in absolute value to $d'/2$ but opposite in sign for the two stimuli. Since $d'$ is the difference between the normal deviates yielded by the two alternative stimuli and since $B$ is their mean, $B$ can be seen as representing the subjects' response propensities when the stimulus alternatives (for example, ethnic character of the applicants) are mixed in equal proportion and, thus, as a logical starting point for a stimulus effect. The $\pm d'/2$ value can be seen as the effect on the performance of a particular stimulus alternative and is given by subtracting $B$ from the normal deviate yielded by that stimulus alternative. Theoretically, $d'$ represents the distance between the discriminal distributions.

Extending to the general stimulus set, 1, 2, . . . , $k$, . . . , $K$, the logic which assigns $d'/2$ as the effect of either of two stimuli, we find subtraction of $B$ from the normal deviate yielded by the $k$th stimulus would furnish a signed quantity which would represent the effect of stimulus alternative $k$. With $B$ as the starting point, this quantity would represent the effect upon the behavior under investigation of presentation of stimulus alternative $k$. More specifically, this quantity would represent the displacement from $B$ along the decision axis of the discriminal distribution associated with stimulus $k$.

In sum, detection theory offers a quantitative model and measures for discrimination in the do context. The basic assumptions of normality and equal variance of the discriminal distributions can be evaluated as described above for discrimination in the can context if four or more unidimensional response alternatives are available. Recently, do applications have begun to appear in experimental psychology. Notably, Grice (1968) has shown how the joint effect on conditioned eyeblink of conditioned stimulus (tone) intensity, unconditioned stimulus (airpuff) intensity, and subjects' anxiety can be parsimoniously reinterpreted using conceptions drawn from detection theory. Detection theory may also prove useful in do applications at the more molar level of interest to sociologists.

## DISCUSSION

Several ways in which detection theory can be applied to problems involving psychosocially-defined stimulus alternatives have been explored. When successful, such applications provide a testable quantitative model which, in turn, yields ratio-scaled measures for two complementary aspects of behavior, discrimination and response bias.

The exploratory experiments were designed for their methodological implications rather than for their content. Careful researchers concerned with substantive aspects of psychosocial discrimination will also be concerned with problems of representative design. Following Brunswik (1956), one must be as careful to sample adequately the psychosocial alternatives in obtaining the stimuli to be used, as one is to sample adequately the human population of interest in obtaining subjects. When representative stimulus samples are obtained, they may need to be shortened or combined to yield a suitable average level of discrimination for tests of the model. For example, whole-sentence units were appropriately difficult in the case of the political dimension, but they proved to be too discriminable for effective tests of theory in the masculinity-femininity case, and therefore, shorter sequences of words were substituted. Of course, the measures pertain to the stimulus sources as represented by the samples drawn, not by any other types of sample (for example, pictures in the Goldwater-Johnson case).

The results of the above exploratory experiments support the utility of detection theory for some types of discrimination between psychosocially defined alternatives. If the theory proves to be generally valid in these applications, it can be used to quantify the discriminability between stimuli of more practical importance. For example, the sociologist concerned with normative or ideological differences between social groups could use the $d'$ measure to index such differences. The approach would include the collection of a representative sample of normative or ideological statements from each of two groups to be compared. The discriminability measure would then be the $d'$ value yielded by the reference subjects in a discrimination paradigm. The set of pairwise comparisons between important subgroups would yield a set of ratio-scaled measures of perceived difference in norms or ideology. Such measures could then be used in further analyses of communication patterns, stereotypes, conflicts, role expectations, or other matters of practical concern.

The stimuli in the experiments discussed above were all samples of text, but the detection-theory model may be applicable to other kinds of stimuli. For example, video displays of actual behavior could constitute stimuli for the discrimination of such psychosocial dimensions as affect, intention, or ideology. Such displays of behaviors and behavioral contexts could also be used to assess a subject's ability to discriminate role-appropriate from role-inappropriate behaviors. Standardized video displays could be used across different subject groups in order to assess the extent to which the role was important to their normative concerns. For example, the same behaviors rendered by a man wearing a policeman's uniform versus civilian clothes could isolate the dependence of behavioral discrimination upon that particular role-oriented dimension. Presumably, such discrimination abilities would vary across age, sex, social class, and ethnic group memberships in predictable ways. Expanding the example to include more role categories or normative dimensions, we see the detection model could be used to map normative or ideological spaces, each of which would reflect referent subject groups' abilities to discriminate the alternatives of interest. This ability might, in turn, be assumed to reflect socially patterned learning experiences.

Although it has never to the authors' knowledge been attempted, it seems feasible to couple detection theory with naturalistic observation. The observer would have to establish criteria for the stimulus and (unidimensional) behavioral alternatives of interest to him. Then, the behavior that accompanies any occurrence of any of the stimulus alternatives would be aggregated to derive the conditional response proportions needed for detection analysis. For example, the investigator might be interested in the propensity of a group of white second-graders to aggress against another child encountered in a playground and in the dependence of such aggression upon the race of the child encountered. The stimulus alternatives could be white versus Negro (as perceived by the observer). The response variable (also as perceived by the observer) could include no aggression, verbal or gestural aggression, physical assault without a weapon, and physical assault with a weapon. The $B$ measure would index the propensity of the subject group to aggress in that setting and could be compared with $B$ yielded by other subjects or other settings. The $d'$ measure would index the dependence of aggression upon the race of the child encountered and could also be compared with $d'$ values obtained from other subject groups or the same group in other settings or at other times. If the assumptions of the model were supported by an operating-characteristic analysis, the $d'$ and $B$ measures would be mutually independent and would reflect appropriate scaling of the covert decision axis which underlies the overt aggressive behavior. The use of naturalistic observation would seem pertinent to a variety of problems of discrimination in the do context, including examples discussed earlier.

In conclusion, several features of detection theory should be noted. First, the user of this model can draw upon the substantial and varied research literature upon which detection theory is based. For example, determinants of criterion location in the perceptual case (Ulehla, 1966) may generalize so as to determine bias in nonperceptual applications.

Second, two complementary aspects of behavior are both expressed in ratio-scaled constructs—$B$ indicates response bias (or propensity for response to occur regardless of the stimulus situation), and $d'$ reflects the dependence of the response on the stimulus present. The generic nature of these constructs provides the potential for diverse applications within a common theoretical framework. This potential diversity is apparent when such applications as Clark's treatment of placebo effects on pain (Clark, 1969) and Grice's analysis of motivational, reinforcement, and stimulus intensity effects on conditioned eyelid responses (Grice, 1968) are contrasted with the applications described in the present chapter.

Third, in detection theory the scale units come from the response distributions of the subject. The ratio-scale properties are, thus, better established than is true when the behavioral model underlying the scale is not well understood or when the scale units reflect the investigator's preconceptions rather than the subject's performance characteristics.

Fourth, detection theory shares with other general approaches to measurement the calibration of the systematic effects under study in terms of unsystematic or uncontrolled variability rather than in terms of measurement scales applied to raw data. For example, the product-moment correlation coefficient $r$ reflects the proportion of variance that is shared (that is, that also exists as covariance). The $F$-ratio used in analysis of variance has in its numerator a composite variance estimate including a term reflecting the possible effect under study; the denominator is a variance estimate in which that term (only) is omitted. In detection theory the measures reflect displacement of a distribution of subject reactions to stimuli or criterion location resulting from systematic effects along an underlying variable scaled in units based on the un-systematic-uncontrolled variability. The strategem of using the uncontrolled variability as a yardstick for systematic effects yields dimensionless constructs as measures—constructs such as $r$, $F$, $d'$, or $B$ which carry the same meaning in a diversity of applications. In contrast, the meaning of simple summary statistics is tied to particular data sets.

Of the foregoing approaches, detection theory has the advantage of not requiring parametric assumptions to be made about the empirical data being analyzed. Its measures, $d'$ and $B$, get their ratio properties from distribution assumptions which can be empirically evaluated, rather than from operations on intervally scaled input data.

Like detection theory, latent-structure analysis can employ distribution assumptions in order to scale an underlying dimension. Both approaches also use a graphic representation of hit rates and error rates associated with different positions on the underlying variable. However, the trace line of latent-structure analysis plots hit rate against the subject's discrimination ability for a given test item; whereas the operating characteristic of detection theory plots hit rate against false positive rate with ability and task held constant. Torgerson provides a technical discussion of similarities in the way distribution assumptions can be used in Thurstonian scaling and latent-structure analysis (Torgerson, 1958). The reader interested in further developing the type of approach presented here may find Torgerson's discussion useful.

## REFERENCES

BRUNSWIK, E.

    1956   *Perception and the Representative Design of Psychological Experiments.* Berkeley: University of California Press.

CLARK, W. C.

    1969   "Sensory-decision theory analysis of the placebo effect on the criterion for pain and thermal sensitivity ($d'$)." *Journal of Abnormal Psychology* 74: 363–371.

DORFMAN, D. D. AND ALF, E.

    1969   "Maximum likelihood estimation of parameters of signal-detection theory and determination of confidence intervals: Rating-method data." *Journal of Mathematical Psychology* 6: 487–496.

ELLIOTT, P. B.

    1964   "Tables of $d'$." Pp. 651–684 in J. A. Swets (Ed.), *Signal Detection and Recognition by Human Observers: Contemporary Readings.* New York: Wiley.

GREEN, D. M. AND SWETS, J. A.

    1966   *Signal Detection Theory and Psychophysics.* New York: Wiley.

GRICE, R. G.

    1968   "Stimulus intensity and response evocation." *Psychological Review* 75: 359–373.

HOHLE, R. H.
    1965    "Detection of a visual signal with low background noise:
            An experimental comparison of two theories." *Journal of
            Experimental Psychology* 70: 459–463.

LEE, W.
    1969    "Relationships between Thurstone category scaling and
            signal detection theory." *Psychological Bulletin* 71: 101–107.

SAFFIR, M.
    1937    "A comparative study of scales constructed by three
            psychophysical methods." *Psychometrika* 2: 179–198.

THURSTONE, L. L.
    1927a   "A law of comparative judgment." *Psychological Review*
            34: 273–286.
    1927b   "Psychophysical analysis." *American Journal of Psy-
            chology* 38: 368–389.

TORGERSON, W. S.
    1958    *Theory and Methods of Scaling.* New York: Wiley.

ULEHLA, Z. J.
    1966    "Optimality of perceptual decision criteria." *Journal of
            Experimental Psychology* 71: 564–569.

ULEHLA, Z. J., CANGES, L., AND WACKWITZ, F.
    1967    "Signal detectability theory applied to conceptual dis-
            crimination." *Psychonomic Science* 8: 221–222.

ULEHLA, Z. J., LITTLE, K. B., AND WEYL, T. C.
    1967    "Operating characteristics and realism of certainty esti-
            mates." *Psychonomic Science* 9: 77–78.

# 3

# CODING RESPONSES TO OPEN-ENDED QUESTIONS

*Kenneth C. W. Kammeyer*

UNIVERSITY OF KANSAS

*Julius A. Roth*

UNIVERSITY OF CALIFORNIA, DAVIS

*This inquiry was initiated with the support of a grant from the Research Committee of the University of California-Davis. Further support was provided by a grant from the University of Kansas General Research Fund. The authors wish to thank Ronald Schwartz and Richard Pardini for their assistance on the study. This paper has been improved by the helpful attention it received from D. Stanley Eitzen and Gary M. Maranell. McKee McClendon provided the computer program that greatly facilitated the analysis of the data.*

Coding is a fundamental task of many sociological studies, but for most researchers it has much less appeal than other parts of the research process. For most it is the uneventful, but necessary, delay that comes between the early enthusiasm of data gathering and the excitement of data analysis.

Although it may be the least pleasant part of a research project, researchers generally recognize the necessity of maintaining a high level of quality control over the coding process. Even when the coding is done by "hired hands," as it almost always is, it is possible to institute cross-check systems that will catch most of the sloppy, inaccurate, or biased coding. Many social researchers employ some cross-check or double-coding system to improve the quality of the data as it goes through the coding process.

Occasionally social researchers have investigated the process of coding, focusing especially on coding accuracy or coding error. Such is the recent research note of Sussman and Haug in which they demonstrated the extent of human and mechanical error in the coding, punching, and tabulating of research data. Their careful examination led them to conclude that "the largest component of processing error occurs in the coding phase of data analysis" (Sussman and Haug, 1967, pp. 55–56). By an independent double coding of 2775 cases (three separate samples), they found the error rate per sample item averaged from 1 per cent to 3 per cent. But, these were averages over all the items of a given study, and there was much variation in the item by item rates of coding error. In some samples certain items had no error at all, while other items had as high as 18 per cent error. The researchers reported that the "Columns [items] with extremely high error represent judgmental coding of responses to open-ended questions" (Sussman and Haug, 1967, p. 55). This finding comes as no surprise because one expects the greatest discrepancies between coders to occur when they have been asked to evaluate and code the responses to open-ended questions. Such responses are usually less than completely clear; they often contain ambiguous words and phrases; and they are frequently ungrammatical and poorly worded. The result is that such responses are read and understood differently by individual coders. This produces a research problem that is troublesome and time consuming, but it is not insurmountable. Given enough time and attention, two independent coders can probably come very close to sharing a common understanding of the meanings of the categories they are using for the coding and can, with some additional effort, share common understandings of the meanings of the words used by the subjects or respondents of a study.

Most researchers settle for something less than the complete socialization of their coders, often using the simple method of comparing the codings of two or more independent coders and then resolving all differences by means of the combined decisions of the coders working together.

One might think that the complete and intensive training of the coders, or the composite judgment of several coders resolving their discrepancies, would be adequate to meet the problem of determining meaning in the coding of responses to open-ended questions. Yet there is another problem of meaning, one much less frequently discussed and, so far as we can discover, not previously investigated. It is to this question that our research is directed: Is the meaning that the coders see in the responses to open-ended questions the same as the respondent himself sees in his words? The task of coding is, after all, one of extracting from the subject's words the essential meaning of his expressed feelings, beliefs, or knowledge about some social object. This essential meaning is then coded in some system of all-inclusive, but mutually exclusive, categories. The question of this research is not what categories the subject himself would employ to categorize his responses—even though this is an important, but even more difficult to investigate, question. The question here is: How would the subject code his answer in a set of categories that are provided by the researcher? If the subject, who provides the answers, could also serve as a coder, would he code his answers differently than other coders, or would there be essentially no difference between the subject-coder's coding and some other coder's coding of the same responses?[1]

## EMPIRICAL INVESTIGATION OF THE QUESTION

The research procedure that can provide the answer to the question is fairly obvious, but it does require a special set of circumstances. Namely, the subjects of a study must also agree to be coders of the data. Normally, this might be difficult to arrange and even somewhat unrealistic. For example, the thought of asking a random sample of community residents to participate in an interview or to answer a questionnaire and then, further, to ask them to become coders of the data is difficult to imagine. In addition, and perhaps this is a more important point, the resultant coders would be very unlike the typical coders in

---

[1] This research question was originally suggested by Sherri Cavan in a personal communication. The practical and methodological issues of the question are also found in the work of Cicourel (1964). His methodological approach to the social world is one that constantly emphasizes that the social researcher must not be too quick to assume that all the words he and his subjects use have shared meanings. The question of meanings has been a long standing methodological problem of content analysis (compare, Berelson, 1952; George 1959).

survey research. An easier approach, indeed one more consistent with customary research procedures, was to use college students as subject-coders. In the present investigation 64 college students enrolled in a social-research methods course were the subjects who answered the questions on a questionnaire and also served as coders of the answers.

The students were asked to complete a questionnaire which included questions on social, family, and personal characteristics (including the occupation of the subject's father) as well as several open-ended questions on student life and direct social action. (The content of these latter questions will be discussed in more detail below.) About one month after the students had completed the questionnaires, they were given instructions on coding. The time spent in this training was minimal but not much less than has typically been given to coders in survey research.

For the actual coding the class of 64 was divided into eight groups of eight persons. Class members, who had been given a sociometric test some days earlier, were combined so that a group did not include friends or acquaintances. The questionnaires were identified only by a code number.

Every subject independently coded the questionnaires of the eight persons in his group. Since each subject was a member of his group he also coded his own questionnaire. No special effort was made to point this out to the coders or to conceal it from them. At the completion of this stage of the study, each questionnaire had been coded eight times—seven times by other subjects acting as coders and once by the subject himself acting as coder.

Following the completion of the coding by the subjects, the two principal investigators and a research assistant independently coded the questions on father's occupation and several open-ended questions. Lastly, the two principal investigators and the research assistant jointly went through all questionnaires and reached a consensus coding of these same questions. At the completion of this stage of the study there were twelve codings of the open-ended questions and the question on father's occupation.

## Content of Open-Ended Questions

Several different types of questions were deliberately selected to provide some variation in the coding tasks. By so doing, we hoped that any results observed would be less likely to be idiosyncratic to the particular type, or form, of the coding procedure. We picked occupational coding as an example of relatively objective data coded with a well-established scale of categories. We included a question on student-role

orientations as an open-ended question that provided highly subjective
data on the subject's attitudes about the student role. The task of the
coder was to evaluate the presence or absence of each of five separate
student roles in the response. The student-action questions were also
open-ended and provided an expression of the subject's opinions about
social action such as protests, sit-ins, demonstrations, and so on. The
coding task differed from the previous one in that the entire response had
to be evaluated for its positive or negative character. Having this variety
of coding tasks, we reasoned if consistent results appeared, we could
make general statements with greater confidence; but if we obtained
varied results, it might be possible to specify some of the coding conditions that produced differences.

  *Father's Occupation.* The occupation of each student's father was
determined from the following set of three questions: (1) What is your
father's (step-father's or guardian's) job or occupation? (2) What does
your father do in this occupation? (Be as specific as you can.) (3) Does
your father work for some business or organization, or does he own his
own business or farm? (He works for_____) (He owns a_____)
(Other (write in)_____). The answers to the questions were coded
using a modified version of Hollingshead's (1957) seven-category system
of occupational prestige. Examples of the specific occupations in each of
the seven categories were provided for the coders.

  *Student Role Orientations.* The next question was designed to draw
from the subjects some indication of their orientation toward the role of
the college student. The question was made up of three parts, but the
answers to the three parts were treated and coded as one continuous
response. The question was: "College students often differ in the things
they value about their college experience. They come to college for different reasons. While they are in college they find features of college life
which become very significant for them. Think for a moment about your
feelings toward college and the college experience. When you are completely honest with yourself, and when you resist the temptation to
respond in cliches, how would you answer the following questions? (1)
What is it about your college experience and education that you value
most? (2) What do you most want and expect from your college experience and education? (3) What are your predominant interests with regard to college life?"

  We had some a priori notions of the types of role orientations that
would be reflected in the responses of the subjects (see Bolton and
Kammeyer, 1967), but a sample of the responses was also examined to see
if any other themes would emerge from them. This procedure produced
one role-orientation theme that had not been anticipated. This theme,
the last one shown below, emphasizes that the college experience allows

the student to meet different kinds of people and to broaden his perspectives. While similar to the social role (C), it seemed to be distinguishable in the coding. These five role orientations may be presented most effectively by simply reproducing the coding instructions given to the coders: "There are five major themes that are often found in the statements that college students use to describe their role orientations. Code the response to the question for each of the following five themes. (A) College as a preparation for an occupation or profession. Viewing college as a place to obtain vocational and occupational training: (1) A predominant or very strong theme in the responses; (2) A clearly indicated theme; (3) A theme that might be inferred from what is said; (4) A theme that is not indicated by the response. (B) An expression of concern with ideas, books, and the pursuit of knowledge. An indication that the person is strongly motivated by intellectual curiosity and is very interested in the world of ideas. (Same responses as A above.) (C) An interest in the social phases of college life. Viewing college as a place to develop social skills, social poise, and competence in interpersonal relations. (Same responses as A above.) (D) An interest in the status and material rewards that may result from the college experience. An emphasis on the personal success and private gain that may come from going to college. (Same responses as A above.) (E) Learning to know different kinds of people, with the emphasis on diversity and difference. The objective is to broaden one's perspectives. (Same responses as A above.)"

*Direct Action.* The remaining set of two open-ended questions focused on the subject's feelings about direct action to change the society and his campus. The two questions on direct action, which were coded separately, were (1) Do you think college students should engage in direct actions (protests, demonstrations, teach-ins, sit-ins, and so on) in order to bring about changes in the society? Elaborate on your answer—why or why not? (2) Do you think students should engage in direct actions (protests, demonstrations, teach-ins, sit-ins, and so on) in order to bring about changes on their own campuses. Elaborate on your answer—why or why not.

While the system for coding the answers to the direct-action questions was more elaborate, we will only report the overall (or global) coding. This coding task required the coder to answer the following question: On the basis of the response to question [1], which position corresponds most closely to the subject's feelings about direct action to change the society? (1) Very positive—without apparent reservations or qualifications; (2) Positive—with some reservations or qualifications; (3) Negative—but only mildly so; (4) Very Negative; (5) Unable to determine from the response. The coding instructions for the second question read: On the basis of the response to question [2], which position corresponds most closely to the subject's feelings about direct action to change his campus? The same coding categories as above were provided.

## Results

Now to answer the research question, which is, again: Will there be a difference between the way in which a subject-coder codes his responses to open-ended questions and the way in which other coders code his responses?

In the analysis that follows we will compare the coding that each subject makes of his own responses with (1) the codings by the other seven student coders, (2) the codings by the two principal investigators and the research assistant (labeled the research supervisors), (3) the composite coding agreed upon by the three research supervisors.

The comparisons will be made by recording the number of times the subject-coder has coded his response the same as other coders, the number of times he has coded his response higher than other coders (for example on the seven-point occupational-prestige scale), and the number of times he has recorded his response lower than other coders.[2]

If there is no systematic difference between the subjects' coding of their own responses and the coding by others, then they should code their responses higher than others about the same number of times as they code them lower. If there is a pronounced tendency for the subject-coders to be either higher or lower than the other coders on any given item, or if there is a pattern of being either higher or lower for a set of items, then this would indicate that others do not see in the responses precisely what the subjects see. This may be clarified by examining the results of the comparisons for father's occupation.

*Father's Occupation.* Before proceeding, however, the reader might try to anticipate the results of the analysis that follows. Will the subject differ systematically from other coders in the way he categorizes his father's occupation? If he does differ from others, will he tend to classify his father's occupation higher on the prestige scale or lower? Remember,

---

[2] The same comparisons were made by comparing the subject-coder's coding of his answer with the arithmetic mean of the codings of the seven other coders and the arithmetic mean of the research-supervisors' codings. This method was open to criticism because of the instability of means for small numbers of cases. It had the additional liability of being difficult to describe accurately and yet clearly. However, this mode of analysis, which focused on the direction of the difference between the subject-coder and the average coding of other coders produced exactly the same results as the method reported here.

For the remaining topics this method of analysis was also followed but will not be reported. Almost exactly the same results were obtained as those reported below.

all subjects were working with a well-established list of the occupations that are typically found in the seven ranked occupational categories.

Table 1 shows that the coding of the subject-coders was the same as other coders (both the other students and the research supervisors) slightly over 70 per cent of the time. We expected a high level of agreement on the coding of this question since the topic was familiar and the methods of the coding system well worked out. However, since there is no established norm or standard for high agreement, it is difficult to say if this is in any way extraordinary until we have compared it with

Table 1

Coding Differences in Father's Occupation Between Subject-Coders
and Other Coders

| Question | The number of times that subject-coders coded their father's occupation: | | | | | |
|---|---|---|---|---|---|---|
| *Father's* *Occupation* | The same as other student coders: | 316 | (70.5%) | | | |
| | Different from other student coders: | 132 | (29.5%) | When different: Higher: | 59 | (44.7%) |
| | Total: | 448ᵃ | (100.0%) | Lower: | 73 | (55.3%) |
| | | | | | 132 | (100.0%) |
| | The same as the research supervisors: | 136 | (70.8%) | | | |
| | Different from the research supervisors: | 56 | (29.2%) | When different: Higher: | 26 | (46.4%) |
| | Total: | 192ᵇ | (100.0%) | Lower: | 30 | (53.6%) |
| | | | | | 56 | (100.0%) |
| | The same as the research supervisors' composite: | 47 | (73.4%) | | | |
| | Different from the research supervisor's composite: | 17 | (26.6%) | When different: Higher: | 8 | (47.1%) |
| | Total: | 64 | (100.0%) | Lower: | 9 | (52.9%) |
| | | | | | 17 | (100.0%) |

ᵃ The total number 448 is obtained from the 56 comparisons ($7 \times 8$) that are made in each of the eight groups.

ᵇ The total number 192 is obtained by making three comparisons (the codings of the two principal investigators and a research assistant) for each of the 64 subjects.

the amount of agreement on the other questions. When we do so we will see that this level of agreement is higher than that obtained on the other open-ended questions in this study.

It was somewhat surprising to us that, among those cases where there were differences between the subject-coders and other coders, the subjects in this study tended to code their own father's occupation in a lower prestige category more often than in a higher prestige category. This tendency was not particularly strong, but both the method of analysis described in footnote 2 and that presented in Table 1 indicated that, when there was a difference between the way a subject coded his father's occupation and the way someone else coded it, about 55 per cent of the time the subject-coder coded it lower on the prestige scale.

We simply make two observations on the basis of this first analysis. First, insofar as there is an overall pattern, it does tend to run counter to what had been expected. We had supposed that if the subject coded his father's occupation differently from others, he would tend to upgrade it rather than downgrade it. Now it appears that something other than status maximization may be operating to produce the observed tendency. Perhaps having additional information (other than what was actually written on the paper), as the subject undoubtedly had about his own father's occupation, had the general effect of reducing the prestige level of the father's work since job labels and occupational titles often tend to be upwardly oriented. (This is exemplified by the well-known janitor to custodian to sanitary engineer progression.)

The second observation grows out of some additional analysis of the extreme cases of difference in which the subject-coder was either distinctly higher or lower than other coders. We noticed that when the subjects had fathers with higher prestige occupations (as judged by the supervisors' composite), the subjects were somewhat more likely to code their fathers' occupations lower than other coders. Conversely, when the subjects had fathers with low prestige occupations, they tended to code their fathers' occupations higher. These findings could be an indication of a strain toward the middle of the prestige range by the subjects when they code their own fathers' occupations. Should this be the case, the general pattern of downgrading observed here could simply reflect the generally higher-status occupations of the subjects in our sample.

This analysis of a relatively structured item has shown that there may be some tendency for the subjects-coders to code their own responses differently from other coders. We have at least a hint of the conclusion that we shall reach in this study: *Respondents see more in their responses than the average objective coder is able to see.* For additional evidence we turn now to the coding of the open-ended questions on college-student role orientations.

*Student Role Orientations.* For the analysis of college-student roles, we did have some notions about the direction of difference that might occur between the subject-coders and other coders. We expected that there would be a tendency for the subject-coders to see more in their responses than others coding the same material, especially if what was to be seen had a generally favorable aura. To put it simply, we supposed that subject-coders might have some tendency to "put the best possible face" on their responses and, therefore, might code their responses to reflect the more valued orientations toward the college role. Of course, the subject-coder might code his responses differently from others simply because, as we suggested above, he had more information about the meaning of his response.

The analysis of the college-role orientation question is presented in Table 2 and follows the basic format presented in Table 1. These tables show that the amount of agreement between the subject-coder and other coders varies greatly from one role orientation to another and, on occasion, from one type of coder to another. The highest amount of agreement occurred with respect to the vocational role orientation where more than 60 per cent of the time there was no difference between the subject-coder and others. The privatist role orientation, which emphasized the status and material rewards of going to college, produced the next highest level of coding agreement with slightly under 60 per cent of the coding the same as the subject-coder. The intellectual and the social role orientations averaged somewhat over 40 per cent agreement between the subject-coder and others coding the same material. Finally, the role orientation that emphasized the importance of college as a place for broadening perspectives showed the lowest levels of agreement—at least between the research supervisors and the subject-coders (31.2 per cent agreement). Other students had an appreciably higher level of agreement with the subject-coders on this last role orientation, about one-half of the time (48.2 per cent) they agreed with the subject's coding of his own response. Except for this item there was relatively little difference in the amount of agreement that the two types of coders (student coders and research supervisors) had with the subject-coders; so it appears that it is the content of the item more than the type of coder that produces most of the differences in coding.

The more important aspect of this analysis is the direction of the difference whenever there is a difference between the subject coding his own questionnaire and some other coder coding it. A persistent or prevailing directionality in the differences may allow some inferences to be made about the causes of differences. Table 2 reveals a clear pattern.

# Table 2

## Coding Differences in College-Student Role Orientations Between Subject-Coders and Other Coders

Role Orientation

The number of times that subject-coders coded their role orientations:

### Vocational: College as Preparation For An Occupation or Profession

| | | | When different: Subject saw the theme | |
|---|---|---|---|---|
| The same as other student coders: | 267 | (59.6%) | more clearly: | 105 (58.0%) |
| Different from other student coders: | 181 | (40.4%) | less clearly: | 76 (42.0%) |
| Total: | 448 | (100.0%) | Total: | 181 (100.0%) |

| | | | When different: Subject saw the theme | |
|---|---|---|---|---|
| The same as the research supervisors: | 123 | (64.1%) | more clearly: | 47 (68.1%) |
| Different from the research supervisors: | 69 | (35.9%) | less clearly: | 22 (31.9%) |
| Total: | 192 | (100.0%) | Total: | 69 (100.0%) |

| | | | When different: Subject saw the theme | |
|---|---|---|---|---|
| The same as the research supervisors' composite: | 47 | (73.4%) | more clearly: | 13 (76.5%) |
| Different from the research supervisors' composite: | 17 | (26.6%) | less clearly: | 4 (23.5%) |
| Total: | 64 | (100.0%) | Total: | 17 (100.0%) |

### Intellectual: Concern With Ideas, Books, and the Pursuit of Knowledge

| | | | When different: Subject saw the theme | |
|---|---|---|---|---|
| The same as other student coders: | 196 | (43.8%) | more clearly: | 130 (51.6%) |
| Different from other student coders: | 252 | (56.2%) | less clearly: | 122 (48.4%) |
| Total: | 448 | (100.0%) | Total: | 252 (100.0%) |

| | | | When different: Subject saw the theme | |
|---|---|---|---|---|
| The same as the research supervisors: | 80 | (41.7%) | more clearly: | 64 (57.1%) |
| Different from the research supervisors: | 112 | (58.3%) | less clearly: | 48 (42.9%) |
| Total: | 192 | (100.0%) | Total: | 112 (100.0%) |

The same as the research supervisors'
composite: 31 (48.4%)
Different from the research supervisors'
composite: 33 (51.6%)

Total: 64 (100.0%)

When different: Subject saw the theme
more clearly: 19 (57.6%)
less clearly: 14 (42.4%)

33 (100.0%)

*Social:*
*An Interest in*
*the Social Phases*
*of College Life*

The same as other student coders: 189 (42.2%)
Different from other student coders: 259 (57.8%)

Total: 448 (100.0%)

When different: Subject saw the theme
more clearly: 120 (46.3%)
less clearly: 139 (53.7%)

259 (100.0%)

The same as the research supervisors: 84 (43.8%)
Different from the research supervisors'
composite: 108 (56.2%)

Total: 192 (100.0%)

When different: Subject saw the theme
more clearly: 77 (71.3%)
less clearly: 31 (28.7%)

108 (100.0%)

The same as the research supervisors'
composite: 29 (45.3%)
Different from the research supervisors'
composite: 35 (54.7%)

Total: 64 (100.0%)

When different: Subject saw the theme
more clearly: 20 (57.1%)
less clearly: 15 (42.9%)

35 (100.0%)

*Privatist:*
*Interest in the*
*Status and*
*Material Rewards*
*of Going to*
*College*

The same as other student coders: 252 (56.2%)
Different from other student coders: 196 (43.8%)

Total: 448 (100.0%)

When different: Subject saw the theme
more clearly: 111 (56.6%)
less clearly: 85 (43.4%)

196 (100.0%)

## Table 2 (*Continued*)

Role Orientation

The number of times that subject-coders coded their role orientations:

The same as the research supervisors: 116 (60.4%)
Different from the research supervisors: 76 (39.6%)
Total: 192 (100.0%)

When different: Subject saw the theme
more clearly: 57 (75.0%)
less clearly: 19 (25.0%)
76 (100.0%)

The same as the research supervisors' composite: 41 (64.1%)
Different from the research supervisors' composite: 23 (35.9%)
Total: 64 (100.0%)

When different: Subject saw the theme
more clearly: 18 (78.3%)
less clearly: 5 (21.7%)
23 (100.0%)

*Broadening Perspectives: Learning to Know Different Kinds of People*

The same as other student coders: 216 (48.2%)
Different from other student coders: 232 (51.8%)
Total: 448 (100.0%)

When different: Subject saw the theme
more clearly: 146 (62.9%)
less clearly: 86 (37.1%)
232 (100.0%)

The same as the research supervisors: 60 (31.2%)
Different from the research supervisors: 132 (68.8%)
Total: 192 (100.0%)

When different: Subject saw the theme
more clearly: 114 (86.4%)
less clearly: 18 (13.6%)
132 (100.0%)

The same as the research supervisors' composite: 15 (23.4%)
Different from the research supervisors' composite: 49 (76.6%)
Total: 64 (100.0%)

When different: Subject saw the theme
more clearly: 46 (93.9%)
less clearly: 3 (6.1%)
49 (100.0%)

When subjects differ from other coders, as they do about half the time, they generally see the role-orientation themes more clearly revealed in their answers than other coders do. Among the 15 comparisons made in Table 2, only one runs counter to this pattern. The exception is found where the subject-coder was less likely to see the social role orientation in his answer than did the other student coders. (In only 46.3 per cent of the differences did the subject see the theme more clearly.) In all other cases where there was a difference between the subject-coder and other coders, the subject-coder saw the role orientation more clearly evidenced in his response.

While it is difficult to say which of these role orientations might be viewed most positively by college students and which viewed less positively, there seems to us to be no clear evidence that the subject-coders are simply seeing in their responses the role orientations that are the most highly valued. In other words, our original assumption that subject-coders would see the more valued role orientations in their responses does not now seem to explain the differences between the subject-coders and others coding their responses. Broadening perspectives (Table 2) does appear to be one role orientation the subject-coder is likely to see more often in his response than other people. Since one can presume that the broadening of perspectives would be positively valued as a role orientation for college students, this could be a case of the subject-coder enhancing his response. But, the next role orientation that the subject-coder sees more often in his response is that of the privatist (Table 2). The privatist role orientation is an explicit concern with "status and material rewards" and an emphasis on "the personal success and private gain that may come from going to college." The self-seeking quality of this orientation is not, it seems to us, particularly flattering, even in a culture that emphasizes materialism. In our view, and we suspect in the view of many students, there is an unseemly self-interest that characterizes this role orientation. Yet this is an orientation that subject-coders see much more often than do others coding their responses. When there was a coding difference between the research supervisors and the subject-coders, 75 per cent of the time the subject-coders saw the privatist role orientation more clearly in their responses. In the same comparison with other student coders it was about 57 per cent of the time. This does not seem to us to be a case of the subject-coder putting the best face on his response.

Furthermore, the intellectual role orientation can be viewed as more evidence that the subject-coder does not differ from other coders simply because he is trying to enhance his own response. Of the five role orientations this was seen relatively less often by the subject-coder in his

## Table 3

### Coding Differences in Attitudes about Direct Action Between Subjects-Coders and Other Coders

The number of times that subject-coders coded their responses:

*Direct Action to Produce Social Change*

| | | When different: Subject saw his response more favorable | |
|---|---|---|---|
| The same as other student coders: | 333 (74.3%) | | |
| Different from other student coders: | 115 (25.7%) | to direct action: | 74 (64.3%) |
| | | less favorable: | 41 (35.7%) |
| Total: | 448 (100.0%) | | 115 (100.0%) |
| | | | |
| The same as the research supervisors: | 155 (80.7%) | When different: Subject saw his response more favorable | |
| Different from the research supervisors: | 37 (19.3%) | to direct action: | 19 (51.4%) |
| | | less favorable: | 18 (48.6%) |
| Total: | 192 (100.0%) | | 37 (100.0%) |
| | | | |
| The same as the research supervisors' composite: | 52 (81.2%) | When different: Subject saw his response more favorable | |
| Different from the research supervisors' composite: | 12 (18.8%) | to direct action: | 9 (75.0%) |
| | | less favorable: | 3 (25.0%) |
| Total: | 64 (100.0%) | | 12 (100.0%) |

**Direct Action to Produce Campus Change**

The same as other student coders: 281 (62.7%)
Different from other student coders: 167 (37.3%)

Total: 448 (100.0%)

When different: Subject saw his response more favorable to direct action: 92 (55.1%)
less favorable: 75 (44.9%)

167 (100.0%)

The same as the research supervisors: 124 (64.6%)
Different from the research supervisors: 68 (35.4%)

Total: 192 (100.0%)

When different: Subject saw his response more favorable to direct action: 30 (44.1%)
less favorable: 38 (55.9%)

68 (100.0%)

The same as the research supervisors' composite: 46 (71.9%)
Different from the research supervisors' composite: 18 (28.1%)

Total: 64 (100.0%)

When different: Subject saw his response more favorable to direct action: 10 (55.6%)
less favorable: 8 (44.4%)

18 (100.0%)

response. While the cynic can argue that anti-intellectualism is widely found among American college students, the favorable connotations of such phrases as concern with ideas, pursuit of knowledge, and intellectual curiosity are readily apparent. If the subject-coder had wanted to code his responses so as to enhance his image, this would certainly have been the place to have done it; yet on the average, he was relatively less likely to see the intellectual orientation in his response than he was to see the privatist, the vocational, or the social orientations. Both this analysis and that of father's occupation run counter to the simplistic notion that differences between subject-coders and other coders can be accounted for by the attempt of the subject-coders to improve or enhance their responses. This will be discussed further in the conclusion.

*Direct Action.* The final two questions asked the subject to indicate his feelings about direct action to change the society and his campus. The coding task in these two instances was to indicate the degree of favorableness or unfavorableness about direct action, the coding categories ranging from very positive to very negative. In this case it was difficult to anticipate the direction of differences between subject-coders and other coders, so it remained to be seen if there would be, as in the previous analysis, systematic directional differences. Table 3 presents the coding differences on the direct action question.

The pattern of the data again is quite consistent although among the nine comparisons there is one exception. The subject-coder generally saw in his responses a more favorable attitude toward direct action than other coders. Only in the comparison with the research supervisors on the question of direct action to change the campus did the subject-coders see their responses as less favorable toward direct action. While the differences were often not great, there did seem to be a systematic directionality in the comparisons, the subject-coders seeing more favorableness toward direct action in their answers.

## Discussion

In some respects this study has concentrated on a very specific and limited methodological issue. Yet, the issue is fundamental for much of the survey research in both sociology and social psychology. The specific issue is whether or not a researcher can discern from the words of a subject exactly how the subject feels about a social object. Usually the objective in a social-psychological survey is to probe the subject's conception of a given issue. It is generally assumed that a subject can tell what his views are better than anyone else. This, in fact, is the common assumption that survey researchers make when they accept the questionnaire response at face value as a measurement of one's position on a given dimension. However, the process of other people coding that response injects another step into this interpretative process. The coding of a response pushes the measured data one more step away from the subject's actual attitude, belief, or opinion. This is a very important step if there is a systematic difference between the subject's feelings and the coding of his response by another person. Our findings clearly suggest that such systematic differences do exist, if we take the subject's coding of his own words as an indication of his position.

Perhaps the implications of these findings for the research processes may be shrugged off with the assertion that in social research the major objective is almost always to make statements about relationships rather than absolute descriptive statements. The argument could then be made that the tendency of coders to misjudge in one direction or another the real meaning of the respondent's words would be unimportant. Since everyone would presumably be measured at a value somewhat off from the value of his true position, the relationship between variables would still be roughly the same. This argument would be valid if the deviation from the meaning that the subject wished to convey was always uniformly in one direction or another, but that is clearly not always going to be the case. In this analysis, for example, the question of father's occupation revealed a tendency for other coders to be more extreme in their categorizations than the subject-coders. The effect that these and other coding differences would have on relationships and correlations between variables is quite complicated. It is clear, however, that if there were countervailing biases in the coding of two cross-classified variables, then the degree, and perhaps the direction, of the relationship would be influenced. It is equally clear that in descriptive research the feelings and opinions of a subject are likely to be distorted and inaccurate after they have been funneled through the perceptions of an objective coder. At least, this is true if the subject's own coding of his response is regarded as the best interpretation of what he is really trying to express by his answer.

Finally, it would be comforting if we could write off the differences between subject-coders and other coders as resulting from the attempts by the former to enhance, embellish, or improve their personal status. Our data do not provide such a comforting conclusion as a total explanation of the differences found. While it cannot be ruled out as a contributory element, it is clear that all of the evidence at hand cannot be so interpreted.

## SUMMARY AND CONCLUSION

Coding is one of the basic steps in the social-research process. While there has been a continuing concern with coding consistency among coders, there has been little or no empirical attention given to the question of whether the subject's words have the same meaning for him as they have for other coders. That has been the question of this inquiry, and from the data it can be seen that there are systematic differences between the coding of subject-coders and other coders, even when they are coding the same words.

There are many questions that this study cannot answer even though the present findings call for many more answers. The study, as planned and executed, sought to learn whether or not systematic differences would occur, and they did. Patterns and differences appeared in each of the three coding tasks, so it does not appear that it was simply a function of what was being coded or how. The interpretations of these differences have been largely ad hoc, and therefore, the direction of further research is clear. Subsequent research must establish more firmly the conditions under which differences will appear and factors that account for the direction of differences. We believe that the findings of this inquiry raise some serious problems regarding the process of coding open-ended questions. The problems are not easily answered or disregarded, and they clearly merit more study.

## REFERENCES

BERELSON, B.
  1952  *Content Analysis in Communication Research.* New York: Free Press of Glencoe.
BOLTON, C. D. AND KAMMEYER, K. C. W.
  1967  *The University Student: A Study of Student Behavior and Values.* New Haven, Conn.: College and University Press.
CICOUREL, A. V.
  1964  *Method and Measurement in Sociology.* London: Collier-Macmillan; New York: Free Press.
GEORGE, A. L.
  1959  "Quantitative and qualitative approaches to content analysis." Pp. 7–32 in Ithiel De Sola Pool (Ed.), *Trends in Content Analysis.* Urbana, Ill.: University of Illinois Press.
HOLLINGSHEAD, A. B.
  1957  *Two Factor Index of Social Position.* New Haven, Conn.: August B. Hollingshead.
SUSSMAN, M. B. AND HAUG, M. R.
  1967  "Human and mechanical error—An unknown quantity in research." *The American Behavioral Scientist* 11: 55–56.

PART TWO

MEASUREMENT ERROR IN
REGRESSION AND
PATH ANALYSIS

# 4

# THE TREATMENT OF UNOBSERVABLE
# VARIABLES IN PATH ANALYSIS

*Robert M. Hauser*

UNIVERSITY OF WISCONSIN, MADISON

*Arthur S. Goldberger*

UNIVERSITY OF WISCONSIN, MADISON

*This paper was prepared for presentation at the 65th annual meetings of the American Sociological Association, held at Washington, D.C., August 31 through September 3, 1970. At that time, it was distributed as Workshop Paper EME 7030 by the Social Systems Research Institute, University of Wisconsin. Work on this project was in part supported by the Graduate School Research Committee of the University of Wisconsin, by the National Institutes of Health, U.S. Public Health Service (M-6275), and by the Social and Rehabilitation Service, U.S. Department of Health, Education, and Welfare (CRD-314).*

Under the rubrics of path analysis (Duncan, 1966; Land, 1969; Heise, 1969) or dependence analysis (Boudon, 1965; 1968), sociologists have recently been introduced to the expression of theories or models as systems of structural equations. In this chapter our purpose is to draw attention to the recurrent problem of estimating the parameters of overidentified path models which feature unobservable variables. Such variables have not been, or perhaps cannot be, measured directly, and the structural coefficients pertaining to their causes and effects must be inferred from the available measurements and the postulated causal structure. While models containing unobservables may be underidentified (Siegel and Hodge, 1968; Duncan, 1969a; Land, 1970) or just-identified (Heise, 1969; Wiley and Wiley, 1970; Land, 1969, pp. 29–33; 1970; Hauser, 1969b, pp. 549–550; and Brewer, Crano, and Campbell, 1970), most frequently they are overidentified (Duncan, Featherman, and Duncan, 1968; Duncan, Haller, and Portes, 1968; Hodge and Treiman, 1968; Duncan, 1969b; Hauser, 1968; 1969a; 1969b; 1970). Overidentification means that alternative estimates of certain parameters can be made (Costner, 1969; Blalock, 1969a; 1970).

Alternative estimates in an overidentified model will not coincide in finite samples even where the model is correct, that is, even where they would coincide in the population. Hence, some means of reconciling the conflicting estimates is required. The theoretical and empirical path-analysis literature tends to slur the sample-population distinction, and it provides little guidance in estimation for overidentified models.[1] Some ad hoc procedures for estimation of overidentified models containing unobservables have been suggested. For example, Blalock (1970) and Land (1970) have advocated that one or more equations be ignored in the estimation process and be introduced only to test for goodness of fit. At least one empirical example using this approach (Hodge and Treiman, 1968; Hauser, 1969b) predates their work. The technique is mentioned in the econometric literature (Christ, 1966, pp. 407–411) but with little enthusiasm. Other analysts have used arbitrary averages of alternative estimators without considering their statistical properties (Duncan, Featherman, and Duncan, 1968; Duncan, Haller, and Portes, 1968; Hauser, 1968; 1969a; 1970).

Principles of estimation imply testing procedures, and the treatment of goodness of fit in the path-analysis literature reflects its casual methods of estimation. In numerous instances we are told only to "see" whether the correlations implied by estimators for an overidentified

---

[1] The sociological literature is occasionally vague on the reasons for discrepancies among alternative estimates (compare Costner, 1969, pp. 252–253, 259, 262). However, the explanation is no more complicated than that required to account for the fact that, in a random sample from a normal population, the mean and the median will be different, despite their coincidence in the population.

model are "close" to the observed correlations. It is not clear how close is close enough. For example, Costner (1969, pp. 252–262) states,

> Failure of the data to satisfy this [overidentification] equation, at least approximately, indicates that, in some respect, the indicators . . . are not appropriate . . . . [T]he several estimates . . . should all be identical except for random error . . . . It may be reasonably asked what is meant when we say that the consistency criterion is satisfied. Do we mean that the two sides of [the overidentification equation] are exactly identical, that they are approximately identical, or that they should not differ to a degree that is statistically significant at the commonly utilized levels of significance?

The sociological literature on path analysis also conveys the misleading impression that certain problems in estimation and testing have not been analyzed or even that they are not amenable to rigorous analysis. For example, Costner (1969, p. 262) states, "Satisfying the additional consistency criteria in the three-indicator model presents an additional statistical inference problem, the solution to which does not appear to be found in the factor analysis literature." Blalock (1970, p. 103) states,

> If there were absolutely no specification or sampling errors, the data would fit the model exactly, and it would make no difference which equations were treated as redundant. However, in practice, no data will fit the model exactly; therefore, there is a certain arbitrariness in one's selection of the particular equations that will be used for estimation purposes and those that will be treated as excess equations used to test the model. This difficulty . . . would seem to admit of no completely satisfactory solution . . . . Perhaps the issue will reduce to the question of whether one assumes specification errors to be more serious than sampling errors . . . .[2]

In fact, the estimation of overidentified models is not an intractable problem, and it is a central topic in the econometric and psychometric literature. There, standard principles of statistical inference are applied to determine efficient estimates, that is, estimates which have minimum sampling variability. Since path models are linear models of the type considered in econometrics and psychometrics, it should

---

[2] These remarks call to mind Boudon's (1968, p. 213) assertion, "Of course, when we are dealing with fallible data, these different possible choices will lead to different estimates, and there is obviously no reason to think that one estimate is better than the other."

not be surprising that the efficient estimating procedures developed there can be applied to problems of estimation in path analysis. Standard principles of statistical inference also imply testing procedures, and these, too, are worked out in the econometric and psychometric literature.[3]

We propose to illustrate the utility of econometric and psychometric estimation techniques for path models containing unobservable variables. Our examples are simple and will not do justice to the more elaborate sociological applications. They can be thought of as components of larger models, and they should suffice to document our basic theme. We shall treat two classes of models, those where unobservables appear only as causes of observable variables and those where unobservables appear as both causes and effects of observable variables. These have been recognized as distinct cases in path analysis.

Following Costner (1969), Blalock (1969a, pp. 264–270) discusses multiple indicators of correlated unobservable variables. Then, under the heading of "the instrumental variable approach" (pp. 270–272), he considers the case where causes of the unobservable variables are also observed. He correctly indicates that this gives an econometric flavor to the model, but his emphasis on instrumental variables is somewhat misleading. Land (1970, p. 507) distinguishes "two general cases for which sociologists will be interested in utilizing unmeasured variables in a causal model." "The first of these," he states, "arises in the study of measurement error . . . . The common characteristic of all of these applications of path analysis is that the hypothetical (unmeasured) variables enter the path models only as causes of the observed variables. A second case in which sociologists will utilize unmeasured variables is as variables which intervene between measured variables in a causal model."

We shall see that the first type of path model translates directly into a confirmatory factor-analysis model which psychometricians have studied and for which computer programs are available. The second type of path model translates into a form studied by econometricians and for which computer programs are also available. There are, we should add, cases which require a blending of the factor-analysis and econometric approaches.

As Blalock has implied, efficient estimation of overidentified path models may not be a very important topic. Perhaps it is more important to settle for some reasonable estimate and to concentrate on improving the model than to search diligently for efficient estimators. Still, it is

---

[3] The idea that path analysis involves a mixture of psychometric and econometric themes is not a new one (see Duncan, 1966, p. 16; Blalock, 1961, pp. 167–169; 1969a; Werts and Linn, 1970; Wright, 1925; 1934; 1954).

worth knowing that there are solutions to some of the puzzles we create, and it is probably worthwhile to build up the stock of tools in advance of the time when rigorous inference becomes the order of the day.

## GENERAL CONSIDERATIONS

In most, and perhaps in all, cases the efficient estimators for an overidentified model may be interpreted as appropriately weighted averages of the several conflicting estimators. The weights are chosen to take account of the sampling variability and covariability of the original estimates. Generally, the weights cannot be determined in advance but must be estimated from a sample. For this reason, the computation required to obtain efficient estimates is often more extensive than that for ordinary regression or ad hoc averaging of estimates. For example, the maximum-likelihood principle offers a standard method for efficient estimation of overidentified models (with or without unobservable variables), and the method implicitly involves the construction of weights with which to reconcile the conflicting estimates. Often, as in factor analysis, iterative computation is required.[4]

To avoid elaborate computations, other estimation procedures have been developed for certain classes of models. Generalized least-squares and two- and three-stage least-squares are econometric examples, and the minres criterion for fitting factor-analysis models is an example from psychometrics. Under some conditions estimates produced by such procedures have the same efficiency as maximum-likelihood estimates.

A simple example may clarify the logic of efficient estimation. Suppose we have two independent, unbiased estimates, $m_1$ and $m_2$, of a parameter $\mu$, which have variances $\sigma_{11}$ and $\sigma_{22}$, respectively. We wish to construct $m$, the minimum-variance unbiased estimator of $\mu$. That is, we want to find weights, $a_1$ and $a_2$, such that $E(m) = \mu$, where $m = a_1m_1 + a_2m_2$ and $\mathrm{Var}(m)$ is minimized. Clearly, we will choose $a_1 + a_2 = 1$, since

$$E(m) = E(a_1m_1 + a_2m_2) = E(a_1m_1) + E(a_2m_2) = a_1E(m_1) + a_2E(m_2)$$
$$= a_1\mu + a_2\mu = (a_1 + a_2)\mu \tag{1}$$

---

[4] The fully recursive model with uncorrelated errors provides an important exception to this pattern. For that model Boudon (1965; 1968) developed an averaging scheme, with weights determined by the sample. However, his estimates are less efficient than those produced by ordinary least-squares regression, which gives all the weight to the regression estimate and ignores the conflicting instrumental-variable estimates (Goldberger, 1970b).

Subject to this, we wish to choose the $a_1$ and $a_2$ which will minimize the sampling variance of $m$, namely,

$$\text{Var}(m) = \text{Var}(a_1 m_1 + a_2 m_2) = a_1^2 \sigma_{11} + a_2^2 \sigma_{22} \tag{2}$$

Multiplying equation (2) by $(m_2 - m_1)^2$, we obtain

$$a_1^2 \sigma_{11}(m_2 - m_1)^2 + a_2^2 \sigma_{22}(m_1 - m_2)^2$$
$$= \sigma_{11}(m_2 a_1 - a_1 m_1)^2 + \sigma_{22}(m_1 a_2 - a_2 m_2)^2 \tag{3}$$

Noting that $a_1 = 1 - a_2$ and $a_2 = 1 - a_1$, we rewrite this as

$$\sigma_{11}(m_2(1 - a_2) - a_1 m_1)^2 + \sigma_{22}(m_1(1 - a_1) - a_2 m_2)^2$$
$$= \sigma_{11}(m_2 - a_1 m_1 - a_2 m_2)^2 + \sigma_{22}(m_1 - a_1 m_1 - a_2 m_2)^2$$
$$= \sigma_{11}(m_2 - m)^2 + \sigma_{22}(m_1 - m)^2 \tag{4}$$

Finally, dividing equation (4) by $\sigma_{11}\sigma_{22}$ and cancelling like terms in the numerator and denominator, we have

$$\sigma^{11}(m_1 - m)^2 + \sigma^{22}(m_2 - m)^2 \tag{5}$$

where $\sigma^{11} = 1/\sigma_{11}$ and $\sigma^{22} = 1/\sigma_{22}$, which we can proceed directly to minimize with respect to $m$. Setting the derivative of expression (5) with respect to $m$ equal to zero, we find that

$$m = \frac{\sigma^{11}}{\sigma^{11} + \sigma^{22}} m_1 + \frac{\sigma^{22}}{\sigma^{11} + \sigma^{22}} m_2 \tag{6}$$

whence

$$a_1 = \frac{\sigma^{11}}{\sigma^{11} + \sigma^{22}} \quad \text{and} \quad a_2 = \frac{\sigma^{22}}{\sigma^{11} + \sigma^{22}} \tag{7}$$

are the desired weights.

While we could have minimized equation (2) directly, we chose the more tortuous path in order to point out that expression (5) gives the function minimized by the principle of generalized least-squares, namely, the weighted sum of squared deviations of the conflicting estimates from the desired estimate, where each weight is inverse to the variance of the corresponding estimate.

If the estimates were not independent but had covariance $\sigma_{12} \neq 0$, then the GLS principle says that the estimate $m$ should be chosen to minimize

$$\sigma^{11}(m_1 - m)^2 + \sigma^{22}(m_2 - m)^2 + 2\sigma^{12}(m_1 - m)(m_2 - m) \tag{8}$$

where the $\sigma$'s with superscripts are elements in the inverse matrix

$$\begin{pmatrix} \sigma^{11} & \sigma^{12} \\ \sigma^{12} & \sigma^{22} \end{pmatrix} = \begin{pmatrix} \sigma_{11} & \sigma_{12} \\ \sigma_{12} & \sigma_{22} \end{pmatrix}^{-1} \tag{9}$$

The resulting estimate, which has the property of minimum-variance unbiasedness, is

$$m = \frac{\sigma^{11} + \sigma^{12}}{\sigma^{11} + \sigma^{22} + 2\sigma^{12}}\, m_1 + \frac{\sigma^{22} + \sigma^{12}}{\sigma^{11} + \sigma^{22} + 2\sigma^{12}}\, m_2 \tag{10}$$

which is again a weighted average of $m_1$ and $m_2$, with the weights now taking account of sampling covariability as well as variability.

In practice, the $\sigma$'s are unknown and must be replaced by estimates of them. When this is done, we refer to the procedure as modified generalized least-squares (MGLS). Under quite general conditions the MGLS procedure produces estimates which are as efficient as those produced by the maximum-likelihood principle.

## MULTIPLE INDICATORS OF CAUSALLY RELATED UNOBSERVABLE VARIABLES

### Specification of the Model

Consider a model in which we observe multiple indicators of two causally related unobservable variables, as shown in Figure 1. In algebraic form the system consists of:

$$y^* = \alpha z^* + \epsilon \tag{11}$$

a linear equation expressing the determination of the unobservable variable $y^*$ by the unobservable variable $z^*$ and an unobservable disturbance $\epsilon$;

$$\begin{aligned} z_1 &= \beta_1 z^* + v_1 \\ &\vdots \quad \vdots \\ z_k &= \beta_k z^* + v_k \\ &\vdots \quad \vdots \\ z_K &= \beta_K z^* + v_K \end{aligned} \tag{12}$$

a set of $K$ linear equations expressing each observable indicator $z_k$ of $z^*$ in terms of $z^*$ and an unobservable disturbance $v_k (k = 1, \ldots, K)$; and

$$\begin{aligned} y_1 &= \gamma_1 y^* + w_1 \\ &\vdots \quad \vdots \\ y_m &= \gamma_m y^* + w_m \\ &\vdots \quad \vdots \\ y_M &= \gamma_M y^* + w_M \end{aligned} \tag{13}$$

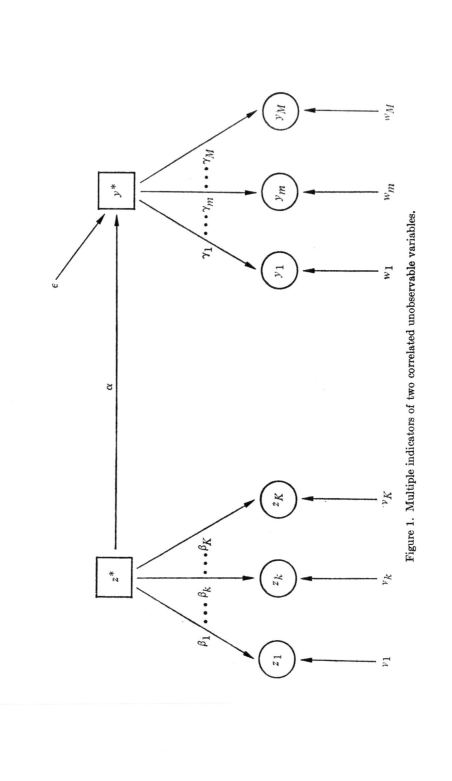

Figure 1. Multiple indicators of two correlated unobservable variables.

a set of $M$ linear equations expressing each observable indicator $y_m$ of $y^*$ in terms of $y^*$ and an unobservable disturbance $w_m (m = 1, \ldots, M)$. It is assumed that the disturbances are independent of $z^*$ and $y^*$ and are mutually independent as well.

The $\alpha$, $\beta$'s, and $\gamma$'s are path coefficients to be estimated along with the disturbance variances, $\sigma_\epsilon^2, \sigma_{v_1}^2, \ldots, \sigma_{v_K}^2, \sigma_{w_1}^2, \ldots, \sigma_{w_M}^2$. We are following the econometric and psychometric convention which leaves the disturbances unstandardized; our variances are just the squares of the residual paths which would appear if the path-analysis convention (in which the disturbances are standardized) had been followed. The unobservables, $z^*$ and $y^*$, are standardized as are the observables (although the latter is not at all essential).

Costner (1969) and Blalock (1969a) considered at length systems of this type without making it clear that such models have already been thoroughly investigated in the psychometric literature. To clarify the situation, a matrix formulation is convenient.

We introduce the vectors

$$x' = (z_1, \ldots, z_K, y_1, \ldots, y_M)$$
$$f' = (z^*, y^*)$$
$$u' = (v_1, \ldots, v_K, w_1, \ldots, w_M)$$

and the matrix

$$\Delta = \begin{pmatrix} \beta_1 & 0 \\ \vdots & \vdots \\ \beta_K & 0 \\ 0 & \gamma_1 \\ \vdots & \vdots \\ 0 & \gamma_M \end{pmatrix} \tag{14}$$

and write equations (12) and (13) compactly as

$$x = \Delta f + u \tag{15}$$

The population variance-covariance matrix of the observable indicators is then

$$\Omega = E(xx') = E(\Delta f + u)(\Delta f + u)' = \Delta E(ff')\Delta' + E(uu')$$
$$= \Delta \Phi \Delta' + \Sigma \tag{16}$$

where we have introduced $\Phi = E(ff')$ as the variance-covariance matrix of the two unobservable variables, $\Sigma = E(uu')$ as the variance-covariance matrix of the disturbances, and used $E(fu') = 0$. It follows from equation (11) that

$$\Phi = \begin{pmatrix} 1 & \alpha \\ \alpha & 1 \end{pmatrix} \tag{17}$$

and from the assumptions on the independence of the disturbances that

$$\Sigma = \begin{pmatrix} \sigma_{v_1}^2 & & & & & \\ & \ddots & & & & 0 \\ & & \sigma_{v_K}^2 & \sigma_{w_1}^2 & & \\ & & & & \ddots & \\ 0 & & & & & \sigma_{w_M}^2 \end{pmatrix} \tag{18}$$

It should now be apparent that what we have is a factor-analysis model (compare Harman, 1967, Chapter 2; Morrison, 1967, Chapter 8). More specifically, the unobservables $z^*$ and $y^*$ represent oblique factors, and the absence of direct paths from $z^*$ to the $y$'s and from $y^*$ to the $z$'s represents certain zero factor loadings.

If we examine the population correlation matrix of the indicators given in equation (16), we see that the model is typically overidentified. The $\frac{1}{2}(K + M)(K + M + 1)$ distinct elements of the symmetric matrix $\Omega$ are expressible in terms of only $1 + 2(K + M)$ parameters, $\alpha, \beta_1, \ldots,$ $\beta_K, \gamma_1, \ldots, \gamma_M, \sigma_{v_1}^2, \ldots, \sigma_{v_K}^2, \sigma_{w_1}^2, \ldots, \sigma_{w_M}^2$; the variance $\sigma_\epsilon^2$ being determined by the standardization of $y^*$. For example, if $M = 2 = K$, we have $\frac{1}{2}(K + M)(K + M + 1) = 10$ and $1 + 2(K + M) = 9$, so that there is one overidentifying restriction.

The maximum-likelihood principle offers a straightforward approach to estimation of the parameters of the model. It must be emphasized that, having specified certain zero factor loadings in advance, we are concerned with confirmatory factor analysis. In the more traditional exploratory factor analysis, various rotations are used to obtain approximate zero factor loadings in the desired places, but these would not do justice to the present model. On the important distinction between confirmatory and exploratory factor analysis, see Jöreskog and Lawley (1968). Computational procedures for confirmatory maximum-likelihood estimation are spelled out in Lawley and Maxwell (1963, Chapters 2, 6) and Jöreskog (1969a).

## Path Analysis Approach to Estimation

Before describing the efficient estimation procedure, we pause to review the path-analysis approach to fitting the model. For the sake of concreteness, we take $K = M = 2$ as in Costner (1969, Figure 4). By inspection of the path diagram, or from equations (11) through (13), the following "estimating equations" are produced:

$$r_{z1z2} = \beta_1\beta_2 \qquad r_{z1y1} = \beta_1\alpha\gamma_1 \qquad r_{z1y2} = \beta_1\alpha\gamma_2$$
$$r_{z2y1} = \beta_2\alpha\gamma_1 \qquad r_{z2y2} = \beta_2\alpha\gamma_2 \qquad (19)$$
$$r_{y1y2} = \gamma_1\gamma_2$$

(compare Blalock, 1969a, p. 251, equations (1) through (6)). In equation (19) there are six equations from which to estimate the five parameters $\alpha$, $\beta_1$, $\beta_2$, $\gamma_1$, $\gamma_2$; the disturbance variances being estimable subsequently. Clearly, the system is overdetermined, there being one excess equation.

In particular, we can estimate $\alpha$ as $a^{(1)}$, the square root of $(r_{z1y1}r_{z2y2})/(r_{z1z2}r_{y1y2})$; and then, with this value in hand, we can go on to solve for estimates of $\beta_1$, $\beta_2$, $\gamma_1$, $\gamma_2$, say $b_1^{(1)}$, $b_2^{(1)}$, $c_1^{(1)}$, $c_2^{(1)}$. Alternatively, we can estimate $\alpha$ as $a^{(2)}$, the square root of $(r_{z2y1}r_{z1y2})/(r_{z1z2}r_{y1y2})$; and with that value in hand, we can go on to solve for estimates of $\beta_1$, $\beta_2$, $\gamma_1$, $\gamma_2$, say $b_1^{(2)}$, $b_2^{(2)}$, $c_1^{(2)}$, $c_2^{(2)}$.

Even if the model is correct in the population, the distinct estimates of the same parameters will fail to coincide in any sample. Sometimes, the advice given is to average them; thus, Blalock (1969a, p. 266) in effect suggests taking $\frac{1}{2}(a_1^{(1)} + a_2^{(2)})$ as the estimate of $\alpha$ and, with this value in hand, going on to solve for estimates of the $\beta_1$, $\beta_2$, $\gamma_1$, $\gamma_2$. Such averaging procedures are obviously arbitrary. In a sense, they put equal weight on conflicting estimates in forming the average. However, the several conflicting estimates are unlikely to have the same sampling variability, and an efficient estimation procedure should take this into account.

## EFFICIENT ESTIMATION OF THE MULTIPLE-INDICATOR MODEL

### Derivation of Procedure

If we consult the factor-analysis literature, we find that the maximum-likelihood principle calls for the estimates to be chosen as the values of $\Delta$, $\Phi$, $\Sigma$, which minimize

$$\log \det(\Omega) + \operatorname{tr}(\Omega^{-1}W) \qquad (20)$$

where $\Omega = \Delta\Phi\Delta' + \Sigma$, $W$ is the sample variance-covariance matrix of the indicators, log stands for natural logarithm, det stands for determinant, and tr stands for trace. Specifically, with $M = 2 = K$, we have from equations (14), (17), and (18),

$$\Delta\Phi\Delta' = \begin{pmatrix} \beta_1 & 0 \\ \beta_2 & 0 \\ 0 & \gamma_1 \\ 0 & \gamma_2 \end{pmatrix} \begin{pmatrix} 1 & \alpha \\ \alpha & 1 \end{pmatrix} \begin{pmatrix} \beta_1 & \beta_2 & 0 & 0 \\ 0 & 0 & \gamma_1 & \gamma_2 \end{pmatrix}$$

so

$$\Omega = \begin{pmatrix} \beta_1^2 + \sigma_{v_1}^2 & \beta_1\beta_2 & \beta_1\alpha\gamma_1 & \beta_1\alpha\gamma_2 \\ & \beta_2^2 + \sigma_{v_2}^2 & \beta_2\alpha\gamma_1 & \beta_2\alpha\gamma_2 \\ & & \gamma_1^2 + \sigma_{w_1}^2 & \gamma_1\gamma_2 \\ & & & \gamma_2^2 + \sigma_{w_2}^2 \end{pmatrix}$$

Also,

$$W = \begin{pmatrix} 1 & r_{z1z2} & r_{z1y1} & r_{z1y2} \\ & 1 & r_{z2y1} & r_{z2y2} \\ & & 1 & r_{y1y2} \\ & & & 1 \end{pmatrix}$$

(Here and throughout the paper we omit the subdiagonal elements of symmetric matrices.)

The equations for minimizing expression (20) and an iterative procedure for solving them can be found in Lawley and Maxwell (1963, pp. 79–81).

The heuristic interpretation is that the maximum-likelihood method seeks parameter values (elements of $\Omega$) which reproduce the observed correlations (elements of $W$) as closely as possible. The over-identifying restriction prevents perfect reproduction, of course.

The estimates produced by the maximum-likelihood method are guaranteed to be efficient, that is, to have minimum sampling variability.

## Numerical Illustration

To illustrate the efficient estimation procedure we draw on Hauser's (1969a) study of schools and the stratification process. The sample consists of some 17,000 white public-school students enrolled in grades 7 through 12. The observed variables (original symbols follow in parentheses) are $z_1$ = arithmetic mark $(A)$, $z_2$ = English mark $(E)$, $y_1$ = educational aspiration $(T)$, and $y_2$ = occupational aspiration $(J)$. The within-school correlations given above the diagonal in Hauser (1969a, Table 3) are presented here in Table 1.

In our model, shown in Figure 2, the marks $z_1$ and $z_2$ are assumed to be indicators of an unobservable variable $z^*$ = academic performance, which determines an unobservable variable $y^*$ = ambition, for which $y_1$ and $y_2$ serve as indicators. The maximum-likelihood estimates are

Table 1
Correlations of Academic Performance and Ambition Indicators
$W$ = Observed Correlations

|       | $z_1$  | $z_2$  | $y_1$  | $y_2$  |
|-------|--------|--------|--------|--------|
| $z_1$ | 1.000  | 0.630  | 0.202  | 0.238  |
| $z_2$ |        | 1.000  | 0.272  | 0.292  |
| $y_1$ |        |        | 1.000  | 0.456  |
| $y_2$ |        |        |        | 1.000  |

reported in Table 2. Our estimates of $\alpha$, $\beta_1$, $\beta_2$, $\gamma_1$, $\gamma_2$ appear as elements of $\hat{\Phi}$ and $\hat{\Delta}$; the residual paths to the indicators are the square roots of the elements in $\hat{\Sigma}$; and the standardization of $y^*$ gives the residual path of $y^*$ as the square root of $1 - a^2$, where $a$ is the estimate of $\alpha$. Also reported in Table 2 is our implied correlation matrix $\hat{\Omega} = \hat{\Delta}\hat{\Phi}\hat{\Delta}' + \hat{\Sigma}$.[5]

Our implied correlations in $\hat{\Omega}$ naturally differ from the observed correlations in $W$; after all, the latter did not satisfy the overidentifying restriction. The differences are rather small, but the sample size is very large. To translate such remarks into a formal test of the causal model, one can simply draw on the likelihood-ratio test of factor analysis (Lawley and Maxwell, 1963, pp. 84–86). The relevant statistic is $T$ log $[\det(\hat{\Omega})/\det(W)]$, where $T$ is the sample size. On the null hypothesis that the overidentifying restrictions are correct, this statistic is distributed as $\chi^2$ with degrees of freedom equal to the number of overidentifying restrictions. In our illustration we have one restriction, a sample size of 17,000, and the determinants are $\det(\hat{\Omega}) = 0.434$ and $\det(W) = 0.423$. This gives a test statistic of 442, which is significant even at the 1

Table 2
Efficient Estimates for Causal Model of Figure 2

$\hat{\Delta}$ = Factor Loadings

|       | $z^*$ | $y^*$ |
|-------|-------|-------|
| $z_1$ | 0.77  | 0     |
| $z_2$ | 0.82  | 0     |
| $y_1$ | 0     | 0.66  |
| $y_2$ | 0     | 0.69  |

$\hat{\Sigma}$ = Unique Variances

|       | $z_1$ | $z_2$ | $y_1$ | $y_2$ |
|-------|-------|-------|-------|-------|
| $z_1$ | 0.64  | 0     | 0     | 0     |
| $z_2$ |       | 0.58  | 0     | 0     |
| $y_1$ |       |       | 0.75  | 0     |
| $y_2$ |       |       |       | 0.72  |

$\hat{\Phi}$ = Factor Correlations

|       |       |       |
|-------|-------|-------|
| $z^*$ | 1.00  | 0.47  |
| $y^*$ |       | 1.00  |

$\hat{\Omega}$ = Implied Correlations

|       |       |       |       |       |
|-------|-------|-------|-------|-------|
| $z_1$ | 1.00  | 0.63  | 0.24  | 0.25  |
| $z_2$ |       | 1.00  | 0.26  | 0.27  |
| $y_1$ |       |       | 1.00  | 0.46  |
| $y_2$ |       |       |       | 1.00  |

[5] Starting with Hauser's correlation matrix, we found the efficient estimation required about three hours on a desk calculator. Computer programs are in fact available (see Jöreskog, 1967).

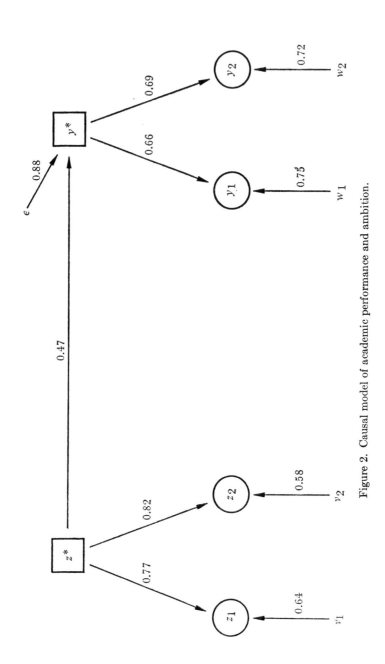

Figure 2. Causal model of academic performance and ambition.

per cent level. Routine procedures of statistical inference, therefore, would lead us to reject the causal model.

## Comments

In Table 3 we present the two conflicting sets of parameter estimates obtained by the path-analysis approach sketched above in the section "Path-Analysis Approach to Estimation" along with our efficient estimates. In this case, the efficient estimates of the individual parameters do not all lie within the range of the two conflicting estimates.

Table 3
Conflicting and Efficient Estimates of $\alpha$, $\beta_1$, $\beta_2$, $\gamma_1$, $\gamma_2$

| $j$ | $a^{(j)}$ | $b_1^{(j)}$ | $b_2^{(j)}$ | $c_1^{(j)}$ | $c_2^{(j)}$ |
|---|---|---|---|---|---|
| 1 | 0.45 | 0.72 | 0.88 | 0.65 | 0.70 |
| 2 | 0.48 | 0.68 | 0.92 | 0.62 | 0.73 |
| Efficient | $a = 0.47$ | $b_1 = 0.77$ | $b_2 = 0.82$ | $c_1 = 0.66$ | $c_2 = 0.69$ |

We have argued that models with multiple indicators of causally related unobservable variables fall directly under the scope of factor analysis, but our illustration was confined to the case of two unobservable variables. Our argument, in fact, requires qualification when there are more than two unobservables bound together in a recursive model. If all direct paths are present in the recursive model, no difficulty arises, there being a one-to-one correspondence between the factor correlations and the paths connecting the unobservables. Estimates of $\Phi$ can be converted directly into estimates of the path coefficients in the main model. But, if some direct paths are ruled out of the recursive system, as in Costner (1969, Figure 6), the one-to-one correspondence breaks down. The structuring of the $\Phi$ matrix will also have to be taken into account in efficient estimation. This can be done by formulating a "second-order factor analytic model" as in Jöreskog's (1970) general method for analysis of covariance structures. The specific device is spelled out in Jöreskog (1969b, pp. 13–18).[6]

## *MULTIPLE CAUSES AND MULTIPLE INDICATORS OF AN UNOBSERVABLE VARIABLE*

### Specification of the Model

We now turn to a model in which we observe multiple causes and

---

[6] His approach also allows for one to specify that certain direct paths be equal as in Blalock (1970, pp. 106–110).

multiple indicators of a single unobservable variable as shown in Figure 3. In algebraic form the model consists of

$$y^* = \alpha_1 x_1 + \cdots + \alpha_k x_k + \cdots + \alpha_K x_K + \epsilon \qquad (21)$$

a linear equation expressing the unobservable variable $y^*$ in terms of its observable causes $x_1, \ldots, x_k, \ldots, x_K$ and an unobservable disturbance $\epsilon$, and

$$
\begin{aligned}
y_1 &= \beta_1 y^* + u_1 \\
&\vdots \qquad \vdots \\
y_m &= \beta_m y^* + u_m \\
&\vdots \qquad \vdots \\
y_M &= \beta_M y^* + u_M
\end{aligned}
\qquad (22)
$$

a set of $M$ linear equations expressing each observable indicator $y_m$ in terms of $y^*$ and an unobservable disturbance $u_m (m = 1, \ldots, M)$. It is assumed that the disturbances are independent of the $x$'s and are mutually independent as well.

The $\alpha$'s and $\beta$'s are path coefficients to be estimated along with the variances of the disturbances $\sigma_{\epsilon\epsilon}, \sigma_{11}, \ldots, \sigma_{MM}$; we are again following the unstandardized-disturbance convention. The unobservable $y^*$ is standardized, as are the observables (although the latter is not at all essential).

We can solve the model into its reduced form by inserting (21) into (22), thus expressing each indicator in terms of the causes and disturbances. The reduced-form equations are

$$
\begin{aligned}
y_m &= \beta_m \alpha_1 x_1 + \cdots + \beta_m \alpha_K x_K + \beta_m \epsilon + u_m \\
&= \pi_{m1} x_1 + \cdots + \pi_{mK} x_K + v_m
\end{aligned}
\qquad (23)
$$

say. Here the reduced-form coefficients are

$$\pi_{mk} = \beta_m \alpha_k \qquad (m = 1, \ldots, M; k = 1, \ldots, K) \qquad (24)$$

and the reduced-form disturbances are

$$v_m = \beta_m \epsilon + u_m \qquad (m = 1, \ldots, M) \qquad (25)$$

The variances and covariances of the $v_m$ are

$$\omega_{mm} = E(v_m^2) = \beta_m^2 \sigma_{\epsilon\epsilon} + \sigma_{mm} \qquad (m = 1, \ldots, M) \qquad (26)$$

and

$$\omega_{mn} = E(v_m v_n) = \beta_m \beta_n \sigma_{\epsilon\epsilon} \quad (m, n = 1, \ldots, M; m \neq n) \qquad (27)$$

Note that the $v$'s are not independent of each other since they all have the disturbance $\epsilon$ in common.

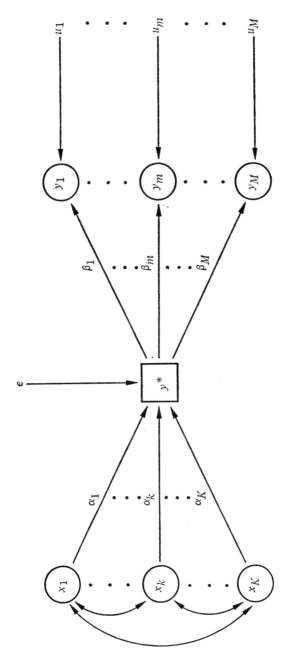

Figure 3. Multiple causes and indicators of an unobservable variable.

A matrix formulation is convenient. We introduce the vectors

$$x' = (x_1, \ldots, x_K) \qquad y' = (y_1, \ldots, y_M)$$
$$\alpha' = (\alpha_1, \ldots, \alpha_K) \qquad \beta' = (\beta_1, \ldots, \beta_M)$$
$$u' = (u_1, \ldots, u_M)$$

and write equations (21) and (22) compactly as

$$y^* = \alpha'x + \epsilon \qquad (28)$$
$$y = \beta y^* + u \qquad (29)$$

with

$$\Sigma = E(uu') = \begin{pmatrix} \sigma_{11} & & 0 \\ & \ddots & \\ 0 & & \sigma_{MM} \end{pmatrix}$$

The reduced form is now

$$y = \beta(\alpha'x + \epsilon) + u = \beta\alpha'x + \beta\epsilon + u$$
$$= \Pi'x + v \qquad (30)$$

where

$$\Pi = \begin{pmatrix} \pi_{11} & \cdots & \pi_{M1} \\ \vdots & & \vdots \\ \pi_{1K} & \cdots & \pi_{MK} \end{pmatrix} = \begin{pmatrix} \alpha_1\beta_1 & \cdots & \alpha_1\beta_M \\ \vdots & & \vdots \\ \alpha_K\beta_1 & \cdots & \alpha_K\beta_M \end{pmatrix} = \alpha\beta'$$

and

$$v' = (v_1, \ldots, v_M)$$

with

$$\Omega = E(vv') = E(\beta\,\epsilon + u)(\beta\,\epsilon + u)' = \sigma_{\epsilon\epsilon}\beta\beta' + \Sigma$$
$$= \begin{pmatrix} \omega_{11} & \cdots & \omega_{1M} \\ \vdots & & \vdots \\ \omega_{M1} & \cdots & \omega_{MM} \end{pmatrix} = \begin{pmatrix} \beta_1^2\sigma_{\epsilon\epsilon} + \sigma_{11} & \cdots & \beta_1\beta_M\sigma_{\epsilon\epsilon} \\ \vdots & & \vdots \\ \beta_M\beta_1\sigma_{\epsilon\epsilon} & \cdots & \beta_M^2\sigma_{\epsilon\epsilon} + \sigma_{MM} \end{pmatrix} \qquad (31)$$

Examination of the reduced form reveals that the model incorporates two sorts of overidentification: (1) The $K \times M$ regression-coefficient matrix $\Pi$ is expressible as the product of a $K \times 1$ vector $\alpha$ and a $1 \times M$ vector $\beta'$. In other words, the $K \times M$ parameters $\pi_{mk}$ are expressible in terms of only $K + M$ parameters $\alpha_1, \ldots, \alpha_K, \beta_1, \ldots, \beta_M$. (2) The $\frac{1}{2}M(M + 1)$ distinct elements of the symmetric variance-covariance matrix $\Omega$ are expressible in terms of the $1 \times 1$ scalar $\sigma_{\epsilon\epsilon}$, the $M \times 1$ vector $\beta$, and the $M$ nonzero elements of the diagonal matrix $\Sigma$. In other words, the $\frac{1}{2}M(M+1)$ distinct parameters $\omega_{mn}$ are expressible in terms of only $1 + 2M$ parameters $\sigma_{\epsilon\epsilon}, \beta_1, \ldots, \beta_M, \sigma_{11}, \ldots, \sigma_{MM}$. Furthermore, the $\beta$'s here are the same as under (1).

Taking the two sorts together and allowing for the standardization of $y^*$, we find that the $(K \times M) + \frac{1}{2}M(M+1)$ distinct reduced-form parameters are expressible in terms of only $2M + K$ distinct structural parameters. This means that the model will typically be overidentified. For example, with $K = 3 = M$ we have $(K \times M) + \frac{1}{2}M(M+1) = 15$ and $2M + K = 9$ so that there are six overidentifying restrictions.

The efficient procedure for estimating the model will have to take account of all these restrictions. Nevertheless, it is instructive to consider the two sorts of overidentification separately.

The first sort of overidentification is of the type dealt with in econometrics (where reduced-form coefficients are combinations of structural coefficients), whereas the second sort of overidentification is of the type dealt with in factor analysis (where covariance matrices are built up from factor loadings, factor variance, and unique variances). Note that $\epsilon$ plays the role of a common factor, $\beta$ the role of factor loadings, and $u$ the role of a unique factor in the expression $v = \beta\epsilon + u$.[7]

The maximum-likelihood principle offers a straightforward approach to efficient estimation of the model, since it takes into account both sorts of overidentifying restrictions. The computation can be performed by Jöreskog's (1970) general method for the analysis of covariance structures.

For present purposes, however, we will be content to consider only the first sort of overidentification. To do so, we simply drop the assumption that the indicator disturbances are mutually independent. In some contexts, no doubt, this is substantively justified and not merely done for the sake of analytical convenience. For example, we might expect to find positively correlated errors among multiple indicators of a single underlying attitude when the indicators are ascertained consecu-

---

[7] This mixture of econometric and psychometric themes is presumably what Blalock (1969a, pp. 270–272) had in mind in asserting that "Once the basic ideas of each approach [instrumental variables and multiple indicators] have become generally familiar, however, it should become possible to apply them in various combinations to a wide variety of causal models." But, as we have seen in the section "Multiple Indicators of Causally Related Unobservable Variables," the multiple-indicator approach essentially is a factor analysis model. Further, the instrumental-variable approach is simply a particular method for estimation of econometric models. Blalock gives no advice for reconciling the alternative instrumental-variable estimates, nor for reconciling the alternative multiple-indicator estimates, let alone for reconciling both sets. The issues involved are sketched in Goldberger (1971).

tively in a survey interview. If the $u$'s are freely correlated, then the correlations of the $v$'s are no longer patterned as they were in equations (26) and (27) or in equation (31), and the factor-analytic considerations disappear.

In that event, we may as well rewrite the model to make the unobservable variable an *exact* function of its causes, absorbing the disturbance $\epsilon$ into the $u$'s and relabelling the latter directly as $v$'s, as in Figure 4. In algebraic form the structural model now reads

$$y^* = \alpha_1 x_1 + \cdots + \alpha_K x_K \tag{32}$$

$$y_m = \beta_m y^* + v_m \qquad (m = 1, \ldots, M) \tag{33}$$

with

$$E(v_m^2) = \omega_{mm} \qquad E(v_m v_n) = \omega_{mn} \tag{34}$$

the $\omega$'s being unrestricted. Forcing an unobservable variable to be an exact function of its observable causes may seem strange. But, once the disturbances in the indicator equations are allowed to be correlated freely, nothing is gained by retaining a disturbance in the causal equation. Partial correlation among the indicators, controlling on the observable causes, is already present. To put it another way, it would be impossible to distinguish empirically whether the partial correlation was attributable to the common disturbance $\epsilon$ or to inherent correlation among the disturbances $u$. We may as well adopt the latter formulation.[8]

On the understanding that the disturbance variances and covariances are unrestricted, we see the reduced-form system (23) or (30) is just a particularly simple example of the reduced forms which arise in the simultaneous equation models of econometrics (Johnston, 1963, Chapter 7). Indeed, examples of this type have been explicitly

---

[8] In the two-indicator situation ($M = 2$) our case may be made more strongly. Even if one made the assumption that $u_1$ and $u_2$ were uncorrelated, nothing would be lost by dropping $\epsilon$ and permitting the $v$'s to be freely correlated; for only two indicators the factor-analysis model is empty. Then, if one insisted on presenting a disturbance in the $y^*$ equation and uncorrelated indicator disturbances, the estimates of the three variances, $\sigma_{\epsilon\epsilon}$, $\sigma_{11}$, $\sigma_{22}$, could be recovered from unrestricted estimates of the three (co)variances, $\omega_{11}$, $\omega_{22}$, and $\omega_{12}$.

Strictly speaking, even in the $M = 2$ case, we find an exception to our argument that a disturbed $y^*$ equation with uncorrelated indicator disturbances is operationally equivalent to an exact $y^*$ equation with correlated indicator disturbances. The former precludes a correlation between $v_m$ and $v_n$ opposite in sign from the product of $\beta_m$ and $\beta_n$, as can be seen from equation (27); the latter has no such restriction. This exception is a version of the "Heywood case" of factor analysis; compare Harman (1967, pp. 117–118).

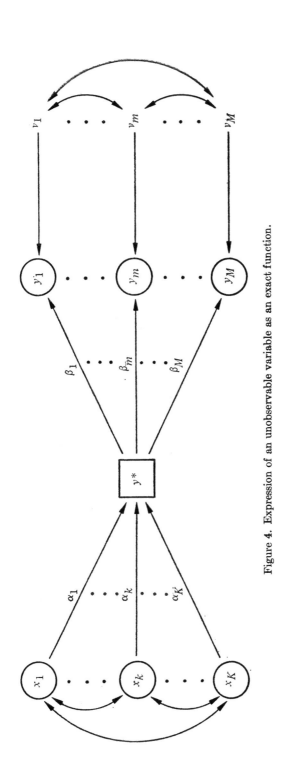

Figure 4. Expression of an unobservable variable as an exact function.

analyzed by Zellner (1970) and Goldberger (1970a). In developing an efficient estimation procedure, we can draw on that literature.

## Path Analysis Approach to Estimation

We pause to sketch how a path-analysis approach to fitting the model might proceed. For the sake of concreteness, we take $M = 2$. By inspection of the path diagram, or from equations (32) and (33), the following "estimating equations" are produced:

$$r_{j*} = \sum_{k=1}^{K} \alpha_k r_{jk} \qquad (j = 1, \ldots, K) \qquad (35)$$

$$r_{**} = \sum_{j=1}^{K} \sum_{k=1}^{K} \alpha_j \alpha_k r_{jk} = 1 \qquad (36)$$

$$r_{jm} = \beta_m r_{j*} \qquad (j = 1, \ldots, K; m = 1, 2) \qquad (37)$$

$$r_{mn} = \beta_m \beta_n r_{**} + \omega_{mn} \qquad (m, n = 1, 2) \qquad (38)$$

Here $r_{j*}$ denotes the correlation of $x_j$ and $y^*$, $r_{jk}$ the correlation of $x_j$ and $x_k$, $r_{**}$ the correlation of $y^*$ with itself, $r_{jm}$ the correlation of $x_j$ and $y_m$, and $r_{mn}$ the correlation of $y_m$ and $y_n$.

In equations (35) through (38) there are $3K + 4$ equations from which to estimate the $2K + 5$ unknowns, $r_{1*}, \ldots, r_{K*}, \alpha_1, \ldots, \alpha_K$, $\beta_1, \beta_2, \omega_{11}, \omega_{22}, \omega_{12}$. After solving out the $r_{j*}$ and $\omega_{mn}$ via equations (35) and (38) respectively, we find there remain $1 + 2K$ equations from which to estimate the $K + 2$ parameters, $\alpha_1, \ldots, \alpha_K, \beta_1, \beta_2$. Clearly the system is overidentified, there being $K - 1$ excess equations.

In particular, for given $r_{j*}$ there are $K$ distinct estimates of $\beta_1$ provided by equation (37), namely

$$b_1^{(j)} = \frac{r_{j1}}{r_{j*}} \qquad (j = 1, \ldots, K) \qquad (39)$$

and similarly, there are $K$ distinct estimates of $\beta_2$, namely

$$b_2^{(j)} = \frac{r_{j2}}{r_{j*}} \qquad (j = 1, \ldots, K) \qquad (40)$$

Even if the model is correct in the population, the distinct estimates will fail to coincide in any sample. One might arbitrarily discard excess equations until a just-determined system obtains which is then solvable for unique estimates. Or, an ad hoc averaging procedure could be adopted (compare Hauser, 1968, pp. 280–287). Thus, equation (37) implies $\beta_1/\beta_2 = r_{j1}/r_{j2}$; so one might estimate $\beta_1/\beta_2$ by

$$\frac{\hat{\beta}_1}{\hat{\beta}_2} = \frac{\displaystyle\sum_{j=1}^{K} r_{j1}}{\displaystyle\sum_{j=1}^{K} r_{j2}} = \frac{\displaystyle\sum_{j=1}^{K} b_1^{(j)}}{\displaystyle\sum_{j=1}^{K} b_2^{(j)}} \qquad (41)$$

Then, for given $\hat{\beta}_1$, $\hat{\beta}_2$, there are two distinct estimates of each $r_{j*}$ provided by equation (37), namely

$$r_{j*}^{m} = \frac{r_{jm}}{\beta_m} \qquad (m = 1,2) \qquad (42)$$

which can be averaged into

$$r_{j*} = \frac{r_{j1} + r_{j2}}{\beta_1 + \beta_2} \qquad (43)$$

With values of the $r_{j*}$ in hand, the normal equations (35) are then solved for estimates of the $\alpha$'s.[9]

Such averaging procedures are obviously arbitrary since they, in a sense, put equal weight on conflicting estimates. An efficient estimation procedure should take into account the differences in the sampling variabilities of the conflicting estimates.

## EFFICIENT ESTIMATION OF MULTIPLE-CAUSE AND MULTIPLE-INDICATOR MODEL

### Derivation of the Procedure

Adopting the econometric approach and proceeding to the general $M$-indicator case, we consider first the estimates of the reduced-form equations obtained by regressing each of the $M$ indicators on all of the observable causes. The normal equations for the typical reduced-form regression equation are

---

[9] In this description, we have skipped a step in going from $\hat{\beta}_1/\hat{\beta}_2$ to $\hat{\beta}_1$ and $\hat{\beta}_2$. This step is a bit awkward in the present formulation in which the $y^*$ disturbance has been absorbed into the $v$'s. Still, from equation (38) we have $r_{12} = \beta_1\beta_2 + \omega_{12}$ whence

$$\hat{\beta}_1\hat{\beta}_2 = \phi r_{12} \qquad (i)$$

where $\phi = 1 - (\omega_{12}/r_{12})$ is temporarily unknown. Combining equations (41) and (i), we have $\hat{\beta}_1$ and $\hat{\beta}_2$ up to a factor of proportionality; then equation (42) gives the $r_{j*}$ up to a factor of proportionality. The solution to the normal equations (35) will then estimate the $\alpha$'s up to a factor of proportionality. Finally, the factor of proportionality is determined by equation (36). A more conventional treatment would have $\omega_{12} = 0$, whence $\phi = 1$, giving $\hat{\beta}_1$ and $\hat{\beta}_2$ separately, and estimating $\sigma_{ee}$ from $\sigma_{ee} = 1 - \Sigma_j\Sigma_k\alpha_j\alpha_k r_{jk}$. The distinction is computational rather than substantive.

$$r_{jm} = \sum_{k=1}^{K} r_{jk} p_{mk} \qquad (j = 1, \ldots, K) \qquad (44)$$

where the $p_{mk}$ denote the least-squares regression coefficients. These $p$'s are estimates of the $\pi$'s but will not satisfy the overidentifying restrictions. According to the model, $\pi_{mk} = \beta_m \alpha_k$; but except by a remarkable coincidence, there will be no set of numbers $b_1, \ldots, b_M, a_1, \ldots, a_K$ such that $p_{mk} = b_m a_k$. Put somewhat differently, the model implies "consistency criteria" such as $\pi_{11}/\pi_{21} = \cdots = \pi_{1k}/\pi_{2k} = \cdots = \pi_{1K}/\pi_{2K}$ (each of these ratios being equal to $\beta_1/\beta_2$), but it will not be true that $p_{11}/p_{21} = \cdots = p_{1k}/p_{2k} = \cdots = p_{1K}/p_{2K}$.

Goldberger (1970a) shows that in the present context maximum-likelihood estimation is identical to modified generalized least-squares estimation. The problem can therefore be posed as follows: Each $p_{mk}$ is an estimate of $\beta_m \alpha_k$; how can we combine them to come up with efficient estimates of the $\beta_1, \ldots, \beta_M, \alpha_1, \ldots, \alpha_K$? In multivariate linear regression models it is well-known that the variances and covariances of the $p_{mk}$ are given by

$$\mathrm{Cov}(p_{mk}, p_{nj}) = \frac{1}{T} \omega_{mn} r^{kj}$$

where $T$ is the sample size, $\omega_{mn}$ are the elements of $\Omega$, and the $r^{kj}$ are the elements of the matrix inverse to the correlation matrix of the $x$'s. It is also well-known that the $\omega_{mn}$ are estimable as the residual variances and covariances $s_{mn}$ from the least-squares regressions. (On these matters, compare Anderson (1958, pp. 178–183) or Goldberger (1964, pp. 207–209).) In view of this, the MGLS procedure calls for estimates of the $\alpha$'s and $\beta$'s to be obtained as follows: choose the values $\alpha_1, \ldots, \alpha_K$, $\beta_1, \ldots, \beta_M$ which minimize

$$\frac{1}{T} \sum_{j=1}^{K} \sum_{k=1}^{K} \sum_{n=1}^{M} \sum_{m=1}^{M} s^{mn} r_{kj} (p_{mk} - \beta_m \alpha_k)(p_{nj} - \beta_n \alpha_j) \qquad (45)$$

where the $s^{mn}$ are the elements of the matrix inverse to the matrix of the $s_{mn}$. In expression (45) the weight attached to the term involving $p_{mk}$ and $p_{nj}$ is inverse to the estimated covariance of $p_{mk}$ and $p_{nj}$ as called for by the MGLS procedure.

In carrying out the minimization, we find a matrix formulation convenient. Let $X'X$ denote the $K \times K$ matrix of the $r_{jk}$, $X'Y$ the $K \times M$ matrix of the $r_{jm}$, and $Y'Y$ the $M \times M$ matrix of the $r_{mn}$. Further, let

$$P = \begin{pmatrix} p_{11} & \cdots & p_{M1} \\ \vdots & & \vdots \\ p_{1K} & \cdots & p_{MK} \end{pmatrix}$$

be the $K \times M$ matrix of the $p_{mk}$. The normal equations (44) are compactly expressed as

$$X'XP = X'Y$$

and their solution as

$$P = (X'X)^{-1}X'Y \tag{46}$$

Further, let

$$S = \begin{pmatrix} s_{11} & \cdots & s_{1M} \\ \vdots & & \vdots \\ s_{M1} & \cdots & s_{MM} \end{pmatrix}$$

be the $M \times M$ matrix of the $s_{mn}$; then

$$S = (Y - XP)'(Y - XP) = Y'Y - Y'X(X'X)^{-1}X'Y \tag{47}$$

The formidable expression (45) can now be compactly written as

$$\frac{1}{T} \operatorname{tr}[S^{-1}(P - \alpha\beta')'X'X(P - \alpha\beta')] \tag{48}$$

A simple manipulation shows that the trace of the $M \times M$ matrix in brackets is, apart from an irrelevant constant, equal to the scalar

$$(\alpha'X'X\alpha)(\beta'S^{-1}\beta) - 2\alpha'X'YS^{-1}\beta \tag{49}$$

The MGLS principle thus chooses $\alpha$ and $\beta$ to minimize expression (49), or rather, if we recall the standardization of $y^*$ as in equation (36), to minimize expression (49) subject to

$$\alpha'X'X\alpha = 1 \tag{50}$$

To minimize expression (49) subject to equation (50), one first forms the expression

$$f = (\alpha'X'X\alpha)(\beta'S^{-1}\beta) - 2\alpha'X'YS^{-1}\beta + \lambda(\alpha'X'X\alpha - 1) \tag{51}$$

where $\lambda$ is a Lagrangean multiplier and then differentiates with respect to $\beta$ and $\alpha$ to find

$$\frac{\partial f}{\partial \beta} = (\alpha'X'X\alpha)2S^{-1}\beta - 2S^{-1}Y'X\alpha \tag{52}$$

$$\frac{\partial f}{\partial \alpha} = (\beta'S^{-1}\beta)2X'X\alpha - 2X'YS^{-1}\beta + 2\lambda X'X\alpha \tag{53}$$

Setting equation (52) at zero, using equation (50), and introducing

$$a' = (a_1, \ldots, a_K) \qquad b' = (b_1, \ldots, b_M)$$

as the symbols for the estimates of $\alpha$ and $\beta$, we find

$$b = Y'Xa \tag{54}$$

Setting equation (53) at zero and using equations (50) and (54), we find that $\lambda = 0$ and, thus, that

$$a = (b'S^{-1}b)^{-1}PS^{-1}b \tag{55}$$

Then, inserting equation (55) into equation (54), we find

$$b = (b'S^{-1}b)^{-1}Y'XPS^{-1}b = (b'S^{-1}b)^{-1}QS^{-1}b \tag{56}$$

where

$$Q = Y'XP = Y'X(X'X)^{-1}X'Y = P'X'XP = Y'Y - S$$

is the matrix of regression moments. What equation (56) says is that

$$(QS^{-1} - \mu I)b = 0 \tag{57}$$

where $\mu = b'S^{-1}b$. In other words, $b$ is a characteristic vector of the matrix $QS^{-1}$. It is not hard to show that $b$ should be a vector corresponding to the *largest* characteristic root $\mu$ (in order to *minimize* the trace) and that it should be normalized by $b'S^{-1}b = \mu$ (in order to ensure $a'X'Xa = 1$).[10] With this value for $b$ in hand, the value for $a$ follows from (55).

The efficient estimates for $\alpha$ and $\beta$ can, in short, be obtained by solving a characteristic root-characteristic vector problem of a type which is prevalent throughout multivariate statistical analysis. Standard computer programs can be adapted for this purpose; a desk calculator will suffice if $M$ is no larger than three or four, once the output of least-squares regressions is available. As shown in the Appendix, the computations are intimately related to those of canonical correlation.

---

[10] When $b$ satisfies equation (57), then premultiplication by $b'S^{-1}$ shows that $b'S^{-1}QS^{-1}b = \mu b'S^{-1}b$; so that when $a$ is computed from equation (55) as

$$a = (b'S^{-1}b)^{-1}PS^{-1}b,$$

we will have $a'X'YS^{-1}b = (b'S^{-1}b)^{-1}b'S^{-1}P'X'YS^{-1}b = (b'S^{-1}b)^{-1}b'S^{-1}QS^{-1}b = \mu$, and $a'X'Xa = a'X'X(b'S^{-1}b)^{-1}PS^{-1}b = (b'S^{-1}b)^{-1}a'X'YS^{-1}b = (b'S^{-1}b)^{-1}\mu$. To make $a'X'Xa = 1$, therefore, we must normalize $b$ according to $(b'S^{-1}b) = \mu$. With these values inserted, expression (49) becomes $(a'X'Xa)(b'S^{-1}b) - 2a'X'YS^{-1}b = 1\mu - 2\mu = -\mu$; since we're minimizing this expression, the desired root is the largest one.

## Numerical Illustration

To illustrate the efficient estimation procedure, we draw on Hodge and Treiman's (1968) study of social participation and social status. The sample consists of approximately 530 adult female residents of a Washington, D.C. suburban county. The observed variables are (original symbols follow in parentheses): $x_1$ = family income ($I$), $x_2$ = main earner's occupation ($O$), $x_3$ = respondent's education ($E$), $y_1$ = frequency of church attendance ($C$), $y_2$ = number of voluntary organization memberships ($V$), and $y_3$ = number of friends seen ($F$). The observed correlations given in Hodge and Treiman (1968, Table 2) are presented here in Table 4.

Table 4
Correlations of Status and Participation Variables

$$\begin{pmatrix} X'X & X'Y \\ & Y'Y \end{pmatrix}$$

|        | $x_1$  | $x_2$  | $x_3$  | $y_1$  | $y_2$  | $y_3$  |
|--------|--------|--------|--------|--------|--------|--------|
| $x_1$  | 1.0000 | 0.3040 | 0.3049 | 0.1000 | 0.2835 | 0.1762 |
| $x_2$  |        | 1.0000 | 0.3444 | 0.1561 | 0.1925 | 0.1357 |
| $x_3$  |        |        | 1.0000 | 0.1580 | 0.3235 | 0.2255 |
| $y_1$  |        |        |        | 1.0000 | 0.3601 | 0.2099 |
| $y_2$  |        |        |        |        | 1.0000 | 0.2654 |
| $y_3$  |        |        |        |        |        | 1.0000 |

The results of unconstrained multiple regression are presented in Table 5. This, in effect, is the estimated model displayed in Hodge and Treiman (1968, Figure 1b); the elements in our $P$ will be found there as paths from causes to indicators, while the elements in our $S$, converted

Table 5
Results of Unconstrained Multiple Regressions

$P$ = Regression Coefficients

|       | $y_1$  | $y_2$  | $y_3$  |
|-------|--------|--------|--------|
| $x_1$ | 0.0335 | 0.1932 | 0.1094 |
| $x_2$ | 0.1078 | 0.0484 | 0.0411 |
| $x_3$ | 0.1107 | 0.2479 | 0.1780 |

$Q = P'X'XP$ = Regression Moments        $S = Y'Y - Q$ = Residual Moments

|       | $y_1$  | $y_2$  | $y_3$  |        |        |        |
|-------|--------|--------|--------|--------|--------|--------|
| $y_1$ | 0.0377 | 0.0660 | 0.0455 | 0.9623 | 0.2941 | 0.1644 |
| $y_2$ |        | 0.1443 | 0.0965 |        | 0.8557 | 0.1689 |
| $y_3$ |        |        | 0.0650 |        |        | 0.9350 |

into standard deviations and correlations, will be found there as residual paths and correlations.

In our model, shown in Figure 5, the influence of status on participation is assumed to be transmitted through a single unobservable variable, $y^*$ = socioeconomic status. The MGLS estimates $a$ and $b$ are reported in Table 6, along with $\hat{\Pi} = ab'$, which is our implied estimate of the compound paths from causes to indicators, and

$$\hat{\Omega} = (Y - X\hat{\Pi})'(Y - X\hat{\Pi}),$$

the matrix of residual moments from the constrained regressions. Converting the elements of $\hat{\Omega}$ into standard deviations and correlations gives the residual paths and correlations displayed in Figure 5.[11]

Our implied estimates in $\hat{\Pi}$ naturally differ from the unconstrained estimates in $P$; the latter, after all, did not satisfy the overidentifying restrictions. The differences, however, are generally small, which suggests that the unobservable-variable model may be appropriate. (Equivalently, one could compare $X'X\hat{\Pi}$ with $X'Y$ to see how closely our model reproduces the correlations between the $x$'s and the $y$'s.) More to the point is the fact that the diagonal elements of $\hat{\Omega}$ are only slightly larger than the corresponding diagonal elements of $S$, which suggests that the fit does not deteriorate much when the overidentifying restrictions are imposed.

### Table 6
### Estimates for Causal Model of Figure 5

$\hat{\Pi} = ab'$ = Constrained Regression Coefficient Matrix

|       | $b$    | $a$    |       | $y_1$  | $y_2$  | $y_3$  |
|-------|--------|--------|-------|--------|--------|--------|
| $x_1$ | 0.1761 | 0.4815 | $x_1$ | 0.0848 | 0.1827 | 0.1226 |
| $x_2$ | 0.3795 | 0.1476 | $x_2$ | 0.0260 | 0.0560 | 0.0376 |
| $x_3$ | 0.2546 | 0.6638 | $x_3$ | 0.1169 | 0.2519 | 0.1690 |

$\hat{\Omega} = (Y - X\hat{\Pi})'(Y - X\hat{\Pi})$ = Implied Residual Moments

|       | $y_1$  | $y_2$  | $y_3$  |
|-------|--------|--------|--------|
| $y_1$ | 0.9690 | 0.2933 | 0.1651 |
| $y_2$ |        | 0.8560 | 0.1688 |
| $y_3$ |        |        | 0.9352 |

[11] Starting with the information in Hodge and Treiman (1968), our efficient estimation required about two hours on a desk calculator. The largest root of $QS^{-1}$, along with the suitably normalized characteristic vector $b$, was extracted by a standard iterative procedure (compare Morrison, 1967, pp. 234–248). The largest root is $\mu = 0.205$, so that the first canonical correlation between the $y$'s and the $x$'s is $0.41 = \sqrt{0.205/1.205}$ (compare the Appendix). When equations (54) through (57) are taken into account, it turns out that $\hat{\Omega} = (Y - X\hat{\Pi})'(Y - X\hat{\Pi}) = Y'Y - bb'$, which facilitates calculations.

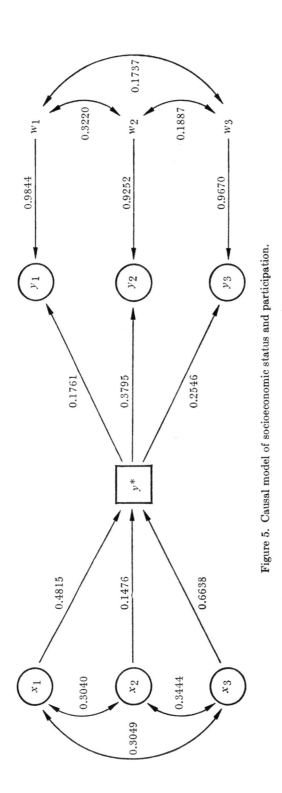

Figure 5. Causal model of socioeconomic status and participation.

To translate such remarks into a formal test of the causal model, we simply draw on the likelihood-ratio test of multivariate analysis (compare Anderson, 1958, Chapter 8). The relevant statistic is $T \log [\det(\hat{\Omega})/ \det(S)]$. On the null hypothesis that the overidentifying restrictions are correct, this statistic is distributed as $\chi^2$ with degrees of freedom equal to the number of overidentifying restrictions. In our illustration we have four restrictions $[4 = (K \times M) - (K + M - 1)]$, a sample size of 530, and the determinants are $\det(\hat{\Omega}) = 0.6549$ and $\det(S) = 0.6607$. This gives a test statistic of 4.5, which is not significant at the 10 per cent level (nor even at the 30 per cent level). Routine procedures of statistical inference, therefore, would not lead us to reject the causal model.

## Comments

We can sketch an interpretation of the efficient parameter estimates in terms of averages of conflicting estimates. Taking for example our efficient estimate of $\beta_1$, we find from equation (54) that

$$b_1 = \sum_{j=1}^{K} r_{j1} a_j$$

where the $a$'s are our efficient estimates of the $\alpha$'s. Defining

$$\hat{r}_{j*} = \sum_{k=1}^{K} a_k r_{jk} \tag{58}$$

as our efficient estimates of the correlations between $x_j$ and $y^*$ [compare equation (35)] we can rewrite $b_1$ as

$$b_1 = \sum_{j=1}^{K} \left(\frac{r_{j1}}{\hat{r}_{j*}}\right) a_j \hat{r}_{j*}$$

Recalling equation (39), we write

$$\hat{b}_1^{(j)} = \frac{r_{j1}}{\hat{r}_{j*}} \qquad (j = 1, \ldots, K)$$

which are $K$ conflicting estimates of $\beta_1$. Multiplying each $r_{j*}$ in equation (58) by $a_j$ and summing gives

$$\sum_{j=1}^{K} a_j \hat{r}_{j*} = \sum_{j=1}^{K} a_j \sum_{k=1}^{K} a_k r_{jk} = \sum_{j=1}^{K} \sum_{k=1}^{K} a_j a_k r_{jk} = 1$$

in view of $a'X'Xa = 1$ [compare equation (36)]. It follows that

$$b_1 = \sum_{j=1}^{K} b_1^{(j)} w^{(j)}$$

where $w^{(j)} = a_j \hat{r}_{j*}$ and $\sum_{j=1}^{K} w^{(j)} = 1$. Thus, $b_1$ is indeed a weighted average of the conflicting estimates $b_1^{(j)}$.

More generally,

$$b_m = \sum_{j=1}^{K} \hat{b}_m^{(j)} w^{(j)} \qquad (m = 1, \ldots, M)$$

where

$$\hat{b}_m^{(j)} = \frac{r_{jm}}{\hat{r}_{j*}} \qquad (m = 1, \ldots, M)$$

It is important to note that the weights $w^{(j)}$ are not determined in advance. Rather, like the $r_{j*}$, they involve the estimates of the $\alpha$'s and, hence, fall out as an incidental part of the efficient estimation computation.

To illustrate the interpretation, Table 7 presents the $r_{j*}$ (elements of $X'Xa$), the $b_m^{(j)}$, and the efficient estimates $b_m$. A similar weighted-

Table 7
Conflicting and Efficient Estimates of $\beta_1, \beta_2, \beta_3$

| $j$ | $\hat{r}_{j*}$ | $b_1^{(j)}$ | $b_2^{(j)}$ | $b_3^{(j)}$ |
|---|---|---|---|---|
| 1 | 0.7287 | 0.1372 | 0.3890 | 0.2418 |
| 2 | 0.5226 | 0.2987 | 0.3683 | 0.2597 |
| 3 | 0.8614 | 0.1834 | 0.3756 | 0.2618 |
|  |  | $b_1 = 0.1761$ | $b_2 = 0.3795$ | $b_3 = 0.2546$ |

average interpretation can be made for the efficient estimates of the $\alpha$'s but will not be demonstrated here.

The present model might be extended by introducing additional observable variables $z_1, \ldots, z_I$ as direct causes of the observable indicators (compare Zellner, 1970, p. 442). That is, equation (33) might be replaced by

$$y_m = \beta_m y^* + \gamma_{m1} z_1 + \cdots + \gamma_{mI} z_I + v_m \qquad (m = 1, \ldots, M)$$

The reduced-form equations would then express the indicators in terms of the $x$'s, $z$'s, and $v$'s. It is not hard to see that only a portion of the reduced-form coefficient matrix would be restricted by the structural model. The restrictions would be precisely of the form that arises in the econometrician's "limited-information" analysis of a single structural equation of a simultaneous equation model (compare Johnston, 1963, pp. 254–258 or Goldberger, 1964, pp. 338–345). As shown by Goldberger and Olkin (1971), the maximum-likelihood and modified generalized least-squares procedures again yield identical parameter estimates in such situations.

## CONCLUSION

In this attempt to spell out procedures for efficient estimation of overidentified unobservable-variable models, we have considered only two simple models in detail. Clearly we have not provided a comprehensive guidebook for the treatment of path models containing unobservable variables. But we think that we have gone far enough to indicate that such a guidebook is feasible. All the models of path analysis are, after all, subsumed under the general linear model of statistics, so the standard principles of statistical inference and the multivariate estimation and testing methods which they entail are relevant. There is no need for a special path-analytic theory of fitting models.

## APPENDIX

The estimation procedure in our numerical illustration of the model with multiple causes and multiple indicators has an interpretation in terms of canonical correlation, suggested to us by O. D. Duncan and by H. W. Watts. Blalock (1969b, pp. 42–43) has also discussed the structure of the proportionally constrained regression model with multiple indicators of the dependent variable and recognized its similarity to canonical correlation. Given a set of variables $y_1, \ldots, y_M$ and a set of variables $x_1, \ldots, x_K$, canonical correlation analysis yields the linear combination of the $y$'s, say $\tilde{y} = \sum_{m=1}^{M} d_m y_m$, and the linear combination of the $x$'s, say $\tilde{x} = \sum_{k=1}^{K} c_k x_k$, which are most highly correlated with one another (compare Morrison, 1967, Chapter 6). Without loss of generality $\tilde{y}$ and $\tilde{x}$ are taken to be standardized. If

$$d' = (d_1, \ldots, d_M) \qquad c' = (c_1, \ldots, c_K)$$

it can be shown that $d$ is chosen to maximize

$$\frac{d'Y'X(X'X)^{-1}X'Yd}{d'Y'Yd} = \frac{d'Qd}{d'(Q+S)d}$$

This leads to the characteristic equation

$$(Q - \lambda S)d = 0 \qquad (59)$$

with the largest root $\lambda$ being the required one and with the standardization $d'Y'Yd = 1$ being imposed. Now, equation (59) is equivalent to

$$(QS^{-1} - \lambda I)Sd = 0 \tag{60}$$

and $d'Y'Yd = 1$ is equivalent to $d'Sd = 1/(1 + \lambda)$. Comparing equation (60) with equation (57), recalling that $b'S^{-1}b = \mu$, and recognizing that $\mu = \lambda$, we conclude that

$$b = \sqrt{\lambda(1 + \lambda)}\, Sd \tag{61}$$

Furthermore, in canonical-correlation analysis it is shown that

$$c = \sqrt{(1 + \lambda)/\lambda}\, Pd \tag{62}$$

Comparing equation (62) with equation (55) and using equation (61), we conclude that

$$a = c \tag{63}$$

Thus, our efficient estimates of $\alpha$ and $\beta$ can be obtained from the $c$ and $d$ of canonical correlation.

If we pursue the point, it follows from equation (63) that the canonical "independent" variable, $\hat{x} = \Sigma_k c_k x_k$, is identical with the constructed unobservable variable, $\hat{y}^* = \Sigma_k a_k x_k$, implied by our estimates of the $\alpha$'s. Further, it follows from equations (59) through (62) that

$$\begin{aligned} Y'\hat{x} = Y'Xc &= \sqrt{(1 + \lambda)/\lambda}\, Y'XPd = \sqrt{(1 + \lambda)/\lambda}\, Qd \\ &= \sqrt{(1 + \lambda)/\lambda}\, \lambda Sd = \sqrt{\lambda(1 + \lambda)}\, Sd \\ &= b \end{aligned}$$

which means that the correlation of each indicator with the canonical "independent" variable (that is, with the constructed $\hat{y}^*$) gives our estimate of the path from $y^*$ to that indicator. Alternatively, it can be shown that

$$b = \sqrt{\lambda/(1 + \lambda)}\, Y'\hat{y}$$

Our estimated paths are proportional to the correlations of indicators with the canonical "dependent" variable $\hat{y} = Yd$. The factor of proportionality arises from the fact that $\hat{y}$ and $\hat{x}$ are not identical; their correlation is just

$$\hat{y}'\hat{x} = d'X'Yc = d'b = \sqrt{\lambda(1 + \lambda)}\, d'Sd = \sqrt{\lambda/(1 + \lambda)}$$

which is the so-called first canonical correlation coefficient.

In summary, a canonical-correlation computer program can be adapted to calculate the parameter estimates for the model in the section "efficient estimation of multiple-cause and multiple-indicator model." In more elaborate unobservable-variable models, however, there is no presumption that the efficient estimates can be deduced from the output of canonical correlation.

## REFERENCES

ANDERSON, T. W.
    1958    *An Introduction to Multivariate Statistical Analysis*. New York: Wiley.

BLALOCK, H. M., JR.
    1961    *Causal Inferences in Nonexperimental Research*. Chapel Hill: University of North Carolina Press.
    1969a    "Multiple indicators and the causal approach to measurement error." *American Journal of Sociology* 75: 264–272.
    1969b    *Theory Construction: From Verbal to Mathematical Formulations*. Englewood Cliffs, N.J.: Prentice-Hall.
    1970    "Estimating measurement error using multiple indicators and several points in time." *American Sociological Review* 35: 101–111.

BOUDON, R.
    1965    "A method of linear causal analysis: Dependence analysis." *American Sociological Review* 30: 365–374.
    1968    "A new look at correlation analysis." Pp. 199–235 in H. M. Blalock, Jr. and A. B. Blalock (Eds.), *Methodology in Social Research*. New York: McGraw-Hill.

BREWER, M. B., CRANO, W. D., AND CAMPBELL, D. T.
    1970    "Testing a single-factor model as an alternative to the misuse of partial correlations in hypothesis-testing research." *Sociometry* 33: 1–11.

CHRIST, C. F.
    1966    *Econometric Models and Methods*. New York: Wiley.

COSTNER, H. L.
    1969    "Theory, deduction and rules of correspondence." *American Journal of Sociology* 75: 245–263.

DUNCAN, O. D.
    1966    "Path analysis: Sociological examples." *American Journal of Sociology* 72: 3–16.
    1969a    "Some linear models for two-wave, two-variable panel analysis." *Psychological Bulletin* 72: 177–182.

1969b   "Contingencies in constructing causal models." Pp. 74–112 in E. F. Borgatta (Ed.), *Sociological Methodology: 1969.* San Francisco: Jossey-Bass.

DUNCAN, O. D., FEATHERMAN, D. L., AND DUNCAN, B.

1968   *Socioeconomic Background and Occupational Achievement: Extensions of a Basic Model.* Final Report No. 5-0074 (EO-191), Contract No. OE-5-85-072. Washington, D.C.: Bureau of Research, Office of Education, Department of Health, Education, and Welfare.

DUNCAN, O. D., HALLER, A. O., AND PORTES, A.

1968   "Peer influences on aspirations: A reinterpretation." *American Journal of Sociology* 74: 119–137.

GOLDBERGER, A. S.

1964   *Econometric Theory.* New York: Wiley.

1970a   "Criteria and constraints in multivariate regression." Workshop Paper EME 7026. Social Systems Research Institute, Madison: University of Wisconsin.

1970b   "On Boudon's method of linear causal analysis." *American Sociological Review* 35: 97–101.

1971   "Econometrics and psychometrics: A survey of communalities." *Psychometrika* 36: 83–107.

GOLDBERGER, A. S. AND OLKIN, I.

1971   "A minimum-distance interpretation of limited-information estimation." *Econometrica* 39: 635–639.

HARMAN, H. H.

1967   *Modern Factor Analysis.* (2nd ed.). Chicago: University of Chicago Press.

HAUSER, R. M.

1968   Family, School and Neighborhood Factors in Educational Performances in a Metropolitan School System. University of Michigan (unpublished doctoral dissertation).

1969a   "Schools and the stratification process." *American Journal of Sociology* 74: 587–611.

1969b   "On 'social participation and social status.' " *American Sociological Review* 34: 549–554.

1970   "Educational stratification in the United States." *Sociological Inquiry* 40: 102–129.

HEISE, D. R.

1969   "Problems in path analysis and causal inference." Pp. 38–73 in E. F. Borgatta (Ed.), *Sociological Methodology: 1969.* San Francisco: Jossey-Bass.

HODGE, R. W. AND TREIMAN, D. J.
 1968 "Social participation and social status." *American Sociological Review* 33: 723–740.
JOHNSTON, J.
 1963 *Econometric Methods.* New York: McGraw-Hill.
JÖRESKOG, K. G.
 1967 "RMLFA: A computer program for restricted maximum likelihood factor analysis." Research Memorandum RM-67-21. Princeton, N.J.: Educational Testing Service.
 1969a "A general approach to confirmatory maximum likelihood factor analysis." *Psychometrika* 34: 183–202.
 1969b "Factoring the multitest-multioccasion correlation matrix." Research Bulletin RB-69-62. Princeton, N.J.: Educational Testing Service.
 1970 "A general method for analysis of covariance structures." *Biometrika* 57: 239–251.
JÖRESKOG, K. G. AND LAWLEY, D. N.
 1968 "New methods in maximum likelihood factor analysis." *British Journal of Mathematical and Statistical Psychology* 21: 85–96.
LAND, K. C.
 1969 "Principles of path analysis." Pp. 3–37 in E. F. Borgatta (Ed.), *Sociological Methodology: 1969.* San Francisco: Jossey-Bass.
 1970 "On the estimation of path coefficients for unmeasured variables from correlations among observed variables." *Social Forces* 48: 506–511.
LAWLEY, D. N. AND MAXWELL, A. E.
 1963 *Factor Analysis as a Statistical Method.* London: Butterworths.
MORRISON, D. F.
 1967 *Multivariate Statistical Methods.* New York: McGraw-Hill.
SIEGEL, P. M. AND HODGE, R. W.
 1968 "A causal approach to the study of measurement error." Pp. 28–59 in H. M. Blalock, Jr. and A. B. Blalock (Eds.), *Methodology in Social Research.* New York: McGraw-Hill.
WERTS, C. E. AND LINN, R. L.
 1970 "Path analysis: Psychological examples." *Psychological Bulletin* 74: 193–212.
WILEY, D. E. AND WILEY, J. A.
 1970 "The estimation of measurement error in panel data." *American Sociological Review* 35: 112–117.

WRIGHT, S.

1925   "Corn and hog correlations." Department Bulletin No. 1300. Washington, D.C.: Department of Agriculture.

1934   "The method of path coefficients." *The Annals of Mathematical Statistics* 5: 161–215.

1954   "The interpretation of multivariate systems." Pp. 11–33 in O. Kempthorne, *et al.* (Eds.), *Statistics and Mathematics in Biology.* Ames, Iowa: Iowa State College Press.

ZELLNER, A.

1970   "Estimation of regression relationships containing unobservable variables." *International Economic Review* 11: 441–454.

# ROBUSTNESS IN REGRESSION
# ANALYSIS

*George W. Bohrnstedt*

UNIVERSITY OF MINNESOTA

*T. Michael Carter*

UNIVERSITY OF WISCONSIN

*This research was funded, in part, by National Institutes of Health grant No. 5-T01-GM-01526. An earlier version of this paper was presented to a symposium, Methodology in Sociology, jointly sponsored by the Methodology Section of the American Sociological Association and Loyola University, Chicago, Illinois, June 10–11, 1970. The authors are especially grateful to G. William Walster for his helpful comments on the earlier version of the paper.*

In the past ten years, there has been a virtual methodological explosion in sociology. Prior to the 1950's one's training at the doctoral level was not likely to include topics such as multiple correlation, covariance analysis, factor analysis, measurement theory, and path analysis, whereas these topics are rapidly being interlarded (if not already included) in the doctoral requirements at major institutions today. Ten or fifteen years ago, one's course was likely to have concentrated on learning a variety of nonparametric and tabular techniques since it was widely assumed that standard parametric statistics were too sophisticated for the quality of data sociological research generated. Like most generalizations, the above statement must be qualified to include the exception. Thus, most demographers were likely to receive considerable training in multivariate parametric techniques. Then too, if one goes back further than 20 years, those sociologists who received training in statistics and methods often did so in departments outside sociology and were taught parametric methods.

While it is difficult to credit one person with reversing this trend, in our judgment the appearance in the early 1960's of a series of articles on causal analysis by Hubert M. Blalock, Jr., probably was the most important single event in reestablishing an interest in parametric techniques since the models he adopted from Herbert Simon (1957) generally required regression analysis. The second person who was extremely important in the revival of interest in parametric statistics is Otis Dudley Duncan, beginning with his 1966 article on path analysis. The rest is all very recent history. The appearance of such volumes as the Blalocks' *Methodology in Social Research* (1968), Edgar Borgatta and George Bohrnstedt's American Sociological Association sponsored *Sociological Methodology: 1969*, and *The American Occupational Structure* by P. M. Blau and O. D. Duncan (1967) have all served to make the move towards parametric statistics even more permanent. Although a formal study has not been done, merely by scanning the major sociological journals, we see that the number of data analyses using parametric techniques has increased dramatically.

It is natural that, with the move towards parametric statistics, there has occurred a greater interest in the estimation of parameters as opposed to a concern merely with the statistical significance of one's findings. We do not mean to imply that statistical significance is less important now than it was 10 or 20 years ago but rather that statistical significance is increasingly being used to indicate the stability of parametric estimates we make. Far too many articles have been published in the major journals in which the level of statistical analysis is a $\chi^2$ test against randomness, hardly very interesting.

Because of our firm belief that the move toward parametric statistics has proven, and will continue to prove, to be a most fruitful approach for data analysis in sociology, we choose not to spend much time on the debate as to whether or not variables in sociology are really measured on interval or ratio scales and, hence, whether or not we can use parametric statistics. Instead, we maintain that our principle concern in sociology is with parameter estimation. As such, we shall present the regression model and the assumptions one must make to use it and then show the effects of systematically violating these underlying assumptions. To the degree that parametric estimates are unaffected by violations of assumptions, we shall say that the model is robust.

## TWO-VARIABLE MODEL

The two-variable regression model we shall consider is

$$Y = \alpha + \beta X + v \tag{1}$$

where $Y$ is the dependent variable, $X$ is the independent variable, and $v$ is the disturbance term. The disturbance term is, in fact, a residual variable—the difference between the actual $Y_i$ and the $Y_i$ predicted from $X_i$ using equation (1). More specifically,

$$\begin{aligned} v &= Y - (\alpha + \beta X) \\ &= Y - \hat{Y} \end{aligned} \tag{2}$$

where $\hat{Y}$ is the estimated $Y$ from $\alpha + \beta X$. Obviously, if there were a perfect linear model linking $X$ with $Y$, then the $v$ would equal zero.

It is assumed that equation (1) is the correct functional form linking $X$ to $Y$. In this assumption we are asserting that there is no specification error; that is, the relationship is linear in the variables rather than curvilinear, and no other variable exists which causes both $X$ and $Y$. We shall have more to say about the effects of specification error later. Also, it is assumed that $X$ and $Y$ are measured without error. At this point we do not concern ourselves with questions of sampling and hence need not concern ourselves with the shape of the distribution of the residuals. We shall address ourselves to this question shortly.

One wants to minimize the distance between the predicted and observed values of $Y$ or, more precisely, to minimize the variance of $v$. The choices of $\alpha$ and $\beta$ which make $\Sigma v^2$ a minimum are (Johnston, 1963, p. 11)

$$\beta = \frac{\text{Cov}(X, Y)}{V(X)} \tag{3}$$

and

$$\alpha = E(Y) - \beta E(X) \tag{4}$$

where

$$\text{Cov}(X, Y) = E(XY) - E(X)E(Y) \tag{5}$$

and

$$V(X) = E(X^2) - E^2(X) \tag{6}$$

and $\text{Cov}(X, Y)$ and $V(X)$ are the covariance of $X$ and $Y$ and the variance of $X$ respectively. Equation (1) might be thought of as the generating model in the population. It can be shown (Goldberger, 1964, p. 159) that the mean of the disturbance is zero and that the disturbance is uncorrelated with $Y$ and $X$.

The preceding discussion, however, is in population terms. When one develops a model for making inferences about population parameters from a sample, additional assumptions are needed. Let the sample consist of $N$ joint observations drawn at random from a population in which there is a conditional distribution of $Y$ for every outcome of $X$. Then, if the sample covariance $s_{XY}$, the sample variances, $s_X^2$ and $s_Y^2$, and the sample means, $\bar{X}$ and $\bar{Y}$, are employed in equations (3) and (4), we obtain sample estimates of $\beta$ and $\alpha$, labelled $B$ and $A$ respectively.[1] Further, when these results are substituted in equation (1), our estimating equation in the sample becomes

$$Y = A + BX + U \tag{7}$$

where $U$ is the sample disturbance or residual term. We then assumed that, in the long run, the disturbance associated with any outcome of $X$ is zero, that the variance at each outcome is a constant, that in repeated sampling the disturbances are independent of each other, and that the independent variable is uncorrelated with the disturbance. More formally, these assumptions are

$$E(U_i) = 0 \qquad \text{for all } i \tag{8}$$
$$E(U_i^2) = \sigma^2 \qquad \text{for all } i \tag{9}$$
$$E(U_i U_j) = 0 \qquad \text{for all } i \text{ and } j \text{ where } i \neq j \tag{10}$$
$$E(UX) = 0 \tag{11}$$

Two other assumptions are needed: (1) It is assumed that the variables are measured without error, and (2) the $X$'s are assumed to be fixed in the

---

[1] Ordinarily these estimates are labelled $a$ and $b$. However, we want to distinguish estimates made in the presence of measurement error from those made in its absence. We shall use $A$ and $B$ when no measurement error is assumed to exist and $a$ and $b$ where the absence of measurement error is not assumed.

sense that all outcomes of $X$ to which generalizations are to be made have been sampled. This assumption means that, when the independent variable is expressed as a set of dummy variables (Suits, 1957), the regression model is exactly the same as a one-way fixed effects analysis of variance (Cohen, 1968).

Now, as shown in Goldberger (1964, pp. 163–167), no further assumptions are necessary to obtain the best linear unbiased estimates of $\alpha$ and $\beta$ where best refers to the estimators with minimum sampling variation. In particular, it can be shown that

$$A = \bar{Y} - B\bar{X} \tag{12}$$

and

$$B = \frac{s_{XY}}{s_X^2} \tag{13}$$

are the best linear unbiased estimates of $\alpha$ and $\beta$. The sampling variances of $A$ and $B$ are (Johnston, 1963, p. 19)

$$V(A) = \frac{\Sigma X_i^2}{N\Sigma(X_i - \bar{X})^2}\,\sigma^2 \tag{14}$$

and

$$V(B) = \frac{\sigma^2}{\Sigma(X_i - \bar{X})^2} \tag{15}$$

In addition, since one does not ordinarily know the variance of the disturbances $\sigma^2$, it can be estimated without bias as

$$\hat{\sigma}^2 = \frac{\Sigma U_i^2}{N - 2} \tag{16}$$

To this point nothing has been indicated about the shape of the distribution of the disturbances (or, equivalently, the shape of the distribution of the dependent variable), and indeed, nothing needs to be said to obtain best linear unbiased estimates of $\alpha$ and $\beta$. However, in order to test hypotheses about $A$ and $B$, one must further assume that the conditional distributions of $U$ are normal for each outcome of $X$. This additional assumption allows one to show that

$$\frac{B - \beta}{\sqrt{V(B)}} \tag{17}$$

is distributed as a central $t$ variable with $N - 2$ degrees of freedom when $\beta$ is known. When the hypothesized $\beta$ is incorrect, equation (17) is distributed as a noncentral $t$, and standard tabled values of $t$ are inappropriate. This simply means that if one is testing the hypothesis that $\beta = 0$, the tabled probabilities are correct only if $\beta$ is indeed zero.

Similarly, a test for the intercept

$$\frac{A - \alpha}{\sqrt{V(A)}} \tag{18}$$

also is distributed as a central $t$ with $N - 2$ degrees of freedom when $\alpha$ is known.

## Violations of Assumptions

Now we can ask the question: What happens when we violate the stated assumptions?

*Normality of Disturbances.* There has been more research done on the effects of nonnormality on robustness than on any violated assumption. In particular, it has been shown by Bartlett (1935), Boneau (1960), Gayen (1949), and Srivastava (1958) that the population distributions of the disturbance term have little effect on obtained $t$ values in repeated samples, given a sufficiently large sample size. That is, the number of significant $t$'s for a given level of significance is about the same regardless of the shape of the parent distribution.

It makes sense to think of the error term as a summary of our ignorance about the variables which cause $Y$ in addition to $X$. This is made clear in the following path diagram:

There are many additional variables which might be thought of as causally related to $Y$, and $U$ is a summary, or surrogate, for them. Given this interpretation of $U$, we can draw on the central-limit theorem which suggests that $U$ should be normally distributed. In particular, this theorem states that the distribution of the sum of $K$ independent random variables tends to be normally distributed regardless of the shape of the original distributions. If we think of $U$, then, as the sum of variables which have been excluded from equation (7) but which are, nevertheless, related to $Y$, it is not unreasonable to assume that $U$ has a normal distribution.

*Homoscedasticity.* It is assumed that for every level of $X$, the variance is a constant, $\sigma^2$. This condition of constant variance is called homoscedasticity, and its absence, heteroscedasticity. Here, too, several investigations have been done to show the effect of nonhomogeneity of variances on the $F$-distribution (Norton, 1952; Cochran, 1947; Godard and Lindquist, 1940), and the results are similar to those reported above for nonnormality. That is, the number of significant $F$-tests and their magnitude are likely to be virtually unaffected unless heterogeneity among the variances is marked.

There are certain cases, however, where one might not be able to assume anything but gross heteroscedasticity. For example, it would seem untenable to suppose that the variance in dollars contributed to local community chest is constant across all categories of income. Specifically, one would hypothesize that there is relatively little variation in donations at the lower-income levels and large variation in the upper-income categories.

What effects can heteroscedasticity have? Estimation of the intercept and regression coefficient remains unbiased regardless of the degree of heteroscedasticity (Johnston, 1963, 208–209). However, unbiasedness is but one desirable characteristic of an estimator. In addition, the best linear unbiased estimator also has the smallest sampling variance. If it has the minimum variance characteristic, it is said to be the most efficient estimator.

Again, suppose we are interested in the relationship between donations to the local community chest and income but suspect that the variance of errors is either proportional to the value of $X$ or to the square of $X$. That is,

$$H_1: E(U_i^2) = \sigma^2 X_i$$

and
$$H_2: E(U_i^2) = \sigma^2 X_i^2$$

There is an implicit third hypothesis that we can investigate that the variance is a constant, as classical least-squares regression assumes; that is,

$$H_o: E(U_i^2) = \sigma^2$$

Goldberger (1964, pp. 235–236) indicates that, when heteroscedasticity is present,

$$E(U_i^2) = \sigma^2 k_i$$

for the $i$th level of $X_i$ and one can transform the original relationship to a homoscedastic one by dividing the $i$th observation on all variables by $\sqrt{k_i}$ and by computing the classical least-squares estimator on the transformed observations. This approach is called a weighted least-squares solution. If the assumed relationship between income and donations is given by

$$Y_i = A + BX_i + U_i \tag{19}$$

but the hypothesis is that $E(U_i^2) = \sigma^2 X_i^2$, then, if we divide equation (19) by $X_i$, we obtain

$$\frac{Y_i}{X_i} = \frac{A}{X_i} + B + \frac{U_i}{X_i} \qquad (20)$$

Now, the disturbance is homoscedastic since $E(U_i/X_i)^2 = [E(U_i^2)]/X_i^2 = \sigma^2$. Or, if we assume that $E(U_i^2) = \sigma^2 X_i$, then equation (19) is divided through by $\sqrt{X_i}$, and we obtain

$$\frac{Y_i}{\sqrt{X_i}} = \frac{A}{\sqrt{X_i}} + B\sqrt{X_i} + \frac{U_i}{\sqrt{X_i}} \qquad (21)$$

which is also homoscedastic.

We can indicate with some fictitious data how one evaluates the relative efficiency of an estimator where heteroscedasticity is present. The data were constructed by increasing the amount of variance as $X$ increased in size roughly by a factor proportional to $X_i^2$. Thus, we would expect the estimated standard error of the regression coefficient in equation (20) to be the smallest, when compared to equations (19) and (21). Also, one would expect that the estimated standard error associated with the untransformed observations, equation (19), to be the largest. The results are shown in Table 1, where $t_{148}$ is a $t$ test with 148 degrees of freedom.

Table 1

| Equation | $N$ | $V(B)$ | $B$ | $t_{148}$ |
|----------|-----|--------|-----|-----------|
| 19 | 150 | 0.204 | 5.0 | 11.06 |
| 20 | 150 | 0.089 | 5.0 | 16.72 |
| 21 | 150 | 0.115 | 5.0 | 14.73 |

We compare the relative efficiency of the standard error associated with the untransformed observations by looking at the ratios of equation (20) and equation (21) to equation (19). If we do this, we see that the efficiency of least squares applied to the original observations is only about 44 per cent of least squares applied to the data using equation (20) (0.089/0.204 = 0.436) and about 56 per cent of least squares applied to equation (21) (0.115/0.204 = 0.564). Note that in each case the estimate of $B$ is the same but that the estimated variance of the sample distribution and, hence, the $t$ values varied considerably.

If one expects that heteroscedasticity exists, one can examine the calculated residuals against the independent variable, and it ought to be evident. Thus, if the $E(U_i^2) = \sigma^2 X_i^2$ as indicated above and equation (19) was used to estimate $B$, the residuals plotted against $X$ would have the following pattern:

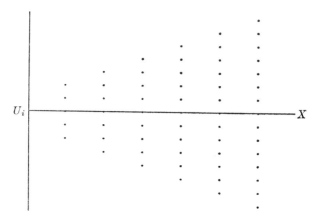

To have confidence in the hypothesis that heterogeneity exists in the population being investigated, one would most certainly need to be able to replicate the pattern of residuals in a new sample.

## Correlations Between Regressors and Disturbances

What happens when one cannot assume that the regressors are uncorrelated with the disturbances? Consider Figure 1 where we assume

Figure 1.

that $X$ is the sole determinant of $Y$. The model assumes that no co-variation exists between $X$ and $U$ and, hence, that

$$\text{Cov}(X, Y) = BV(X) \tag{22}$$

or

$$\rho_{XY} = P_{YX} \tag{23}$$

where $\rho_{XY}$ is the correlation between $X$ and $Y$ and $P_{YX}$ is the path coefficient (Duncan, 1966) linking $X$ and $Y$. The point is that in Figure 1 only $X$ is responsible for variation in $Y$, and we can easily estimate $\beta$ (or $P_{YX}$) since $\text{Cov}(X, Y)$ and $V(X)$ are observables. Now, consider Figure 2. Whereas the correct model underlying Figure 1 is given by equation (7), this is not appropriate for the situation in Figure 2 where

Figure 2.

a second variable $U$, which is correlated with $X$, also must be included. It can be shown by multiplying equation (7) through by $X$, taking expectations, and using equation (5) that

$$\text{Cov}(X, Y) = \beta V(X) + E(XU)$$
$$= \beta V(X) + \text{Cov}(X, U) \tag{24}$$

since $E(U) = 0$ by assumption, and

$$\rho_{XY} = P_{YX} + P_{YU}\rho_{XU} \tag{25}$$

That is, the covariation in $X$ and $Y$ is now due to two variables and not one, and if we try to estimate $\beta$ with $B = s_{XY}/s_X^2$, we will obtain a biased estimator since it follows from equation (24) that when $X$ and $U$ are correlated,

$$\beta = \frac{\text{Cov}(X, Y) - \text{Cov}(X, U)}{V(X)} \tag{26}$$

That is, the true $\beta$ shown in equation (26) differs from that which classical least-squares estimators yield as a function of the size of $\text{Cov}(X, U)$. Examples of the effects are shown in Table 2. Notice that the estimated $\beta$ is 0.30 but that the actual value of $\beta$ varies considerably as a function of the magnitude and sign of $\text{Cov}(X, U)$. When the correlation between $X$ and $U$ is large, the errors in estimating $\beta$ are likely to be large. Thus, when $\rho_{XU} = -0.8$, the estimate of $\beta$ is only two-thirds as large as it should be $(0.30/0.46 = 0.652)$. On the other hand, if $\rho_{XU} = +0.8$, then the estimate of $\beta$ is over twice as large as it should be $(0.30/0.14 = 2.14)$. Obviously, when the regressors are correlated with the disturbance, gross errors in estimating $\beta$ can arise, as this simple example shows. The need for the assumption is shown clearly in equation (25). One has an observed correlation $(\rho_{XY})$ with which to try to estimate both $P_{YX}$ and $P_{YU}$. Without assuming that $\rho_{XU} = 0$, the equation is underidentified; that is, we have too many unknowns for the number of equations (Goldberger, 1964, pp. 306–318). Had we believed that some variable was causally related to $Y$, we should have included it in our model and made measurements on it. Then, estimates of both parameters in equation (25) could have been made.

Table 2
Effect on True $\beta_{YX}$ of $\rho_{XU} \neq 0$ and Estimated $\beta_{YX}$ Under False
Assumption $\rho_{XU} = 0$

| $\beta_{YX}$ | $\mathrm{Cov}(Y, X)$ | $V(X)$ | $\rho_{XU}$ |
|---|---|---|---|
| 0.34 | 1.2 | 4 | $-0.2$ |
| 0.38 | 1.2 | 4 | $-0.4$ |
| 0.42 | 1.2 | 4 | $-0.6$ |
| 0.46 | 1.2 | 4 | $-0.8$ |
| 0.26 | 1.2 | 4 | $+0.2$ |
| 0.22 | 1.2 | 4 | $+0.4$ |
| 0.18 | 1.2 | 4 | $+0.6$ |
| 0.14 | 1.2 | 4 | $+0.8$ |

Note: $B_{YX} = 0.30$ under assumption $\rho_{XU} = 0$.

## Specification Errors

When one has mistakenly either omitted or included variables in an equation assumed to capture the true causal structure to $Y$, or when the functional form chosen to represent the variables is incorrect, we say that one has made a specification error. We can now move on to consider what happens to one's parametric estimates when certain kinds of specification errors are made. Most of us begin by assuming that we know something about the causal determinants of some $Y$ of interest and fit a linear model to the observations. Obviously, the resulting estimates are descriptions of reality only to the degree that we have correctly specified the determinants of $Y$ and that the linear model is the correct functional form. Otherwise, we will be fitting the wrong observations into the wrong model, and the obtained estimates will be relatively meaningless. These facts underscore the role of theory in solving the specification problem. If we do not have a theory or hypothesis which carefully specifies the variables related to $Y$, merely putting every conceivable variable into the regression equation generates junk since it does not take the logical ordering of the variables into account (Gordon, 1969).

Theil (1957) has indicated that one can compare competing models by examining their respective sums of squares of the residuals corrected for degrees of freedom. The smaller is the sum, the larger the $\bar{R}^2$, and the better the derived predictions fit the data. This in turn suggests that the specification may be better.

Suppose that our true underlying model is of the form

$$Y = A + B_1X + B_2X^2 + U_1 \tag{27}$$

but we try to estimate $Y$ instead with

$$Y = A' + B'_1 X \qquad (28)$$

Clearly we have made a specification error and are estimating the wrong parameters. In that sense the linear model will not be robust at all. However, if we compare the $R^2$s corrected for degrees of freedom $\bar{R}^2$, it may tell us that equation (27) gives a better fit than equation (28). One examines the multiple-correlation coefficients which have been corrected for degrees of freedom since the observed $R^2$ is a function not only of the true correlations in the population but also the number of predictor variables. That is, a regression which includes the same predictors plus one as a previous regression will necessarily have an $R^2$ at least as large as that associated with the previous regression, even though the latter regression is not a better estimate of the multiple correlation in the population. The relationship between the corrected and uncorrected estimates is

$$R^2 = \bar{R}^2 + \frac{K}{N - K - 1} (1 - R^2) \qquad (29)$$

where $R^2$ is the observed estimate, $\bar{R}^2$ is the estimate corrected for degrees of freedom, and $K$ is the number of independent variables (Goldberger, 1964, p. 217).[2] The last term to the right indicates how the unbiased estimate is inflated by the relationship of the number of predictors to the sample size. We can simply solve equation (29) for $\bar{R}^2$ to get an unbiased estimate of the multiple correlation. Hence,

$$\bar{R}^2 = R^2 - \frac{K}{N - K - 1} (1 - R^2) \qquad (30)$$

We can illustrate by a fictitious example how equation (30) could help us decide between equation (27) and (28) as the better fit to the data. We generated some fictitious data to fit roughly the line $Y = 2X + X^2$. Hence, the multiple correlation associated with equation (27) ought to be higher when corrected for degrees of freedom than that associated with equation (28). The results are in Table 3.

---

[2] We avoid using biased and unbiased to describe $R^2$ and $\bar{R}^2$ respectively since, strictly, $\bar{R}^2$ is not unbiased. However, one does not necessarily want an unbiased estimator. For example, if in the population the multiple correlation is zero, then for $\bar{R}$ to be unbiased it must assume some values less than zero. Quite patently, however, any estimate less than zero can be improved by estimating the parameter to be zero since zero will always be closer to the true parametric value than a negative estimate. However, following this procedure would yield biased estimates of the parameter, even though this procedure represents an improvement over using an estimate which takes on negative values (Darlington, 1968, pp. 172–173).

Table 3

| Model | $R^2$ | $N$ | $K$ | $\bar{R}^2$ |
|---|---|---|---|---|
| equation (27) | 0.9942 | 80 | 2 | 0.9940 |
| equation (28) | 0.9021 | 80 | 1 | 0.9008 |

Notice that the $R^2$ corrected for degrees of freedom does indeed tell us that equation (27) produces a better fit to the observation than did equation (28).

To summarize this section, we began this chapter by assuming that we knew the correct variables to account for $Y$ and the correct functional form for linking the variables. Obviously, if we specify either the variables or the functional form incorrectly, we will be estimating the wrong parameters entirely, and in that sense, robustness does not exist at all. However, we see that a method does exist for helping to determine which of several rival models is the best.

### Errors in Measurement

As indicated in the introduction to this paper, social scientists in the mid 1950's were cautioned against using parametric statistics since they assumed the existence of an underlying interval or ratio scale, something we rarely, if ever, see in sociology. At best, most of our measuring instruments measure at the ordinal level. We do not have new information to contribute to the continuing debate on the subject although we believe that the arguments for the use of parametric statistics far outstrip the arguments against. Thus, we will merely review some of them here.

It is argued that, while the researcher may assign 1, 2, 3, and 4 to the categories strongly disagree, probably disagree, probably agree, and definitely agree as though the psychological distances between the categories were the same, they may not be. Thus, the real situation may be

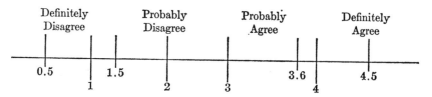

Labovitz (1967, 1970) has shown that, as long as one assumes a monotonic relationship between the measurement scale and the underlying psychological scale, the application of tests of significance to ordinal data yields few aberrations. Essentially, the same conclusions are reached

by Baker, Hardyck, and Petrinovich who draw the three following conclusions (1966, pp. 299–300):

> (1) The percentage of $t$'s reaching the theoretical 5 per cent and 1 per cent levels of significance is not seriously affected by the use of nonequal interval measurements. (2) To the extent that there is any influence of the scale transformation on the percentage of $t$'s reaching theoretical significance levels, the influence is more marked when intervals in one broad region of a scale are larger than intervals in another region of the scale than it is when interval sizes vary randomly. (3) If an investigator has a measuring instrument which produces either an interval scale or an ordinal scale with randomly varied interval sizes, he can safely use $t$ for statistical decisions under all circumstances examined in this study. The single exception is that $t$ should not be used to do a one-tailed test when samples of unequal size have been done from a badly skewed population.

There are three other similar conclusions the authors list but more important is their conclusion: "The research worker who has nothing better than an ordinal scale to work with may have an extremely poor fit to reality, but at least he will not be led into making incorrect probability estimates if he observes a few simple precautions" (1966, p. 301).

In our judgment these two empirical studies make the point best. Others who have been in this debate are Burke (1953), Senders (1953), Borgatta (1968, 1970), and Jacobson (1970) to name a few. The point is that, under almost any conceivable research situation, statistical tests are robust enough to allow the researcher to use them with little fear of gross errors regardless of whether or not he has an interval or ratio scale so long as his ordinal measure is monotonically related to the underlying true scale.

Two other points seem worth mentioning: (1) The statistical power of parametric statistics over nonparametric statistics is well-known, and the above findings suggest that, even though some errors in inference may occasionally be made by using ordinal data with parametric techniques, the increase in power makes the risk seem small. See Borgatta (1970) on this point. (2) However, if one is still unconvinced, he still can use parametric statistics with ordinal measures and even nominal variables by using dummy variables as long as the dependent variable is not nominally measured. (Boyle, 1970; Lyons and Carter, 1971; Suits, 1957; Cohen, 1968.) This point seems to bother research sociologists since it is thought (incorrectly) that to use multiple regression one must assume a multivariate normal distribution, and this clearly cannot be assumed with dichotomous variables, which dummy variables are. However, we saw in our stated assumptions for the fixed-effects model (which is appropriate for most dummy-variable analysis) that the assumption is for the conditional distributions to be normal, nothing else.

Therefore, we conclude that, when one has a variable which is measured at least at the ordinal level, parametric statistics not only can be, but should be, applied.

While it seems clear that errors in measurement affect the number of statistically significant $t$'s in only minor ways, we shall now show that parameter estimation in regression analysis can be seriously affected by such errors. This will not lead us to conclude that parametric analyses should be avoided, but instead, to suggest that estimates should include adjustments to correct for errors in measurement.

We can now examine more carefully how errors in measurement affect estimation. In this section a population rather than a sample is assumed, although all the conclusions apply to samples as well.[3] If, instead of assuming that $X$ and $Y$ are measured without error, we allow that

$$x = X + e_x \quad \text{and} \quad y = Y + e_y \qquad (28)$$

where $x$ and $y$ are the observed variables and $e_x$ and $e_y$ are the errors in measurement of $x$ and $y$ respectively, then our regression model is

$$y = a + bx + u \qquad (29)$$

where $a$ and $b$ are used to indicate estimates of $\alpha$ and $\beta$ when errors of measurement are present and where u is the disturbance term. Now we assume that the true scores are uncorrelated with the measurement errors and that measurement errors in $x$ are uncorrelated with measurement errors in $y$.

It now can be shown that

$$b = \frac{\text{Cov}(x, y)}{V(x)} \qquad (33)$$

and

$$\beta = \frac{\text{Cov}(x, y)}{V(x) - V(e_x)} \qquad (34)$$

That is, the formula for $b$ and the $\beta$ measured without error, equation (3), differ in the denominator by the variance of the measurement errors in $X$. We can more clearly see how $b$ and $\beta$ differ by looking at the ratio

---

[3] In the remaining sections of this chapter the term *bias* may be better than *robustness* since, strictly speaking, robustness applies only to sample statistics and not to population models.

of $b$ to $\beta$. Clearly, if $X$ and $Y$ were measured without error, then $b/\beta = 1$ and $[V(x) - V(e_x)]/V(x) = 1$. We now can define the reliability of $x$ and will denote it $\rho_{xx'}$.

DEFINITION: The reliability of a random variable $x$ is

$$\rho_{xx'} = \frac{V(x) - V(e_x)}{V(x)} = 1 - \frac{V(e_x)}{V(x)} \tag{35}$$

This is the definition of reliability provided by Lord and Novick (1968, p. 61). It is seen, then, that when $b = \beta$, $\rho_{xx'} = 1.0$, which implies no measurement error in $X$. But, in general,

$$b = \beta \rho_{xx'} \tag{36}$$

This result indicates the effect unreliability has on the regression coefficient in the two-variable case. To show how nonrobust the estimate of the regression coefficient can be in the presence of measurement error, let us assume that $\beta = 3.0$. We then note from Table 4 how severely attenuated $b$ can become when reliability is low. Clearly one's estimates of $\beta$ can be grossly underestimated when unreliability exists. Unfortunately, most of our measures in sociology seldom have reliabilities above 0.8. That is, one can expect estimates in the two-variable case to be attenuated by 20 per cent or more.

We now can examine the effects of unreliability on the estimate of the intercept constant. It can be demonstrated that

$$a = \mu_y - b\mu_x = \mu_y - \beta \rho_{xx'} \mu_x \tag{37}$$

assuming that $E(e_x) = E(e_y) = 0$. Now, if $\mu_y$ and $\mu_x \geq 0$, it is easily shown that

$$a \geq A \tag{38}$$

That is, if the means are greater than or equal to zero, then the intercept of variables measured with errors will be equal to or larger than the intercept of the true underlying variables.

Table 4
Effect of Measurement Error on Estimated $\beta_{YX}$

| $b_{yx}$ | $\rho_{xx'}$ | $\beta_{YX}$ |
|---|---|---|
| 2.7 | 0.9 | 3.0 |
| 2.1 | 0.7 | 3.0 |
| 1.5 | 0.5 | 3.0 |
| 0.9 | 0.3 | 3.0 |

Both the intercept and the regression coefficient tend not to be particularly robust when measures are unreliable. We now can consider the effects of measurement error on the correlation coefficient. The correlation of $X$ and $Y$ is defined as

$$\rho_{XY} = \frac{\mathrm{Cov}(X, Y)}{\sqrt{V(x)V(y)}} = \frac{\rho_{xy}}{\sqrt{\rho_{xx'}\rho_{yy'}}} \qquad (39)$$

Equation (39) is often referred to as the correction of $\rho_{xy}$ for errors in the measurement of $X$ and $Y$. Rearranging (39), we see that

$$\rho_{xy} = \rho_{XY} \sqrt{\rho_{xx'}\rho_{yy'}} \qquad (40)$$

and that the observed correlation between $x$ and $y$ is attenuated by errors in both variables, whereas the regression coefficient is attenuated by errors in the independent variable. It should be noted in passing that the standardized regression coefficient (beta weight) is affected by measurement in both $X$ and $Y$. This is obvious since the beta weight equals the correlation coefficient in the two-variable case. Table 5 shows

Table 5
Effect of Measurement Error on $\rho_{xy}$ for Various Values of $\rho_{XY}$

| $\rho_{xy}$ | $\rho_{XY}$ | $\rho_{xx'}$ | $\rho_{yy'}$ |
|---|---|---|---|
| 0.08 | 0.20 | 0.40 | 0.40 |
| 0.12 | 0.20 | 0.60 | 0.60 |
| 0.16 | 0.20 | 0.80 | 0.80 |
| 0.16 | 0.40 | 0.40 | 0.40 |
| 0.24 | 0.40 | 0.60 | 0.60 |
| 0.32 | 0.40 | 0.80 | 0.80 |
| 0.24 | 0.60 | 0.40 | 0.40 |
| 0.36 | 0.60 | 0.60 | 0.60 |
| 0.48 | 0.60 | 0.80 | 0.80 |
| 0.32 | 0.80 | 0.40 | 0.40 |
| 0.48 | 0.80 | 0.60 | 0.60 |
| 0.64 | 0.80 | 0.80 | 0.80 |

how badly $\rho_{XY}$ can be underestimated when reliabilities are even quite high (for example, $\rho_{xx'} = \rho_{yy'} = 0.8$).

That errors in measurement will lead to biased estimates of $\alpha$ and $\beta$ can be shown in another way also. Johnston (1963, pp. 148–149) demonstrates that even though we assume that the errors in measurement in $X$ and $Y$ are uncorrelated and that the $X$'s and $Y$'s are uncorrelated with their respective errors in measurement, when measurement error exists,

$$\mathrm{Cov}(u, x) = -\beta V(e_x) \qquad (41)$$

which implies that a correlation exists between the disturbance term and the regressor. But, we recall that one of our assumptions for applying classical least squares was that this covariance be zero. This demonstrates that, when $e_x = e_y \neq 0$, applying classical least squares to equation (32) will yield biased estimates of $\alpha$ and $\beta$. See equation (26) and

Table 1 for the effects of disturbances correlated with the regressor.

It might be of interest for the reader to see precisely what the formula for the regression coefficient is when some assumptions cannot be met. It is given by

$$\beta = \frac{\text{Cov}(x, y) - \text{Cov}(e_x, Y) - \text{Cov}(X, e_y) + \text{Cov}(e_x, e_y)}{V(X)} \quad (42)$$

In particular, we must assume that the measurement errors in $X$ are uncorrelated with $Y$, the measurement errors in $Y$ are uncorrelated with $X$, and the measurement errors in $X$ and $Y$ are uncorrelated with each other. Then, in order to show that equation (42) equals equation (34), we must further assume that the measurement error in $X$ is uncorrelated with $X$ and that the measurement errors in $Y$ are uncorrelated with $Y$. Obviously, this is a lot of assumptions to be met. For example, let $\text{Cov}(x, y) = 1.21$ and $V(X) = 4.36$. Then, our estimate of $\beta$ is 0.30. However, the true $\beta$ could be substantially different from 0.30 if all of the above assumptions are not met, as Table 6 shows.

Table 6

Actual Values of $\beta_{YX}$ when Correlated Measurement Error Exists Whereas its Estimate Equals 0.30 under Assumption of Random Measurement Error

| $\beta_{YX}$ | $\text{Cov}(e_x, Y)$ | $\text{Cov}(X, e_y)$ | $\text{Cov}(e_x, e_y)$ |
|---|---|---|---|
| 0.208 | +0.1 | +0.1 | +0.1 |
| 0.139 | +0.2 | +0.2 | +0.2 |
| 0.071 | +0.3 | +0.3 | +0.3 |
| 0.300 | −0.1 | +0.1 | −0.1 |
| 0.323 | −0.2 | +0.2 | −0.2 |
| 0.346 | −0.3 | +0.3 | −0.3 |
| 0.346 | −0.1 | −0.1 | −0.1 |
| 0.415 | −0.2 | −0.2 | −0.2 |
| 0.483 | −0.3 | −0.3 | −0.3 |

We now move on and show the effects of errors in measurement in the case of two independent variables. In this case, the model is assumed to be

$$Y = \alpha + \beta_1 X_1 + \beta_2 X_2 + U \quad (43)$$

where $Y$, $X_1$, and $X_2$ are measured without error and $\alpha$, $\beta_1$, and $\beta_2$ are the population parameters. If the variables are measured with error, classical least-squares regression is applied to

$$y = a + b_1 x_1 + b_2 x_2 + u \quad (44)$$

instead of equation (43). Now, we can express the regression coefficients, $\beta_1$ and $\beta_2$, as functions of observables. In particular,

$$\beta_1 = \sqrt{\frac{V(y)}{V(x_1)}} \left[ \frac{\rho_{22'}\rho_{y1} - \rho_{y2}\rho_{12}}{\rho_{11'}\rho_{22'} - \rho_{12}^2} \right] \tag{45}$$

and

$$\beta_2 = \sqrt{\frac{V(y)}{V(x_2)}} \left[ \frac{\rho_{11'}\rho_{y2} - \rho_{y1}\rho_{12}}{\rho_{11'}\rho_{22'} - \rho_{12}^2} \right] \tag{46}$$

Notice, first of all, that similar to the two-variable case, errors in measurement in the dependent variable do not affect the regression coefficients, only errors in measurement in the independent variables. It is clear from equation (45) and equation (46) that, where reliability is perfect, the formulas for $\beta_i$ and $b_i$ would be identical since

$$b_i = \sqrt{\frac{V(y)}{V(x_i)}} \left[ \frac{\rho_{Yi} - \rho_{Yi}\rho_{ij}}{1 - \rho_{ij}^2} \right] \tag{47}$$

The second point to be made is that $\beta_i$ and $b_i$ bear no simple relationship to each other when measurement error is present. That is, either one could be the larger, whereas in the two variable case, it is true that $|b| \le |\beta|$—$b$ is always attenuated because of measurement error in the independent variable. We show by example in Table 7 using fictitious

Table 7
Effect of Measurement Error and Correlation Among the Independent Variables
on Estimates of $\beta_{YX\cdot Z}$, $\rho_{YX\cdot Z}^*$, and $R_{Y\cdot XZ}^{2*}$[a]

| $\beta_{YX\cdot Z}$ | $b_{yx\cdot z}$ | $\rho_{YX\cdot Z}^*$ | $\rho_{yx\cdot z}$ | $R_{Y\cdot XZ}^{2*}$ | $R_{y\cdot xz}^2$ | $\rho_{zy}$ |
|---|---|---|---|---|---|---|
| −0.186 | 0.029 | −0.113 | 0.031 | 0.257 | 0.161 | 0.7 |
| 0.139 | 0.125 | 0.146 | 0.167 | 0.264 | 0.183 | 0.4 |
| 0.309 | 0.225 | 0.333 | 0.300 | 0.382 | 0.250 | 0.0 |

[a] $\rho_{xx'} = \rho_{zz'} = 0.81$ and $\rho_{yy'} = 1.0$.

data that it is possible for $b_i$ to be greater than $\beta_i$, or vice versa, depending upon the values of the correlations among the variables and their reliabilities. Thus, in one case $\beta_1 = -0.186$ and $b_1 = 0.029$. Notice that in this case even the sign of the regression coefficient has changed. In the other examples $\beta_i$ is greater than $b_i$, and usually the absolute value of $\beta_i$ will be greater than that of $b_i$. Practically, this means that it is only when $\beta_i$ is near zero that sign changes are likely to occur.

The partial-correlation coefficient is affected by errors in measurement in all three variables. It is given by

$$\rho_{ij\cdot k}^* = \frac{\rho_{kk'}\rho_{ij} - \rho_{jk}\rho_{ik}}{\sqrt{\rho_{jj'}\rho_{kk'} - \rho_{jk}^2} \sqrt{\rho_{kk'}\rho_{ii'} - \rho_{ik}^2}} \tag{48}$$

where $\rho_{ij\cdot k}^*$ is the true partial as opposed to the observed partial $\rho_{ij\cdot k}$. The partial-correlation coefficients operate much the same way in the presence of error as do the regression coefficients. That is, it is possible for $\rho_{ij\cdot k}$ to overestimate or underestimate $\rho^*_{ij\cdot k}$. Which situation will, in fact, occur depends on the size of the reliabilities and the observed correlations $\rho_{ij}$. This can be seen by comparing equation (48) with the formula for the observed partial correlation uncorrected for measurement errors.

$$\rho_{ij\cdot k} = \frac{\rho_{ij} - \rho_{jk}\rho_{ik}}{\sqrt{1 - \rho_{jk}^2}\,\sqrt{1 - \rho_{ik}^2}} \qquad (49)$$

Table 7 presents examples of the effect of unreliability on the estimates of $\rho^*_{ij\cdot k}$.

Finally, we turn to the multiple-correlation coefficient. It is stated, without proof, that the coefficient of determination $R^{2*}_{i\cdot jk}$ is always attenuated when errors in measurement are present. This can be understood intuitively from the fact that the observed variances are inflated by measurement error. That is,

$$V(x) = V(X) + V(e_x) \qquad (50)$$

Further, since the measurement error is assumed to be random, it has no predictive power with respect to other variables. Examples of the attenuation of $R^{2*}_{ij\cdot k}$ are given in Table 7 for various levels of reliability.

## SIMULTANEOUS EQUATION MODELS

Since Duncan's now classic article on path analysis in 1966, sociologists seeking to speak to the question of causality among sociological variables have tended to regard the technique as a panacea. Indeed, to some extent at least, the use of path analysis has reached fad proportions. The sobering fact is that, although path analysis is indeed a most powerful inferential technique, it is based on a series of highly restrictive assumptions. Heise (1968) has made this point quite strongly, but few people apparently took him seriously. We intend, therefore, to extend his argument somewhat to show in more detail exactly what happens to the estimates of the path coefficients when the assumptions are violated.

In order to keep this presentation within reasonable limits, we will take the simple three-variable recursive model that is defined by the system of structural equations:

$$\begin{aligned} Y &= P_{YX}X + U_Y \\ Z &= P_{ZX}X + P_{ZY}Y + U_Z \end{aligned} \qquad (51)$$

or, diagrammed,

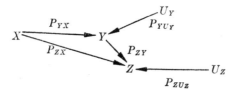

In this system our purpose is to estimate the values of the three paths, $P_{YX}$, $P_{ZY}$, and $P_{ZX}$. The following are required assumptions for solution: (a) equation (51) is the correct causal model in the population, (b) the relations linking the variables are linear, (c) no reciprocal causation exists among the variables, (d) the disturbances $U_Y$ and $U_Z$ are uncorrelated with each other and with the independent variables in the equations in which the residuals appear, (e) the three variables are measured without error, and (f) the remaining assumptions in equations (8) through (11) above.

To the extent that these assumptions are not met, our results, based on this model, will tend to be invalid. As we have seen previously, the regression model is, in fact, fairly robust in the presence of violations of many of the required assumptions. However, in most cases other than the normality assumption, we have been forced to make certain corrections in our estimating procedures in order to insure that our estimates will, in fact, be the best unbiased linear estimate. We shall come to the same conclusion in this section.

### Violation of Assumptions

As Heise (1969) has pointed out, the assumptions of linearity and no reciprocal relationships are relatively easy to bypass. It can be shown, for instance, that while the regression of income on education is only approximately linear, the regression of the logarithm of income on education is almost perfectly linear. Likewise, the econometricians have long used the technique of two-stage least squares in order to solve the problem of reciprocal relationships. Thus, with the use of data transformations and subsidiary procedures, we could easily transform the structure of equation (51) in order to offset the effects of violations of these two assumptions.

### Errors in Measurement

Assumptions (a), (d), and (e) above are quite highly interrelated. In fact, we shall show that, if measurement error exists, or if relevant variables have been omitted from the model, the disturbance terms will be correlated. We will take first the case of measurement error in all three variables. If we let $x = X + e_x$, $y = Y + e_y$, and $Z = z + e_z$, then equation (51) can be rewritten as

$$y = P_{YX}x + w_y$$
$$z = P_{ZX}x + P_{ZY}y + w_z \tag{52}$$

where $w_y = U_Y + e_y - P_{YX}e_x$ and $w_z = U_Z - P_{ZX}e_x - P_{ZY}e_y$. Then it is easy to show that

$$\text{Cov}(w_y, x) = -P_{YX}V(e_x)$$
$$\text{Cov}(w_z, x) = -P_{ZX}V(e_x)$$
$$\text{Cov}(w_z, y) = -P_{ZY}V(e_y)$$

and

$$\text{Cov}(w_y, w_z) = P_{YX}P_{ZX}V(e_x) - P_{ZY}V(e_y) \tag{53}$$

Thus, when measurement errors are present in the observed values, we guarantee that the disturbance terms will be correlated with the independent variables and with themselves. Further, this insures that our estimates of the path coefficients themselves will be biased.

It is extremely difficult to assess precisely how our estimates will be affected. If we could be sure that they would only be attenuated and not increased, we might feel, to some degree, secure in our estimates. This, unfortunately, is not the case. We have seen from equation (36) that $P_{YX}$ can only be attenuated. On the other hand, we have seen from equations (45) and (46) that $P_{ZX}$ and $P_{XY}$ can be either attenuated or increased, depending on the precise unobservable relations in the data. This situation is further compounded by the fact that the existence of a correlation between $w_y$ and $w_z$, which we fail to account for in our routine estimation procedures, causes us to misestimate $P_{ZX}$. Thus, we could very easily find ourselves in the position of rejecting $Y$'s importance as an intermediate variable solely on the basis of measurement error in all three variables.

### Correcting Path Coefficients

As before, we can express the true unbiased estimate in terms of observed quantities and reliability coefficients. The resulting equations for the three path coefficients would be

$$P_{YX} = \frac{\rho_{xy}}{\sqrt{\rho_{yy'}}\sqrt{\rho_{xx'}}}$$

$$P_{ZX} = \frac{\sqrt{\rho_{xx'}}}{\sqrt{\rho_{zz'}}}\left[\frac{\rho_{yy'}\rho_{xz} - \rho_{xy}\rho_{yz}}{\rho_{xx'}\rho_{yy'} - \rho_{xy}^2}\right] \tag{54}$$

$$P_{ZY} = \frac{\sqrt{\rho_{yy'}}}{\sqrt{\rho_{zz'}}}\left[\frac{\rho_{xx'}\rho_{yz} - \rho_{xy}\rho_{zx}}{\rho_{yy'}\rho_{xx'} - \rho_{xy}^2}\right]$$

As we have shown for the two- and three-variable single-regression equations, such a correction procedure removes the correlation between the disturbance term and the independent variables in the equation. It can similarly be shown that this procedure will also eliminate the correlation between $U_y$ and $U_z$ that is due to measurement error. It should be noted at this point that any correlation between the original disturbance terms $U_Y$ and $U_Z$, of course, will remain even after we have corrected for the effects of measurement error.

Table 8 presents the results of fictitious data to show the effect

### Table 8
#### Effects of Measurement Error on the True Path Coefficients[a]

|  | $\rho_{ii'} = 0.81$ | $\rho_{ii'} = 0.64$ |
|---|---|---|
| $P_{yx} = 0.40$ | $P_{YX} = 0.49$ | $P_{YX} = 0.63$ |
| $P_{zx} = 0.13$ | $P_{ZX} = 0.17$ | $P_{ZX} = 0.13$ |
| $P_{zy} = 0.33$ | $P_{ZY} = 0.41$ | $P_{ZY} = 0.54$ |

[a] $\rho_{xy} = 0.40$, $\rho_{xz} = 0.30$, $\rho_{yz} = 0.40$.

of measurement error on the true path coefficients in the three variable recursive system. As was noted earlier and is evident in the case of $P_{ZX}$, measurement error does not affect the values of partial path coefficients in a consistent manner.

### Effect of Specification Error

We indicated earlier in our single-equation model that specification problems obviously have a serious effect. On the one hand, we may in fact be trying to estimate the wrong parameter if we have included a variable in our model which in fact is causally unrelated to the others, and on the other hand, we will obtain biased estimates of the parameters if we have excluded from our model variables which are causally related to the dependent variable. It is this latter situation which can be explored with simultaneous equation models.

Suppose the true specification is

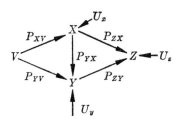

Now, the set of equations which correctly represents this model is

$$X = P_{XV}V + U_X$$
$$Y = P_{YV}V + P_{YX}X + U_Y \tag{55}$$
$$Z = P_{ZX}X + P_{ZY}Y + U_Z$$

However, instead of recognizing this model, we suppose that we were ignorant of the fact that $V$ was operating in the system. That is, we supposed incorrectly that the model was

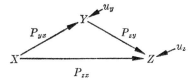

In this case we would have incorrectly represented the model as

$$Y = P_{yx}X + u_y$$
$$Z = P_{zx}X + P_{zy}Y + u_z \tag{56}$$

Rewriting equation (56) by substituting in for $X$ and $Y$ from equation (55), we have

$$Y = P_{yx}(P_{XV}V + U_x) + u_y$$
$$Z = P_{zx}(P_{XV}V + U_z) + P_{zy}(P_{YV}V + P_{YX}X + U_y) + u_z \tag{57}$$

It is easy to show that correlations exist between $X$ and $u_y$; $X$, $Y$, and $u_z$; and $u_y$ and $u_z$. The latter three correlations are quite complex and are not shown, but the first is relatively simple and makes the point well. Specifically,

$$\text{Cov}(X, u_y) = \rho_{XY}(1 - \rho_{XV}^2 - \rho_{XU_z}) \tag{58}$$

Obviously, if this correlation exists, it will bias our estimate of the path coefficient linking $X$ to $Y$. Similar arguments could be made for the biases accruing to the other correlations, referred to above, which result from misspecification of the model.

Thus, as was noted verbally in Heise's discussion, specification errors can seriously affect our estimates of the true structural parameters operating in the system. This situation is further complicated by the fact that, unlike the previous situation of measurement errors, we cannot apply a correction factor to our estimates to re-establish their unbiased property. Or, stated more simply, if we hypothesize the wrong model, then our estimation of that model will yield meaningless estimates.

## SUMMARY

In this chapter we have attempted to examine systematically what happens to the validity of our regression estimates when the assumptions underlying the technique are violated. We feel there is ample evidence to suggest that regression analysis is adequately robust except in the presence of measurement and specification error. It has been shown that the problems of heteroscedasticity and nonnormality do not, in fact, generally cause serious distortions. In cases where they do, on the other hand, adequate correction procedures exist to minimize these distortions.

We have not, however, dealt with the problem of autocorrelated errors in time-series or panel data. It appears reasonable to expect that the errors in such cases are in fact correlated. Such a situation, of course, violates the assumption that the disturbance term is not correlated with the independent variable. Heise (1970) has examined this problem in the panel design with simulated data. Neither have we dealt with the effect of using the fixed-effects model when a random-effects or mixed model is needed.

Our regression estimates, however, are rather seriously distorted by measurement error. It should be noted explicitly at this point that we have dealt primarily with random measurement error. The situation, of course, becomes much more serious if nonrandom error exists, as has been pointed out by Costner (1969) and Blalock (1969). Fortunately, in the case of random measurement error, we can correct our estimates by utilizing observed reliability coefficients to obtain unbiased estimators of the regression parameters.

An additional problem which we have ignored to this point is the sampling distribution of the estimates when they have been corrected for attenuation. Equation (47) for the corrected partial regression coefficient contains six separate statistics, each of which has its own sampling distribution. To date, we know of no one who has even been willing to speculate on the parameters of the ultimate sampling distribution. This, however, is a problem that must be solved before we can attach definite probability statements to our estimates.

On the whole, it appears reasonable to assume then that, with a modicum of technical competence and diligence, the sociological researcher can obtain reasonably accurate estimates of the regression parameters. Except for a few noted exceptions, sociologists seem to be blatantly unconcerned with the problems of measurement error. The most cursory review of the major journals should convince one of this fact. Yet, it is measurement error which produces the most serious distortions in our regression estimates. We can only come to the sobering conclusion, then, that many of the published results based on regression analysis in the sociological literature are possibly distortions of whatever reality may exist.

Our plea is for sociologists engaged in substantive research to confront the unreliability of their measurement instruments. It is obviously unrealistic to anticipate the construction of error-free instruments. However, we do not feel it is either unrealistic or unreasonable to expect sociologists to recognize explicitly the error existent in their instruments and to take this error into account in their analyses. At the very minimum, researchers ought to report the reliability of their measuring instruments.

## BIBLIOGRAPHY

BAKER, B. O., HARDYCK, C., AND PETRINOVICH, L.

1966  "Weak measurements vs. strong statistics: An empirical critique of S. S. Steven's proscriptions on statistics." *Educational and Psychological Measurement* 26: 291–309.

BARTLETT, M. S.

1935  "The effect of non-normality on the *t* distribution." *Proceedings of the Cambridge Philosophical Society* 31: 223–231.

1949  "Fitting a straight line when both variables are subject to error." *Biometrics* 5: 207–212.

BLALOCK, H. M., JR.

1964  *Causal Inference in Non-Experimental Research.* Chapel Hill: University of North Carolina Press.

1969  "Multiple indicators and the causal approach to measurement error." *American Journal of Sociology* 74: 264–272.

BLALOCK, H. M., JR., AND BLALOCK, A. B. (Eds.)

1968  *Methodology in Social Research.* New York: McGraw-Hill.

BLAU, P. M. AND DUNCAN, O. D.

1967  *American Occupational Structure.* New York: Wiley.

BONEAU, C. H.

1960  "The effects of violations of assumptions underlying the *t* test." *Psychological Bulletin* 57: 49–64.

BORGATTA, E. F.

1968  "My student, the purist: A lament." *Sociological Quarterly* 9: 29–34.

1970  "Reply to Jacobson: A dirty handkerchief is not what I always really wanted." *Sociological Quarterly* 11: 270–271.

BORGATTA, E. F. AND BOHRNSTEDT, G. W. (Eds.)
1969    *Sociological Methodology 1969.* San Francisco: Jossey-Bass.

BOX, G. E. P.
1953    "Non-normality and tests on variances." *Biometrika* 40: 318–335.

BOX, G. E. P. AND ANDERSEN, S. L.
1955    "Permutation theory in the derivation of robust criteria and the study of departures from assumption." *Journal of the Royal Statistical Society*, 17: 1–34.

BOX, G. E. P. AND TIAO, G. C.
1964    "A note on criterion vs. inference robustness." *Biometrika* 51: 168–173.

BOYLE, R. P.
1970    "Path analysis and ordinal data." *American Journal of Sociology* 75: 461–480.

BURKE, C. J.
1953    "Aptitude scales and statistics." *Psychological Review* 60: 73–75.

COCHRAN, W. G.
1947    "Some consequences when the assumptions for the analysis of variance are not satisfied." *Biometrics* 3: 22-38.

COHEN, J.
1968    "Multiple regression as a general data-analytic system." *Psychological Bulletin* 70: 426–443.

COSTNER, H. L.
1969    "Theory, deduction and rules of correspondence." *American Journal of Sociology* 75: 245–263.

DARLINGTON, R. B.
1968    "Multiple regression in psychological research and practice." *Psychological Bulletin* 69: 161–182.

DUNCAN, O. D.
1966    "Path analysis: Sociological examples." *American Journal of Sociology* 72: 1–16.

EISENHART, C.
1947    "The assumptions underlying the analysis of variance." *Biometrics* 3: 1–21.

ELASHOFF, R. M.
1968    "Effects of errors in statistical assumptions." Pp. 132–142 in D. L. Sills (Ed.), *International Encyclopedia of the Social Sciences* (Volume 5). New York: Macmillan and The Free Press.

GAYEN, A. K.
1949    "The distribution of 'student's' *t* in random samples of any

size drawn from non-normal universes." *Biometrika* 36: 353–369.

GODARD, R. H. AND LINDQUIST, E. F.
1940 "An empirical study of the effect of heterogeneous within-groups variance upon certain *F*-tests of significance in analysis of variance." *Psychometrika* 5: 263–274.

GOLDBERGER, A. S.
1964 *Econometric Theory*. New York: Wiley.

GORDON, R. A.
1969 "Issues in multiple regression." *American Journal of Sociology* 73: 592–616.

HEISE, D. R.
1969 "Problems in path analysis and causal inference." Pp. 38–73 in E. F. Borgatta and G. W. Bohrnstedt (Eds.), *Sociological Methodology 1969*. San Francisco: Jossey-Bass.
1970 "Causal inference from panel data." Pp. 3–27 in E. F. Borgatta and G. W. Bohrnstedt (Eds.), *Sociological Methodology: 1970*. San Francisco: Jossey-Bass.

HOTELLING, H.
1961 "The behavior of some standard statistical tests in non-standard conditions." *Fourth Berkeley Symposium on Mathematical Statistics and Probability* 1: 319–359 (1960). Berkeley and Los Angeles: University of California Press.

JACOBSON, P. E., JR.
1970 "Some comments to console Edgar F. Borgatta." *Sociological Quarterly* 11: 265–259.

JOHNSTON, J.
1963 *Econometric Methods*. New York: McGraw-Hill.

KAHNEMAN, D.
1965 "Control of spurious association and the reliability of the controlled variable." *Psychological Bulletin* 64: 326–329.

KERRICH, J. E.
1966 "Fitting the line $Y = aX$ when errors of observation are present in both variables." *The American Statistician* 20: 24.

LABOVITZ, S.
1967 "Some observations on measurement and statistics." *Social Forces* 46: 151–160.
1970 "The assignment of numbers to rank order categories." *American Sociological Review* 35: 515–524.

LORD, F. M. AND NOVICK, M. R.
1968 *Statistical Theories of Mental Test Scores*. Reading, Mass.: Addison-Wesley.

LYONS, M. AND CARTER, T. M.
1971 "Comment on Boyle's Path analysis and ordinal data." *American Journal of Sociology* 76: 1112–1132.

MALINVAUD, E.
1966 *Statistical Methods of Econometrics.* Chicago: Rand McNally.

NORTON, D. W.
1952 An Empirical Investigation of Some Effects of Non-Normality and Heterogeneity on the F-Distribution. State University of Iowa (unpublished doctoral dissertation).

SCHEFFE, H.
1959 *The Analysis of Variance.* New York: Wiley.

SENDERS, V. L.
1953 "A comment on Burke's additive scales and statistics." *Psychological Review* 60: 423–424.

SIEGEL, S.
1956 *Non-Parametric Statistics for the Behavioral Sciences.* New York: McGraw-Hill.

SIMON, H.
1957 *Models of Man.* New York: Wiley.

SNEDECOR, G. W. AND COCHRAN, W. G.
1967 *Statistical Methods.* Ames, Iowa: Iowa State University Press.

SRIVASTAVA, A. B. L.
1958 "Effects of non-normality on the power function of the *t*-test." *Biometrika* 45: 421–429.

STEVENS, S. S.
1946 "On the theory of scales of measurement." *Science* 103: 677–680.

STOUFFER, S. A.
1936 "Evaluating the effects of inadequately measured variables in partial correlation analysis." *Journal of the American Statistical Association* 31: 348–360.

SUITS, D. B.
1957 "Use of dummy variables in regression equations." *Journal of the American Statistical Association* 52: 548–551.

THEIL, H.
1957 "Specification errors and the estimation of economic relationships." *The Review of the International Statistical Institute* 25: 41–51.

WOLD, H. AND FAXER, P.
1957 "On the specification error in regression analysis." *The Annals of Mathematical Statistics* 28: 265–267.

# ❧6❧

# TECHNIQUES FOR USING ORDINAL MEASURES IN REGRESSION AND PATH ANALYSIS

*Morgan Lyons*
THE FLORIDA STATE UNIVERSITY

*I would like to thank T. Michael Carter and Warren O. Hagstrom for their helpful comments on an earlier version of this paper. Important revisions were suggested by two anonymous readers. The final content is, of course, the sole responsibility of the author.*

Since the introduction of techniques of path analysis to sociologists less than a decade ago (Blalock, 1964; Duncan, 1966), a number of important elaborations in the use of these techniques have been offered. Among them are recent statements applying the path-analysis framework to the study of item reliability (see Werts and Linn, 1970), the incorporation of techniques for estimating models containing nonrecursive or feedback properties (Duncan, Haller, and Portes, 1968; Duncan, 1970a), and the estimation of coefficients in overidentified unobservable-variable models (see Hauser and Goldberger, 1971).

Another elaboration that has proven useful for certain analysis problems is the set of techniques proposed by Boyle (1970) which allows the examination of the ordinal properties of measures within the standard regression and path analysis frameworks (see also Lyons and Carter 1971). The purpose of this chapter is to provide a detailed guide to the use of ordinal measures in regression and path analyses. Included in the discussion are comments on the translations among interval, ordinal, and nominal measures, the choice of standardized versus unstandardized coefficients, and procedures for adjusting the scale of a measure to maximize predictability (effect-proportional recalibration).

A bivariate, linear regression of some dependent variable $Y$ on some independent variable $X$ may be represented graphically as in Figure 1 where $b_{YX}$ represents the slope of the linear regression of $Y$ on $X$.

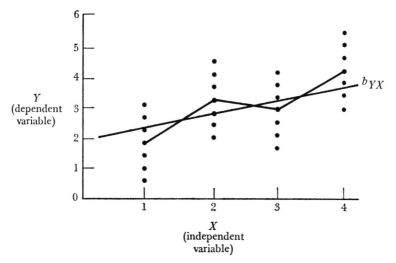

Figure 1. Graphic representation of the regression of $Y$ on $X$ ($b_{YX}$) and of the path of conditional means of $Y$ across categories of $X$.

The position of the regression line is derived to minimize the sum of squared deviations of observations about the line (the least-squares criterion), which also maximizes its fit to the weighted conditional means of $Y$ of the $X_i$ categories. Generally, the path of means will be found to deviate from linearity to some extent, and therefore, the prediction of $Y$ is not as close using a linear function as it would be if we used a nonlinear function.

Suppose, however, that we wish to attend to the linear segments connecting the means, that we disregard the linear least-squares rule applied to the full set of means. In doing so, we may gain the full predictability of $Y$ given $X$ (as described by the correlation ratio $\eta^2$ as opposed to the linear correlation $r^2$) and observe the relative contribution to $b_{yx}$ made by each interval of $X$—the slope of each regression segment connecting the conditional $Y$ means for successive categories of $X$. Through this we have obtained a detailed analysis of the effects of $X$ as an ordinal variable.

## INTERVAL, ORDINAL, AND NOMINAL CODING

Table 1 illustrates the decomposition of a continuous parent variable $V$, assumed to be measured as an interval scale, into sets of ordinal and nominal binary (or dummy) variables $V_i$. Following the required constraint for all decomposition procedures, we find, in each case, one fewer dummy variable than there are categories of the parent variable. This satisfies the restriction that there be no linear dependence among the dummy variables. (See Melichar, 1965, for a useful alternative constraint, one used in nominal dummy-variable analysis when it is called multiple-classification analysis.) One important feature of each decomposition is that each category or value of the parent variable is uniquely represented by a pattern of values among the dummy set. Thus, an individual (unit) in category 2 of the parent variable is coded ordinally as one in $V_2$ and $V_1$ and zero in all the other $V_i$; the same individual is coded nominally as one in $V_2$ only. No other category of the parent variable has the same coding in either case. As we shall see, the

Table 1

The Decomposition of $N+1$ Categories of a Parent Variable Into Sets of $N$ Ordinal and $N$ Nominal Dummy Variables

| Category of the Parent Variable[a] | Dummy Variables of an Ordinal Decomposition | | | | | Dummy Variables of a Nominal Decomposition | | | | |
|---|---|---|---|---|---|---|---|---|---|---|
| | $V_n$ | $V_{n-1}$ | $\cdots$ | $V_2$ | $V_1$ | $V_n$ | $V_{n-1}$ | $\cdots$ | $V_2$ | $V_1$ |
| $V = n$ | 1 | 1 | $\cdots$ | 1 | 1 | 1 | 0 | $\cdots$ | 0 | 0 |
| $V = n-1$ | 0 | 1 | $\cdots$ | 1 | 1 | 0 | 1 | $\cdots$ | 0 | 0 |
| $\vdots$ | | | $\vdots$ | | | | | $\vdots$ | | |
| $V = 2$ | 0 | 0 | $\cdots$ | 1 | 1 | 0 | 0 | $\cdots$ | 1 | 0 |
| $V = 1$ | 0 | 0 | $\cdots$ | 0 | 1 | 0 | 0 | $\cdots$ | 0 | 1 |
| $V = 0$ | 0 | 0 | $\cdots$ | 0 | 0 | 0 | 0 | $\cdots$ | 0 | 0 |

[a] Parent variable categories need only be exhaustive of the sample and mutually exclusive; their specific values are irrelevant to the two decompositions, although we typically decompose a variable that might have an interval scale.

particular manner in which the set of categories is represented creates the special interpretive characteristics of the ordinal-coding scheme.

A set of empirical data may be used to illustrate these applications more clearly. A recent survey of campus reactions to a student-protest strike (Lyons, 1971) provides both ordinal and interval measures. The assumed-interval measures are self-reported political position (POL), boycotting classes (BOYCOTT), and exposure to protest-relevant information (INF); the two measures used ordinally are strike participation (PT) and strike identification (ID).[1] Table 2 shows how the two

Table 2

Examples of Ordinal-Coding Decompositions for Strike Participation and Strike Identification

Strike Participation

| Categories of Strike Participation (PT) | Ordinal Decomposition | | | |
|---|---|---|---|---|
| | $PT_4$ | $PT_3$ | $PT_2$ | $PT_1$ |
| Obstruction = 5 | 1 | 1 | 1 | 1 |
| March or Picket but not Obstruction = 4 | 0 | 1 | 1 | 1 |
| Rally or Meeting only = 3 | 0 | 0 | 1 | 1 |
| No Participation = 2 | 0 | 0 | 0 | 1 |
| Antistrike Participation = 1 | 0 | 0 | 0 | 0 |

Strike Identification

| Categories of Strike Identification (ID) | Ordinal Decomposition | |
|---|---|---|
| | $ID_1$ | $ID_2$ |
| Prostrike = 2 | 1 | 1 |
| No Identification = 1 | 0 | 1 |
| Antistrike = 0 | 0 | 0 |

[1] Information was taken from a 2 per cent systematic sample of the student body ($N = 547$). The variables are defined as follows: Political position (POL)— "With respect to other students at the University of Wisconsin, my own political views are: radical left (1), left of center (2), moderate (3), right of center (4), very conservative (5)." Boycotting classes (BOYCOTT)—"Did you *deliberately* miss any classes at any time out of sympathy to the strike? yes (0), no (1)." Exposure to strike information (INF)—"How closely did you follow developments during the first week of demonstrations? up-to-the-minute (1), at least four or five times per day (2), two or three times per day (3), about once a day (4), little attention (5)." Strike participation (PT)—active in antistrike activities (1), no participation (2), only attended prostrike meetings or rallies (3), marched or picketed prostrike but did not obstruct classroom entrances (4), obstructed (5)." Strike identification (ID)— "Regardless of the extent of your active participation in the demonstrations, (a) Did you feel a general identification with the protestors? (b) with the antistrike? (a) only (2), neither (a) nor (b), or both (a) and (b) (1), (b) only (0)."

ordinal variables were coded for their ordinal decompositions. As can be seen, the ordinal decomposition forms a cumulative pattern vis-à-vis the categories of the parent variable. Thus, for example, $PT_4$ codes the distinction between obstructors and others; $PT_3$ distinguishes obstructors and marchers and picketers from others; $PT_2$ adds on persons attending rallies or meetings; and $PT_1$ distinguishes all but antistrikers from antistrikers. Note, however, that this is not a cumulation of items in the Guttman scalogram sense. What cumulates is not individual respondents' endorsements of more and more extreme participation items—here each respondent is in only one of the participation categories that have been constructed—but the inclusiveness of the aggregate of persons as we move toward more and more extreme forms of leftist participation. The behavior of this cumulative coding in a regression equation will be shown to be basic to the interpretation of ordinal coefficients.

## INDEPENDENT VARIABLES

In a regression equation a variable may become either independent (predicting) or dependent (predicted). In a recursive (one-way) path model—whose estimates are derived from a series of separate regression equations—a variable may, in addition, be both dependent on a previous predictor and a predictor itself, and as such, it may define indirect causal paths in the model. Conventionally, variables that are independent variables only are termed exogenous, while variables that are dependent on any other variable in the model are termed endogenous. Since the ordinal decomposition has special features as independent, dependent, and intervening variables, each of the uses will be treated separately.

When an ordinal decomposition is used as a set of independent variables $V_i$ predicting a dependent variable $Y$ the following equation results:

$$\hat{Y} = a + b_n(V_n) + b_{n-1}(V_{n-1}) + \cdots + b_2(V_2) + b_1(V_1) \qquad (1)$$

where each $b_i$ represents the net regression coefficient for the corresponding $V_i$. Equation (1) is identical in form to the one used for predicting $Y$ from a set of nominal dummies. Since the ordinal $V_i$ are coded differently, however, the values of the $b_i$ will be different from the nominal case. (The intercept $a$ has the same value in both cases and is the conditional mean of $Y$ for the same omitted category of $V$.)

The source of the differences in a given $b_i$ from the ordinal to the nominal case should be evident from an inspection of Table 1. Whereas a

Table 3
Predicted $Y$ Values for Persons in Each Category of the Parent Variable,
When the Ordinal and Nominal Codings from Table 1 are Used

| Observed Parent Category | Predicted $Y$ (Conditional Means) | |
|---|---|---|
| | Ordinal Coding | Nominal Coding |
| $V = n$ | $\hat{Y} = a + b_n(V_n) + b_{n-1}(V_{n-1}) + \cdots$ $+ b_2(V_2) + b_1(V_1)$ | $\hat{Y} = a + b_n(V_n)$ |
| $V = n - 1$ | $\hat{Y} = a + b_{n-1}(V_{n-1}) + \cdots + b_2(V_2) + b_1(V_1)$ | $\hat{Y} = a + b_{n-1}(V_{n-1})$ |
| $\vdots$ | $\vdots$ | $\vdots$ |
| $V = 2$ | $\hat{Y} = a + b_2(V_2) + b_1(V_1)$ | $\hat{Y} = a + b_2(V_2)$ |
| $V = 1$ | $\hat{Y} = a + b_1(V_1)$ | $\hat{Y} = a + b_1(V_1)$ |
| $V = 0$ | $\hat{Y} = a$ | $\hat{Y} = a$ |

person in a given category of the parent variable will be weighted by
only one $b_i$ in the nominal equation (all other $b_i$ will be weighted zero), in
the ordinal equation he may be coded 1 in more than one $V_i$ and thus
accumulate more than one of the $b_i$. For example, a person in category
$V = n$ from Table 1 will have the value 1 for all the $V_i$, and thus, his
predicted $Y$ will be the sum of all the $b_i$ plus the intercept $a$. This is
illustrated in Table 3, which shows the predicted $Y$ value (the conditional
mean of $Y$) for persons in each category of the parent variable $V$. Predicted $Y$ values from the nominal coding also are shown in Table 3.

Table 3 illustrates the cumulative nature of ordinal regression.
Persons in the category $V = 0$ are predicted to have the $Y$ value $a$;

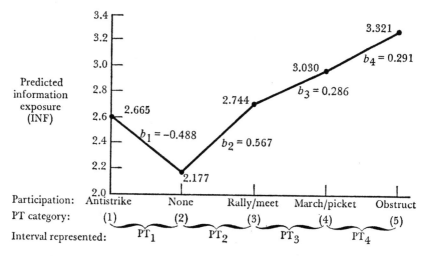

Figure 2. Predicted information exposure (INF) for each of the five categories
of strike participation. From Table 4.

Table 4

Illustration of the Cumulative Nature of Ordinal Coefficients Presented in
Table 3, Predicting Information Exposure (INF) From Strike
Participation (PT)

| Observed Participation Category | Predicted Value of Information Exposure[a] |
|---|---|
| PT = 5 | $\widehat{INF} = 2.665 - 0.488 + 0.567 + 0.286 + 0.291 = 3.321$ |
| PT = 4 | $\widehat{INF} = 2.665 - 0.488 + 0.567 + 0.286 = 3.030$ |
| PT = 3 | $\widehat{INF} = 2.665 - 0.488 + 0.567 = 2.744$ |
| PT = 2 | $\widehat{INF} = 2.665 - 0.488 = 2.177$ |
| PT = 1 | $\widehat{INF} = 2.665$ |

[a] Conditional means of INF; from unstandardized coefficients net of $ID_1$ and $ID_2$ [see equation (2), below].

persons in each successive category of $V$ have $\hat{Y}$ values equal to the previously predicted $Y$ plus an additional $b_i$ (times the value of the additional $V_i$ category, which is always one). Thus, each successive $b_i$ represents the change in predicted $Y$ from the previous category of $V$. Whereas a nominal coefficient under this constraint is interpreted as the difference (change in $\hat{Y}$) between the corresponding $V$ category and the omitted $V$ category, an ordinal coefficient is interpreted as the difference (change in $\hat{Y}$) between the given category of $V$ represented and the previous category of the parent variable $V$ with regard to some dependent variable $Y$. The predicted $Y$'s ($\hat{Y}$'s) are, again, the conditional means of $Y$ for the categories of the parent variable $V$, which allows for an easy plotting of the path of $Y$ means for the variable $V$. This has been done in Figure 2, which is taken directly from the data in Table 4; Table 4 presents an empirical example for Table 3.

Equation (1) for these data is

$$\widehat{INF} = 2.665 - 0.488PT_1 + 0.567PT_2 + 0.286PT_3 + 0.291PT_4$$
$$- 0.156ID_1 + 0.291ID_2 \quad (2)$$

with the inclusion of the ordinal $ID_i$ set making the $b_i$ weights for $PT_i$ net of $ID_1$ and $ID_2$ as well. Note that had the additional $ID_i$ set not been included in the equation, the paths described in Figure 2 would have been the unadjusted true path of INF means for each category of the predictor PT.

The well-known formula for translating unstandardized ($b_{YX}$) into standardized ($B_{YX}$) coefficients is given in equation (3)

$$B_{YX} = b_{YX} \frac{S_X}{S_Y} \quad (3)$$

where $S_X$ and $S_Y$ are the standard deviations (square roots of the variances) for variables $X$ and $Y$, respectively. The formula generalizes, with the same ratio of $S_X$ to $S_Y$, to net regression coefficients.

In standardized form equation (2) becomes

$$\widehat{INF} = -0.137PT_1 + 0.286PT_2 + 0.132PT_3$$
$$+ 0.072PT_4 - 0.062ID_1 + 0.141ID_2 \quad (4)$$

with the intercept now zero. Understandably, none of the signs of the coefficients change in the standardized form. (A positive difference does not become a negative difference, and vice versa, simply by correcting for variances.) The contrast between equations (2) and (4) does illustrate the possibility that the ranking of the magnitudes of coefficients may be different in unstandardized and standardized forms. Thus $PT_4$ goes from second largest positive $PT_i$ coefficient in the unstandardized equation to third largest in the standardized equation (though this coefficient is necessarily nonsignificant beyond 0.05 in both cases). The reason for this is that $PT_4$ has relatively low variance, since there are few obstructors, and therefore, the standardization procedure penalizes it as an independent variable. This can easily be seen from an examination of equation (3).

There is a straightforward transition from equation (1) to the full linear (assumed-interval) regression of $Y$ on $V$. In contrast to the ordinal decomposition illustrated in Figure 2, the usual assumed-interval regression fits a single regression line to the full set of weighted conditional means. Letting $b_V$ represent this single weight applied to every interval of $V$, and substituting it for each of the $b_i$ in equation (1), we obtain

$$\hat{Y} = a + b_V(V_n + V_{n-1} + \cdots + V_2 + V_1) \quad (5)$$

or

$$\hat{Y} = a + b_V \sum_{i=1}^{n} V_i \quad (6)$$

where

$$\sum_{i=1}^{n} V_i$$

is equivalent to the parent variable $V$ (as in Table 1) or $V$ plus some positive or negative constant. (This is an important qualification on this transition. Note, however, that the ordinal-coding scheme may be applied to any set of ordered categories, regardless of its original coding.)

The important distinction here is that the ordinal procedure does not force a uniform $b_V$ on each interval of $V$, as the least-squares procedure does for the full range of $V$, but instead allows a separate prediction of each interval (a separate $b_i$) and thus a maximum nonlinear prediction of $Y$ given $V$. Thus, the linear $R^2$ derived from equation (6) will be less than, or equal to, the $R^2$ from equation (1), the latter being identical to the nonlinear $\eta^2$ for predicting $Y$ from $V$. The ordinal procedure, therefore, gains both detail in the predictability of each segment of $V$ and, usually, overall predictability.[2] Note, however, that the ordinality of this regression procedure is not reflected in $\eta^2$—which is identical for both ordinal and nominal decompositions. The ordinality is found in the interpretation of the $b_i$, which goes beyond the assessment of overall ordinal association commonly applied to cross-tabular data, for example. On the other hand, we must here assume that the dependent variable is basically interval in metric, an assumption not required of standard measures of ordinal association.

The $R^2(\eta^2)$ is identical for ordinal and nominal decompositions and is the same for standardized or unstandardized forms of the equations. This means that the correlation between a set of dummy independent variables and another independent variable is also invariant under nominal versus ordinal coding. It then follows that the choice between a nominal versus an ordinal coding will not affect the values of coefficients of other variables in an equation, since the same amount of variance is controlled in either case. For example, the coefficients for $ID_1$ and $ID_2$ would not change if the $PT_i$ were nominally, and not ordinally, coded in equation (2).

The relationship between the $b_i$ in equation (1), the ordinal decomposition, and $b_V$ in equation (6), the assumed interval scale, is given in Figure 3. What is shown (in the path analysis algebra of total indirect effects given in the formula under parts (a) and (b) of Figure 3) is that, if the $b_i$ predicting $Y$ from the ordinal decomposition are weighted by the regressions of the corresponding $V_i$ on the parent variable $V$, the sum of their effects on $Y$ is exactly the zero-order linear regression of $Y$ on $V$. This is substantiated by Figure 3(c) and (d) and by a proof given in Lyons and Carter (1971).

Thus, it is possible to derive the linear effect of the parent variable through the conventional path analysis algebra of indirect effects if the

---

[2] One reader has suggested that the techniques of multiple partials (see Cowden, 1952; Hamilton, 1965) would provide a statistically cleaner interpretation of effects within the ordinal-regression framework. However, that alternative does not address itself to the ordinal interpretation of single coefficients, and as does any technique, it requires its own theoretical justification (Duncan, 1970b).

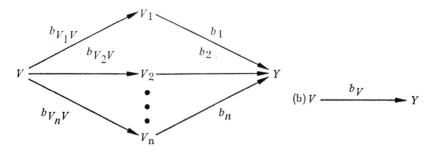

(a)  Total effect of $V$ on $Y$ through $V_i = \sum_{i=1}^{n} b_{V_i V} b_i = b_V$

(b) $V \xrightarrow{\quad b_V \quad} Y$

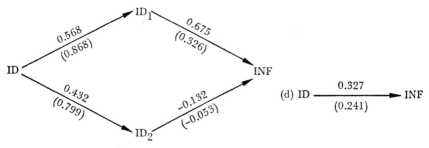

(d) $ID \xrightarrow[\quad (0.241) \quad]{\quad 0.327 \quad} INF$

(c)  Total effect (unstandardized) $= (0.568)(0.675) + (0.432)(-0.132) = 0.327$
     Total effect (standardized)    $= (0.868)(0.326) + (0.799)(-0.053) = (0.241)$

Figure 3. Reconstituting the bivariate linear effect of $V$ on $Y$ by including the parent variable $V$ in the model for its ordinal decomposition: general model and empirical example.

parent variable is included in the model as a prior predictor of its ordinal dummies. However, this procedure is complicated whenever there are extraneous variables operating. As it turns out, the net linear regression of $Y$ on $V$ can be derived through conventional path-analysis algebra only if all extraneous variables directly and causally linked to either the $V_i$ or to $Y$ are directly linked, at least for algebraic purposes, to both simultaneously—a proof found in Lyons and Carter (1971). Figure 3 also reveals the possibility for reconstituting linear standardized effects (in parentheses) using the same procedure used for unstandardized ones. It should be noted that the dummy variables in an ordinal (or nominal) decomposition are necessarily intercorrelated, and the conventions of path analysis would have this indicated by the use of curved, double-headed arrows connecting each pair of dummies in a path diagram, at least when the decomposition represents exogeneous influences. These intercorrelations are, of course, central to the derivation of any partial coefficients, including the ordinal $b_i$. The use of double-headed arrows might, therefore, be advisable, except perhaps for the additional cluttering of already complicated diagrams.

## TRANSLATING BETWEEN ORDINAL AND NOMINAL COEFFICIENTS

The translation between ordinal and nominal coefficients, when the data have been coded by either procedure has already been suggested in comments about the interpretation of the coefficients as differences between dependent variable values predicted by the different categories of the parent variable $V$. Table 5 presents a formalization of the translation procedure, and an empirical example is provided in Table 6.

Ordinal coefficients in Table 5 are represented by the $b_i$, nominal coefficients by the $b_i'$. The omitted category, $V = 0$ in this illustration,

Table 5

The Translation Between Unstandardized Ordinal and Nominal Regression Coefficients for a Given Ordering of the Parent Variable $V$
(With the Lowest-Ordered Category Omitted)

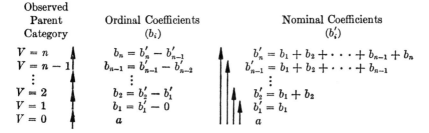

| Observed Parent Category | Ordinal Coefficients $(b_i)$ | Nominal Coefficients $(b_i')$ |
|---|---|---|
| $V = n$ | $b_n = b_n' - b_{n-1}'$ | $b_n' = b_1 + b_2 + \cdots + b_{n-1} + b_n$ |
| $V = n - 1$ | $b_{n-1} = b_{n-1}' - b_{n-2}'$ | $b_{n-1}' = b_1 + b_2 + \cdots + b_{n-1}$ |
| $\vdots$ | $\vdots$ | $\vdots$ |
| $V = 2$ | $b_2 = b_2' - b_1'$ | $b_2' = b_1 + b_2$ |
| $V = 1$ | $b_1 = b_1' - 0$ | $b_1' = b_1$ |
| $V = 0$ | $a$ | $a$ |

Table 6

Empirical Illustration of the Procedure Given in Table 5 for Translating Between Ordinal and Nominal Coefficients. Prediction of Information Exposure (INF) from Participation (PT) Categories

| Observed Participation Category | Net Unstandardized Ordinal Coefficients $(b_i)$ Predicting INF | Net Unstandardized Nominal Coefficients $(b_i')$ Predicting INF |
|---|---|---|
| PT = 5 | $0.291 = 0.656 - 0.286$ | $0.656 = -0.488 + 0.567 + 0.286 + 0.291$ |
| PT = 4 | $0.286 = 0.365 - 0.079$ | $0.365 = -0.488 + 0.567 + 0.286$ |
| PT = 3 | $0.567 = 0.079 - (-0.488)$ | $0.079 = -0.488 + 0.567$ |
| PT = 2 | $-0.488 = -0.488 - 0$ | $-0.488 = -0.488$ |
| PT = 1 | $(2.665)$ | $(2.665)$ |

is the base in both cases—the starting point for the cumulation of ordinal coefficients and the reference category for all nominal coefficients. Arrows indicate the two categories of $V$ referenced by the dummy coefficients—the coefficient is interpreted as the difference between the mean of the dependent variable predicted by the $V$ category at the base of the arrow and the mean predicted by the $V$ category at the head of the arrow.

Given the ordering of categories of the parent variable $V$, we translate nominal coefficients into ordinal coefficients by subtracting the next lowest coefficient (zero if the next lowest is the omitted category). Nominal coefficients may be created by cumulating (summing) ordinal coefficients from the omitted category (zero) up to the given category of $V$. A simple modification is required if the omitted category is not the lowest ranked one—a change of sign going from ordinal to nominal coefficients for categories ranked below the omitted one. The rescaling effected by the standardization procedure does *not* permit this translation between ordinal and nominal coefficients in standardized form.

## DEPENDENT VARIABLES

Ordinal and nominal decompositions of dependent variables do not serve as sets in the same sense as decompositions serve as independent variables. As a set of independent variables in the same regression equation, the ordinal variables receive weights net of, or controlling for, the other ordinal variables and any other variables in the equation. It is this regression-control procedure that transforms the series of cumulatively coded dichotomies of the ordinal decomposition (see Table 1) into the cumulative interpretation that is given their derived $b_i$'s. This control procedure works differently for the nominal coding, which is not constructed from an ordered series of dichotomous cutting points, thus the difference in interpreting the $b_i$ derived from the two decompositions.

Effects on separate dependent variables, dichotomous or otherwise, are estimated separately, and not as sets, in regression or path analyses. This means that if we were to omit one of the variables in a decomposition it would have no bearing on the effects estimated for some independent variable on the other members of the decomposition. Ordinal dependent variables form a set, then, only in that they have been decomposed from the same parent variable.

Thus, the interpretation of an ordinal, or nominal, dependent variable is simply the interpretation of a dichotomous dependent variable of any kind, except that each member of the decomposition represents a specific dichotomization of the same parent variable. For example, the coefficients in Figure 4(a) are interpreted as the influence of politi-

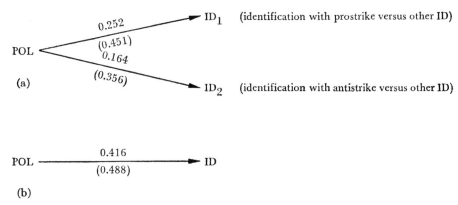

Figure 4. Illustration of the separate estimation of the effects of political position (POL) on the ordinally decomposed dichotomies for strike identification ($ID_1$ and $ID_2$) and the parent variable ID.

cal position on neutral and antistrike versus prostrike identification ($b_{ID_1 \cdot POL} = 0.252$) and antistrike versus neutral and prostrike identification ($b_{ID_2 \cdot POL} = 0.164$). Dummy-variable decompositions of ordinal dependent variables are not interpreted as the intervals between successive parent variable categories. Rather, they are representations of the parent variable dichotomized at a particular interval, the same interval represented when the ordinal dummy is used as an independent variable.

There is, however, a cleaner interpretation when the ordinally coded dependent variable happens to have been a trichotomy, such as ID. In that case, the ordinal coding still uniquely represents each parent category. One ordinal dummy represents the omitted category versus the others, and the second ordinal dummy represents the highest-ordered category versus the others, as with the strike identification variable just mentioned. As a result, one may discern from their separate estimates the relative distinctiveness of the two end categories from the middle one. For example, it may be concluded from Figure 4 that POL is more predictive of prostrike identification ($ID_1$) than antistrike identification ($ID_2$).

However, even though the effects on any single variable of an ordinal decomposition cannot be interpreted ordinally (they are not predicting to an interval of the parent variable), the effects of a given independent variable on the variables of an ordinally coded decomposition sum to a familiar and informative quantity—when, at any rate, the coefficients are in unstandardized form. As Figure 4 illustrates, the sum of a variable's unstandardized effects on a decomposed ordinal

variable is equal to the bivariate linear effect [Figure 4(b)]. That this
generalizes to unstandardized net effects (with other independent variables present) but to neither bivariate nor controlled standardized
effects is shown in the following two proofs. Fortunately, we are not
interested in the variances of decomposed variables, and so, we are
not interested in standardized coefficients.

Referring to the general models shown in Figure 5(a) and (b),

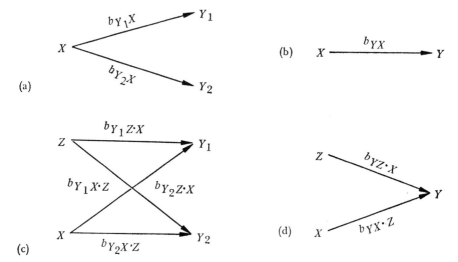

Figure 5. General models for assumed-interval and ordinally decomposed
dependent variables.

we let $Y$ be the parent dependent variable and $Y_1$ and $Y_2$ its full ordinal
decomposition. Coded as in Table 1, this means $Y = Y_1 + Y_2$. We
can also allow $Y' = Y_1 + Y_2$ where $Y' = Y + c$, $c$ being some positive
or negative constant. The unstandardized regression of $Y$, $Y_1$, and $Y_2$
on $X$ diagrammed in Figure 5 may be expressed in terms of covariances
($C_{ij}$ = covariance of variables $i$ and $j$) and variances ($V_i$ = variance
of variable $i$) as follows:

$$b_{YX} = \frac{C_{XY}}{V_X} \tag{7}$$

$$b_{Y_1X} = \frac{C_{XY_1}}{V_X} \tag{8}$$

$$b_{Y_2X} = \frac{C_{XY_2}}{V_X} \tag{9}$$

Therefore,

$$b_{Y_1X} + b_{Y_2X} = \frac{C_{XY_1}}{V_X} + \frac{C_{XY_2}}{V_X} \tag{10}$$

$$b_{Y_1X} + b_{Y_2X} = \frac{C_{XY_1} + C_{XY_2}}{V_X} \tag{11}$$

Since $Y = Y_1 + Y_2$, $C_{XY_1} + C_{XY_2} = C_{XY}$. (The covariance of the sum of two variables with a third variable is equal to the sum of their covariances with the third variable.) Therefore,

$$b_{Y_1X} + b_{Y_2X} = \frac{C_{XY}}{V_X} \tag{12}$$

or

$$b_{Y_1X} + b_{Y_2X} = b_{YX} \tag{13}$$

Thus, the sum of unstandardized effects on the ordinal decomposition of a variable must be equal to the unstandardized effect on the parent variable, at least when no other independent variables are operating simultaneously. To show that this is also true for net regression coefficients in unstandardized form [controlling, in this case, for one other independent variable $Z$, as represented in Figure 5(a) and (b)], we begin with the following formulas:

$$b_{YX \cdot Z} = \frac{V_X C_{XY} - C_{XZ} C_{ZY}}{V_X V_Z - (C_{XZ})^2} \tag{14}$$

$$b_{Y_1X \cdot Z} = \frac{V_X C_{XY_1} - C_{XZ} C_{ZY_1}}{V_X V_Z - (C_{XZ})^2} \tag{15}$$

$$b_{Y_2X \cdot Z} = \frac{C_X C_{XY_2} - C_{XZ} C_{ZY_2}}{V_X V_Z - (C_{XZ})^2} \tag{16}$$

Again relying on the fact that $Y = Y_1 + Y_2$, we can write

$$b_{Y_1X \cdot Z} + b_{Y_2X \cdot Z} = \frac{V_X C_{XY_1} + V_X C_{XY_2} - C_{XZ} C_{ZY_1} - C_{XZ} C_{ZY_2}}{V_X V_Z - (C_{XZ})^2} \tag{17}$$

$$b_{Y_1X \cdot Z} + b_{Y_2X \cdot Z} = \frac{V_X (C_{XY_1} + C_{XY_2}) - C_{XZ} (C_{ZY_1} - C_{ZY_2})}{V_X V_Z - (C_{XZ})^2} \tag{18}$$

$$b_{Y_1X \cdot Z} + b_{Y_2X \cdot Z} = \frac{V_X C_{XY} - C_{XZ} C_{ZY}}{V_X V_Z - (C_{XZ})^2} \tag{19}$$

or

$$b_{Y_1X \cdot Z} + b_{Y_2X \cdot Z} = b_{YX \cdot Z}$$

This proof generalizes to the $n$ independent variable case such that

$$b_{Y_1X \cdot Z_1 Z_2 \ldots Z_n} + b_{Y_2X \cdot Z_1 Z_2 \ldots Z_n} = b_{YX \cdot Z_1 Z_2 \ldots Z_n} \tag{20}$$

## PROOF OF THE INEQUALITY OF STANDARDIZED EFFECTS

Again referring to the models diagrammed in Figure 5, we can show that standardized coefficients for a set of ordinally coded dependent variables do not sum to the value of the coefficient predicting the parent variable as they do in the case of unstandardized coefficients.

Equation (4), which shows the translation from unstandardized to standardized coefficients, may be combined with equation (7) to show this translation in variance-covariance terms. ($B_{YX}$ is, again, the standardized form for $b_{YX}$.) Thus,

$$B_{YX} = \frac{C_{XY}}{V_X} \cdot \frac{S_X}{S_Y} \tag{21}$$

Analogous to the previous proof,

$$B_{Y_1X} + B_{Y_2X} = \frac{C_{XY_1}}{V_X} \cdot \frac{S_X}{S_{Y_1}} + \frac{C_{XY_2}}{V_X} \cdot \frac{S_X}{S_{Y_2}} \tag{22}$$

If $S_{Y_1} = S_{Y_2} = S_Y$, then the right side of equation (22) could be transformed into the right side of equation (21), which shows the equivalence of the standardized linear coefficient with the sum of the standardized coefficients predicting the decomposition. But the ratio $S_X/S_{Y_i}$ will always be larger than the ratio $S_X/S_Y$ because the standard deviation of a three-or-more category parent variable is always larger than the standard deviation of the variable dichotomized in any fashion. Therefore, the sum of the standardized effects on a set of ordinals will be greater than the linear effect of the same independent variable on the parent variable. Therefore,

$$B_{YX} < B_{Y_1X} + B_{Y_2X} \tag{23}$$

The same conclusion is reached regarding net standardized coefficients. The net regressions of $Y$, $Y_1$, and $Y_2$ on $X$, if we control for $Z$, are given by

$$B_{YX \cdot Z} = \frac{V_X C_{XY} - C_{XZ} C_{ZY}}{V_X V_Z - (C_{XZ})^2} \cdot \frac{S_X}{S_Y} \tag{24}$$

$$B_{Y_1X \cdot Z} = \frac{V_X C_{XY_1} - C_{XZ} C_{ZY_1}}{V_X V_Z - (C_{XZ})^2} \cdot \frac{S_X}{S_{Y_1}} \tag{25}$$

$$B_{Y_2X \cdot Z} = \frac{V_X C_{XY_2} - C_{XZ} C_{ZY_2}}{V_X V_Z - (C_{XZ})^2} \cdot \frac{S_X}{S_{Y_2}} \tag{26}$$

As before, the only condition under which we can factor out the ratio of variances and illustrate the equivalence of the coefficient predicting $Y$ with the sum of the coefficients predicting the ordinal $Y_i$ set is if $S_{Y_1} = S_{Y_2} = S_Y$, which, again, cannot be true. Thus,

$$B_{YX \cdot Z} < B_{Y_1 X \cdot Z} + B_{Y_2 X \cdot Z} \qquad (27)$$

All this of course makes standardized coefficients no less correct than unstandardized ones. However, it is convenient to be able to discern an overall linear effect from a simple inspection of the separate (linear) effects of an independent variable on a set of ordinal dependent variables. As has been shown, this can be done with variables in their original metric but not with the equations in standardized form (when the metrics have been variance equated) in which case, it has been argued, the coefficients are less interesting anyway.

A caution should be interjected at this point regarding the special statistical properties of dichotomous dependent variables generally. First, it is quite possible in such an equation to produce predictions of the dependent variable that fall outside its actual range, that is, greater than 1 or less than 0 for a 0, 1 coding. A number of ad hoc remedies have been suggested, including one called probit analysis, a technique for forcing low and high predicted values to approach zero and one asymptotically. Most references to these techniques are found in the econometrics literature (see, for example, Goldberger, 1964). A second problem is to make tests of statistical significance using ordinal or other dichotomous dependent variables. Specifically, there is a primary concern with the extreme violation of the homoscedasticity of error variances assumption when dichotomies are used as dependent variables.

## INTERVENING VARIABLES

The ordinal decomposition has been found to function differently as independent versus dependent variables. As an independent variable, each ordinal dummy in the set comes to represent the interval between two successive categories of the parent variable, and each corresponding regression coefficient tells us the predictibility of that interval of the parent variable. As a dependent variable, on the other hand, each ordinal dummy represents the parent variable dichotomized at a particular category, not the interval between that category and a contiguous one. Nevertheless, it was found that unstandardized predictions from a given independent variable to a set of ordinal dependent dummies sum to the prediction of the parent variable.

What happens when an ordinal set serves simultaneously as a dependent and independent variable, that is, intervenes between two other variables? Unfortunately, the indirect effect through any one member of the ordinal decomposition has no clear interpretation. The path analysis algebra of indirect effects would have us multiply the effect of an independent variable on a particular dichotomization of a parent intervening variable (the ordinal dummy as a dependent variable) times the effect of a specific interval of the same parent variable on some dependent variable. Thus, the inconsistent representation of an ordinally coded dummy as independent versus dependent variable confuses the combination of the two in an intervening variable sequence.

As it turns out, the indirect effects through an ordinal decomposition taken as a set of intervening variables may have a very clear interpretation, one very similar to the sum of effects on a set of ordinal dependent variables. This is illustrated in Figure 6, in which the total indirect effect through an ordinal set, Figure 6(a), is seen to be larger than the linear indirect effect, Figure 6(b), but exactly equal to the in-

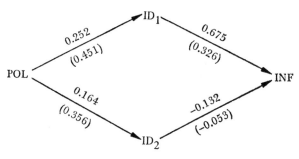

(a)          Total effect = $(0.252)(0.675) + (0.164)(-0.132) = 0.149$

$$POL \xrightarrow[\ (0.488)\ ]{\ 0.416\ } ID \xrightarrow[\ (0.241)\ ]{\ 0.327\ } INF$$

(b)          Total effect = $(0.416)(0.327) = 0.136$

$$POL \xrightarrow{\ 1.27\ } ID' \xrightarrow{\ 0.117\ } INF$$

(c)          Total effect = $(1.27)(0.117) = 0.149$

Figure 6. Indirect unstandardized effect of political position (POL) on information exposure through (a) the ordinal decomposition of strike identification (ID), (b) the parent variable ID, and (c) ID effect proportionally rescaled to its maximum effect on INF.

direct effect through the linear parent variable effect proportionally recalibrated on the dependent variable, Figure 6(c)—that is, rescaled to have its maximum effect on INF. The following section will deal with effect-proportional recalibration.

No proof is given for the findings in Figure 6, findings which have been empirically replicated using other variables, partly because they represent fairly restricted models. One might not produce the effect-recalibrated result if, for example, the models specified the existence of extraneous variables affecting INF. The conclusions are simply that an indirect effect through a single ordinal variable has no clear interpretation and that total indirect effects through an ordinal decomposition may have a straightforward interpretation only in the absence of other extraneous variables.

## EFFECT-PROPORTIONAL RECALIBRATION

As already noted, a variable's linear effect on some dependent variable can only be less than or equal to its nonlinear effect. In other terms, a straight regression line does a poor job of describing a path of means to the extent that the means do not lie in a straight line. This was illustrated earlier in Figure 1, and the argument readily generalizes to the $n$-variable case.

We may, if we wish, offer two opposing explanations for the nonlinear or curvilinear path of means in Figure 1: (1) there is a true nonlinear relationship between $Y$ and $X$ or (2) the observed nonlinearity is due to the fact that $X$ has been improperly scaled; that is, if we could stretch or contract the $X$ axis to its "true" scale, we would find the relationship linear. Of course, we might argue that *both* conditions are true to some extent, but that leaves us with the problem of how much of which.

The name given the procedure for stretching or contracting an independent variable to a linear relationship with some dependent variable is effect-proportional recalibration (see Boyle, 1970). As implied, this procedure essentially makes the width of each $X$ interval proportional to its effect on the dependent variable, as compared with other intervals of $X$. Since the procedure results in a perfect linear fit to the conditional means of $Y$, it achieves a maximum prediction of $Y$ (but not a perfect one since there will still be some scatter about these conditional means). The new linear correlation between the $Y$ and the $X$ recalibrated on it is now equal to the nonlinear correlation ratio. For this reason, effect-proportional recalibration is useful not just for discovering the true intervals of $X$—a rather mystical enterprise—but also for estimating the nonlinear effect of $X$ on $Y$.

Since effect-proportional recalibration uses the relative effects of different intervals of an independent variable, its link with ordinal regression analysis is obvious. The ordinal coefficient represents the effect of an interval; so a ratio of ordinal coefficients is a ratio of effects. Obtaining the ratio of effects from an ordinal regression analysis, these ratios can then be used to recode the parent variable effect proportionally.

Table 7 shows how an independent variable, strike identification (ID), may be recalibrated on a dependent variable, whether the respondent boycotted classes (BOYCOTT), using any number of recoding values. The regression of BOYCOTT on the ordinal set $ID_i$ is given in equation (28). The two intervals represented by $ID_1$ and $ID_2$ predict increments in BOYCOTT of 0.110 and 0.484, respectively, a ratio of 1 to 4.4. Each set of recoding values for ID in Table 7 meets the effect-proportional criterion: the ratio of 1 to 4.4—taken directly from the ordinal coefficients—the ratio of effects for the two ID intervals on BOYCOTT, is maintained by each coding. In each effect-proportional coding in Table 7, the difference between the first and second versus the second and third coded values is always 1 to 4.4. The general rule is that any linear transformation of an effect-proportional scale is an effect-proportional scale.

Standardized regression coefficients are insensitive to linear transformations of variables, such as alternative effect-proportional recalibrations, as is evident in the first column of Table 7. However, the specific effect-proportional recalibration used on a given independent variable makes a big difference in its unstandardized effect as is evident in column

Table 7
Two Models Illustrating Standardized and Unstandardized Total Effects Using Alternative Effect-Proportional Recalibrations for Strike Identification (ID).

| CALIBRATION OF ID | ID AS AN INDEPENDENT VARIABLE ID → BOYCOTT | | ID AS AN INTERVENING VARIABLE POL → ID → BOYCOTT | |
|---|---|---|---|---|
| | standardized | unstandardized | standardized | unstandardized |
| *Original Coding* | | | | |
| (a) 0, 1, 2 | 0.537 | 0.322 | 0.262 | 0.134 |
| *Effect-Proportional Coding* | | | | |
| (b) 0, 1, 5.4 | 0.574 | 0.110 | 0.273 | 0.140 |
| (c) −1, 0, 4.4 | 0.574 | 0.110 | 0.273 | 0.140 |
| (d) 0.773, 1, 2 | 0.574 | 0.482 | 0.273 | 0.140 |
| (e) −9, 1, 45 | 0.574 | 0.011 | 0.273 | 0.140 |
| (f) 2, 2.11, 2.594 | 0.574 | 1.000 | 0.273 | 0.140 |
| (g) 2, 2.34, 3.844 | 0.574 | 0.322 | 0.273 | 0.140 |

two. Thus, we are able to produce unstandardized regression coefficients for BOYCOTT on ID of from 0.011 to 1.000, all through legitimate effect-proportional rescalings. We could have achieved an effect anywhere between near zero and near infinity. The point is that unstandardized coefficients reflect the basic metric, and an effect-proportional rescaling changes the metric in an arbitrary way.

There is thus no best effect-proportional rescaling, but there is a very simple one, which has a certain intuitive appeal, that is achieved by substituting the predicted means of the dependent variable for the corresponding categories of the independent variable. This is what has been done in *row f* of Table 7 in which coding values were derived from the unstandardized prediction equation

$$\widehat{\text{BOYCOTT}} = 2.0 + 0.110\text{ID}_1 + 0.484\text{ID}_2 \tag{28}$$

Since ID was ordinally coded (see Table 2), the value of the intercept 2.0 is the predicted BOYCOTT level for ID = 0, the predicted value for ID = 1 is 2.0 + 0.110 = 2.11, and for ID = 2, 2.0 + 0.100 + 0.484 = 2.584. The unstandardized prediction from this effect-proportional ID variable is then 1.0 because a given increase in ID predicts the same increase—in fact, the same value—in BOYCOTT, an arbitrary but intuitively appealing outcome.

Another intuitively appealing solution, though one involving more effort, achieves an unstandardized effect-proportional coefficient equal to the original unstandardized coefficient. This may be done by multiplying each variable's coefficient in the ordinal equation by the reciprocal of the linear equation coefficient. For example, since $b_{\text{BOYCOTT·ID}} = 0.322$, equation (28) becomes

$$\text{BOYCOTT} = 2.0 + \left(\frac{1}{0.322}\right)(0.110)\text{ID}_1 + \left(\frac{1}{0.322}\right)(0.484)\text{ID}_2 \tag{29}$$

or,

$$\text{BOYCOTT} = 2.0 + 0.341\text{ID}_1 + 1.503\text{ID}_2 \tag{30}$$

and the new effect-proportional coding values for ID become 2.0, 2.0 + 0.341 = 2.341, and 2.341 + 1.503 = 3.844—replacing the 0, 1, 2 coding of the original ID variable. This is shown in row (g) of Table 7. (Note that these procedures may be applied to ordinal coefficients net of other independent variables as well.) The appeal of this solution is that it emphasizes the complete irrelevance of the effect-proportional recoding procedures for the unstandardized metric.

There is at least one other interesting finding from Table 7 which is that both unstandardized and standardized indirect effects remain constant across any legitimate effect-proportional recalibration of an intervening variable. And, as was found in Figure 6, in the simple case where there are no other independent variables, these effects are equivalent to the total indirect effect through the decomposed intervening variable. The interesting finding implicit in the last column of Table 7 is that the fluctuations in unstandardized effect-proportional coefficients in the ID → BOYCOTT segment are compensated for by the POL → ID segment by which the former coefficient is multiplied to arrive at the total indirect effect. Thus, whereas each segment represents a different coefficient for each different effect-proportional recoding, the product of the two segments is identical for all effect-proportional recodings.

A final point should be made regarding the technique of effect-proportional rescaling. A variable whose ordinal decomposition reveals a nonmonotonic curvilinear relationship with another variable (a change in sign across ordinal coefficients) cannot be effect-proportionally recalibrated without rearranging the categories of the parent variable. Graphically, there is no way to straighten a deflected path of means through stretching or contracting the metric of the independent variable. More intuitively, a basically ordinal variable whose segments do not consistently predict increments (or decrements) in a dependent variable on which it is defined as ordered is either a nonmonotonic predictor or is improperly ordered. Note, however, that there is nothing in the recalibrating technique presented above—going from ordinal coefficients to recalibrated category values—that requires monotonicity of effect. The order (magnitude and sign) of the predicted dependent variable means simply becomes the (perhaps new) order of the rescaled independent variable. If nonmonotonicity exists, the rescaling also implicitly becomes a reordering. This in no way vitiates the technique for deriving non-linear effects. It does point out that using effect-proportional rescaling for finding a true scale for a variable may require some radical alterations of the variable.

## ADVANTAGES AND DISADVANTAGES

The single justification of any scientific methodology is its pragmatic utility. Techniques of ordinal regression and path analysis, being quite new, have not had the benefit of much practical application, but still we may profit from an attempt to assess their potential for social research.

The possibility of incorporating assumed-ordinal variables into the regression analysis framework while retaining ordinality of the variables should be attractive to many sociologists. Even more useful is the facility with which this procedure allows us to analyze the ordinality of such variables—to discover which intervals, if any, are making greater or lesser contributions than others. Beyond this useful information about the behavior of various steps of a variable, these techniques leave the researcher with basic data for performing effect-proportional rescalings, for deriving through simple transformations nominal coefficients for the categories, or for making an empirically based decision to accept the more parsimonious linear assumption about the original parent variable. If we wish to employ an ordinal decomposition, perhaps together with other variables, in a standard recursive path analysis, technically an interrelated set of regression analyses, we have seen that there are certain useful interpretations of total effects for such an ordinal set, particularly as a set of dependent variables.

However, as with most data-analysis techniques, these advantages of ordinal regression may in some cases be offset by concomitant disadvantages. Without entering into the controversy over the desirability of standardized versus unstandardized regression (or path) coefficients, we have seen that by far the most easily interpreted ordinal coefficients are unstandardized ones. This is not really to be taken as a disadvantage, however, since generally we would be ordinally decomposing only a variable for which we were interested in the original metric. That is, we use the ordinal analysis to discover the effect of, or on, a unit change from one category of a variable to another, not the role of a change in one standard deviation unit.

A more troublesome property of ordinal techniques is the added complexity of an ordinal as opposed to an interval path analysis. Considerably more coefficients are produced in an ordinal decomposition—though no more than in the conventional nominal (dummy) variable analysis, including multiple classification analysis. In a path diagram, this may mean a tremendous clutter of numbers and arrows, which defeats the purpose of the diagram as a visual model. This suggests the advisability of presenting a table of path coefficients for analyses incorporating ordinal estimates, perhaps together with a carefully designed diagram. This gain in detail of information thus brings with it a certain loss in parsimony, though an ordinal path analysis is still far more condensed than a corresponding cross-tabular presentation, which may contain little more useful information.

Another disadvantage lies in the failure of certain arrangements of ordinal decompositions in independent and intervening variable positions to produce simple interpretations of effects. A more serious disadvantage of ordinal regression techniques is, unfortunately, not just a matter of inconvenience. This is the problem of inaccuracy of estimates for ordinal parameters, a consequence of the fractionation that occurs when a multi-category variable is decomposed into separate component variables. This instability has two sources, one in sampling fluctuations and the other in the extent to which the parent variable is unreliable. The standard error of a parent variable will be smaller than the standard error of any of its decomposed ordinal coefficients, which are always partial regression coefficients, net of the other ordinal variables in the set. A parent variable, being a linear composite of its component ordinal segments, is necessarily more reliable than any one of these segments.

The caveat should be clear. Regression and path analyses, as other techniques, are fairly demanding of both the adequacy of sampling and the quality of variables. It must be emphasized that the ability to incorporate assumed-ordinal variables into these powerful techniques in no way opens up possibilities for poorly constructed or inadequately applied measures. Nor does ordinal regression supplant techniques *theoretically* more suited to particular measures and problems. Used with discretion, however, ordinal techniques may prove useful additions to the array of analytic procedures now available to the social scientist.

## REFERENCES

BLALOCK, H. M., JR.
1964 *Causal Inferences in Nonexperimental Research*. Chapel Hill: University of North Carolina Press.

BOYLE, R. P.
1970 "Path analysis and ordinal data." *American Journal of Sociology* 75: 461–480.

COWDEN, D. J.
1952 "The multiple-partial correlation coefficient." *Journal of the American Statistical Association* 47: 442–456.

DUNCAN, O. D.
1966 "Path analysis: sociological examples." *Americal Journal of Sociology* 72: 3–16.
1970a "Duncan's corrections of published text of 'peer influences on aspirations: a reinterpretation.'" *American Journal of Sociology* 75: 1042–1046.
1970b "Partials, partitions, and paths." Pp. 38–47 in E. F. Borgatta and G. W. Bohrnstedt (Eds.), *Sociological Methodology 1970*. San Francisco: Jossey-Bass.

DUNCAN, O. D., HALLER, A. O., AND PORTES, A.
1968 "Peer influences on aspirations: a reinterpretation." *American Journal of Sociology* 74: 119–137.

GOLDBERGER, A. S.
  1964   *Econometric Theory.* New York: Wiley.
HAMILTON, C. H.
  1965   "County net migration rates." *Rural Sociology* 30: 13–17.
HAUSER, R. M. AND GOLDBERGER, A. S.
  1971   "Treatment of unobservable variables in path analysis."
         Chapter 4 in this volume.
LYONS, M.
  1971   "Campus Reactions to Student Protest." University of
         Wisconsin (unpublished doctoral dissertation).
LYONS, M. AND CARTER, T.
  1971   "Further comments on Boyle's 'Path analysis and ordinal
         data.' " *American Journal of Sociology* 76: 1112–1132.
MELICHAR, E.
  1965   "Least-squares analysis of economic survey data." *Proceedings of the Business and Economic Statistics Section,
         American Statistical Association, 1965* pp. 1–13.
WERTS, C. E. AND LINN, R. L.
  1970   "Cautions in applying various procedures for determining
         the reliability and validity of multiple-item scales." *American Sociological Review* 35: 757–759.

# PART THREE

# PATH AND PROCESS
# MODELS

# 7

# FORMAL THEORY

## Kenneth C. Land

COLUMBIA UNIVERSITY AND RUSSELL SAGE FOUNDATION

*This paper was presented to a symposium on "Methodology in Sociology" jointly sponsored by the Methodology Section of the American Sociological Association and Loyola University, Chicago, Illinois, June 10 and 11, 1970. Otis Dudley Duncan, Robert McGinnis, and Paul F. Lazarsfeld and the editors of this volume made valuable comments on earlier drafts of the paper.*

The topic of this chapter is so broad that I should like to specify, at the outset, the problems I shall consider under this title. My primary goal here is to explicate the role of formal sociological theory as it impinges on the scientific sociological enterprise as a whole. Although sociologists have utilized numbers and statistics in the description and measurement of relations among social phenomena at least since the time of Adolphe Quetelet (1796–1874), concerted efforts to formalize sociological theories in general and to develop mathematically formulated sociological theories in particular have gotten seriously underway only in the past two decades. In the process of developing principles of formalizing, and criteria for evaluating, sociological theories, a number of new terms, such as structural equations, generating processes, identification of structural equations, and so on, have entered the lexicon of professional sociological jargon. Moreover, the precise interrelationships of such paraphernalia to the broader goals of the empirical investigation of social phenomena have often been less than clear.

Therefore, I shall attempt in this essay to explicate as clearly as possible the interplay of the processes of theoretical specification, model solution, reduced-form and structural parameter estimation, and model testing or evaluation with the traditional processes of theorizing and data collection. Hopefully, this demonstration will convince the non-methodologist of the benefits to be gained by the application of the relatively complicated procedures of which the profession has recently become aware. On the other hand, methodologists will be, in general, at least implicitly aware of the ideas I shall present. However, my presentation of the material may provide a useful organization even for the specialist. Indeed, the only claim to originality I can make for this essay lies precisely in its organization; for, the general topic and approach taken here have been developed and used in several scientific disciplines over the past two or three centuries.

After delineating a scheme for the place of formal theory in the process of scientific explanation, I shall discuss several examples which illustrate the general principles. Moreover, in order to illustrate the generality of the scheme, I shall briefly consider an example from physics as well as sociology. Finally, on the basis of the general principles of the use of formal theory to be presented and the illustrative examples to be reviewed, I shall consider some constraints which are imposed on model building in sociology. The constraints on model construction arise from several sources and will be of considerable importance for some time in sociology.

## INTERPLAY OF THEORETICAL SPECIFICATION, MODEL SOLUTION, PARAMETER ESTIMATION, AND MODEL APPRAISAL IN MATHEMATICAL SOCIOLOGY

### Theoretical Specification

The philosophy of science, like sociology, is an ongoing and active intellectual enterprise. As such, one could hardly expect to find complete consensus among philosophers of science on the methodology of scientific explanation. Furthermore, since the present essay is concerned with problems of sociology, the discussion cannot become lost in the debates of philosophers of science. Rather, I shall choose to follow the arguments of an essay which has had considerable influence on the development of the philosophy of science since its publication in 1948— Carl Hempel and Paul Oppenheim's "The Logic of Explanation" (1953). According to Hempel and Oppenheim, *a scientific explanation* of an empirical phenomenon consists of two major constituent parts, the explanandum and the explanans (1953, p. 321). That is, the explanandum consists of a set of sentences describing the phenomenon to be explained while the explanans consists of the set of sentences constructed to account for the phenomenon. Moreover, the explanans contains two subsets of sentences, those sentences that state specific antecedent conditions, denoted by $C_1$, $C_2$, . . . , $C_k$, and those sentences that represent laws or general statements about behavior, denoted by $L_1$, $L_2$, . . . , $L_r$. Finally, Hempel and Oppenheim propose that a scientific explanation must satisfy four necessary conditions of logical and empirical adequacy in order to be judged sound (1953, pp. 321–322): (1) The explanandum must follow as a logical consequence of the information contained in the explanans. (2) The explanans must contain at least one general law, and all of the laws contained in the explanans must actually be required for the derivation of the explanandum. (3) The explanans must have empirical import; that is, the content of the explanans must be capable, at least in principle, of confirmation by test or observation. (4) The sentences in the explanans must be highly confirmed by all evidence at the time in question.

In brief, Hempel and Oppenheim's description of scientific explanation is summarized in Figure 1 (1953, p. 322).

Two essential components of Hempel and Oppenheim's views on the logic of scientific explanation are that an explanation is unacceptable if it does not allow predictions and that there is a structural equality or symmetry of scientific explanation and scientific prediction (Hempel and Oppenheim, 1953, pp. 322–323):

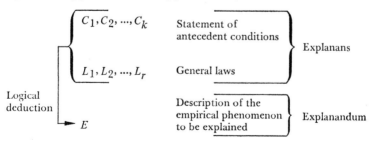

Figure 1. From Hempel and Oppenheim (1953).

Let us note here that the same formal analysis including the four necessary conditions, applies to scientific prediction as well as to explanation. The difference between the two is of a pragmatic character. If $E$ is given, i.e. if we know that the phenomenon described by $E$ has occurred, and a suitable set of statements $C_1, C_2, \ldots, C_k, L_1, L_2, \ldots, L_r$ is provided afterwards, we speak of an explanation of the phenomenon in question. If the latter statements are given and $E$ is derived prior to the occurrence of the phenomenon it describes, we speak of a prediction. It may be said, therefore, that an explanation is not fully adequate unless its explanans, if taken account of in time, could have served as a basis for predicting the phenomenon under consideration.

Thus, according to Hempel and Oppenheim, explanation and prediction are formally equivalent because they rest on the same information, that is, the relevant generalizations or covering laws and the statements of initial conditions. This position has been criticized in recent years (see, for example, Kaplan, 1964; Rescher, 1966; Sheffler, 1960) as methodologists and philosophers of science have sought to emphasize distinctions between explanation and prediction. The most fundamental difference, according to Kaplan (1964, p. 350), derives from the basis of the claims:

The most basic difference between explanation and prediction, however, is with respect to the grounds they each offer for their claims. An explanation rests on a nomological or theoretical generalization, or on an intelligible pattern, but a prediction need not have such a basis. I am not speaking of guesses, even of those that rest on knowledge of which the guesser is unaware. A prediction, as distinct from a guess, is reasoned—a basis is put forward, some premise from which what is predicted is being inferred. The point is that the basis may be a merely empirical generalization. We can give a reason for making some specific prediction rather than another, but we may be able to give no reason other than past successes for expecting the prediction to come true. Analyses of voting behavior, for example, may have identified certain counties or states as barometers of the political weather, thereby allowing the computer to make early predictions; but making predictions from them is very different from having an explanation of the vote.

In order to avoid such methodological controversies in the present chapter, I shall generally distinguish theoretical predictions from nontheoretical predictions. A major goal of the paper is to show how mathematical models facilitate theoretical explanation in the social sciences. In such a context it is natural to equate theoretical explanations with theoretical predictions and to use the terms interchangeably.

The Hempel-Oppenheim formulation of the logic of explanation has also been critized as being an excessively rigid, formal, and incomplete conception of scientific explanation (see, for example, Hanson, 1958, Chapter 4; Kuhn, 1962, Chapter 2; and Nagel, 1961, Chapter 4, for alternative views on the nature of scientific theories and scientific explanation). Indeed, in his more recent writings, Hempel (1965) himself seems to have modified his views on these topics. Although it is impossible to discuss these various critiques here, suffice it to say that they do not generally imply that the strategy suggested by the Hempel-Oppenheim conception is inappropriate for scientific research. In particular, the Hempel-Oppenheim emphasis on the statement of covering laws and conditions of observation is especially useful for illuminating certain properties and functions of mathematical models in empirical science.

Up to this point the discussion has been quite informal. However, I will argue in this essay that the mathematical model is an even more crucial aspect of theory building and research methodology in sociology than in physical science. The basic argument to be developed is that sociologists typically are not able to perform controlled experiments—a type of physical model which can easily be given a mathematical description—to collect data from which to estimate parameters and test theories. Consequently, any meaningful test of sociological theory must take into account the various conditions under which observations are made. Furthermore, the mathematical model is particularly capable of performing this function. That is, if a mathematical model can be shown to have the properties discussed below, then we can perform certain logical operations (mathematical transformations) on the model with the assurance that the results have a high correspondence to the results we would observe from the corresponding physical manipulation of the objects of the theory. For example, one can study the relationship of certain variables of the theory while controlling for others. Although this is a typical feature of empirical sociological analysis, it is often executed without any explicit theoretical rationale (compare, Gordon, 1968). The contribution of the mathematical model lies in its capacity theoretically to inform empirical research procedures. Therefore, it will be worthwhile to explore the relationship of model to theory and data in more detail by introducing some formal definitions and subjecting them to logical analysis. We begin with theory, the conceptual source of any scientific explanation.

The general problem to which the remainder of this section of the chapter is addressed is illustrated in Figure 2. To begin, I assume that we

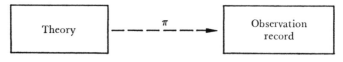

Figure 2.

are confronted with a theory which purports to account for the behavior of a class of empirical events. I also assume that this class of events is represented by a sample of empirical observations. Beginning with the theory is more a matter of convenience than of necessity. Of course, one could also begin with a set of observations for which one desired to construct a theoretical explanation. However, since I am here concerned primarily with the process of scientific explanation, I will assume that we begin with the theoretical side of the matter, and later in the discussion, I will return to the interplay of theorizing and empirical observation.

Put simply, the basic issue in scientific explanation is the relationship of the theory to the observations of the empirical events, expressed in Figure 2 as a dashed arrow, labeled $\pi$, from the theory to the observation record. Essentially, we would like to have assurances that there exists some degree of correspondence between the assertions of the theory and the structure of relationships among the observations. We want to be confident that such a correspondence exists in order that the theory can serve as a representation of the empirical relationships. In brief, we desire to be able to assert that $\pi$ in Figure 2 is, in some sense, a mapping of the elements of the theory onto the elements of the observation record in such a way that the former can serve as a representation of the latter. However, in order to give a precise meaning to these rather loosely stated desiderata, we shall have to examine these objects and their interrelationships in considerably more detail. Let us begin with an examination of the components of a theory and of an observation record.

*A scientific theory* is a set of concepts and propositions asserting relationships among the concepts. The basic building blocks of a theory are its concepts, that is, the ideas or notions with which it is concerned. Detailed discussions of the various forms of conceptualization in scientific theories are available elsewhere in the sociological literature (see, for example, Zetterberg, 1965, Chapter 3; Stinchcombe, 1968, Chapter 2; and Blalock, 1969, Chapter 7), and I shall not attempt to enter into those arguments here. For the purposes of the present essay, it suffices to assert that the concepts of a theory can be useful in a scientific explanation only if they are defined so as to have some measurable real-world counterpart. That is, there must be some specifiable event in the real world which corresponds to the theoretical concept, or the concept must be causally linked to other concepts which are measurable (see, for example, Costner, 1969).

The other basic subset of the elements of a theory consists of propositions which assert relationships among the concepts of the theory. For present purposes, it suffices to require that such propositions be of the "if . . . then" logical form, which asserts that a change (or some function thereof) in one concept is associated in some regular and specifiable way with a change (or some function thereof) in another concept. Furthermore, it is convenient for purposes of formalization to label some, or all, of the theoretical propositions as axioms. Blalock's criterion (1969, p. 18) for selecting axioms is that they be propositions involving concepts that are taken to be directly linked causally. Finally, in order that the axioms form a theory relating to the entire set of concepts, it suffices to require that each axiom contain at least one concept which also appears in at least one other axiom in the theory. Otherwise, the theory will have no logical connectiveness, and it will break into discrete subsets of propositions.

A distinguishing characteristic of a theory is that it cannot explain specific empirical events without prior transformation. That is, theoretical propositions are general statements about causal relationships among the concepts of the theory. However, specific empirical events occur, and are observed, under varying conditions (compare, Hempel and Oppenheim, 1953; this statement holds whether the events are produced experimentally in the laboratory or nonexperimentally in natural environments), and these conditions must be taken into account before the theory can be utilized deductively to explain a given empirical observation of a phenomenon. Therefore, the set of elements we call the observation record must contain, or be capable of producing, measurements of the parameters under which the observations were made in addition to measurements of the events corresponding to the concepts of the theory. Furthermore, with regard to the quality of the observations, I shall make the epistemological assumption that the measurements do not consist primarily of measurement error. More specifically, we must stipulate that the observations have error components which are negligible or estimable. Finally, in order to relate the observations of events and the conditions or parameters of observation, I shall make the ontological assumption that some unknown, but presumably knowable, structure of relationships among the parameters and the variables that produced the observed events exists in the real world.

These specifications regarding the attributes of a scientific theory and an observation record can be summarized in the following two definitions.

DEFINITION 1: The statement that a set, denoted in this paper by $A$, is a theory means that $A$ consists of the following two subsets of elements: (1) concepts defined so as to have some measurable real-world counterpart and (2) propositions which assert relationships among the concepts of the theory. The concepts and propositions together contain an implicit explanation of the behavior of a given class of empirical phenomena.

DEFINITION 2: The statement that a set, denoted in this paper by $E$, is an observation record means that $E$ consists of two subsets of measurements describing (1) the empirical events corresponding to the concepts of set $A$ and (2) the conditions under which the events are observed. With regard to the observations, we assume that the measurements do not consist primarily of measurement error. Furthermore, we make the ontological assumption that some structure exists in the real world that produced the observed events.

Given the measurements of the concepts and observation conditions from the observation record and the general propositions of a theory, the goal is the logical deduction of the measurements describing the events of interest. The question now is: How does one traverse the gap between general theory on the one hand and description of specific observations of empirical events on the other? The answer is given in three related but distinct steps. The first step is the specification of the theory. Put simply, *theoretical specification* is the expression of a theory in mathematical form. In actual practice, this process is often arduous and, for some theories, intractable. If successful, however, it provides us with a third set which we shall call a mathematical model.

If the specification of a scientific theory results in a mathematical model of the theory, then there must exist some correspondence between the elements of the theory and the elements of the model. First of all, to each concept of the theory there must correspond either a variable or a parameter in the mathematical model. *Variables and parameters* are quantities which can assume a specified range of numerical values. Since we have specified above that the concepts of a scientific theory must have a real-world counterpart and we now impose the constraint that to each concept in the theory there corresponds a variable or a parameter in a mathematical model of the theory, it follows that one can tell by means of observations which value the variable or parameter has in a particular empirical occurrence (Stinchcombe, 1968, pp. 29–30, makes this attribute a condition in his definition of a variable).

In terms of their nexus in mathematical models, both the variables and the parameters can assume a specified range of values. Thus, the variables and parameters of a mathematical model can be distinguished only by the further specification that the magnitudes of the parameters can be fixed and manipulated by the model builder whereas the magnitudes of the variables are solved for within the model as functions of the parameters (compare, Brems, 1968, p. 3). For this reason the parameters are termed *free parameters* when used in the construction and investigation of a mathematical model. Furthermore, although one can observe the values of both the parameters and the variables in a particular empirical application, it is the fact that the values of the variables can be solved for within the model when the parameters are measured which provides a check on the empirical validity of the model as will be shown below.

A second correspondence which must be established between elements of the theory and elements of the model pertains to the relation of propositions of the theory to equations of the model. In general, to each axiom of the theory there must correspond an equation of the model involving the variables and parameters of the model. Mathematically, the equations of the model are constrained by the requirements that they be both functionally independent and consistent. That is, although the equations can involve each of the variables and parameters, they must be consistent in the sense that they do not place contradictory requirements on the relations of the variables and parameters. Also, the equations must be independent in the sense that it is impossible to write one of the equations as a mathematical function of the others. A necessary, but not sufficient, condition that the model meet these requirements of consistency and independence is that the number of equations in the model be equal to the number of variables as defined above. If there is a larger number of equations in the model, then it is mathematically impossible for the equations to be both independent and consistent. On the other hand, if the number of equations is smaller than the number of variables in the model, then the system of equations will be underdetermined, and it will be impossible to solve it. A final requirement on the model, corresponding to the constraint on the axioms of the theory, is that each one of the equations must include at least one variable which also appears in at least one other equation which is part of the model.

Corresponding to the implicit explanation of a class of empirical events which a theory possesses, a mathematical model or representation of a theory is capable of producing a general description of the class of events. That is, because the free parameters of a mathematical model can assume a specified range of values (in general, an infinite number of unique values), it follows that, when the model is solved for the variables as a function of the parameters, the variables will also assume a range of numerical values (also an infinite number, in general). Thus, the explanations provided by a mathematical model are of a very general nature and are not capable, without further knowledge, of producing descriptions of specific empirical occurrences.

It should be emphasized at this point that I have assumed throughout this section that the goal of our analysis is the theoretical explanation of a given set of empirical observations. Moreover, by a theoretical explanation, I mean the derivation of a description of the observations from a set of theoretical laws defining the causal relations between variables and parameters. Thus, I have assumed that we are dealing with what have come to be known in the social-science literature as structural (or causal) models (see, in particular, Simon, 1957, Chapters 1, 2, 3, for a discussion of structural models). The essential identifying characteristic of a structural model is that it attempts to define a set of equations which corresponds to actual causal relations in the real world. Each equation in a structural model represents a causal mechanism which is assumed to relate the parameters and variables of the equation.

The *degenerate structural model* consists of one equation relating one variable to one or more parameters. This is the structural representation which underlies the typical scientific laboratory experiment. However, sociological theories are generally concerned with processes which occur in natural social settings and which are observed in ongoing social systems. Given such a goal of explanation, it follows that sociological models will generally involve more than one variable, and hence, they will consist of more than one equation. Therefore, structural models in sociology should be viewed as a generalization of the classical experiment. Moreover, even though this is a fairly straightforward and innocent form of generalization, it will be shown below that it introduces some rather extensive complications of the inferential process. Before proceeding to this analysis, however, I should like to summarize the comments of the past several paragraphs in the following definition.

DEFINITION 3: The statement that a set, denoted in this paper by $B$, is a *mathematical model* of a theory means that $B$ consists of the following two subsets: (1) variables and free parameters representing the concepts of the theory and (2) equations which relate the variables and parameters and represent the logical structure of the theoretical propositions. Together, these subsets yield a general description of the behavior of the class of events corresponding to the variables of the model.

Thus, the mathematical model is an expression of the theory in a form that permits an analysis of its logical implications. Moreover, model building is concerned almost solely with this process of specification of theoretical relationships. Therefore, the terms model building and theorizing are not necessarily identical and, in general, should not be used interchangeably.[1] For example, Durkheim's treatise on the division of labor (1933) is a theory, not a model. On the other hand, Coleman's analysis of change and response uncertainty (1964b) can be both; however, when portrayed as a model, it is ready to give quantitative descriptions of empirical events if its free parameters are given specific values. Coleman's general behavioral propositions cannot yield that kind of information. Finally, it should be noted that much can often be learned about a theory at this stage of the theoretical explanation of empirical phenomena. For example, Bartholomew's (1967) presentation of some stochastic models for social processes is an excellent illustration of the kinds of knowledge which can be produced by model building. Essentially, he analyzes the mathematical implications of various structural assumptions about social processes (stratification, mobility, diffusion of information) in a stochastic-process framework. Furthermore, many of the results derived by Bartholomew are not at all obvious from verbal theoretical discussions of the social phenomena. In brief, the logical analyses made possible by a mathematical model of a theory may reveal unforeseen implications if the logical structure of the theory is sufficiently nontrivial. Moreover, the model may point to logical contradictions or to the necessity of additional assumptions not obvious from an examination of the verbally stated propositions of the theory.

This general discussion of the process of theoretical specification could be enlightened at this point by the introduction of a specific example. Therefore, I shall consider a formalization of a part of Durkheim's treatise on the division of labor from the present author's experience (Land, 1970). This specific model is certainly no more virtuous than many other representations in the literature. However, it does serve to illustrate the general rules which have been stated above. Furthermore, several other examples of model construction will be discussed

---

[1] It should be noted that there is apparently no consensus on this point in the sociological literature. For example, both Stinchcombe (1968) and Blalock (1969) have recently written books concerned with the problem of theoretical explanation in sociology. Stinchcombe's title is *Constructing Social Theories* while Blalock's is *Theory Construction*. From the similarity of the titles, one would expect that the books treat similar material. However, there is very little overlap between the coverage of the two volumes. Stinchcombe deals primarily with problems of concept formation and the establishment of propositions, which I would term theorizing. Blalock, on the other hand, deals with the techniques of moving from verbal to mathematical representations of sociological theories, which I would call theoretical specification or model building. Clearly, we need both more adequate theorizing and better model construction in sociology.

in detail in the next section of the paper, and the present example can be compared with them.

An expository analysis (Land, 1970) of Durkheim's theory of the causes of the division of labor (1933, Book II) revealed that the theory could be restated in terms of three concepts (dynamic or moral density, competition, and the division of labor) and three propositions relating these concepts as follows: (1) The level of dynamic density of a society refers to the number of interacts of the members of the society per unit of time where an interact is a specific action-reaction sequence between two individuals. The variable corresponding to this concept will be designated by $D(t)$. (2) The level of competition in a society refers to the level of scarcity of sustenance goods among the members. The corresponding variable will be denoted by $C(t)$ below. (3) The level of the division of labor in a society is the degree of differences among members of the society with regard to their sustenance activities. The division of labor variable will be denoted by $L(t)$. (4) The level of dynamic density in a society will tend to increase if its existing level is lower than that appropriate to the level of the division of labor. That is, if there is an increase in the level of the division of labor and the level of dynamic density is no longer in equilibrium with the level of the division of labor, then there will be a subsequent increase in the level of dynamic density which will tend to move it back towards equilibrium with the new level of the division of labor. The postulated relationship will be assumed to require time for its adjustment. (5) The level of competition in a society depends upon, and increases with, the level of dynamic density in the society. I will also postulate that the level of competition adjusts itself almost simultaneously to the level of dynamic density in the society. (6) The level of the division of labor in a society will increase if its existing level is lower than that appropriate to the level of competition in the society. Furthermore, I will postulate that the adjustment of the division of labor to the level of competition in a society requires time to be effected.

Now these three restated propositions from Durkheim's theory are formulated in such a manner as to yield rather easily to the following three equations (where $dx/dt$ represents the derivative of $x$ with respect to time) and the corresponding constraints:

$$\frac{dD(t)}{dt} = f[D(t), L(t)] \tag{1}$$

$$C(t) = g[D(t)] \tag{2}$$

$$\frac{dL(t)}{dt} = h[C(t), L(t)] \tag{3}$$

where we impose the following constraints on the functions $f$, $g$, and $h$:

$$\frac{\partial f}{\partial L} > 0 \tag{4}$$

$$\frac{\partial f}{\partial D} < 0 \tag{5}$$

$$\frac{dC}{dD} = \frac{dg}{dD} > 0 \tag{6}$$

$$\frac{\partial h}{\partial C} > 0 \tag{7}$$

$$\frac{\partial h}{\partial L} < 0 \tag{8}$$

In words, equation (1) states that the time rate of change in dynamic density is a function of the existing level of dynamic density and the level of the division of labor, whereas the constraints (4) and (5) restrict the form of $f$ such that it increases with an increase in $L$ and decreases with an increase in $D$. A similar interpretation holds for equation (3) and the constraints (7) and (8). On the other hand, equation (2), an algebraic rather than a differential equation, corresponds to the assumption that the adjustment of the level of competition to the level of density is instantaneous relative to the other two relations. Therefore, its only constraint requires that the function $g$ be such that an increase in $D$ induces an increase in $C$.

This example will be returned to in the analysis to be pursued below. At this point, it suffices to note that it illustrates the general principles involved in the process of theoretical specification as outlined above. First, corresponding to each concept of the theory, there is a variable in the mathematical model. Second, corresponding to each proposition asserting a direct causal link between the concepts, there exists a structural equation in the model. Finally, although the restatement of Durkheim's theory does not specify precise forms for the equations of the model, at least we were able to derive certain qualitative constraints which explicit forms of the functions must satisfy. (Durkheim's original verbal essay is even less specific. This example illustrates the fact that the mathematical modeler must often make verbal restatements of existing theories before he can proceed to construct a model).

The Durkheim example illustrates another theme which will be reiterated below. That is, even though there is a variable in the model corresponding to each of the concepts of the theory, the functions $f$, $g$, and $h$ will contain various mathematical coefficients. These will be termed the structural parameters, and the point is that the verbal theory does not have a corresponding component. Thus, there is not a complete structural equality between the theory and the model, and this seems to be the case for most theories and models in the current social science literature. In general, the model will contain elements not found in the verbal theory.

In concluding this discussion of the process of theoretical specification, I should note that the Durkheim example provides an illustration of the differences in the explanations given by general verbal theories and mathematical models in social science. First of all, the verbal propositions given above, if highly confirmed by empirical investigations, provide an implicit theoretical description or explanation of the class of phenomena referred to by the concepts. The explanation is implicit because the propositions must be operated on logically before any deductions can be inferred. Furthermore, as Hempel and Oppenheim (1948) have emphasized, some account must be taken of the conditions of observation. On the other hand, if the functions of the mathematical model are given a specific form, then the model provides a general theoretical description of the class of empirical events referred to by the variables. The explanation is general because, even though the mathematical equations provide a logical calculus from which deductions follow, it is still true that the coefficients of the functions are free structural parameters. In other words, because the coefficients can assume any value in a specified range, the model will provide a theoretical description of the behavior of the density and division of labor variables of all societies for which the forms are accurate. This point is that, in order to theoretically explain the behavior of the variables in a given society, we must find specific values for the structural parameters of the mathematical model, that is, we must take account of the conditions of observation. Thus, we are led naturally to the next topic of the chapter.

## Model Solution and Parameter Estimation

The process of theoretical specification has advanced us one step of the distance from theory to data. Yet, the mathematical model, even though it is ideal for logical analysis, is still too general a system to produce a specific prediction which can be compared with the empirical description of the variables of the model. The problem has been seen to lie in the free parameters of the model. In general, each parameter can take on an infinite number of values which in turn imply an infinite number of descriptions of the variables. In short, generality, the very property of the model which gives it analytical power, also restrains its capacity to produce specific predictions. Although theory and past empirical research will often contain information about the algebraic signs and relative values of the parameters, it is not possible, in general, to know the precise values for given empirical settings. Indeed, it would be quite destructive to the claims of sociology as an empirical science if we were able to deduce specific predictions of empirical events without any concern for the conditions of observation. This argument leads us to the second and third steps in the journey from theory to data. That is, in order to get specific deductions from the model, we must first engage in model solution and reduced-form parameter estimation.

*Model solution* is the mathematical reduction of the structural equations of the model to an expression of the variables as functions of the free parameters. This is essentially a mathematical transformation, and the full range of modern mathematical techniques can be brought to bear on the question of whether or not there exists a solution for the particular mathematical model. If the model builder is so fortunate as to have a model which yields to modern algebraic and analytic techniques, then the model can be solved for an explicit expression of the variables as a function of the free parameters. If the model is so complex that it cannot be solved by known mathematical techniques, then the model builder must turn to techniques of numerical analysis such as numerical integration or computer simulation in order to explore the mathematical implications of the model. The point is that it is the model-solution process which facilitates the exploration of the implications (including unforeseen contradictions) of various assumptions about the forms of the structural equations and the range of values of the free parameters. The processes of theoretical specification and model solution are typically subsumed under the general notion of *model building*. However, the theoretical-specification process is generally concerned with the theoretical plausibility of various structural equations, whereas the model solution is a more specifically mathematical problem, that is, it takes a theoretical specification process as given and works out its implications. If successful, the process of model solution yields a fourth set which we shall call the *reduced-form* of the mathematical model.

Because the reduced-form is derived by a transformation of the structural equations of the mathematical model, the components of the reduced-form are transformations of the elements of the model. First of all, since the structural equations are solved for the variables as a function of the parameters, it follows the parameters of the reduced-form equations will be functions of the structural parameters. This implies, in turn, that the reduced-form equations are not necessarily functionally independent as were the structural equations.

Consider again the Durkheim model sketched above as an example. If we follow Land (1970), one possible specification of the functions $f$, $g$, and $h$ proceeds by first absorbing the function $g$ into the function $h$ and then specifying that the two differential equations of the model are linear with constant coefficients and possess algebraic signs appropriate to the constraints on the equations. The model then reduces to the following two differential equations:

$$
\frac{dx_1}{dt} = a_1 + b_{11}x_1 + b_{12}x_2
$$

$$
\frac{dx_2}{dt} = a_2 + b_{21}x_1 + b_{22}x_2
$$

(9)

where $x_1 = D$, $x_2 = L$, $a_1$, $a_2$, $b_{12}$, $b_{21}$ are constrained to be positive constants, and $b_{11}$ and $b_{22}$ are negative constants. Then, let the column vector of derivatives of the $x_1$ with respect to $t$ be denoted by $x'$; let the column vector of the constants $a_i$ be denoted by $A$; let the vector of the $x_{it}$ where the subscript $t$ refers to the time of observation be denoted by $x_t$; and let the matrix of coefficients $b_{ij}$ be denoted by $B$. With this notation equation (9) can be written as

$$
x' = A + Bx
$$

(10)

Furthermore, the solution of equation (10) can be written as[2]

$$
x_t = e^{Bt}C - B^{-1}A
$$

(11)

where $C$ is a vector of constants satisfying the following equation, which is found by setting $t = 0$ in equation (11)

$$
C = x_0 + B^{-1}A
$$

(12)

and where $e^{Bt}$ is defined as the infinite sum

$$
e^{Bt} = I + Bt + \frac{B^2t^2}{2!} + \frac{B^3t^3}{3!} + \ldots
$$

(13)

Equation (11) shows clearly that the reduced-form parameters of this model are functions of the structural-equation parameters and, therefore, that the reduced-form equations are not functionally independent.

Some additional terminology must be introduced now in order to facilitate the discussion of model solution and the reduced-form of a mathematical model. The equations of a model may assume one of

---

[2] This solution is different from that reported in Land (1970) which was in error. I am grateful to Neil W. Henry for kindly pointing this out to me in a personal communication.

several general forms depending primarily upon the characteristics of the theory which is formalized and upon the particular theoretical specification. A first basic distinction concerns whether the model is static or dynamic. *A model is static* if, and only if, all of its structural equations are algebraic equations relating the values of the variables and parameters measured simultaneously, that is, without regard to time. On the other hand, *a model is dynamic* if, and only if, it relates the values of the variables and parameters measured at different points in time and its structural equations contain at least one difference, differential, difference-differential, integral, or integro-differential equation.

A second basic dimension of classification of the equations of a mathematical model concerns whether the model is exact or stochastic. *A model is exact* if, and only if, all of its structural equations describe the relations among the variables and parameters exactly, without error or approximation. If the model is not exact, then it is stochastic. *A model is stochastic* if, and only if, at least one of its structural equations describes the relations among the variables and parameters only approximately as a result of the presence of disturbing factors that act in a random, or stochastic, fashion.

These two basic dimensions of classification (the terminology here follows that of Christ, 1966) of structural equations yield the following four basic classes of mathematical models: (1) static and exact, (2) static and stochastic, (3) dynamic and exact, and (4) dynamic and stochastic. The importance of such characteristics of structural equations lies in their consequences for the process of model solution and the properties of the reduced-form equations.

Consider first the case of static and exact structural equations. In this case, the solution of the model will yield a set of reduced-form algebraic equations—one equation for each variable—which give the values of the variables as a function of the values of the free parameters of the model. Since the equations of the model are exact, the reduced-form equations define equilibrium values for the variables. That is, if the values of the free parameters are specified, then the reduced-form equations will specify a value for each variable. Since the model is static, it is impossible to study the path of the system as it moves from one equilibrium position to another. That is, as soon as a new value is given for one of the free parameters, then a new equilibrium value is implied for the variables. This is, in fact, the basis of the method of comparative statics, an analytical procedure which has been developed and applied to such models in biology and economics (see, in particular, Samuelson, 1965, for an exposition of the technique). In brief, comparative statics is a method for "the investigation of changes in a system from one position of equilibrium to another without regard to the transitional process involved in the adjustment" (Samuelson, 1965, p. 8).

Since the reduced-form equations give the values of the variables as a function of the free parameters, it is possible to utilize the data from the observation record to estimate statistically the values of the parameters for the specific conditions under which the observations were made. The process of parameter estimation will be analyzed below. However, this is a strategic point at which to make a terminological distinction which has been alluded to above and which will be necessary for the subsequent discussion of parameter estimation. Up to this point, I have discussed only the processes of theoretical specification, model solution, and the exploration of the sensitivity of the values of the variables to changes in the parameters of the model (comparative statics). For such model-building purposes the distinction between free parameters and variables is sufficient. In order to measure or estimate the parameters from a particular observation record, however, we must refine the category of the free parameters of the model into two categories: (1) structural parameters and (2) exogenous variables. Also, we will refer to the variables of the model as *jointly endogenous variables*, that is, those variables the values of which are solved for or determined within the model. The *exogenous variables*, on the other hand, are those free parameters of the model which are given observed values in the observation record, that is, their values are determined outside of the model. Finally, the *structural parameters* are those free parameters of the model which correspond to the coefficients or constants of the structural equations of the model and whose exact values for given conditions of observation must generally be estimated from the observation record. For the degenerate case of the classical single-linear-additive-equation laboratory experimental model, the endogenous variable is the dependent variable, the exogenous variables are the independent variables, and the structural parameters are the regression coefficients. The more general case of a multiple-equation model merely requires a more general terminology.

Consider now the analysis of static and stochastic structural equations. Such models can be formulated in one of two ways: (1) they can be generalized from static-exact models by the addition of random or stochastic disturbance terms which possess specified joint probability distributions to the systematic determination of the variables by the exact equations; (2) they can be formulated solely in terms of probabilities and joint probability distributions. In either case, the model-solution process results in an equilibrium reduced-form solution because of the static character of the model. The reduced-form does differ, however, from the reduced-form of a static-exact model. That is, the solution in the case of static-stochastic structural equations gives the conditional probability distribution of the jointly endogenous variables for given values of the exogenous variables and the structural parameters of the random variables due to the stochastic character of the model.

In the case of dynamic and exact structural equations, the solution of the model results in a mathematical expression for the values of the endogenous variables as in the case of static-exact equations. However, the solution of a dynamic-exact model will generally express the values of the endogenous variables as a function of the structural parameters and the values of the endogenous variables at a previous point in time as in equation (11) for the Durkheim example. In this case, the previously-determined endogenous variables clearly are not exogenous since they were determined within the model at an earlier point in time. Therefore, the concept of endogenous variables must be redefined for dynamic models to exclude values of the endogenous variables at a previous point in time. In this case, we speak of lagged endogenous variables, and the endogenous variables at a particular point in time are called currently endogenous variables. Also, we call the lagged endogenous variables and the exogenous variables (if any) of the model by the generic label predetermined variables. Because the equations of dynamic models relate values of the variables over time, the solution of such a model is often mathematically more rich than the solution of a static model. Without going into details of mathematical methods or results, it may be stated that, if the model yields to currently available mathematical theory, then one can find the equilibrium positions of the systems, the conditions under which the equilibrium points are stable and unstable, and the precise time path the system will follow from any initial position. (See any textbook on the theory of differential equations for a statement of these results, for example, Coddington and Levinson, 1955). In brief, in addition to a solution for the equilibrium values of the endogenous variables as in static models, one can also study the properties of the equilibrium points and the transition from one equilibrium point to another.

Dynamic-stochastic models can be viewed as generalizations of dynamic-exact models as static-stochastic models are generalizations of static-exact models. One can derive a dynamic-stochastic model by either the addition of a stochastic component to a dynamic-exact model or by formulating the equations in terms of probabilities as in the case of a

Markov chain. Since the model is dynamic, the reduced-form solution will trace the time path of the variables over time as in the case of dynamic-exact equations. However, because the model is stochastic, the reduced-form solution will give the conditional probability distributions as well as the expected values of the currently endogenous variables as a function of the structural parameters, the parameters of the random variables, and the predetermined variables.

The last few paragraphs have introduced a large set of terminological distinctions for describing various mathematical models and their reduced-form. If the terms are somewhat less than clear to the reader at this point, I should point out that the examples in the next section of the paper will illustrate most of the concepts in concrete form. For the present, I shall summarize the foregoing discussion in the following formal definition.

DEFINITION 4: The statement that a set, denoted in this paper by $D$, is a reduced-form of a mathematical model means that $D$ consists of three subsets of elements: (1) a set of predetermined variables, (2) a set of endogenous variables, and (3) a set of reduced-form equations each one of which expresses an element of (2) as a function of (1) and the reduced-form parameters which, in turn, are functions of the structural parameters of the mathematical model, set $B$.

As stated above, the process of model solution is primarily a mathematical procedure for deriving the reduced-form equations from the structural equations of the model. However, since the reduced-form equations express each endogenous variable as a function of predetermined variables and the reduced-form parameters, they are in a form which is susceptible to classical statistical procedures of least-squares parameter estimation (see Christ, 1966, pp. 358–380). As will be emphasized below, such a procedure is not optimal under certain conditions. However, it is acceptable for a number of models.

Consider, for example, the following version of the solution—equation (11)—of the Durkheim example discussed above. Use equation (11) for $t$ and $t - 1$ so that[3]

$$
\begin{aligned}
0 = x_t &- e^B x_{t-1} \\
= e^{Bt}C &- B^{-1}A - e^B e^{B(t-1)}C + e^B B^{-1}A \\
= e^{Bt}(x_0 + B^{-1}A) &- B^{-1}A - e^B e^{B(t-1)}(x_0 + B^{-1}A) + e^B B^{-1}A \\
= e^{Bt}x_0 + e^{Bt}B^{-1}A &- B^{-1}A - e^B e^{B(t-1)}x_0 - e^B e^{B(t-1)}B^{-1}A + e^B B^{-1}A \\
= -B^{-1}A &+ e^B B^{-1}A \qquad (14)
\end{aligned}
$$

---

[3] Again, this derivation (due to Neil W. Henry) differs from that reported in Land (1970), which was in error.

or, equivalently,

$$x_t = e^B x_{t-1} + e^B B^{-1} A - B^{-1} A$$
$$= e^B x_{t-1} + (e^B - I) B^{-1} A \tag{15}$$

Equation (15) can be written

$$x_t = A^* + B^* x_{(t-1)} \tag{16}$$

where $A^* = (e^B - I) B^{-1} A$ and $B^* = e^B$. This matrix equation expresses the values of the current endogenous variables $x_t$ as a function of the predetermined variables $x_{(t-1)}$ and the reduced-form parameters, $A^*$ and $B^*$. Since there are two current endogenous variables, equation (13) can also be written

$$x_{1t} = a_1^* + b_{11}^* x_{1(t-1)} + b_{12}^* x_{2(t-1)}$$
$$x_{2t} = a_2^* + b_{21}^* x_{1(t-1)} + b_{22}^* x_{2(t-1)} \tag{17}$$

In this form the reduced-form equations are readily susceptible to least-squares parameter estimation procedures from an observation record containing time-series observations on the two variables. Land (1970) obtained the following reduced-form structure from a time series of observations of the variables for the United States, 1900–1950:

$$x_{1t} = -169.079 + 0.096 x_{1(t-1)} + 2.288 x_{2(t-1)} \ (R = 0.983)$$
$$x_{2t} = \phantom{-}69.946 + 0.109 x_{1(t-1)} + 0.221 x_{2(t-1)} \ (R = 0.989) \tag{18}$$

The reduced-form parameters do not suffice, however, as a theoretical explanation of an observation record. The goal set earlier in this paper was to provide such a theoretical explanation by obtaining estimates of the structural parameters of the model. Thus, the question now is whether or not the parameters of the structural equations can be uniquely derived from the reduced-form or the observation record. The pursuit of this question in general leads us to the next topic of the paper.

## Structural-Parameter Estimation and Model Appraisal

As we have seen, the process of model solution gives us a set of reduced-form equations which determine expected values of the endogenous variables as a function of the values of the predetermined variables and the reduced-form parameters which can be estimated statistically from an observation record. However, because the parameters of the reduced-form equations are functions of the basic causal parameters of the structural equations of the model, we can derive only a limited amount of information from the reduced-form parameters. In particular, suppose that there is a structural change in one of the basic structural relationships of the mathematical model, that is, suppose that one or more of the numerical values of the coefficients of a structural equation change for a particular social system for which the structural relationships hold. Then the values of all of the reduced-form parameters which are a function of this structural parameter will also change. Yet, since the reduced-form parameters are, in general, functions of more than one structural parameter, it may be impossible to identify which particular structural relationship has changed, and by how much, from an examination of the estimated reduced-form parameters alone. If we refer back to the Durkheim example, the question is whether or not it is possible to identify which of the parameters of the structural equations (9) has changed when we observe a change in the parameters of the reduced-form equations (17).

From another perspective the basic point is that the structural equations (and their parameters) refer to the independent causal relationships assumed to be operating in a particular empirical setting whereas the reduced-form equations (and their parameters) are not necessarily independent nor do they represent causal mechanisms in general. Thus, although the reduced-form equations are generally such that their parameters may be easily estimated, they also provide a limited amount of information, in general, about the basic structural or causal mechanisms of the phenomenon. Hence, one purpose of this section of the chapter is to specify the conditions under which the structural parameters can be recovered from the reduced-form parameters and the conditions under which other estimation procedures must be utilized. In brief, structural-parameter estimation is concerned with the estimation of the numerical values of the parameters of the structural equations of a mathematical model from the parameters of its reduced-form or, more generally, from a given observation record. This process yields a fifth set which we shall call the mathematical structure corresponding to a given mathematical model and a given set of conditions of observation.

The mathematical structure bears a close correspondence to the mathematical model; it is, in fact, a given instance of the general set (possibly infinite) of structures allowable by the model. Contrariwise, a mathematical model can be defined as a set of mathematical structures (see, for example, Christ, 1966, p. 21). Furthermore, if data on predetermined variables from an observation record are fed into the mathematical structure, then predicted values of the endogenous variables will emerge which can be compared with the actual description from the observation record as in the case of the reduced-form equations. However, the advantage of the mathematical structure when used for such purposes is that it enables one to trace the causal processes by which changes in the values of the predetermined variables and structural parameters are transformed into changes of the values of the endogenous variables. This is a consequence of the estimation of specific numerical values of the structural parameters of the basic causal processes of the system as specified in the following definition.

DEFINITION 5: The statement that a set, denoted in this chapter by $C$, is a *mathematical structure* corresponding to a given mathematical model and a given observation record means that $C$ is a set consisting of two subsets: (1) structural equations as specified by the mathematical model, and (2) estimated values of the structural parameters (including the parameters of the joint-probability distributions if the model is stochastic) from the observation record. Taken together, these two subsets are sufficient to determine uniquely the values (in the case of exact structures) or the conditional probability distributions (in the case of stochastic structures) of the endogenous variables conditional on the values of the predetermined variables.

Before proceeding to analyze the conditions under which the mathematical structure can be reproduced from a reduced-form which is specific to a particular observation record, we find it useful to formalize the notions about a close correspondence among the five sets which have been defined to this point in the chapter. That is, I have defined five different sets—theory, mathematical model, mathematical structure, reduced-form, and observation record—and I have assumed that a more or less exact correspondence can be established among them. However, this nebulous notion should be given a more precise formulation. In particular, such an analysis will facilitate the discussion of structural-parameter estimation and model appraisal. The concept of a mapping from one set to another provides the necessary logical apparatus for analyzing the relationships of our sets.

DEFINITION 6: The statement that $\sigma$ is a *mapping* from a nonempty set $X$ *into* a nonempty set $Y$ means that $\sigma$ is a rule which associates a unique element in $Y$ with each element in $X$. Henceforth, it will be assumed that all sets are nonempty.

DEFINITION 7: The statement that the mapping $\sigma$ of $X$ into $Y$ is from $X$ *onto* $Y$ means that for every element $y$ in $Y$ there exists an element $x$ in $X$ such that $x$ is mapped to $y$ by $\sigma$.

DEFINITION 8: The statement that the mapping $\sigma$ of $X$ into (or onto) $Y$ is *one-to-one* means that if two elements $x_1$ and $x_2$ in $X$ are distinct then the elements $y_1$ and $y_2$ to which $\sigma$ maps $x_1$ and $x_2$ are distinct.

The problem of relating the five sets defined in definitions (1), (2), (3), (4), and (5) is now seen to be an issue of deciding what class of properties the mappings of elements among the sets should possess. Specifically, it was stated earlier that a mathematical model should reflect the structure of the theory under consideration. Furthermore, if the theory is to explain successfully the events described in the observation record, then the model must of necessity have some correspondence to the structure of relations among the real entities which produced the record. This implies, for example, that the transformations carried out on theoretical entities in the model must have a strong correspondence to the relationships among the real phenomena if the predictions of the model are to conform well to the observation description. In short, this discussion implies that the mappings among the five sets defined above should preserve the structure of relations among the elements. The following three definitions employ this criterion and various combinations of the properties of mappings.

DEFINITION 9: The statement that $\phi$ is a *homomorphism* from a set $X$ to a set $Y$ means that $\phi$ is a mapping from $X$ into $Y$ which preserves logical structure. Because the discussion is intended to be general, the properties of the logical structures are not specified. But, for example, suppose that the operation of multiplication is defined on the elements of each set. This definition then asserts that if $x_1$ and $x_2$ are in $X$, then $\phi(x_1 \cdot x_2) = \phi(x_1) \cdot \phi(x_2)$ where the product on the left side is the product in $X$ while that on the right side is the product in $Y$.

DEFINITION 10: The statement that $\phi$ is an *isomorphism* from a set $X$ to a set $Y$ means that $\phi$ is a homomorphism from $X$ into $Y$ and that $\phi$ is one-to-one.

DEFINITION 11: The statement that the set $X$ is *isomorphic* to the set $Y$ means that there exists an isomorphism $\phi$ of $X$ onto $Y$.

The three types of mappings delineated in definitions (9), (10), and (11) possess varying degrees of structural correspondence. Clearly, it is most desirable to have sets which are isomorphic. For when two sets are isomorphic, then, in some sense, they are equal. Isomorphic sets differ in that their elements are labeled differently. However, the isomorphism gives us the program which assigns the labels, and with it, if we desire a given logical transformation in one set, we can carry out the analogous transformation in the other set and rest assured that the result will be meaningful in the former set. On the other hand, a mapping which is merely an isomorphism from a set $X$ into (but not onto) a set $Y$ does not provide quite the degree of correspondence as does an onto isomorphism. The reason is that the set $Y$ may contain elements to which no corresponding element in $X$ is mapped if the isomorphism is merely into $Y$. Finally, if the mapping from $X$ into $Y$ is but a homomorphism, then there is even less structural correspondence of the sets. In this case it is not even certain that an element in $Y$ will have a unique counterpart in $X$.

Figure 3 shows six maps denoted by $\rho$, $\tau$, $\sigma$, $\phi$, $\psi$, and $\pi$ connecting the five sets: theory, mathematical model, mathematical structure, reduced-form, and observation record. The question at this point is which of the definitions (9), (10), (11) can reasonably be expected to apply to the maps in mathematical sociology as it stands today. As stated earlier, it would be preferable to have maps which established the sets as isomorphic to each other. However, it is unlikely that we can find maps which show the sets to be isomorphic, particularly at the present crude level of theorizing in sociology. Consider, for example, the map from the theory (set $A$) to the model (set $B$). It is quite unlikely that this map can be onto since, as pointed out above in the discussion of theoretical specification, it is often the case that the model must include assumptions not present in the theory, for example, assumptions about the stochastic disturbances in the relationships produced by variables not included in the model. Furthermore, a similar analysis shows that the map from the mathematical structure (set $C$) to the observation record (set $E$) also will not establish the sets as isomorphic. As a matter of fact, in this case the structural relationships of the latter set are not even known.

All is not lost, however, by our incapacity to set up isomorphic correspondences among the five sets. For, to the extent that we can show that unique elements in one set map to unique elements in another set, we can establish that our homomorphisms are one-to-one and, therefore, that they are isomorphisms. Furthermore, it is easily shown that the subsets of the parent sets for which we have established isomorphisms are actually isomorphic. We are then in a position to receive a payoff from this rather extended analysis. The payoff is in terms of a concise specification of the conditions under which the mathematical structure corresponding to a mathematical model and a given observation record can be recovered from its estimated reduced-form and in terms of a specification of the checks on the empirical validity of the theory (set $A$) provided by the application of various techniques of model appraisal to the isomorphism from set $C$ (mathematical structure) to set $E$ (observation record).

Consider first the estimates of the structural parameters of the mathematical model from a given observation record. Suppose that the model has been solved to obtain the reduced-form equations, that is, as in Figure 3, suppose that set $B$ has been transformed into set $D$ by a suitable transformation $\sigma$. Suppose further that the reduced-form parameters have been estimated statistically from an observation record. Then a necessary and sufficient condition that the parameters of set $C$ (mathematical structure) be recoverable from the estimated

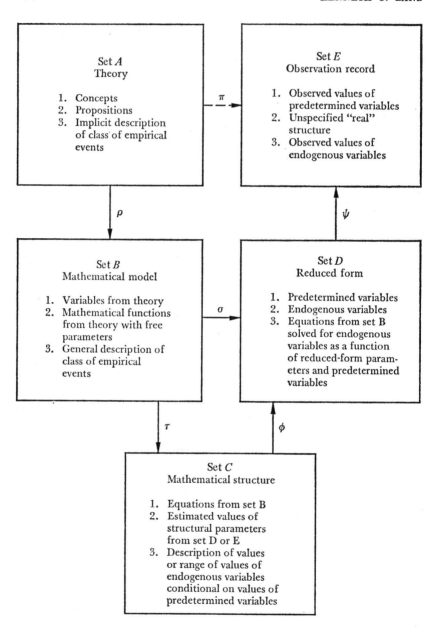

Figure 3.

parameters of set $D$ (reduced-form) is that the inverse of the mapping from $B$ to $D$ $\sigma^{-1}$ exist and that $\phi^{-1} = \sigma^{-1}$, where $\phi$ is the mapping from set $C$ (mathematical structure) to the set $D$. This set of relationships illustrates the position of the reduced-form as a transformation of either the mathematical model or the mathematical structure. If the reduced-form is defined as the solution of the mathematical model, then its parameters are merely formal functions of the free structural parameters of the model. On the other hand, if the values of the structural coefficients are known (that is, if they have been estimated), then the values of the reduced-form parameters can be derived by the application of the same transformation to the mathematical structure. Thus, we could specify in Figure 3 that $\sigma = \phi$. Finally, if the reduced-form parameters are given specific numerical values, either by reduced-form parameter estimation or by solution of the estimated mathematical structure, then we have what is properly called the *reduced-form structure* which is related to the reduced-form as the mathematical structure is related to the mathematical model. That is, the reduced-form structure is a given instance of the reduced-form, or the reduced-form is the set of all allowable reduced-form structures (for example, compare the reduced-form structure of equations (18) with the general reduced-form of equations (15) or (17).

The condition stated in the previous paragraph for the estimation of the structural parameters from the reduced-form parameters is equivalent to the condition that the mathematical model be just-identified. Various necessary and sufficient conditions for the identification of a large variety of mathematical models have been derived in the econometrics literature (see, for example, Fisher, 1963, for a detailed discussion of such results). The importance of this condition lies in the ease of estimation of the structural parameters if such an inverse mapping exists. For example, because such an inverse transformation existed for the reduced-form equations, Land (1970) was able to estimate the mathematical structure from equations (18) above corresponding to equations (9) for the Durkheim model.[4] Furthermore, it is a highly

---

[4] Because of the algebraic errors reported above, the mathematical structure reported in Land (1970) is incorrect. By applying the formulas reported above, one finds the following estimates of the structural coefficients:

$$A = \begin{bmatrix} -98.20 + 595.002i \\ 62.78 - 112.846i \end{bmatrix} \quad B = \begin{bmatrix} -0.7745 + 1.7666i & 1.4866 - 7.1573i \\ 0.0703 - 0.3350i & -0.6818 + 1.3574i \end{bmatrix}$$

These matrices have complex components which are necessary to capture the oscillating patterns in the observed data. Note, however, that the real components of the $B$ matrix are the same as those reported in Land (1970) except that they are now

significant finding for the process of structural parameter estimation that the application of least-squares estimation procedures to the reduced-form, in the case of just-identification of all equations in the model, is an optimal method of estimation known as indirect least-squares (see, for example, Christ, 1966, p. 403). On the other hand, if such an inverse mapping does not exist, then either it is impossible to estimate the structural parameters or one must utilize the vastly more complicated statistical estimation procedures which have been derived for simultaneous structural-equation estimation (see, for example, Christ, 1966, Chapter 9, for an exposition of simultaneous-equation estimation procedures). Such problems of structural estimation will be illustrated in the examples of the next section of the chapter.

Consider now the problem of model appraisal via checks on the mapping from set $C$ (mathematical structure) to set $E$ (observation record). Given that the model is just-identified so that the reduced-form parameters can be estimated directly from the observation record or that the structural-equation parameters have been estimated by other means, we find the check very simple. If the theory is valid, then there must be a close correspondence between the values of the endogenous variables which are deduced from the reduced-form (conditional on the observed values of the predetermined variables) and the observed values. Of course, we must avoid the logical fallacy of affirming the consequent; therefore, the fit of the theoretically derived values must be judged by appropriate statistical procedures. As Stinchcombe (1968, Chapter 2) has emphasized, another classical canon of scientific inference in model appraisal is to compare theoretically derived and observed values from as many different theoretical structures as possible. If the fit of the sets of observed and predicted values is close enough (as determined by statistical criteria), then we may fail to reject the null hypothesis that the theoretically imposed relationships in the mathematical structure are similar to the real structure which produced the observation record. Thus

---

estimated relative to the decennial observations. The real components of the $A$ vector are considerably different from those reported earlier because the algebraic errors reported above affect its estimation. As a further check on the meaningfulness of this structure, one can solve for the equilibrium solution implied by the above values for $A$ and $B$. Solving $x' = 0 = A + Bx_e$, we find $x_e = -B^{-1}A$, giving the following equilibrium values:

$$x_e = \begin{bmatrix} 62.2698 + 2.2090i \\ 98.5016 - 9.7583i \end{bmatrix}$$

which is a meaningful equilibrium position for the set of observed $x_t$ values from which the coefficients were computed.

we have some confidence that the mapping from the mathematical structure to the observation record is an isomorphism. But we can say more; specifically, even though there are elements in the empirical structure (real world) which do not correspond to any elements in the mathematical structure under our mappings, we are justified in failing to reject the null hypothesis that the structures are isomorphic in all relevant respects. There are many other technical aspects of model appraisal which cannot be discussed here (see, for example, Christ, 1966, Chapter 10). Finally, since the mappings from the theory to the model, from the model to the mathematical structure, and from the structure to the observation record establish isomorphic relationships among the subsets in the parent sets, we may fail to reject the theory as an explanation of the empirical phenomenon. This follows from the fact that the mapping from the theory to the observation record is one-to-one and onto since it is a composition of one-to-one and onto maps. Hence we have some confidence in assuming that the map $\pi$ in Figure 3 is an isomorphism from set $A$ (theory) onto a subset of set $E$ (observation record). In brief, we may assume that our theory represents a segment of empirical reality. On the other hand, if we reject the null hypothesis, then we lack confidence in $\pi$ as an isomorphism and are spurred on to a reformulation of theory and model.

In summary, I have sought here to spell out the formal relationship of scientific theory to empirical observations. The basic argument has been that some kind of formal representation of a theory is a necessary condition to an accurate theoretical representation of an empirical phenomenon. Consequently, I have defined the structures obtained at the related stages of specification of a theory and the empirical estimation of its parameters as well as the interrelationships of the obtained structures. This is not to imply that the typical researcher is aware of the formal distinctions which I have drawn. Rather, one could detect work on each of these aspects of explanation in the total scientific enterprise. At various points in the development of a specific discipline, moreover, work is likely to be concentrated on some of the structures which I have delineated to the relative neglect of the others. For example, comparatively little work in modern physics is verbal theorizing. Rather, physicists tend to theorize almost solely by use of mathematical models. Furthermore, modern economists tend to work in all five structures. That is, in the current economic literature, one finds a mixture of verbal theory, mathematical models of verbal theory, empirical estimation of the parameters of mathematical models, and tests of the fit of mathematical models to observation records. On the other hand, work in sociology has tended to concentrate on the propagation of verbal theories and the collection of observation records with only a loose connection between the two structures. The major work of specification of theories and empirical estimation of theoretical parameters (sociological constants) remains to be accomplished. Undoubtedly, a greater proportion of the efforts of sociologists will be devoted to these latter two tasks as sociologists become more facile in the use of mathematical and statistical methods.

It is now possible to compare the scheme of the four steps of theoretical specification, model solution, reduced-form and structural parameter estimation, and model appraisal presented above with alternative outlines in the methodological literature. Essentially, the scheme presented here is that which is used in modern econometrics although I am not aware of a unified presentation in the econometrics literature such as that presented here. In the sociological literature a somewhat similar treatment in the context of measurement models was given by Lazarsfeld (1959). Briefly, Lazarsfeld (1959, pp. 506–528) delineated the following nine steps of latent structure analysis: (1) choice and specification of the model, (2) accounting equations specialized for the model, (3) the conditions of reducibility, (4) identifiability, (5) identification, (6) computation—the fitting procedure, (7) evaluation of the fit, (8) the recruitment pattern, and (9) classification and scores. In comparing the two schemes, we find three of Lazarsfeld's steps—(3), (8), and (9)—seem to be peculiar to measurement models whereas steps (1) and (2) are aspects of the process of theoretical specification and steps (4) and (5) are aspects of the process of model solution. Thus, the four processes outlined above can subsume Lazarsfeld's more detailed outline of steps in latent structure analysis. Supplemented with Lazarsfeld's steps (8) and (9), the present scheme can, in fact, subsume measurement models as a particular class of structural models. However, because of limitations of space and because of the existence of a large literature on the subject, I will not give a specific treatment of measurement models in this chapter.

## EXAMPLES OF USE OF MATHEMATICAL MODELS

In the preceding section of this essay, I have given a rather elaborate discussion of the processes of theoretical specification, model solution, reduced-form and structural parameter estimation, and model appraisal. These processes were seen to interrelate the five sets: theory, mathematical model, mathematical structure, reduced-form, and observation record. Furthermore, it should be emphasized that all four processes and all five sets are integral elements in the process of scientific explanation as outlined by Hempel and Oppenheim (1948). Specifically, it is essential that the mathematical model incorporate the covering laws which are thought to govern a particular phenomenon. However, as Hempel and Oppenheim demonstrated, covering laws alone are not sufficient to explain the behavior of empirical events. Rather, one must also measure the conditions of observation in order to explain a particular occurrence of a phenomenon. This requirement includes the measurement of the initial conditions and exogenous forces which influence the observed values of the events of interest. In terms of research procedure, this stipulation means that the researcher must engage in various techniques of parameter estimation in order to specify either the mathematical or reduced-form structures from which theoretically derived values of the events of interest can be compared with the observed values by various statistical techniques of model appraisal.

In this section of the chapter, I shall briefly discuss three specific substantive examples of the use of mathematical models and parameter estimation procedures in scientific explanation. I should like to state certain boundaries on this discussion. First, the few models to be discussed here cannot be taken as representative of the use of models in science (or even in social science). Rather, they are chosen to illustrate the generality of the scheme outlined in the first part of the chapter. Second, the present discussion cannot be taken as a definitive exposition of any of the models. Rather, I shall emphasize either those aspects of model building or model evaluation which highlight the scheme presented above. To begin, I shall review very briefly a simple application of classical mechanics which illustrates some aspects of theoretical specification, model solution, and parameter estimation in physics.

## Classical Mechanics

Consider the horizontal motion of a physical particle in a resisting medium, a problem which is treated in any elementary textbook on classical mechanics (see, for example, Marion, 1965). The physical theory which is assumed to govern the behavior of such a phenomenon is Newton's famed three laws of mechanics (Marion, 1965, pp. 57–58):

> (1) A body remains at rest or in uniform motion unless acted upon by a force. (2) A body acted upon by a force moves in such a manner that the time rate of change of momentum equals the force. (3) If two bodies exert forces on each other, these forces are equal in magnitude and opposite in direction.

Simple as they are, these three propositions have been found to be sufficient to describe the motion of physical particles for a large variety of conditions. Specifically, Newtonian mechanics provides an accurate description of physical motion with the important exceptions of microscopic particles and particles at high velocities in which cases one must employ the modern theories of quantum mechanics and relativity, respectively.

In the case of the motion of a physical particle in a resisting medium, Newton's Second Law provides us with the equation $F = ma$ which is the covering law presumed to govern the motion of the particle, where $F$ represents the force on the particle, $m$ represents the mass of the particle, and $a$ represents the time rate of change of the velocity of the particle (or the rate of change of the rate of change of the position particle with respect to time). In some expositions of classical mechanics (for example, Marion, 1965), this equation is, in fact, considered as a definition of the concept of force when mass is given an operational definition.

The additional specification that the retarding force in the medium be proportional to the velocity of the particle yields the following equation of motion as a mathematical model:

$$ma = \frac{mdv}{dt} = -kmv \tag{19}$$

where $kmv$ is the magnitude of the resisting force ($k$ is constant of proportionality, $m$ is mass of the particle, and $v$ is velocity of the particle). Then from equation (19) we get

$$\int \frac{dv}{v} = -k \int dt \tag{20}$$

where $\int$ is the indefinite integral operator, or, if we carry out the integration,

$$\ln v = -kt + C_1 \tag{21}$$

where $\ln v$ designates the natural logarithm of the velocity and $C_1$ is a constant of integration which can be evaluated if we prescribe the initial condition that the velocity at the beginning is $v_0$ or $v(t = 0) = v_0$. Then $C_1 = \ln v_0$, and on taking antilogarithms, we derive the following equation for the description of the velocity of the particle at any time $t$:

$$v = v_0 e^{-kt} \tag{22}$$

where $e = 2.7183 \ldots$ (the base of the natural logarithms). Equation (22) can be integrated to obtain the displacement $x$ as a function of time,

$$v = \frac{dx}{dt} = v_0 e^{-kt}$$

or

$$x = v_0 \int e^{-kt} dt = -\frac{v_0}{k} e^{-kt} + C_2 \tag{23}$$

The initial condition that the displacement of the particle at the beginning is zero or $x(t = 0) = 0$ implies that $C_2 = v_0/k$.

Therefore,

$$x = \frac{v_0}{k}(1 - e^{-kt}) \tag{24}$$

This result shows that $x$ asymptotically approaches to value $v_0/k$ as $t \to \infty$.

Thus we have seen that a very elegant single-equation model for the description of the horizontal motion of a physical particle in a resisting medium can be specified out of the general Newtonian principles of mechanics, which have the virtue of being applicable to an enormous number of physical problems. In addition to the illustration of theoretical specification and model solution in physical science provided by this example, I should like to emphasize that, in order to deduce specific numerical values for the velocity and displacement variables in equations (22) and (24) one first must estimate empirically the two parameters of the model, $v_0$ and $k$. The initial condition from which the system develops is represented by the initial velocity $v_0$, and the constant $k$ corresponds to the coefficient of resistance of the medium in which the particle is moving. These are the parameters or conditions of observation which must be estimated before predictions from the model can be compared with the observed values of the variables for accuracy of description. The main point is that, even for such a simple application of Newtonian mechanics, *descriptions of specific events cannot be derived from the model without engaging in the process of parameter estimation*. In brief, parameter estimation is not a new difficulty encountered in mathematical social science as is sometimes assumed by individuals who are generally not familiar with the way mathematics is applied in science (compare, Atkinson, Bower, and Crothers, 1965, pp. 15–18). On the other hand, the social sciences can make a strong case for their greater complexity by pointing to their vastly more complicated estimation problems and procedures.

## Reward Structures and Allocation of Effort

Coleman (1962) began an examination of how the structure of rewards in a group affects the effort expended by members of the group in the rewarded (or punished) activity. He began with the informal observation that in society, just as in the laboratory, men work to gain rewards and escape punishments. However, in society there is no experimenter to establish the reward schedule. Rather, the peculiar character of social systems is that the various members are, for one another, the purveyors of rewards and punishments. From this general perspective Coleman then specified his problem to be the examination of the allocation of group members' efforts between two or more activities under two different reward structures, when one member's efforts help bring success to others who are engaging in that activity and when his efforts subtract from their success.

Coleman's general approach to a model of the process of allocation of effort is to conceive of each group member as vacillating between two activities, allocating his effort to one or the other. Conceptually, the individual can be characterized as being in one of two states, $A$ or $B$, with the possibility of movement from each to the other. With the further assumption that the probability of an individual's movement from $A$ to $B$ in a very small period of time is independent of the length of time he has been in $A$ (and similarly for the reverse movement), Coleman is able to specify that the system is a continuous-time Markov process governed by the following two equations:

$$\frac{dp_A(t)}{dt} = -\beta p_A + \alpha p_B \tag{25}$$

and

$$\frac{dp_B(t)}{dt} = -\alpha p_B + \beta p_A \tag{26}$$

where $p_A$ is the probability of being in state $A$, $\alpha$ is the transition rate from $B$ to $A$, independent of time $(0 \leq \alpha < \infty)$, $\beta$ is the transition rate from $A$ to $B$, independent of time $(0 \leq \beta < \infty)$, and $p_B = 1 - p_A$.

In brief, Coleman's model, as specified in equations (25) and (26), says that, as an individual, each member of the group has tendencies $\alpha$ and $\beta$ toward states $A$ and $B$, respectively. If there were no encouragement or discouragement from other group members, then the individual's probability of being in each state at any time $\tau$ after initially being observed in one of the two states could be calculated and the relative amounts of time he would spend in each state at stochastic equilibrium could be found by setting equation (25) or equation (26) equal to zero. This gives

$$\frac{p_A}{p_B} = \frac{\alpha}{\beta} \tag{27}$$

and

$$p_A = \frac{\alpha}{\alpha + \beta} \qquad p_B = \frac{\beta}{\alpha + \beta} \tag{28}$$

as the relative amounts of time in each state and the probability of being in each state, respectively.

On the basis of this model of individual-level processes, Coleman (1962, p. 121) points out that, if a group of $N$ members consisted merely of $N$ persons governed independently by this process, then the distribution of group members among the two activities would be the following binomial distribution:

$$p_i = \binom{N}{i} p_A^i p_B^{N-i} \tag{29}$$

where $p_i$ is the probability that $i$ persons will be carrying out activity $A$, given $N$ persons in the group, $p_A$ is the probability that each will carry out $A$ (will be in state $A$), and $p_B = 1 - p_A$. Hence, if we observed this group a number of times, we would expect to find the distribution in equation (29).

It is clear that Coleman is not interested in the independence model of activities as represented by equation (29). Rather, his basic assumption is that the activities of group members are interrelated. Consider first his model of structures with mutual reward. Coleman arrives at this model by modifying equations (25) and (26) to include an additive transition rate $\gamma$ toward an activity from every person engaging in the activity. If there are $i$ persons in activity $A$, and if an individual is in $B$, then his transition rate to $A$ will be $\alpha + i\gamma$; the remainder of the $N - 1$ persons, $N - 1 - i$, are in activity $B$, so that if he finds himself in $A$, then the transition rate to $B$ will be $\beta + (N - 1 - i)\gamma$.

However, Coleman's goal of studying the group allocation of effort is not fully attained by the study of how the individual's behavior is influenced by others in his group under a particular assumption about individuals' effects on one another. Rather, he is interested in how the *group's* behavior is affected by this reward structure. To answer this question, Coleman (1962, p. 122) distinguishes the group-level stochastic process from the individual-level processes. Thus, although the group members can vacillate only between two states (activity $A$ or $B$), the group can be in one of $N + 1$ states ($0, 1, 2, \ldots, N$ members engaged in activity $A$). By imposing the stochastic equilibrium condition that the flow of group members across each of the $N$ boundaries separating the $N + 1$ group states must be equal in the two directions, Coleman (1962, p. 123) was able to solve for the following expected distribution of groups (where $a = \alpha/(\alpha + \beta)$ and $c = \gamma/(\alpha + \beta)$):

$$p_i = \binom{N}{i} \frac{\displaystyle\prod_{j=0}^{i=1} (a + jc) \prod_{j=0}^{N-i-1} (1 - a + jc)}{\displaystyle\prod_{j=0}^{N-1} (1 + jc)} \tag{30}$$

The rather complicated expression of equation (30) is characterized by Coleman (1962, p. 123) as a kind of "contagious binomial" for the rewards act so as to induce more and more of the group into the activity that most of the people are doing. Thus, the parameter $c$ represents the value of $\gamma$ relative to $\alpha$ and $\beta$. On experimenting with values of this parameter, Coleman (1962, p. 124) found that the contagious distribution did not differ markedly from the simple binomial with respect to the average allocation of effort in the group—it remains divided proportionally to the individual transition tendencies $\alpha$ and $\beta$. Coleman did find a considerable difference in the group's stability around this average. If the reward coefficient $\gamma$ is large relative to $\alpha$ and $\beta$ (that is, if $c$ is greater than 1.0), then the group is highly unstable near its mean and finds stability only at one or the other extremes, when *all* group members are engaging in $A$ or all in $B$. Thus, the allocation of effort under these conditions of interdependence differs sharply from that of the aggregate of independent persons.

In a similar analysis of reward structures with mutual punishments, Coleman (1962, p. 125) assumed a negative additive transition intensity for each person engaging in an activity. For this model he found another contagious binomial distribution as the solution for the expected distribution of groups that would be found at stochastic equilibrium. However, because the additive reward parameter is negative in this model, Coleman (1962, p. 126) also showed that it distorts the mean of the distribution in the direction of $N/2$ members of the group engaged in each activity with a smaller variance than in the case of independent group activities as represented by the simple binomial distribution.

Finally, on the basis of his model of additive rewards, Coleman (1962, pp. 129–131) analyzes some naturally occurring distributions of the number of shops of size $N = 1, 2, \ldots, 8$ in the New York Typographical Union in which $i = 1, \ldots, 8$ men voted for the winning candidate in a union election. He found that the two parameters of the model were capable of giving a fairly accurate representation of the observed data. Furthermore, he found that the size of the reward parameter decreased with increasing size of the shop.

There are two reasons for including this brief review of Coleman's models of reward structures in this chapter. First, he utilizes a type of mathematical analysis which seems especially appropriate for the study of social-psychological processes (that is, discrete-state Markov processes). Indeed, Coleman (1964a) dealt almost solely with this type of mathematics in his defining work on mathematical sociology. Second, his paper illustrates substantively how assumptions or propositions about individual behavior can be transformed into theorems about group behavior much in the pattern of economists in modern microeconomic theory.

## Process of Social Stratification

In a series of papers, Otis Dudley Duncan (Blau and Duncan, 1967; Duncan, 1968a; 1968b; 1969; Duncan, Featherman, and Duncan, 1968) has considerably enriched professional sociological theory regarding the process of social stratification as well as knowledge of the numerical values of some of the stratification parameters for contemporary American society. Modern sociological theory provides a characterization of stratification systems in terms of the processes by which individuals become located, or locate themselves, in positions in the system (see, for example, Svalastoga, 1965, pp. 36–70). One conceptually extreme stratification system could be called a pure ascription system in which the circumstances of a person's birth are sufficient to determine unequivocally his ranked status in a hierarchical system. The other conceptual extreme is a pure achievement system in which an individual's prospective adult status would be completely undetermined at birth. Under these conditions his status would be found only on reaching adulthood as a consequence of his own actions. In short, in such a system, an individual's adult status would not be conditioned, much less determined, by the circumstances of his birth or rearing. As Duncan notes (Blau and Duncan, 1967, p. 163), the stratification system of any moderately large and complex society involves both ascriptive and achievement principles.

On the basis of such generalizations regarding stratification, Duncan began the construction of his basic model of stratification (Blau and Duncan, 1967, p. 164):

> The governing conceptual scheme in the analysis is quite a commonplace one. We think of the individual's life cycle as a sequence in time that can be described, however partially and crudely, by a set of classificatory or quantitative measurements taken at successive stages. . . . Given this scheme, the questions we are continually raising in one form or another are: how and to what degree do the circumstances of birth condition subsequent status? and, how does status attained (whether by ascription or achievement) at one stage of the life cycle affect the prospects for a subsequent stage?

For the construction of his basic model of stratification, Duncan (Blau and Duncan, 1967, p. 165) examined the interrelationships of five variables: father's educational attainment, father's occupational status, respondent's educational attainment, status of respondent's first job, and status of respondent's occupation in 1962. The sample on which these variables were measured consisted of approximately 20,000 American men aged 20–64 surveyed as an adjunct to the monthly "Current Population Survey" of the U. S. Bureau of the Census in March 1962 (Blau and Duncan, 1967, pp. 10–12).

As a final set of theoretical-methodological assumptions pursuant to the construction of a model of the stratification process, Duncan prescribed a temporal or causal ordering of these variables on the basis of his conception of their sequential operation in the individual's life cycle (Blau and Duncan, 1967, p. 166). Since the focus of concern is not the father's career but, rather, the set of statuses that comprised the origin conditions of sons, it was sufficient to make no assumption as to the causal priority of father's education and father's occupation. On the other hand, since the son's education is supposed to follow in time, Duncan assumed that it was susceptible to causal influences from the measures of family status. Furthermore, while recognizing the possibility of exceptions, Duncan assumed that the son's first full-time job was subsequent to, and susceptible to causal influences from, the family background as well as son's educational attainment. Finally, it was easily seen that the son's occupation in 1962 was subject to causal influences from the first full-time occupation.

In the terminology which has been developed in this chapter, Duncan assumed that father's educational attainment and father's occupation were exogenous variables whereas the son's education, first full-time occupation, and occupation in 1962 were taken as jointly endogenous variables in a static-stochastic model of the process of social stratification. In order to write the equations of Duncan's model, I shall fix the following notation:

$x_1$ = father's education
$x_2$ = father's occupation
$y_1$ = son's education
$y_2$ = son's first full-time occupation
$y_3$ = son's occupation in 1962
$u_i$, $i$ = 1, 2, 3, = stochastic-disturbance terms assumed to be mutually independent

Then Duncan's basic model of social stratification can be written as the following set of equations (Blau and Duncan, 1967, p. 170):

$$y_1 = 0.310x_1 + 0.279x_2 + 0.859u_1$$
$$y_2 = 0.440y_1 + 0.224x_2 + 0.818u_2 \qquad (31)$$
$$y_3 = 0.281y_2 + 0.394y_1 + 0.115x_2 + 0.753u_3$$

The structural parameters are estimated from the basic sample of approximately 20,000 American men aged 20–64 in 1962. All variables, including the stochastic-disturbance terms, are measured in standard-deviation units. Hence, the structural coefficients are path coefficients which, in a particular equation, represent the proportion of its standard deviation by which the endogenous variable will change when one of the other variables is changed by one standard deviation. In brief, the path coefficients are measures of the direct or net effects of the variables. Note, in particular, the father's education is represented in equations (31) as having a zero direct effect on the son's first and subsequent occupations. However, this does not imply that the variables are un-correlated in the sample because father's education has a considerable direct effect on son's education which, in turn, has direct effects on the son's occupations. Thus, the correlation of these variables is seen to be composed entirely of the indirect effects of father's education via the son's education. Finally, note that the stochastic-disturbance terms in equations (31) possess rather large path coefficients. As Duncan (Blau and Duncan, 1967, p. 203) has emphasized, however, the path coefficients of the disturbance terms have an important theoretical meaning in a model of the process of stratification. Specifically, these path coefficients represent the cumulative effects of other unmeasured variables on the educational and occupational achievement of the sons. Presumably, such unmeasured variables are aspects of the son's behavior with respect to the stratification hierarchy and are thus representative of unmeasured elements of the achievement principles of stratification in American society.

One of the chief virtues of Duncan's work on models of stratification has been his continuous efforts to elaborate the basic model presented above. In particular, he has explored the effects of other variables such as intelligence, aspirations and motives, and parental and peer social influences on son's educational and occupational achievement (see, in particular, Duncan, Featherman, and Duncan, 1968; see also Duncan, 1968a; Duncan, Haller, and Portes, 1968). He has also shown recently (Duncan, 1968b, p. 707) that the prestige scores of occupations in the United States are remarkably stable over time so that comparisons of such scores are meaningful for periods of a half or three quarters of a century. In short, Duncan's work on models of stratification is one of the outstanding theoretical and empirical contributions to modern sociology. It is impossible to summarize all of his work in this brief statement, but its effect on formal theory in sociology goes far beyond the study of stratification. For the mathematical-modeling techniques he has used so well are now being used in the study of many other sociological phenomena.

## CONSTRAINTS ON DEVELOPMENT

In this chapter I have outlined in a fairly detailed fashion what I believe is a balanced framework within which formal theory in sociology can be developed. Thus, I have emphasized parameter-estimation and model-appraisal problems as much as theoretical specification and model solution in the process of the mathematical explanation of specific sociological events. I believe that this is one of the critical issues in the development of mathematical sociology. Mathematical methods have been acclaimed as potentially capable of bridging the long-standing gap between theory and empirical research in sociology. Yet, if mathematical sociology is to perform this service, it must be as intimately concerned with problems of model evaluation as it is with model building. For, it is in the evaluation of parameters of empirical social systems that mathematical sociology can both empirically inform sociological theory and theoretically inform social research. Thus, we must be careful not to reproduce the theory-research dichotomy in mathematical sociology. There are some indications that such a distinction has emerged in economics where mathematical economics tends to be concerned primarily with model building while econometrics is concerned with the methods and results of parameter estimation and model testing on empirical economic data.

This chapter has already become longer than originally desired. However, because the space devoted to the problems of formal theory above facilitates (if not demands) it, I should like now to outline briefly some contemporary constraints on the construction of formal theory in sociology. As I have emphasized throughout this chapter, there are several correspondences or isomorphisms which must be established in the process of building formal theories, and these isomorphisms, in turn, impose certain severe constraints on what can be done.

A first isomorphism must be established in the processes of theoretical specification and model solution. There are two kinds of constraints which are imposed on these processes. A first constraint is imposed by the existing theoretical base in contemporary sociology. In brutal terms, the state of conceptualization in sociology is often so poor that the mathematical modeler must improvise at the very beginning of the construction of a model. One possibility for the ameliorization of this constraint lies in the development of new theoretical conceptualizations. However, there is little assurance that such developments will be more amenable to mathematical methods than existing constructs. Therefore, it would be well if those sociologists who specialize in theorizing were to become better informed as to the necessary requirements of a theory in order that it be mathematically and empirically useful. In particular, it would help matters considerably if theorists were to become familiar with, and use, the elementary mathematical notion of function so that they could begin to specify the functional forms which sociological relations are presumed to take. As it is now, the mathematical modeler typically must specify functional forms for a theory because the theorist has failed to perform this task. A second constraint on the process of theoretical specification and model solution derives from the existing base of mathematical techniques from which a model may be specified and solved. As I have emphasized above, these processes are essentially mathematical in character, and the model builder must draw on the body of existing techniques in order to specify and solve his model. It is my judgment, however, that the range of techniques in modern mathematics is sufficiently large that mathematical sociologists will be able to work with existing theory for many years to come. On the other hand, if they are sufficiently persistent and creative in their tasks, then we may expect that model building in sociology will induce the development of new mathematics. Certainly, this has been the experience with the application of mathematics in other scientific disciplines. Modern mathematical economics, for example, has encouraged the development of two subdisciplines of modern mathematics—the theory of games and the theory of linear inequalities or linear programming.

As I have emphasized in this chapter, the processes of parameter estimation and model appraisal are vital aspects of the use of mathematical models to explain specific empirical observations of sociological phenomena. This is another crucial point at which an isomorphism must be established, this time between the mathematical model and the observation record. The vehicle for the establishment of such an isomorphism must be statistical techniques of parameter estimation and hypothesis testing. However, since sociological models are likely to be multiple-equation models, the classical statistical procedures for controlled experiments may not be optimal procedures. In fact, it was a similar situation which stimulated the vigorous development of the subdiscipline of econometrics in modern economics. Although mathematical sociologists can draw on the vast body of techniques which now exists in econometrics, as Duncan has done in the development of his models of stratification, there are indications (compare, Bartholomew, 1967, p. 9) that the existing statistical theory is very meager for the kinds of stochastic-process models which often are useful in sociology. Alternatively, consider the problems of multicollinearity discussed by Gordon (1968). Because of these and other problems, I would venture the judgment that there will exist a need for the systematic development of statistical theory in sociology as our models become more fully developed.

A final set of serious constraints on the development of formal theory in sociology lies in the adequacy of sociological observations. Briefly, there is very little need to be concerned with parameter estimation and model testing if the basic data of our observation records do not meet certain standards of accuracy. Anyone concerned with parameter estimation for theoretically informed mathematical models must be concerned with the quality of observation records. In the present context two comments are pertinent.

First, the requirement stated above that error components of observations be estimable seems to be a fruitful approach to measurement problems. In brief, given some estimate of the error components of an observation record, the observations can be adjusted so that parameter estimation and model evaluation can proceed on the basis of the adjusted observations. Recently, this has taken the form of an adjustment of methods of parameter estimation (see, for example, Heise, 1969; Costner, 1969; Blalock, 1970).

Second, I should like to emphasize that past scientific experience has been that the development of formal theory both requires and stimulates measurement accuracy. Moreover, the first indications are that this is the experience in sociology (see, for example, Blau and Duncan, 1967, p. 166; Siegal and Hodge, 1968; Goodman, 1969). In brief, I believe that the scientific maturity of sociology will be signaled by our increasing ability to understand the implications of measurement error for the inferential process rather than by the complete eradication of measurement inaccuracy.

## SUMMARY AND CONCLUDING COMMENTS

In this chapter I have been concerned with the methodology of the construction and evaluation of formal theory in sociology. Without discussing technical matters of mathematics and statistics, I have introduced the four processes of (1) theoretical specification, (2) model solution, (3) reduced-form and structural parameter estimation, and (4) model appraisal as the means by which one may interrelate the five sets: (1) theory, (2) mathematical model, (3) mathematical structure, (4) reduced-form, and (5) observation record. Furthermore, I have discussed several examples from contemporary sociology which are illustrative of the general processes of model building and model evaluation. Finally, on the basis of the correspondences which must be established among the above sets, I have outlined some constraints on the development of formal theory in sociology.

I hope that this presentation has been neither too optimistic nor too pessimistic about the prospects for formal sociological theory. Let there be no illusions about the difficulties of following the path which has been displayed here. Furthermore, there is no guarantee that formal theory will enhance sociological understanding. On the other hand, I suggest that formal theories have already advanced the state of sociological knowledge in at least some of those few areas in which such techniques have been employed. Moreover, I believe that the methodology of formal theory provides the most opportune context in which the checks and balances of scientific method can function—perhaps the strongest possible argument for the continued development of formal theory in sociology.

## REFERENCES

ATKINSON, R. C., BOWER, G. H., AND CROTHERS, E. J.
  1965 *An Introduction to Mathematical Learning Theory.* New York: Wiley.
BARTHOLOMEW, D. J.
  1967 *Stochastic Models for Social Processes.* New York: Wiley.
BLALOCK, H. M., JR.
  1969 *Theory Construction: From Verbal to Mathematical Formulations.* Englewood Cliffs, N.J.: Prentice-Hall.
  1970 "Estimating measurement error using multiple indicators and several points in time." *American Sociological Review* 35: 101–112.
BLAU, P. M. AND DUNCAN, O. D.
  1967 *The American Occupational Structure.* New York: Wiley.
BREMS, H.
  1968 *Quantitative Economic Theory.* New York: Wiley.
CHRIST, C. F.
  1966 *Econometric Models and Methods.* New York: Wiley.
CODDINGTON, E. A. AND LEVINSON, N.
  1955 *Theory of Ordinary Differential Equations.* New York: McGraw-Hill.
COLEMAN, J. S.
  1962 "Reward structures and the allocation of effort." Pp. 119–132 in J. H. Criswell, H. Solomon, and P. Suppes (Eds.), *Mathematical Methods in Small Group Processes.* Stanford, Calif.: Stanford University Press.

1964a  *Introduction to Mathematical Sociology.* New York: Free Press.
1964b  *Models of Change and Response Uncertainty.* Englewood Cliffs, N.J.: Prentice-Hall.

COSTNER, H. L.
1969  "Theory, deduction, and rules of correspondence." *American Journal of Sociology* 75: 245–263.

DUNCAN, O. D.
1968a  "Ability and achievement." *Eugenics Quarterly* 15: 1–11.
1968b  "Social stratification and mobility." Pp. 675–719 in E. B. Sheldon and W. E. Moore (Eds.), *Indicators of Social Change: Concepts and Measurements.* New York: Russell Sage Foundation.
1969  "Contingencies in constructing causal models." Pp. 74–112 in E. F. Borgatta (Ed.), *Sociological Methodology: 1969.* San Francisco: Jossey-Bass.

DUNCAN, O. D., FEATHERMAN, D. L., AND DUNCAN, B.
1968  *Socioeconomic Background and Occupational Achievement: Extensions of a Basic Model.* Ann Arbor: Population Studies Center, University of Michigan.

DUNCAN, O. D., HALLER, A. O., AND PORTES, A.
1968  "Peer influences on aspirations: a reinterpretation." *American Journal of Sociology* 74: 119–137.

DURKHEIM, E.
1933  *The Division of Labor in Society.* New York: The Free Press.

FISHER, F. M.
1963  *The Identification Problem in Econometrics.* New York: McGraw-Hill.

GOODMAN, L. A.
1969  "On the measurement of social mobility: an index of status persistence." *American Sociological Review* 34: 831–849.

GORDON, R. A.
1968  "Issues in multiple regression." *American Journal of Sociology* 73: 592–616.

HANSON, N. R.
1958  *Patterns of Discovery.* Cambridge: Cambridge University Press.

HEISE, D. R.
1969  "Separating reliability and stability in test-retest correlation." *American Sociological Review* 34: 93–101.

HEMPEL, C. G.
 1965  *Aspects of Scientific Explanation.* New York: The Free
       Press.
HEMPEL, C. G. AND OPPENHEIM, P.
 1953  "The logic of explanation." *Philosophy of Science* 15 (1948).
       Reprinted in H. Feigel and M. Brodbeck (Eds.), *Readings
       in the Philosophy of Science.* New York: Appleton-Century.
KAPLAN, A.
 1964  *The Conduct of Inquiry.* San Francisco: Chandler.
KUHN, T. S.
 1962  *The Structure of Scientific Revolutions.* Chicago: University
       of Chicago Press.
LAND, K. C.
 1970  "A mathematical formalization of Durkheim's theory of
       the causes of the division of labor." Pp. 257–282 in E. F.
       Borgatta and G. W. Bohrnstedt (Eds.), *Sociological Method-
       ology: 1970.* San Francisco: Jossey-Bass.
LAZARSFELD, P. F.
 1959  "Latent structure analysis." Pp. 476–543 in Sigmund Koch
       (Ed.), *Psychology: A Study of a Science,* Volume 3. New
       York: McGraw-Hill.
MARION, J. B.
 1965  *Classical Dynamics.* New York: Academic Press.
NAGEL, E.
 1961  *The Structure of Science.* New York: Harcourt, Brace and
       World.
RESCHER, N.
 1966  "On prediction and explanation." *British Journal for the
       Philosophy of Science* 8: 281–290.
SAMUELSON, P. A.
 1965  *Foundations of Economic Analysis.* New York: Atheneum.
SIEGAL, P. M. AND HODGE, R. W.
 1968  "A causal approach to the study of measurement error."
       Pp. 28–59 in H. M. Blalock, Jr. and A. B. Blalock (Eds.),
       *Methodology in Social Research.* New York: McGraw-Hill.
SHEFFLER, I.
 1960  "Explanation, prediction, and abstraction." In A. Danto
       and S. Morgenbesser (Eds.), *Philosophy of Science.* New
       York: Meridian Books.
SIMON, H. A.
 1957  *Models of Man.* New York: Wiley.

STINCHCOMBE, A. L.

1968    *Constructing Social Theories.* New York: Harcourt, Brace, and World.

SVALASTOGA, K.

1965    *Social Differentiation.* New York: McKay.

ZETTERBERG, H. L.

1965    *On Theory and Verification in Sociology.* Totowa, N.J.: Bedminster.

# 𝕏8𝕏

# KEY VARIABLES

*Phillip Bonacich*

UNIVERSITY OF CALIFORNIA, LOS ANGELES

*Kenneth D. Bailey*

UNIVERSITY OF CALIFORNIA, LOS ANGELES

Sociologists frequently formulate theories that postulate the signs of relations between variables but not the magnitudes of these relations. We then attempt to draw from these models implications about the signs of relations not postulated in the theory. Under certain conditions, however, assumptions only about the signs of relationships are insufficient to draw testable implications. For example, if variables $A$ and $B$ are positively correlated and variables $B$ and $C$ are positively correlated, it does not follow that $A$ and $C$ are positively correlated. In this chapter we will examine quite a different circumstance, namely that in which no inferences can be made about the relationship between two variables despite the fact that the theory postulates a positive (or a negative) relationship. This will be shown to occur because of the effects of the system within which these variables are embedded. Variables involved in such paradoxes will be called key variables, and methods for locating them will be described below.

## ILLUSTRATION OF PROBLEM

We can illustrate the problem by drawing on the small-group theories of George Homans and Robert Bales. Homans (1950) has proposed that the amount of friendliness, the amount of interaction, and the amount of goal-directed group activity all tend to be in positive reciprocal relations to each other and that the level of these variables for a group is also affected by additional features of the situation. To give specific illustrative content to these additional features, we might propose that the amount of free time that group members have has an additional effect on the amount of interaction, that psychological compatibility has an additional effect on the level of friendliness, and that common interests among group members have an additional effect on the amount of goal-directed activity. We use the following symbols:

$$x_1 = \text{rate of interaction}$$
$$x_2 = \text{level of friendliness}$$
$$x_3 = \text{rate of goal-directed group activity}$$
$$b_1 = \text{amount of free time}$$
$$b_2 = \text{psychological compatibility}$$
$$b_3 = \text{common interests}$$

The theory could be diagramed as shown in Figure 1.

Now let us introduce an insight from Bales (1950). Goal-directed group activity can lead to competition between group members for recognition and leadership. Goal-directed activity can put a strain on the relations between group members. In Homans' terms activity can have a negative effect on friendliness. Therefore, we will make one modification of Homans' theory. This combined Homans-Bales theory is diagramed in Figure 2, in which the broken line symbolizes a negative effect.

We have no a priori reason to suppose that the relations are linear, but it is convenient to suppose that they are, and linear relationships can be treated as a first approximation to more complex relationships. The theory can be expressed as follows:

$$x_1 = \qquad\quad + a_{12}x_2 + a_{13}x_3 + b_1$$
$$x_2 = a_{21}x_1 \qquad\quad - a_{23}x_3 + b_2$$
$$x_3 = a_{31}x_1 + a_{32}x_2 \qquad\quad + b_3$$

Note that the model is static rather than dynamic. Time, or more particularly change over time, is not part of the model. It is obvious that

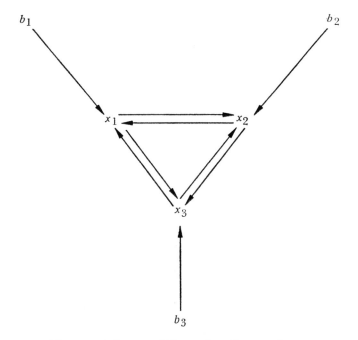

Figure 1. A diagram of Homans' small-group theory.

most sociological theories are of this sort. We theorize about what we think are stable configurations. Since time is not a variable in the above theory, to test it we would sample groups we assume have reached some kind of equilibrium, so that time no longer mattered. It would be a mistake, for example, to sample newly formed groups, because although the level of psychological compatibility might be high, it might not yet have produced the appropriate level of friendliness, so that the true equilibrium relations would be obscured.

The direct postulated effect of $b_1$ on $x_1$ (of free time on rate of interaction) is positive, but we see in Figure 2 that there is a negative causal loop in the theory from $x_1$ to $x_3$ to $x_2$ and back to $x_1$. We may wish to find the net or total effect of $b_1$ on $x_1$ taking into account that a change in $b_1$ will also change $x_3$ and $x_2$ indirectly which also affect $x_1$.

It might seem that the total effect of $b_1$ on $x_1$ could be negative because of the negative loop. In this chapter we will show that the net effect of $b_1$ on $x_1$ must be positive, even though the theory contains no assumptions about the particular values of the coefficients in the equations. However, we will show that no inferences can be made about the sign of the total effect of $b_3$ on $x_3$. This is important because it means that an

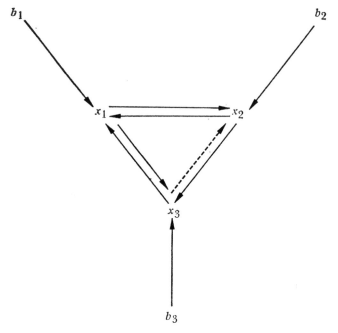

Figure 2. A diagram of the combined Homans-Bales theory. The broken line indicates a negative relationship.

observed positive, or negative, correlation between common interests $b_3$ and the rate of goal-directed activity $x_3$ is irrelevant to the truth or falsity of the theory as it is now stated.

To find the total effect we take the partial derivatives of the variables in the equations with respect to $b_1$. We will assume that $b_1$ is not a cause of $b_2$ and $b_3$, that is, $\partial b_2/\partial b_1 = \partial b_3/b_1 = 0$. The other partial derivatives are

$$\frac{\partial x_1}{\partial b_1} = \frac{a_{12}\partial x_2}{\partial b_1} + \frac{a_{13}\partial x_3}{\partial b_1 + 1}$$

$$\frac{\partial x_2}{\partial b_1} = \frac{a_{21}\partial x_1}{\partial b_1} - \frac{a_{23}\partial x_3}{\partial b_1}$$

$$\frac{\partial x_3}{\partial b_1} = \frac{a_{31}\partial x_1}{\partial b_1} + \frac{a_{32}\partial x_2}{\partial b_1}$$

These three equations can be solved for $\partial x_1/\partial b_1$. Using Cramer's rule (Hadley, 1961, pp. 166–167), we find

$$\frac{\partial x_1}{\partial b_1} = \frac{\begin{vmatrix} -1 & a_{12} & a_{13} \\ 0 & -1 & -a_{23} \\ 0 & a_{32} & -1 \end{vmatrix}}{\begin{vmatrix} -1 & a_{12} & a_{13} \\ a_{21} & -1 & -a_{23} \\ a_{31} & a_{32} & -1 \end{vmatrix}} = \frac{\begin{vmatrix} -1 & -a_{23} & a_{32} \end{vmatrix}}{\begin{vmatrix} -1 & a_{12} & a_{13} \\ a_{21} & -1 & -a_{23} \\ a_{31} & a_{32} & -1 \end{vmatrix}}$$

The numerator is negative, but the sign of $\partial x_1/\partial b_1$ is unknown because the sign of the denominator is unknown. However, as Samuelson (1965, pp. 257–283) has pointed out, there is an intimate relation between static models (as ours is at this point) and dynamic models. Indeterminate static models can be solved if the stability conditions for an underlying dynamic process are specified. Samuelson calls this strategy the correspondence principle. If the equilibria described by the static model were not stable, there would be little point in using the static model in the first place.

In this case it makes particular sense to put the model in dynamic terms because this is how Homans and Bales actually phrase their own theories. For the sake of illustration we have put the theories in static form.

We will put the model in the form of a set of linear differential equations with constant coefficients so that the static model describes all the equilibrium configurations of the variables.

$$x_1' = -x_1 + a_{12}x_2 + a_{13}x_3 + b_1$$
$$x_2' = a_{21}x_1 - x_2 - a_{23}x_3 + b_2$$
$$x_3' = a_{31}x_1 + a_{32}x_2 - x_3 + b_3$$

The main diagonal terms are negative because we assume that in the absence of system effects each variable would have equilibrium values for each combination of the variables that affect it.

By setting all derivatives equal to zero, as they are at equilibrium, we derive the static model. If the coefficients are restricted so that the equilibria are stable, we may be able to find the sign of $\partial x_1/\partial b_1$.

The stability condition for the above linear differential equations is that the eigenvalues of the matrix of coefficients have negative real parts (Sokolnikoff and Redheffer, 1966, p. 213). Since the eigenvalues come in conjugate pairs and the determinant of a matrix is also the product of its eigenvalues, the sign of the determinant of the matrix of coefficients is $(-1)^n$, where $n$ is the number of equations in a stable system.

In this three variable case, the denominator has a negative sign if the system is assumed to be stable, and consequently, $\partial x_1/\partial b_1$ is positive. The direct and the total or net relationships between $b_1$ and $x_1$ are both positive. It is a valid implication of the model that $b_1$ and $x_1$ are positively related among all possible stable equilibria.

The case is very different for the effect of $b_3$ on $x_3$. We will show that from this theory, containing assumptions only about the signs of relationships, no inferences can be made about the sign of the total effect of $b_3$ on $x_3$. The importance of this is that a positive correlation observed between $b_1$ and $x_1$ (between free time and rate of interaction) supports the theory, but that a positive or a negative correlation between $b_3$ and $x_3$ (between common interests and group goal-directed activity) does not prove or disprove the theory.

$$
\frac{\begin{vmatrix} -1 & a_{12} & 0 \\ a_{21} & -1 & 0 \\ a_{31} & a_{32} & -1 \end{vmatrix}}{\begin{vmatrix} -1 & a_{12} & a_{13} \\ a_{21} & -1 & -a_{23} \\ a_{31} & a_{32} & -1 \end{vmatrix}} = \frac{\begin{vmatrix} a_{12} & a_{21} & -1 \\ -1 & a_{12} & a_{13} \\ a_{21} & -1 & -a_{23} \\ a_{31} & a_{32} & -1 \end{vmatrix}}{} = \frac{\partial x_3}{\partial b_3}
$$

In order to know the sign of $\partial x_3/\partial b_3$ we must know the sign of $a_{12}a_{21} - 1$. However, given only that we assume that the static signed model is stable, there is no way in which we can infer whether $a_{12}a_{21}$ is greater than, less than, or equal to one. We can not infer *anything* about the sign of the total relationship between $x_3$ and $b_3$. Observations about the sign of the relationship between $b_1$ and $x_1$ do confirm or refute the theory, but observations about the sign of the stable relationships between $b_3$ and $x_3$ have no bearing on the truth of the theory as it is stated.

One can get an intuitive feel for the distinctiveness of $x_3$ and why it can have either a positive or a negative net relationship to its external cause $b_3$ while $x_1$ has a positive relation to its external cause. An increase in activity (through an increase in common interests) will reduce friendliness. This reduction in friendliness will be multiplied by its positive relation to interaction; reduced friendliness will lead to reduced interaction leading to reduced friendliness, and so on. This multiplied reduction in friendliness and interaction may be sufficiently large to cause a reduction in activity that is larger than the initial increase. The key idea is that activity is in a sort of negative relationship to variables that can reinforce each other and whose compounded reciprocal reduction can lead to a reduction in activity larger than the initial increase. Thus we may find (or may not find—we can not tell which) that the greater the common interests the less the goal-directed activity, and this would not be inconsistent with an assumption that the immediate effect of increased common interests is increased goal-directed activity.

Is this a plausible conclusion? Anything that would magnify the effect that Bales predicts would reduce the positive effect of common interests on the amount of goal-directed activity. Suppose, for instance, that competition within an academic department is intense. If two faculty members work on projects together, there is a tendency for both of them to want to be dominant. A history of these competitive struggles could lead to a situation in which only minor collaboration between those with distantly related interests occurs. On the other hand, to the extent that collaboration does not involve unpleasant struggles for domination, common interests and common action will be more strongly related.

It is clearly important to be able to distinguish a variable like $x_1$ whose relationship to its independent variable $b_1$ can be inferred from the theory (as shown above) from a variable like $x_3$, which has an indeterminate relationship to its independent variable. Can one distinguish these two types easily by a visual inspection of the graph of the theory? This chapter will give a partial answer.

## GENERAL CASE

Most sociological theories are static in that they describe relations between variables but not change over time. A simple static model is of the form $Ax + b = 0$, where $x$ is a column vector of $n$ variables in mutual interdependence, $b$ is a column vector of independent variables that are assumed to be unrelated to each other, and $A$ is a square matrix of coefficients giving the relations among the dependent variables.

Not only are many, or most, sociological theories static, but they are likely to contain assumptions only about the existence and sign of relationships; all that is likely to be specified by the sociologist about the matrix $A$ is whether the coefficient $a_{ij}$ is positive, negative, or zero. We call such a theory $A^*$. The matrix $A^*$ contains only the symbols $+$, $-$, and $0$. Any $A$ consistent with the constraints described by $A^*$ must be allowable because only the existence and sign of relationships has been postulated.

As a further constraint, a dynamic model underlying the static model is assumed to be in stable equilibrium. The static model is assumed to describe all the equilibrium configurations of the dynamic model. If the equilibria were assumed to be unstable, there would be little point in using a static model.

The dynamic model is $x' = Ax + b$. The static-equilibrium model is found by setting $x' = 0$. Any allowable $A$ must not only satisfy the constraints of $A^*$ but also must have stable equilibria.

One implication one may wish to draw from a theory of this sort is the sign of the total or net relationship between $x_i$ and one of its independent causes $b_i$, taking into account the effects of the system within which $x_i$ is inextricably embedded. The total effect is $\partial x_i / \partial b_i$. Let $A_i$ be the matrix of order $n - 1$ with the $i$th row and column deleted. It is easily shown that if the independent causes $b$ are unrelated to each other, $\partial x_i / \partial b_i = -|A_i|/|A|$.

If $A$ is a stable system, then $|A|$ has sign $(-1)^n$, as was shown in the last section. The sign of $\partial x_i / \partial b_i$, thus, depends on the sign of the numerator. In the illustration in the last section, we showed that for some variables the sign of $|A_i|$ can be inferred from $A^*$ and thus that the sign of $\partial x_i / \partial b_i$ can be inferred from the theory. These will be called nonkey variables. For other variables the sign of $|A_i|$ can not be inferred from $A^*$, and consequently, the sign of $\partial x_i / \partial b_i$ can not be inferred either. These will be called key variables. In the illustration above $x_1$ is a nonkey variable, and $x_3$ is a key variable.

Many theories include assumptions only about the signs of relationships between variables. The difficulty is that no inferences can be drawn about the sign of the relationship between the key variable and one of its causes because of the effect of the system in which the key variable is embedded. To put the problem in a more optimistic manner, inferences can be drawn about the sign of the total relationship between nonkey variables and their causes.

The problem in the remainder of this chapter is to devise an easy test to determine which variables are key and which are nonkey. From the illustration it appears that one feature of key variables might be that they are in a kind of negative relationship with variables that reinforce one another so that an initial increase in the key variable is overwhelmed by the negative reaction it provokes.

## RECOGNIZING KEY VARIABLES

The same assumptions will be made as before. Each variable has an equilibrium value toward which it would tend in the absence of system effects, so that $a_{ii} < 0$. The independent variables $b$ are all independent of one another.

One type of key variable is discussed in this section. Although there may well be other types, the kind described here seems likely to arise in practice. This type may exist when there are positive and negative causal loops in a theory.

A positive loop in a dynamic system $Ax + b = x'$ is any sequence of $m$ variables $x_1, x_2, \ldots, x_m$ such that $a_{12}a_{23} \ldots a_{m-1,m}a_{m1} > 0$. In a positive loop there are an even number of negative causal relationships. A common type of positive loop is one in which all links are positive; $x_1$ exerts a positive effect on $x_2$, $x_2$ has a positive effect on $x_3$, and so on, and variable $x_m$ has a positive effect on $x_1$. Positive loops can be a cause of instability because increases in any one variable are compounded by the loop. Negative loops are sequences of variables $x_1, x_2, \ldots, x_m$ such that $a_{12}a_{23} \ldots a_{m1} < 0$. Negative loops have an odd number of negative relationships.

Let $P^*$ be a positive loop of $m$ variables in which only the directions of relationships have been specified. We will show that some matrices $P$, consistent with $P^*$, have a determinant with sign $(-1)^m$ while other matrices $P$, consistent with $P^*$, have determinants with sign $-(-1)^m$.

A matrix $P$, consistent with $P^*$, has the following form:

$$P = \begin{pmatrix} -a_{11} & a_{12} & 0 & \ldots\ldots & 0 & 0 \\ 0 & -a_{22} & a_{23} & \ldots\ldots & 0 & 0 \\ \cdot & \cdot\cdot\cdot\cdot & \cdot & \ldots\ldots & \cdot\cdot\cdot\cdot & \cdot \\ \cdot & \cdot\cdot\cdot\cdot & \cdot & \ldots\ldots & \cdot\cdot\cdot\cdot & \cdot \\ 0 & 0 & 0 & & -a_{m-1,m-1} & a_{m-1,m} \\ a_{m1} & 0 & 0 & & 0 & -a_{mm} \end{pmatrix}$$

$$|P| = \Pi(-a_{ii}) + (-1)^{m-1} a_{m1}a_{12}a_{23} \ldots a_{m-1,m}$$
$$= (-1)^m [\Pi a_{ii} - a_{12}a_{23} \ldots a_{m-1,m}a_{m1}]$$

The second term within the brackets is positive because in a positive loop an even number of the coefficients are negative. The determinant $|P|$ can be either positive or negative depending on whether the product of the main-diagonal terms is greater than, or less than, the product of the off-diagonal elements. This corresponds, respectively, to situations in which $P$ is stable or unstable. If $\Pi a_{ii} > a_{12}a_{23}a_{34} \ldots a_{m1}$, then $P$ is stable and sign $|P| = (-1)^m$. If $\Pi a_{ii} < a_{12}a_{23} \ldots a_{m1}$, then sign $|P| = -(-1)^m$ and $P$ is unstable. Thus, one can not infer from $P^*$ whether $|P|$ is positive or negative. Moreover, we can easily show that for any system containing a positive loop plus other variables that are not part of any loop, the sign of $|A|$ cannot be determined.

On the other hand, a negative loop of $m$ elements always has a determinant of sign $(-1)^m$. The formula for the determinant of the negative loop is the same as the formula for the positive loop. However, this time the second term within the brackets contains an odd number of negative coefficients, the whole term within the brackets is always positive, and the sign of the determinant is always $(-1)^m$. It is easy to show that any system of $m$ variables containing a negative loop plus other variables not a part of any loop will always have the sign $(-1)^m$.

The positive loops consistent with a given $P^*$ have both positive and negative determinants. Suppose that a system $A_i^*$ consists of a positive loop plus variables not a part of any loop. The determinant $|A_i|$ can either be positive or negative. Let us add a new variable $x_i$ to produce the system $A^*$. Suppose that the coefficients can be chosen so that $A$ is stable while $|A_i|$ is positive and that other coefficients can be chosen so that $A$ is stable while $|A_i|$ is negative. Then, it is clear that the removal of $x_i$ from $A^*$ produces a system $A_i^*$ so that $|A_i|$ can be either positive or negative even if it is assumed that $A$ is stable. Since $\partial x_i / \partial b_i = -|A_i|/|A|$, $x_i$ is a key variable because $\partial x_i / \partial b_i$ can be either positive or negative in the stable system $A$.

In simpler language, if the addition of a variable to an unstable positive loop can produce a stable system, or equivalently, if removal of a variable from a stable system can leave an unstable positive loop, the variable is key. One way in which an otherwise unstable positive loop can be part of a stable system is through the presence of negative loops as in Figure 3.

The loop $P^*$ consisting of variables $x_1, x_2, \ldots, x_k, x_{k+1}, \ldots, x_m$ is a positive loop, and the loop $N^*$ consisting of the variables $x_1, \ldots, x_k, x_{m+1} \ldots, x_n$ is a negative loop.

Although it has not been proved to be generally true, in every case examined by the authors, for suitable choices of the coefficients, such a negative loop can change any loop consistent with the constraints de-

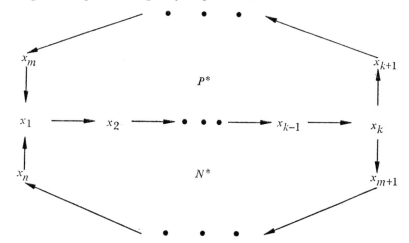

Figure 3. A stable system containing both a positive loop and a negative loop.

scribed by $P^*$ into a stable system. Thus, all the variables that are in the negative loop but not in the positive loop (variables $x_{m+1}$ through $x_n$) are key variables because their removal from $A^*$ can change a stable system into a system $A_i^*$ such that $|A_i|$ could be either positive or negative.

The diagrams in Figure 4 show some of the structures that have been examined by the authors. Solid lines are positive relations, and broken lines are negative relations. Key variables are circled. The reader can verify that all key variables are on negative loops that share variables with positive loops.

To illustrate how it was shown that these were key variables, let us look at structure $b$. We want to show that variable $x_4$ is a key variable. In order to do this we must show that the subsystem composed of variables $x_1$, $x_2$, and $x_3$ can have either a positive or a negative determinant whereas the system as a whole is stable.

The following simplifications make the job of identifying key variables easier. The one relationship shared by both loops, $a_{31}$ between $x_1$ and $x_3$, is arbitrarily given the value one. It is assumed that all main-diagonal elements are equal; $a_{ii} = -r$ for every $x_i$. The other two relationships in the positive loop, $a_{12}$ and $a_{23}$, are given the identical values of $a$, and the other relationships in the negative loop, $a_{43}$ and $a_{14}$, are given the values $b$ and $-b$.

If there are values of $a$, $b$, and $r$ such that $|A_4|$, the determinant of the system without $x_4$, is positive while $A$ is stable (for example, all eigenvalues of $A$ have negative real parts, and consequently, $|A|$ is positive), then $\partial x_4/\partial b_4 = -|A_4|/|A|$ can be negative while $A$ is stable.

CONDITION 1:

$$A_4 = \begin{vmatrix} -r & a & 0 \\ 0 & -r & a \\ 1 & 0 & -r \end{vmatrix} > 0$$

An expansion of this determinant shows that this condition is $a^2 > r^3$.

CONDITION 2: $|A - \lambda I| = 0$ implies that the real part of $\lambda$ is negative. The characteristic equation is

$$(r + \lambda)^4 - a^2(r + \lambda) + b^2(r + \lambda) = 0.$$

We must show that it is possible for all four solutions to this characteristic equation to have negative real parts for some choice of $a$, $b$, and $r$ while condition 1 is not contradicted.

The first root of the characteristic equation is simply $-r$, and since $r$ is positive, $\lambda_1$ clearly has a negative real part no matter what particular values are chosen for $a$, $b$, and $r$

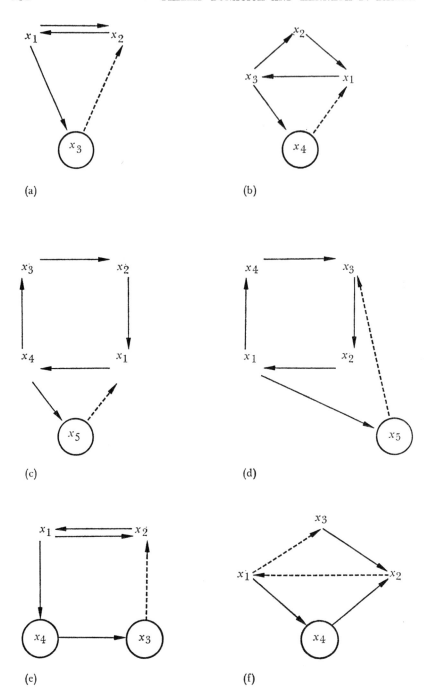

Figure 4. Causal structures containing key variables.

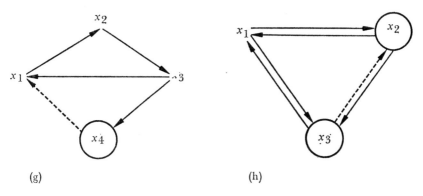

(g)                                    (h)

FIG. 4. (*Continued*)

$$\lambda_2 = (a^2 - b^2)^{1/3} - r.$$

Let $a^2 > b^2$. Then, if $\lambda_2$ is to be negative, $a^2 < r^3 + b^2$.

$$\lambda_3 = \frac{-(a^2 - b^2)^{1/3}}{2} - r + i\sqrt{3}\,\frac{(a^2 - b^2)^{1/3}}{2}$$

$$\lambda_4 = \frac{-(a^2 - b^2)^{1/3}}{2} - r - i\sqrt{3}\,\frac{(a^2 - b^2)^{1/3}}{2}$$

$\lambda_3$ and $\lambda_4$ always have negative real parts.

Thus, the real parts of the eigenvalues of $A$ are negative when $b^2 < a^2 < r^3 + b^2$. The determinant $|A_4|$ is positive when $r^3 < a^2$. It is easily seen that these two conditions do not contradict one another. Therefore, it is possible for $\partial x_4/\partial b_4$ to be negative when $A$ is stable. On the other hand, $\partial x_4/\partial b_4$ is positive if $a^2 < r^3$, and this does not contradict condition 2. Therefore, $x_4$ is key.

## RECOGNIZING NONKEY VARIABLES

In this section some types of nonkey variables will be described. If a variable is not any of these types, the theorist will have to carefully examine the individual case.

First, it is easy to show that if $A^*$ contains no loops at all, then every variable is nonkey. If there are no loops, then $A_i$, the structure in which $x_i$ has been removed, also has no loops. The matrix $A_i$ can then be arranged in the form of a triangular matrix in which all the main-diagonal elements are negative. $|A_i|$ is the product of these main diagonal elements and therefore sign $|A_i| = (-1)^{n-1}$. This is important because many theories contain no loops and so there are none of the ambiguities of the type described here. However, one point of this paper is that such ambiguities do not always exist even when a theory contains loops.

If there is just one positive loop plus other variables that do not belong to any loop, $A$ can be put in the form of a modified triangular matrix with a square matrix in its middle containing the coefficients between the variables in the positive loop. The determinant $|A|$ equals the product of the main diagonal elements times the determinant of the square matrix. The removal of any variable $x_i$ not in the loop will produce $|A_i| = |A|/(-a_{ii})$. Since sign $|A| = (-1)^n$, sign $|A_i| = (-1)^{n-1}$, and $x_i$ is not a key variable. If the variable is in the positive loop, its removal will create a system with no loops for which sign $|A_i| = (-1)^{n-1}$, as was shown above.

Finally, let us examine the type of structure, discussed in the last section, in which there were interacting positive and negative loops. It was shown that variables that were in the negative loop but not in the positive loop were key variables. Now we will show that all the other variables, the variables in the positive loop, are nonkey. The removal of any of the variables $x_i$ from the structure $A^*$ leaves a structure $A_i^*$ in which there is either a negative loop plus other variables not a part of any loop or no loops at all. In the former case we showed previously that sign $|A_i| = (-1)^{n-1}$ for all $A_i$ consistent with $A_i^*$. In the latter case we have already shown that a structure of $n-1$ variables with no loops will have a determinant of sign $(-1)^{n-1}$.

A few types of key and nonkey variables for which there were general rules have been discussed in this section and in the last section. There will be situations not covered by these general rules for locating key and nonkey variables. They can be examined individually.

## IMPLICATIONS

The problem of drawing testable implications from theories that contain assumptions only about the signs of relationships has long plagued sociologists because we are often able only to make these weak assumptions. In this chapter a logical problem with drawing implications from these types of theories is described. One may not be able to infer the net relationship between an independent variable and a variable embedded in a system of variables because of the effects of the system; the net relationship, including system effects, and the direct or postulated relationships may not agree in sign.

The most important aspect of the paper is not this general point but rather the exact description of some of the types of variables whose relationships to other variables cannot be inferred, and the exact description of some types of variables whose relationships to other variables can be inferred. The types are based on the variable's relation to causal loops in the theory. This should be of value to the theorist faced with causal loops.

This chapter, however, analyzes only one important type of problem in one type of model. Other problems remain. For example, how could self-generating variables that are unstable in the absence of system effects be included? How would a relaxation of the assumption that the independent variables $b$ are independent of each other affect the conclusions? Most importantly, when can one draw implications about the relationship between independent variable $b_i$ and system variable $x_j$ from $A^*$ where no direct relationship between $b_i$ and $x_j$ is postulated? All these questions and other modifications remain to be examined.

## REFERENCES

BALES, R.
  1950  *Interaction Process Analysis.* Reading, Mass.: Addison-Wesley.
HADLEY, G.
  1961  *Linear Algebra.* Reading, Mass.: Addison-Wesley.
HOMANS, G. C.
  1950  *The Human Group.* New York: Harcourt, Brace and World.
SAMUELSON, P. A.
  1965  *Foundations of Economic Analysis.* New York: Atheneum.
SOKOLNIKOFF, L. S. AND REDHEFFER, R. M.
  1966  *Mathematics of Physics and Modern Engineering.* New York: McGraw-Hill.

# 𝕏 9 𝕏

# COLEMAN'S PROCESS APPROACH

*Martin Jaeckel*

UNIVERSITY OF PITTSBURGH

*I am grateful to Thomas Fararo for introducing me to the topic and for his guidance throughout.*

This chapter deals with a number of social-process models developed and presented by James Coleman in *Introduction to Mathematical Sociology* (1964a). However, it is intended neither as a direct general summary of these models, nor as a comprehensive introduction to them. Its purpose is to review the models in generic terms, that is, to present and inspect them as a family or type and to discuss briefly what appear to be their major characteristics and functions. An important aim is to arrive at some assessment, however limited, of their nature, relevance, and scope.

## SUBSTANTIVE BACKGROUND

The kind of applied problem that has led to the development of the models to be discussed is perhaps best represented by a study conducted by Coleman, Katz, and Menzel (1957) on variations in the rates at which certain categories of medical practitioners adopted the use of a new drug. As Coleman (1964a, pp. 43f) describes it:

> The general problem concerned the process of the adoption of a new drug by doctors in four midwestern communities. One variable which was found to play a very important part in the time at which the doctor introduced the drug was his integration or isolation in the local medical community, as measured by the number of times other doctors named him as a social friend or as a frequent fellow-discussant of medical cases. Those doctors who were highly integrated with their colleagues adopted the drug much more quickly—on the average, about four months sooner—than their socially or medically isolated fellows.

This finding may in itself seem fairly obvious, but the investigators found themselves faced with alternative hypotheses that would explain it. Coleman (1964a, p. 44) says:

> Two alternative hypotheses appeared reasonable in explanation of the difference: (a) The integrated doctors were different kinds of doctors on the whole, doctors who were more up-to-date and quicker to pick up new things. That is, the same traits which made them integrated made them quick to use new drugs. (b) The integrated doctors were in a social position to learn about the drug and be persuaded to use it quickly, while the isolated doctors, out of contact with their fellows, had to depend upon advertising and the drug salesman to be persuaded to use the drug.

In order to decide between the two hypotheses, the investigators proceeded to inspect the cumulative distribution curves representing the gradual adoption of the drug by the separate subsets of doctors and to match the form of each of these curves against that theoretically expected on the basis of certain assumptions concerning the nature of the diffusion process at work. For the socially integrated doctors, the rate of adoption was postulated to be proportional to the number already having adopted the drug *and* to the number who as yet had not. This corresponds to the *logistic* version of the process of population growth. For the socially isolated doctors, diffusion of the drug was postulated

to proceed from a *constant source* independent of the number already
having adopted the drug and, hence, at a rate proportional only to the
number who as yet had not. The researchers reasoned as follows (Coleman, 1964a, p. 44):

> If hypothesis (a) were true, and the difference in introduction
> were due to individual differences, then the process of diffu-
> sion would be much the same for the isolated and integrated
> doctors, and the resulting shapes of the cumulative curves
> of introduction should be roughly the same, differing only in
> the size of [an individual parameter $k$] . . . . If, however,
> hypothesis (b) were true, then the very process of introduc-
> tion should be different: the integrated doctors should be
> persuaded to use the drug by their colleagues who have al-
> ready come to use it—a diffusion process in accordance with
> the logistic law; the isolated, in contrast, should be persuaded
> by the drug salesman and advertising, in accordance with
> the constant-source law [of diffusion].

It turned out that the cumulative distribution obtained for the integrated doctors fit the logistic growth curve reasonably well, as did
the isolates' cumulative adoption curve fit that for constant-source
diffusion (Coleman, 1964a, pp. 44f). The individual-qualities hypothesis
was, hence, rejected, and the alternative hypothesis, "which postulated
social location rather than individual differences as the cause of the
difference in drug introduction between integrated and isolated doctors"
(Coleman, 1964a, p. 44), was considered confirmed.

Our reason for dwelling on this particular research effort is that
it incorporates a number of features that are representative for the
models Coleman subsequently introduced and developed.[1] To begin,
interest is focused on the rate at which members of a group reach a
certain state and on the composition of this rate. Furthermore, the
models applied are standard and well-known forms of processes of
diffusion (or population growth). For the process of interest, the rate
of diffusion is set in relation both to the number of members not yet,
and to the number of those already, reached. These formal assumptions
correspond to the exhaustion of the available population and to the
effects of social contact that were to be studied. But it is the incorporation of precisely these characteristics—exhaustion and contagion—on

---

[1] The fact that the equations used in this study are algebraic, and the construction of processes, therefore, deterministic rather than stochastic, is the main
reason why this research is not included in the main set of models presented by
Coleman and to be discussed in this chapter. See the section below on the stochastic-
process assumption.

which Coleman's models are largely built. It is in fact their combination that makes certain models particularly applicable to social phenomena, Coleman maintains, because it includes "two elements which are crucial in social phenomena: nonindependence of actions and limited populations" (Coleman, 1964a, p. 308). And finally, the above example demonstrates the simultaneous use of several models for a comparison and a general identification of process structures and their consequences.

The more sophisticated versions of diffusion or population-growth processes are stochastic in nature, that is, they are built on probabilistic postulates and equations, and it is these that Coleman has adapted to sociological inquiry. He has not only applied them, but as is often the case with substantive applications of formal constructs, he has developed them further as well. The direction this work has taken can perhaps be indicated by means of another example: the application of one of Coleman's models to the problem of cleavage in union elections in small shops (Coleman, 1966). The phenomenon of interest was the observation—made on a large number of records of elections in a printers' union—that the within-shop distribution of votes cast for alternative candidates did not vary randomly about the overall average proportion for the winner. Far too many groups instead displayed vote proportions at one of the extremes (Coleman, 1966, p. 169). Since the particular union concerned was known to have been operating under an internal two-party system for a considerable time, the competition between the two parties could be assumed to underlie the observed polarization. But did such knowledge suffice as an explanation of the particular form the distribution of the various groups had taken over vote frequencies for the winner? And, more generally, how was one to account for how such distributions came about and, furthermore, for the fact that the phenomenon was more marked in smaller shops? Presumably it is questions such as these that led to a focusing on the nature of the influence processes at work as the general problem, and it is to this question that Coleman applies the formalizing approach.

In the diffusion and population-growth processes mentioned above, the alternative to the state of interest is usually some residually defined state such as nonexistence or unaffectedness. If one relates the characteristics boundedness of the population and contagion to modes of social organization, however, both the total group situation and the influences leading to individual transitions from one state to the other gain in interest. If one furthermore applies such conceptualization, as does Coleman, to a situation of political competition, then the resulting model will include the possibility of transitions into, and not only from, the state (or states) alternative to the primary state of interest.

Since in the particular case at hand the voting was limited to the choice
between candidates of two parties, the normal two-state model of diffusion with exhaustion and contagion could be applied. The further assumptions were: (1) that individual voters had a certain given tendency
toward favoring the candidate of each of the two parties and (2) that
the voting behavior of each member was subject to influence (of an
as yet undetermined kind) by the shop members taking the opposite
stand. The formal statement corresponding to this conceptualization
included as distinctive postulates: (1) the definition of the process as a
stochastic one, that is, the formulation of action tendencies in terms of
probabilities, (2) the partitioning of the rate expressing the basic probability of an individual's shifting his vote into two components, one
expressing his intrinsic preference, the other the effects of social influence
or contagion, and (3) transition probabilities defined for change-overs
in both directions between the two alternative states, that is, each party
could both gain and lose adherents in a shop at a certain probabilistic
rate. (This feature of including losses as well as gains was, in a general
way, already preformed in the birth-and-death process models of population growth.)

   With this construction of the voting and influence process, Coleman was able to generate distributions of group-specific proportions
roughly approximating those observed, and fitting them particularly
well for the smaller shops.

   As for the nature of the influence mechanism assumed to be
operating, Coleman broaches the subject under the heading of "Reward
Structures and the Allocation of Effort" (Coleman, 1966, pp. 159–173).
He develops a framework of assumptions concerning the mutually
supportive structure of a certain type of group activity and the concomitant encouragement of such an activity in individuals by the other
group members already engaged in it. By relating rewarders and potential performers via the common activity of interest, he then arrives at
positive effects, upon the transition tendencies towards an activity, of
the number of members already engaged in it (1966, p. 160). Besides
applying this framework to the political situation under discussion,
Coleman also generalizes the consideration of reward structures to
include the case when similarity of activities between group members
means competition between them and, hence, mutual inducement
("punishments") to shift to the alternate one(s). As we shall see in the
section "An Overview of the Structural Variants," Coleman again
utilizes several models to study the distributions over separate activities
resulting from such processes and to identify the general character of
the structures governing them.

## BASIC FORMAL ASSUMPTIONS

After the above brief sketch of the kind of substantive problems involved in the development of Coleman's models, we now turn to an abstract characterization of the general approach embodied in the models. This characterization will take the form of a discussion of the overall formal assumptions that define the models as a family or type. The delimiting assumptions are given with the conceptualization of the processes in question as continuous-time, discrete-state and stochastic processes of the Markov type. We shall consider these assumptions in turn and shall present them in terms of their alternatives, that is, in terms of the decisions involved in conceptualizing the processes in the manner indicated.

### Continuous-Time

The continuous-time assumption asserts that, for the duration of the process, states are defined at each instant of time and that transitions can occur at any particular instant. Once it has been explicitly formulated, this assumption seems rather obvious and generally valid. To conceptualize social processes as occurring in continuous time agrees well with our intuitive conceptions of them. We naturally think of social processes (modernization, for example) as occurring continually, that is, in the form of ongoing changes in the properties of individuals and in the relations among individuals. Whether continuous occurrences are intrinsic to social processes or not, the point to be emphasized is that to think of the constituent changes as occurring at arbitrary times is the reasonable assumption. There is no a priori reason for excluding any particular time points from those at which changes occur. The alternative assumption that the changes in question occur at fixed discrete points in time would seem to hold for social phenomena only under special conditions, in particular under synthetic regularizing conditions such as those of an experiment.

The collection of data, it is true, is mostly conducted not continuously but at separate time points, and this necessarily imparts a discrete-time form to what ordinarily exists in the way of indicators of the phenomena of interest. But it seems questionable whether such discrete-time observations can be considered representative for the phenomena and the relationships they purport to depict. Aggregate cross-sectional or over-time data may be satisfactory for some purposes, and some of the problems involved can be dealt with by increasing the number of observations or the fineness of their spacing. But when it comes to the principal conceptualization of processes in social reality, an all too close identification of the processes in question with what discrete-time observational procedures yield displays obvious weaknesses. The issue, then, is whether or not the extant paucity and limitations in the quality of observations should be allowed to induce corresponding primary restrictions on the general theoretical conceptualization of what is actually going on. What Coleman suggests is the converse—that the continuous-time conceptualization of social processes be taken as the general conceptual framework and that cross-sectional survey and discrete-time panel data be treated as variants within this comprehensive framework. The conceptual unification envisioned by Coleman constitutes one of his goals in developing the models under discussion. As Coleman (1964a, p. 132) says:

> One of the primary aims in developing this continuous-time . . . model has been the desire to tie together the inferences about relationships which we make from cross-sectional data with the similar inferences we make from over-time data. The resulting model as presented . . . allows just such a tying-together: it is conceived in terms of processes operating over time, but it can equally mirror the states of aggregate equilibrium which our cross-sectional studies describe. Such a linkage is an important one, because all our analysis of "effects" of variables upon one another should ultimately be referable to the same theory about the processes involved, whether the data are cross-sectional or over-time.

### Stochastic

As was the case with the continuous-time assumption, so also the stochastic assumption. The assumption that social processes "develop in time according to probabilistic laws" (Bartholomew, 1967, p. 1; see also, Fararo, 1969a) seems a fairly natural one to make. It appears intuitively reasonable to think of the individual behaviors of which these processes consist as not strictly determined in any single case and, yet, as corresponding, on the average, to the social and environmental conditions under which they take place. And apart from the intuitive plausibility of the stochastic assumption, there appear to be advantages intrinsic to stochastic models which make them theoretically preferable to their deterministic counterparts. Conceiving of such processes as developing in the form of a flow of probability distributions through time enlarges the range of what the models can handle. The stochastic assumption implies that variability is itself conceptually included in the model and not just added as an extrinsic error term to an equation the primary structure of which has already been determined. Since stochastic models are defined in terms of probability distributions over system states, they generate such distributions as predictions, which is more than just the single expected values that deterministic models are able to generate. This surplus means an increase both in explanatory relevance and in testability. Thus, more is asserted about the form of the phenomena, and the projected distributions themselves indicate a way of testing the model.

Of course deterministic models generally possess the advantage that they employ simpler mathematics and, hence, are more readily solved. Simplified deterministic versions are often used as approximations by means of which to arrive at solutions for stochastic models, especially if not more than the expected values is desired. Coleman (1964a, pp. 527f) in fact recommends using them for this purpose. But again, the levels should be distinguished: there is no reason why the mathematical procedures usefully employed in gaining inferences and in generating predictions should also determine the principal conceptualization of the phenomena. It could be clearer and, in the long run, less misleading to conceptualize a social-process model in stochastic terms if that seems generally appropriate, to carry its development as far as possible under that assumption, and only then to turn to deterministic simplifications, if they promise enlightenment not to be gained otherwise.

### Discrete-State

The discrete-state assumption asserts that the variable in question is represented in such a manner that there is, in principle, only a finite number of values that can be assigned to it (usually integers). Compared with the previous two assumptions, which are in part programmatic in character, Coleman's reasons for the discrete-state assumption appear to be relatively pragmatic. His major argument for concentrating on a special type of discrete-state variable, namely, the frequency of group members in alternative states at a given time, is that much, if not most, sociological data comes either in the form of counts of numbers of individuals possessing or satisfying some qualitative attribute or in the form of aggregate measures based on such counts. This argument is presumably informed by an assessment of the state of sociology as a discipline that for the most part has not yet determined its basic concepts, that is, concepts that satisfy both the criterion of theoretical relevance and the classical criteria for (cardinal fundamental) measurement.[2]

[2] It is perhaps an open question whether the search for basic concepts should necessarily be oriented to a type comparable to those denoting elementary properties in the physical sciences. Relational concepts, such as the division of labor, may turn out to be more useful.

The major strategy Coleman pursues to arrive at some form of quantitative measurement in spite of the general dearth of adequately measurable concepts is an indirect one. It consists of two steps: first, the identification of individuals on dichotomous qualitative attributes (for example, holding some specified political preference, or not) and, second, the summing up, for the group, of the number of individuals that are in one of the alternative states at a given time. It is this super-imposition of a counting process upon an essentially nominal primary classification of individuals that yields the discrete states and the equivalence classes of the correspondingly defined variable (the number of group members in the alternative state of interest at a given time). Whatever may have been gained by this procedure, the label discrete-state for process models built on this kind of measurement is clearly a wide one, since the variables to which it refers are of a specially constructed type, the magnitude dimension of which is not intrinsically social in character.

## Markov

The final major assumption defining Coleman's process models is the Markov assumption, that is, the assumption that the probability of a system's being in a certain state at a given time depends only on the system's state at the previous time and the corresponding transition probability. Data concerning states of the system at any earlier time are irrelevant in the sense that they cannot alter the probability distributions for the states of the system from the given time onward. In other words, knowledge of the present state of a system and of the transition probabilities suffices to determine its future development (Coleman, 1964a, p. 23, footnote 21).

The notion that a system "has no memory" in the sense that its past enters into its future development only via the form the present state displays may not always correspond to our intuitions of what individuals and social systems generally are like. For the occupational mobility of individuals and of families, for example, this condition seems very unlikely (Coleman, 1964a, p. 460). But the advantage of the Markov assumption lies in the simplicity it introduces into the handling of over-time transition probabilities.[3] In particular, it is a very convenient tool for projecting a system's development forward over time and for arriving at predictions for some future point in time, predictions

---

[3] Technically, the Markov assumption implies that transitions in nonoverlapping time intervals are statistically independent, which conveniently allows one to multiply corresponding probabilities (Feller, 1949, p. 415).

which can then be examined. It is presumably for such reasons that Coleman makes use of the Markov assumption, but he is quick to point out that it would be one of the first assumptions that continuous observation would allow us to test (Coleman, 1964a, p. 133). For the purpose of designing initial base-line models which can then be modified, however, he is willing to begin with this assumption.

## SETTING UP AND APPLYING A MODEL

The previous section was intended to serve as an introduction to the general character of Coleman's models and the nature of the underlying approach. In this section the basic procedure and the operations involved in setting up such models will be explicated and described. The voting and influence process discussed above will continue to serve as our example. It is selected as representative of the structural type to which it belongs, namely, the general birth-and-death class. Our presentation will not extend to a direct demonstration of the operations and techniques involved in analytically developing and in applying such a model, but it will instead concentrate on the logic of the general procedure. The major stages in the sequence of steps to be explicated are formulating the assumptions of the model, deducing consequences to obtain predictions, and testing it against data.

### Formulating Assumptions

Since stating the postulates not only defines a model but also largely determines the substantive conceptualization of the process, this step is of crucial significance. It, in effect, constitutes the last stage of defining the phenomenon of interest, or at least the version to be tried out. This obviously includes the definition and identification of the system and its elements and of both their states. As has already been indicated above, the voting model in question refers to bounded social groups (union shops) and their members. It posits two alternative states (political allegiances) for individuals, and defines as the state of a system the aggregate number of individuals in the state of interest. Its representation postulates consist of statements to that effect.

The transition postulates define the possibilities of change. These are conceptualized in terms of probabilities for individual transitions from one alternative state to the other (and for corresponding transitions on the level of system states) in given small intervals of time. Transition probabilities are set equal to the product of an assumed transition rate and the length of the time interval within which it is conceived to be operating. Two distinctive features of the transitions in question together represent the form and the effects of social influence that Coleman is investigating. First, transitions are defined to be possible in both directions (between the two states for individuals and from a given system state), and it is this feature that places the voting model in the birth-and-death process class. The second main feature is the partitioning of individual transition rates into two components, one representing prior individual tendencies toward either party, the other representing social-influence effects, effects defined to be proportional to the number of group members found in the alternative state at the time. It is this last specification that circumscribes the source of the dynamics of interest. To otherwise simplify matters, Coleman assumes that the intrinsic individual rate components are homogeneous over all individuals and over time and even that they are constant and, therefore, independent of the system state prevailing at a given time. But, to relate transition rate components to the number of elements in the alternative state is to make them dependent on the state of the system at a given time and, thus, largely to delimit the character of the process.[4]

The conditions assumed to hold for individual transitions in this process can be visualized in Figure 1, with $A$ and $B$ denoting alternative individual states (partly allegiances), $\alpha$ and $\beta$ intrinsic tendencies toward each of these states, and $\gamma$ the influence effect attributable to each group member in the opposite camp; $N$ denotes the (limited) size of the group, $i$ (or $N - i$) the number of group members favoring party $A$ or $B$ and $i$ (or $N - i$)$\gamma$ their cumulative effect.

Since system states are defined in terms of the number of elements in a basic individual state, they are obviously affected by individual transitions. Such individual transitions are, however, to be conceived of as occurring one at a time. This is one of the consequences of the continuous-time assumption, which allows one to conceptually reduce the

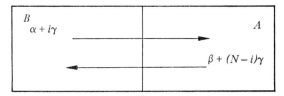

Figure 1. Transition diagram for an individual (voting model with two-way contagion, Coleman, 1964a, p. 343).

[4] It is this dependency specification together with the limitation on the population and the just-mentioned simplifying restrictions that distinguish this particular process from the general birth-and-death paradigm, which leaves the (group) rates unspecified.

time interval in which such transitions occur to the infinitesimal proportions necessary to limit such occurrences to at most one. Hence, transitions from a given system state $E_i$ are restricted to those to the adjacent states $E_{i+1}$ or $E_{i-1}$, respectively, at any one time. The rates for transitions between adjacent system states are obtained by summing up the rates for the individuals for which transitions could occur, that is, by multiplying the individual transition rate from state $A$ to $B$ (or $B$ to $A$) by the number of individuals in state $A$ or $B$. The resulting compound transition rates between system states are visualized in Figure 2, for which the same general notation applies as for Figure 1. The system states are represented by numbered boxes, and outside coefficients (to the left) denote the number of individuals available (in a source state) to which the individual transition rates (the inside components on the right of an expression) apply.

To give an example: "when the group is in state 2, this means that two persons are . . . [in state $A$], each of them characterized by a transition rate of $B$ to $\alpha + (N - 2)\gamma$. Thus the group transition rate to state 1 is simply the sum of these two (for, if either transition occurred, the group would move into state 1), i.e., $2[\alpha + (N - 2)\gamma]$" (Coleman, 1966, pp. 162f).

## Deducing Consequences

Once the assumptions that define the structure of the process have been formulated, the task becomes that of deducing the consequences, that is, the state of affairs the structure generates over time. As was indicated above, the transition probabilities are conceived of as the products of assumed transition rates operating over time. From these transition probabilities and the state(s) the system is in at given initial times, a general expression can, in principle, be derived for the states the system can be expected to be in at arbitrary later times. Both the initial conditions and the predictions are themselves stated as probabilities that the system is in the various states, that is as probability distributions over these states at a given time, denoted $P(E_i)$ at time $t$ or $P_i(t)$. The goal

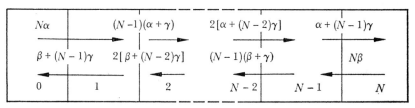

Figure 2. Transition diagram for a group (voting model with two-way contagion, Coleman, 1964a, p. 344).

then is to deduce a general expression for $P_i(t)$ or, in other words, the form this probability distribution takes on as it flows through time in terms of the parameters involved in the assumed transition rates. If this goal is achieved, then the general expression for the form of the process can be used to generate predictions for the distributions $P_i(t)$ in concrete cases, predictions which can then be tested against the form observed distributions actually show.

The indicated analytical task itself consists of two subtasks.

First, one must derive expressions for the limiting, or instantaneous, rates of change (at time $t$) in the probability of the system's being in the various states $E_i$. This is done by working with the notion of an arbitrarily small interval of time $\Delta t$ within which changes in the probabilities $P_i(t)$ occur and by formulating the relationship expressed by the difference quotient $[P_i(t + \Delta t) - P_i(t)]/\Delta t$ as $\Delta t$ goes to zero. The intuitive statement that corresponds to the resulting system of differential equations is that gains into, and losses from, a particular system state can be expected to occur from, and into, adjacent states at the transition rates initially specified and weighted by the probability of the system's being in the various source states from which transitions occur. Second, one solves these equations (that is, matching the expressed conditions) to obtain the desired general expression for the probability (distribution) that the system is in state $E_i$ at a time $t$.

In order to arrive at the desired general solution for the voting process in question, Coleman makes the simplifying assumption that the system has reached equilibrium when the vote is taken. Analytically, the condition of statistical equilibrium says that the probability (for one system or the expected proportion of a sample of identical systems) of being in each state remains the same.[5] In other words, at equilibrium the probability distribution $P_i(t)$ is stationary. Time can thus be disregarded and the restriction at time $t$ be dropped. The further derivation of the general expression for $p_i$ is based on the fact that at equilibrium the flow of transitions between adjacent system states must be equal in the two directions (Coleman, 1966, p. 163 and pp. 172f). This implies that the various probabilities for the separate system states can be expressed in terms of each other (and of the corresponding transition rates); and since their sum can be set equal to one, it is possible to solve for one of them ($p_0$) and then to obtain a general expression for $p_i$, namely,

---

[5] Formally, the equilibrium assumption states that the rate of change in the probability distribution $P_i(t)$ is zero. Its conceptual equivalent is the notion that the mechanism that generates the process drives the process into itself, that is, that the vector representing the probability distribution over system states is continually being regenerated.

$$p_i = \binom{N}{i} \frac{\prod_{j=0}^{i-1} (a + jc) \prod_{j=0}^{N-i-1} (1 - a + jc)}{\prod_{j=0}^{N-1} (1 + jc)}$$

with $a = \alpha/(\alpha + \beta)$ and $c = \gamma/(\alpha + \beta)$ (Coleman, 1964a, p. 345). The parameter $a$ represents the relative strength of the assumed intrinsic individual tendencies toward state $A$, the parameter $c$ the comparable effects of contagion or social influence.

## Testing

The manner in which such a model is applied to data will only be briefly explicated. Given our empirical voting process, the structure of which the model is assumed to properly represent, we can use the above-listed expression for the general form of the process to generate a theoretical prediction as to the probability distribution to be expected over the various states (at equilibrium). The primary identification between model and empirical process is arrived at partly by definition (the conceptualization of system states is formally identical for both) and partly on the basis of the plausibility of the key assumptions the model makes concerning transitions between states (that is, constant individual, and system-dependent "contagion," rate components). Conclusive identification between the model and the structure of the empirical process is arrived at by (relative) validation of these assumptions via a comparison between the form of the theoretically predicted probability distribution and that of the empirically observed distribution over the various states. Since the prediction is stated as a distribution of probabilities (that is, expected relative frequencies), the comparison occurs in terms of observed relative frequencies, and this implies observations must be replicated (by repetition either on the same system or over identical systems).

The actual distribution to be predicted is obtained by entering estimates for the basic parameters into the general equation above, estimates that are obtained from summary statistics for the set of sample data obtained on the observations. For the present model the equations relating the parameters $a$ and $c$ to the distribution of system states $i$ are

$$a = \frac{\Sigma i p_i}{N} \quad \text{and} \quad c = \frac{\sigma^2 - Na(1 - a)}{N^2 a(1 - a) - \sigma^2}$$

where $\sigma^2$ is the variance of $i$: $\sigma^2 = \Sigma i^2 p_i - (\Sigma i p_i)^2$ (Coleman, 1964a, p. 345). Thus, "$a$, which is simply the average proportion of persons in position $A$, and $c$, which is an estimate of the size of the contagion parameter $\gamma$, relative to $\alpha$ and $\beta$, can be estimated from the mean [$\bar{x}$] and variance [$s^2$], respectively, of the distribution of the groups" (Coleman, 1964a, p. 345). The goodness-of-fit between the correspondingly generated theoretical distribution and the distribution actually observed (that is, the differences between them) can then be tested according to standard statistical procedures (for example, the general chi-square or the cumulative Kolmogorov-Smirnov test) in order to decide whether the process observed should be considered to be of the kind initially assumed, or not.

As it turned out, the present model's predictions fit the union-election data fairly adequately and, thus, indicate that groups of that kind do in fact behave as if there were contagion or social influence of the sort assumed (Coleman, 1964a, pp. 347f). The fit was better, however, for the smaller groups than for the larger ones. Upon listing the values for the parameters $a$ (average proportion in the state of interest) and $c$ (relative size of the contagion parameter) for the various group sizes, Coleman noticed that the value of $c$ decreased steadily from group size two to group size seven and then remained roughly constant for sizes eight to eleven. Since the contagion parameter is proportional to the influence each group member exerts upon each other member, Coleman reasoned that perhaps its decrease (from group size two to seven) was a result of each person's influence decreasing per other person as the groups increased in size. He therefore tried multiplying $c$ by $N - 1$ to obtain a measure for the total influence exerted by each group member. He then found that the quantity $c(N - 1)$ remained roughly constant up to group size seven, beyond which there was a tendency for it to increase (Coleman, 1964a, p. 348). This then suggested that personal influence is perhaps relatively stable, or at least additive per other group member in undifferentiated small groups, and that at about size seven some kind of structural differentiation occurs that changes the influence pattern. This very tentative suggestion would have to be tested under various aspects and conditions for it to gain in precision and validity. The general point to be made, however, is that working with the conceptualization and the model indicated can lead to empirically based insights concerning the basic parameters and, thus, raise further questions concerning their relationships to each other and to other boundary conditions.

## OVERVIEW OF STRUCTURAL VARIANTS

After the explication just presented of the general method and the procedures followed in developing and applying a stochastic model, we

Table 1
## COLEMAN'S PROCESS MODELS: An Overview of the Structural Variants

### THE PURE-BIRTH PROCESSES

| NAME | TRANSITION RATE: $E_i \to E_{i+1}$ | TRANSITION DIAGRAM | DISTRIBUTION at $t$ |
|---|---|---|---|
| 1. POISSON | $\alpha$ | $0 \xrightarrow{\alpha} 1 \xrightarrow{\alpha} 2 \xrightarrow{\alpha} 3 \to$ | $P_i(t) = \dfrac{e^{-\alpha t}(\alpha t)^i}{i!}$ |
| 2. PURE BIRTH | $\alpha_i$ | $0 \xrightarrow{\alpha_0} 1 \xrightarrow{\alpha_1} 2 \xrightarrow{\alpha_2} 3 \to$ | compare Karlin, 1966, p. 179 |
| 3. YULE (Linear Birth) | $\alpha_i = i\alpha$ | $h \xrightarrow{h\alpha} h+1 \xrightarrow{(h+1)\alpha} h+2 \xrightarrow{(h+2)\alpha} h+3 \to$ | $P_i(t) = \binom{i-1}{i-h} e^{-h\alpha t}(1 - e^{-\alpha t})^{i-h} \quad (i = h, h+1 \cdots)$ ; $h$ is the initial population size, $\neq 0$ |
| 4. PURE BIRTH with EXHAUSTION | $\alpha_i = \alpha(N-i)$ | $0 \xrightarrow{N\alpha} 1 \xrightarrow{(N-1)\alpha} 2 \;\cdots\; N-1 \xrightarrow{\alpha} N$ | $P_i(t) = \binom{N}{i}(1 - e^{\alpha t})^i e^{-\alpha t(N-i)}$ |
| 5. PURE BIRTH with CONTAGION | $\alpha + i\beta$ | $0 \xrightarrow{\alpha} 1 \xrightarrow{\alpha+\beta} 2 \xrightarrow{\alpha+2\beta} 3 \to$ | $P_i(t) = \dfrac{\alpha(\alpha+\beta)\cdots(\alpha + (i-1)\beta)e^{-\alpha t}(1 - e^{\beta t})^i}{i!\beta^i}$ |
| 6. PURE BIRTH with CONTAGION (simplified) | $\beta_i = i\beta$ | $1 \xrightarrow{\beta} 2 \xrightarrow{2\beta} 3 \xrightarrow{3\beta} 4 \to$ | $P_i(t) = e^{-\beta t}(1 - e^{-\beta t})^{i-1}$ |
| 7. PURE BIRTH with CONTAGION and EXHAUSTION | $(N-i)(\alpha + i\beta)$ | $0 \xrightarrow{N(\alpha)} 1 \xrightarrow{(N-1)(\alpha+\beta)} 2 \xrightarrow{(N-i)(\alpha+i\beta)} i \xrightarrow{} i+1 \;\cdots\; N-1 \xrightarrow{\alpha+(N-1)\beta} N$ | compare Bailey, 1957, p. 41 |
| 8. PURE BIRTH with CONTAGION and EXHAUSTION (simplified) | $(N-i)(i\beta)$ | $1 \xrightarrow{(N-1)\beta} 2 \xrightarrow{(N-2)2\beta} 3 \xrightarrow{(N-i)i\beta} i \xrightarrow{} i+1 \;\cdots\; N-1 \xrightarrow{(N-1)\beta} N$ | compare Coleman, 1964a, p. 311 and Bailey, 1957, p. 43 for the equation for the *mean* |

## Table 2
## COLEMAN'S PROCESS MODELS: An Overview of the Structural Variants

### The BIRTH-and-DEATH PROCESSES

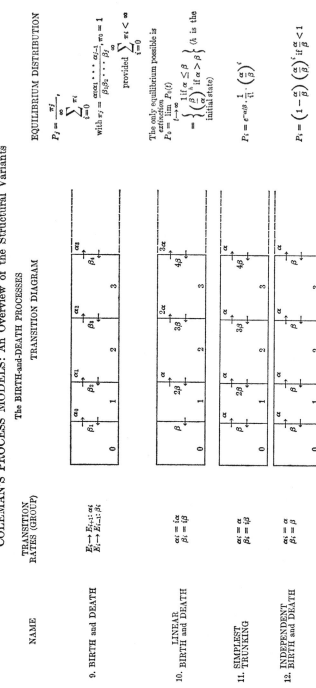

| NAME | TRANSITION RATES (GROUP) | TRANSITION DIAGRAM | EQUILIBRIUM DISTRIBUTION |
|---|---|---|---|
| 9. BIRTH and DEATH | $E_i \to E_{i+1}: \alpha_i$ <br> $E_i \to E_{i-1}: \beta_i$ | | $P_j = \dfrac{\pi_j}{\sum_{i=0}^{\infty} \pi_i}$, <br> with $\pi_j = \dfrac{\alpha_0 \alpha_1 \cdots \alpha_{i-1}}{\beta_1 \beta_2 \cdots \beta_j}$, $\pi_0 = 1$ <br> provided $\sum_{i=0}^{\infty} \pi_i < \infty$ |
| 10. LINEAR BIRTH and DEATH | $\alpha_i = i\alpha$ <br> $\beta_i = i\beta$ | | The only equilibrium possible is *extinction* <br> $P_0 = \lim_{t\to\infty} P_0(t)$ <br> $= \left\{ \begin{array}{l} 1 \text{ if } \alpha \leq \beta \\ \left(\frac{\beta}{\alpha}\right)^h \text{ if } \alpha > \beta \end{array} \right\}$ ($h$ is the initial state) |
| 11. SIMPLEST TRUNKING | $\alpha_i = \alpha$ <br> $\beta_i = i\beta$ | | $P_i = e^{-\alpha/\beta} \cdot \dfrac{1}{i!} \cdot \left(\dfrac{\alpha}{\beta}\right)^i$ |
| 12. INDEPENDENT BIRTH and DEATH | $\alpha_i = \alpha$ <br> $\beta_i = \beta$ | | $P_i = \left(1 - \dfrac{\alpha}{\beta}\right)\left(\dfrac{\alpha}{\beta}\right)^i$ if $\dfrac{\alpha}{\beta} < 1$ |

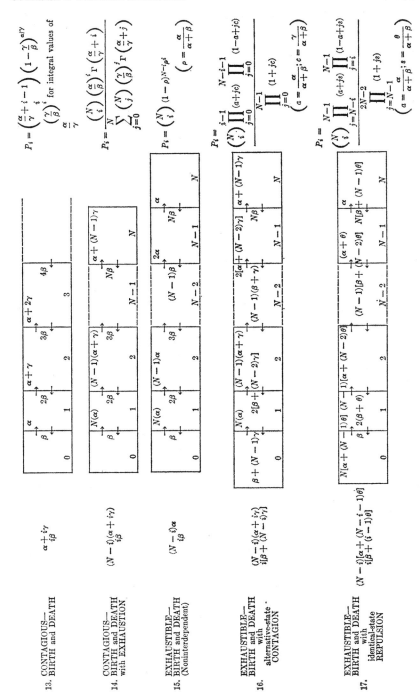

now turn to an overview of the models Coleman has constructed. The purpose of this section is to present a synopsis of the various models in terms of the way they are built, in order both to indicate what is characteristic for each of them within the general framework outlined in the first section and to show how they are related to each other. It appears there is an analytical sequence to the particularizing assumptions which define them. A summary presentation of these models in concise and partly visual form can, therefore, serve to reproduce this sequence for the reader. It can serve as a guide to the points at which the specifications from which the various models have been obtained have been introduced and can, thus, demonstrate to which general types these models belong and how the different subtypes are interrelated.

Tables 1 and 2 attempt to fulfill this task. They are meant to be read serially as well as horizontally. The models are presented in the sequence in which Coleman presents them and, hence, can perhaps serve both to reproduce his general demonstration of how such models are developed and to indicate somewhat the direction in which this work is leading. Apart from such synthesizing functions, however, a synopsis can also simply serve as a quick general orientation and as a basis for desired comparisons of the analytical features of the models.

## Organization of Tables

The processes fall into two main groups according to whether transitions occur in only one, or in both, directions from a given system state $E_i$. Table 1 presents the former, the pure-birth processes, and Table 2 the latter, the birth-and-death processes.

Not included in the tables are two models ("brand loyalty in consumer purchasing" (Coleman, 1964a, pp. 321ff) and "freely forming groups" (1964a, pp. 361ff)) which incorporate modifications that place them beyond the confines of these general structural types and, therewith, of this presentation of variants within them. The main assumption that is vitiated in their case is the limitation of instantaneous transitions to those to adjacent states only.

The processes are numbered continuously for easy reference. The upper parts of the tables (processes 1–3 and 9–10) do not present Coleman's specific models, but classic stochastic-process models by modification of which his models have been derived. They are included to indicate the general nature of the analytical relationships involved.

The notation is the same as that introduced for the transition diagrams above with the following modifications: in Table 1, $\beta$ denotes the contagion component of pure-birth transitions; in Table 2, $\beta$ denotes the constant individual component of loss transitions in birth-and-death processes; in Table 2, $\gamma$ denotes a positive contagion component in either direction; and in Table 2, $\theta$ denotes a negative one (repulsion, mutual punishment, see the explication below).

The synopsis proceeds as follows: Column 1 labels the particular process model in terms of its type and its differentiating assumption(s). Since system states are defined alike for all the models (that is, as numbers of individuals in an alternative state of interest), these defining and differentiating assumptions concern the transitions. (Process 16, the exhaustible birth-and-death process with alternative-state contagion, will be recognized as the abstract version of our voting-process example.)

Column 2 expresses the characteristic transition rates algebraically. It presents them in terms of their basic components, $\alpha$, $\beta$, $\gamma$, or $\theta$, the relationship(s) between these components, whether they are dependent on (states of) the system or not, and if so, how this relationship has been specified. In other words it constitutes a concise representation of the defining and differentiating assumptions and of the structural relationships implied in combining them. (To explicate our example, process 16, $(N - i)(\alpha + i\gamma)$ represents the system transition rate to $E_{i+1}$, the next higher system state in which one more person is in state $A$. $(N - i)$ indicates for how many individuals a shift to state $A$ is conceivable; namely, for those in state $B$, $(\alpha + i\gamma)$ is the individual transition rate into state $A$ and is composed of the intrinsic transition component towards $A$, $\alpha$, and the overall contagion component $i\gamma$, which represents the cumulative influence of the individuals in state $A$, numbering $i$. Similarly, $i[\beta + (N - i)\gamma]$ represents the system transition rate from $E_i$ to $E_{i-1}$.) The transition rates characteristic for the various structural types have been set equal to the unspecified rates ($\alpha_i$ or $\beta_i$) of the general pure-birth or birth-and-death processes in order to indicate that the former have been arrived at by restrictive specifications upon the latter.

Column 3 contains the transition diagrams for the various processes and thus constitutes an initial explication of what a model's assumptions together imply. Among other things, it indicates the lower and the upper limits (if any) of these processes. Its main function, however, is to demonstrate the relative size and composition of a model's total transition rates at various states as they vary in terms of their constant and their system-dependent components. (For the voting process, process 16, for example, the transition diagram indicates a structural symmetry for transitions from, and toward, both extremes, that is, states $E_0$ and $E_N$, a symmetry that is reflected in a certain similarity the structure of the equilibrium solution obtained displays with that of the binomial distribution. On the further implications of this observation, see below.) Taken together, columns 1, 2, and 3 in different ways present the structure of the various models and indicate what the models have in common and where they differ.

*Column 4* lists general solutions for the probability distribution predicted for a process at a time $t$ (for pure-birth type processes, which reach equilibrium only in case the number of unaffected elements is exhausted) or at equilibrium (for birth-and-death type processes). With birth-and-death type processes, however, equilibrium is not reached in all cases, nor does it always mean substantively the same thing for the system concerned; with the linear birth-and-death process, it implies extinction.

Some of these solutions can be recognized as identical or similar in form to certain well-known probability distributions; the simplest trunking model, process 11, for example, has a Poisson distribution as its equilibrium prediction. The implications can then be followed through in the further analysis, evaluation, and application of these models. (For an example, see below.)

## The Analytical Sequence

The further commentary will be restricted to a few brief remarks on the interrelatedness of the structural aspects.[6] The Poisson process (process 1) serves as the basic paradigm for defining and representing the transitions to an adjacent state. The pure-birth process (process 2) indicates the generalization obtainable if the restriction that the transition rate be constant is dropped. It is by means of specifications introduced on its undetermined transition rate $\alpha_i$ that the other pure birth process models are defined.

The Yule (linear-birth) process (process 3) supplies a classic example of how this rate can be linked to the state of the system (that is, the size of the birth rate depends upon the size of the population). The next two processes (the first of Coleman's models proper) introduce two important modifications—a limitation on the number of elements in a system, thus making the state space exhaustible, (process 4) and the introduction of the assumption that contagion between elements influences the transition rates (process 5).

In case the independent component is negligible compared to the ever-increasing effects of contagion, a simplified version of the pure-

---

[6] For general commentaries on these processes, the formulas for parameter estimates, and examples of applications the reader is referred to Chapters 10 and 11 of Coleman (1964a) and to Feller (1949), Feller (1968, Chapter 17), and Karlin (1966, Chapter 7).

birth process with contagion can be constructed by dropping the independent component (the $\alpha$ parameter). Since in the resulting model (process 6) the transition rate is based on nothing but contagion $i\beta$, it cannot begin in state $E_0$. In this model, moreover, another difficulty is encountered. Since the transition rate for the noncontagious Yule (linear-birth) process is identically constructed ($\alpha_i = i\alpha$), the algebraic properties of the probability distributions and the empirical form of the process cannot be used to decide between the two. The contagion assumption must stand on its own or be verified by other observations, for example, by sociometric observations on the existence of line of influence.

The last two entries in Table 1, processes 7 and 8, represent modifications of processes 5 and 6, respectively, and are obtained by introducing a limit on the population, and thereby, exhaustion of the state space. This feature is represented by the $(N - i)$ coefficient.

For the group of processes with two-way transitions (Table 2), the general birth-and-death process (process 9) serves as the paradigm, and the linear version (process 10) again demonstrates a simple, but classic, form of the dependence of transition rates on the states of the system. (It perhaps represents the form which we first conceive of for the growth of human populations, that is, births and deaths as simply being proportional to the size of the population, before other factors—for example, limits on the food supply, differentiation according to age and fertility cohorts, and the like—complicate the picture.)

The simplest trunking model (process 11) combines independence of the acquisition rate with system dependence of the loss rate and the independent birth-and-death process (process 12) independence (that is, constancy) of both rates, whereas the linear birth-and-death process above (process 10) combined system dependence of both. The natural complement to these three models to complete the classificatory pattern would seem to be a process that combines (linear) dependence of the acquisition with independence of the loss rate—except that it would not reach equilibrium.

As for the pure-birth processes, so also for the birth-and-death process models Coleman introduces the assumptions of contagion (process 13) and of exhaustion (process 15) and combinations of them (for example, process 14), the principal new feature being that contagion is possible both in one and in two directions. An example for one-way contagion is sociometric choices a person receives in a group, with observed popularity leading to further choices and other gains or losses simply proportional to the number of choices one could yet receive or has already received (see Coleman, 1964a, p. 332, table).

The final distinction Coleman makes is that between positive contagion between elements in alternative states (process 16) and negative contagion (mutual repulsion) between elements in identical states (process 17), which distinction he uses to study types of reward structures.

## Structural Comparisons: An Example

We shall now present Coleman's application of this distinction in the study of reward structures, as a partial parallel to the analytical uses to which these tables can be put. This application is a prime example of the kind of theoretical results that can follow from structural observations and between-model comparisons of the kind such tables facilitate.

As was pointed out above, the equilibrium distribution for the voting process (process 16) displays an algebraic structure analogous to that of the binomial distribution, the difference residing mainly with additional $jc$ terms that represent the effects $(i\gamma)$ of contagion. There is nothing surprising about the appearance of these terms since contagion between alternative states had been the distinctive assumption made for the voting-and-influence process. Nor is the "binomial" character of the rest of the expression surprising, if one reflects upon the further assumptions of the model (that is, exhaustion and intrinsic individual transition components not dependent upon the state of the system) and, furthermore, upon the fact that "intuitively they correspond, for a process continuous in time, to the 'independent trial' assumptions of the binomial" (Coleman, 1964a, p. 342). The previously listed noninterdependent birth-and-death process with exhaustion (process 15), which incorporates these other assumptions, in fact arrives at a binomial distribution in equilibrium. But, if the two processes differ by the contagion assumption in their basic structures and by corresponding contagion effect terms in the equilibrium solutions, what will be the difference in the forms of the distributions these solutions prescribe? What will such a difference imply? How will the effects of related structures compare?

It appears analytical questions such as these together with substantive questions concerning the forms of social influence led Coleman to the consideration of reward structures and their differential effects. The distribution he develops between activity structures with mutual reward and with mutual punishment is based on the type of within-group competition envisioned. If it is sub-groups that are competing for supporters, then influence is exerted to make converts. If, on the other hand, it is individuals who are competing for preferred activities or benefits, then competitors are discouraged; that is, in the two-state situation they are pushed toward the alternative state. Everybody in state or activity $A$, $i$ persons, is influenced by everybody else in that state, $i - 1$ persons, to make the transition to state $B$. If $\theta$ represents the corresponding unit of influence, then the group transition rate to state $E_{i-1}$, one less individual in state $A$ because he has shifted to $B$, can be expressed as $i[\beta + (i - 1)\theta]$ (process 17, column 2). And, conversely, the $N - i$ individuals in state $B$ are having influence exerted on them by each other $(N - i - 1)$ to shift to state $A$. Hence, the transition rate $E_i \rightarrow E_{i+1}$ equals $(N - i)[\alpha + (N - i - 1)\theta]$.

As for the differential effects of the two reward structures, Figures 3 and 4 (adapted from Coleman, 1964a, p. 358) indicate the forms of the equilibrium distributions that correspondingly defined influence processes reach (for groups of size five and an $a = \alpha/(\alpha + \beta)$ parameter of 0.6). These are plotted for positive contagion parameters $c = \gamma/(\alpha + \beta)$ and negative contagion parameters $s = \theta/(\alpha + \beta)$ of 0.4 and 1.6 each and are compared to the binomial distribution reached by the contagion-free exhaustive birth-and-death process (process 15) representing a collection of individuals independent of each other.

As the graphs indicate, the distributions obtained for the two types of influence processes diverge from the binomial distribution in opposite directions. Whereas positive alternative-state contagion leads to more frequent proportions of group members at either extreme, negative identical-state contagion (repulsion) leads to higher relative fre-

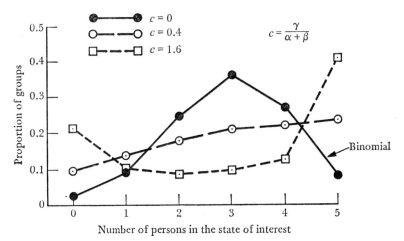

Figure 3. Equilibrium distribution of exhaustible birth-and-death processes with two-way contagion (for equations see Table 2). Distribution of groups under varying conditions of positive alternative-state contagion. (Adapted from Coleman, 1964a, p. 358.)

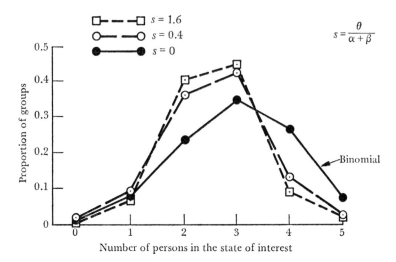

Figure 4. Equilibrium distribution of exhaustible birth-and-death processes with two-way contagion (for equations see Table 2). Distribution of groups under varying conditions of negative identical-state contagion (repulsion). (Adapted from Coleman, 1964a, p. 358.)

quencies for a more balanced break down per group. The overall implication is clear: opposite directions in the transitions effected by contagion produce (equilibrium) probability distributions conversely divergent from the baseline of randomness. The contagion models under discussion can, hence, not only be used separately to study the consequences of certain assumptions and to predict the precise form corresponding phenomena will take, but also the three models combined can be used as an instrument to identify general features of the influence structure operating in a group, namely, whether rewards or punishments prevail, or more precisely, whether alternative-state or identical-state transition-rate dependency prevails.

For an empirical application, Coleman shifted the framework to the level of individuals. He studied the number of evenings per week that a sample of middle-class teenagers spent going out with each other and was able to determine correspondingly diverging distributions for boys versus girls, which he then attributed to spontaneity versus constraint as the characteristic structures underlying the intrapersonal reward processes assumed to be operating. The details of this application need not concern us here; the main point is simply that it demonstrates that broad distinctions made between general features of analytically related models can guide one to empirically identifying and differentiating corresponding distribution phenomena and to determining the nature of the structures generating them.

## Structural Comparisons: General Uses

To return to the general overview of the structural variants, the above digression into the simultaneous application of several contagion models was intended to demonstrate the potential utility of comparisons between process structures. Such comparisons constitute one of the main uses that can be made of Tables 1 and 2. Another main use, demonstrated in the section "The Analytical Sequence," is the retracing and analysis of the manner in which the various models have been developed by means of specifications upon more general structures. Combined, such analysis and comparisons can lead to a consideration of the classificatory scheme itself and to the observation that the models presented consist of various combinations of a rather limited number of alternative assumptions. The alternatives involved are essentially three: transitions in one direction or in two, contagion or not, exhaustion or not. The various process models can therefore be arranged in a table, the classifications of which are set up along the line of these alternatives. Table 3 represents this result. It is yet another overview of the models in question, but one that locates and presents their particular structures as combinations of assumptions and that emphasizes the interrelatedness of the different subtypes. Certain supplementary distinctions are implicitly included for ordering certain further specified separate forms of contagion: pure versus mixed, one-way versus two-way, and positive versus negative. Their proliferation is a formal indication of the point at which Coleman is concentrating his analytical efforts.

## DISCUSSION: UTILITY OF THE MODELS

Thus far this exposition of Coleman's process approach has, for the most part, consisted of a relatively straightforward presentation of its general features, namely, the major assumptions and the method underlying the development of the models, the classificatory pattern of the structural variations involved, and some of the main uses to which such models can be put. Perhaps a generalization of this last-mentioned aspect, the utility of these models, can serve as a suitable perspective for their discussion and review. In the following we shall attempt to assess the nature of the models and the approach in question in terms of their relevance and principal scope.

### Conceptualization

To begin with a general point, the introduction by Coleman of continuous-time models into sociology quite definitely constitutes an innovation and an achievement of considerable general significance. For

Table 3
Coleman's Models classified according to alternative core assumptions

| | Transitions in *one direction* only Processes Pure-Birth | | Transitions in *two directions* Birth-and-Death Processes | |
|---|---|---|---|---|
| | No Exhaustion | Exhaustion | No Exhaustion Simplest Trunking | Exhaustion |
| *No Contagion:* | (Yule) | Pure Birth with Exhaustion | Independent Birth and Death | Exhaustible—Birth and Death (Noninterdependent) |
| *Contagion:* | Pure Birth with Contagion<br>Pure Birth with Contagion (simplified) | Pure Birth with Contagion and Exhaustion<br>Pure Birth with Contagion and Exhaustion (simplified) | Contagious—Birth and Death | Contagious—Birth and Death with Exhaustion<br>Exhaustible—Birth and Death with alternative-state Contagion<br>Exhaustible—Birth and Death with identical-state Repulsion |

what the conceptualization involved—the combination of the stochastic and the continuous-time assumptions—implies is nothing less than a rethinking of the relationship between states, variables or distributions of interest, as something that occurs as a continuous flow of transitions over time the form of which can, in principle, be seen while it is unfolding. Coleman calls this notion that of a "causal relationship acting through time" (1964a, p. 105). This conception so readily matches our everyday observations and our natural intuitions of what is actually going on that it is easily taken for granted, and the corresponding continuous-time conceptualization is overlooked. Even apart from the question of direct consequences for the operationalization of research problems, the import of Coleman's further suggestion that this conceptualization be taken as the framework for handling noncontinuous-time observations also, has yet to be fully realized. As a paradigm for modes of conceiving of the relationships involved, this conception can lead to greater flexibility and care in theoretically assuming such relationships and to closer scrutiny and more accurate representation of the form the observed developments actually take.

## Principal Uses

As for the models themselves and their uses, even the few examples given above already indicate the advance they represent in the tools at our disposal. To be able to simply, but accurately and comprehensively, describe a process, and to generate alternate forms, significantly increases the range of our capacity to probe the fine details of data and to determine the nature of the relationships involved. In the case of the non-stochastic drug-diffusion process cited initially, it was inspection of the over-time form of the process that permitted a decision between reasonable alternative generating conditions (social location versus individual character) for the observed differential adoption rates. In the case of the polarization observed in certain union elections, it was the reconstruction of the equilibrium distribution of the underlying influence process that made possible an initial identification of a major factor (within-group contagion). The same example also served to demonstrate certain general uses of such models: the application of a neutral model not expected to fit as a baseline of randomness from which to distinguish, and thus more precisely determine, the phenomenon of interest and the deliberate juxtaposition of divergent generating structures in order to compare their consequences and to arrive at broad distinctions of more general interest (for example, distinctions concerning reward structures and their effects).

These uses of the models are based on the fact that, generally speaking, the models consist of analytical relationships that link sets of assumptions that define generating structures with sets of consequences expressed as kinds of probability distributions. The formal structure of the models can, hence, be utilized in several ways and, so to speak, from both ends. We can, thus, compare assumptions with consequences, assumptions (as alternative explanations) against each other, consequences (that is, expectations) against each other, and finally, comparisons of the two kinds with each other. Of course, the uses made of such models are not limited to those closely linked to the structure of the models. They can consist of studies in the variations induced by changes in a parameter or boundary condition (for example, in the voting example above the decrease in the person-to-person influence parameter $c$ parallels an increase in group size).

### Advantages of Formal Structures

The formal nature of these models implies advantageous flexibility in yet another direction: not only can they be transposed from applications in one substantive area to applications in another but the level at which they apply can be shifted as well. A considerable number of applications deal with cases in which the individual constitutes the entity or system referred to, and the frequency with which certain events occur (the number of sociometric choices received, for example, or evenings spent out a week; see examples above) defines the overall state, with contagion defined as the effect that such an event has on the likelihood of the event happening again. This framework has been applied, in particular, to the study of repeaters in industrial or traffic accidents and of similar phenomena in consumers' buying patterns (Coleman, 1964a, pp. 319ff).

Certain further extensions of the uses to which such models can be put are linked to the generalization obtainable if the restriction is lifted that the overt responses of individuals be direct indicators of the (overall) state they are in and if this relationship is instead defined as being probabilistic. Relativizing the relationship in this manner of course complicates the constructive interpretation of data on individuals' responses and especially of the variability of responses. But, it appears this elaboration is valuable for handling data from multiwave panels for which such variability over time constitutes a central problem (Coleman, 1964a, p. ix). In further works not treated here, Coleman (1964a, Chapters 12 and 13; 1964b) develops a model for handling this dimension. The conceptualization involved essentially consists of considering the individual as a collection of attitudinal elements that undergo a continuous-time stochastic process similar to that outlined above for individuals in groups. This generalization thus appears as a consequent extension of the guiding notion delineated in the above section "Basic Formal Assumptions" that behavioral processes occur in fluid, probabilistic form.

## Difficulties

On the other hand, the abstract and formal character of such models engenders certain problems in the verification of their substantive interpretations. These problems are variants of the general methodological problem of establishing the uniqueness of an explanation. The first difficulty concerns the validity of the identification of a generating mechanism with an observed distribution. Given a model which has successfully been matched with the overall form of an empirical process, what can one conclude? The deductions may be precise, and the form of the predictions detailed, but the question that remains, especially with equilibrium distributions, is whether the mechanism posited is the only one capable of generating the results obtained. The distributions obtained for the contagious pure-birth and the contagious birth-and-death processes, for example, are of negative-binomial form (Tables 1 and 2, processes 5 and 13), which can also be generated by other processes with different underlying assumptions (Coleman, 1942a, pp. 300ff and 329ff).

The notion of *contagion* is itself a prime example for the vulnerability of certain explanatory assumptions. In the case of the industrial accidents application, for example, the Polya distribution deduced from this assumption can also be obtained from the assumption of heterogeneity. In other words, both interpretations fit the overall predictions of the model that each accident increases the probability of another accident for that individual and that proneness to accidents has a fixed prior probability value for each individual and is Poisson distributed throughout the population (Feller, 1949, pp. 413f). As Coleman points out, the solution to this difficulty (that is, the test for confirmation of the assumed contagion effects) resides with continuous observation and/or a detailed comparison of the over-time data obtained for different time intervals (1964a, p. 376).

But even if the formal equivalent of contagion, system dependency of transition rates, can be shown to hold, a second ambiguity remains: To what influence mechanisms exactly are the ascertained changes in transition rates to be attributed? Thus, if individuals can be shown, for the voting-process example, to shift their preference at a rate proportional to the number of group members in the alternative state, this still leaves undecided what is to be understood by the social influence envisioned to be effecting these changes. Alternative versions are conceivable as to who and what are the agents and the medium. On the one

hand, it could be the proselytizing activity of party supporters that gains
further supporters; on the other hand, such gains could simply be due to
efforts toward conformity by individual members reacting to the number
of opponents they face. Mixed modes are conceivable as well. Such problems of interpretation are, of course, best decided by the introduction of
further evidence. For the case at hand, evidence can be adduced to support the first alternative and make it plausible. It could be shown that,
for the union and the size of shops in question, the consensus (or cleavage) phenomenon was higher where members were relatively active in
union politics than where they were not (Lazarsfeld and Menzel, 1969,
pp. 511f).

One could even go a step further and say that this kind of interpretation problem is subsidiary, if not irrelevant, to the use of the model
itself, since the model deals simply with formal characteristics of transition rates and their consequences, once they have been assumed or
identified. But, what the discussion of this example indicates is that such
a model does not in itself necessarily embody all the substantively relevant features and perhaps not even a direct representation of the de-
clared phenomenon of interest (for example, social influence).

This readily occurring partial divergence between guiding substantive notions and their simplified representation in models can
perhaps be illustrated by reference to the topic toward which Coleman's
work on reward structures appears to be leading—the regulation of
social behavior by group norms (1964a, pp. 333 and 335f). It is not
immediately apparent why only transitions into other states should be
encouraged by group members (an assumption the models discussed
appear to make) and not continuance in the desired activity or state
as well. Sanctions are, after all, known to be applied both to induce
and to maintain desired performance. Coleman suggests that what is
needed is a concept analogous to that of pressure in gases, for which
both the tendencies to remain in and to leave a vessel (or state) are a
function of one and the same parameter, that is, the relative difference
in pressure as compared to the surroundings (1964a, p. 361). But if any
of the pressures involved are to be designated as "normative" (Coleman,
1964a, p. 333), the derived pressures resulting from certain subgroup
constellations would seem to qualify for the label, rather than the primary pressures that constitute the initial competition between these
subgroups. This holds all the more for the envisioned generalization to
more than two activities or states, each with its own reward structure,
and the equilibrium distribution over activities expected to result
(Coleman, 1966, pp. 168f). On the one hand, the constancy of such a
distribution would make it a prime candidate for a standard for group

members to orient themselves by; and on the other hand, this state of affairs matches our intuition concerning norms, as usually not simply and absolutely constraining in some direction, but rather toward a certain distribution, level, or amount in what is desired. What we have, then, is closer to a model of the genesis of certain norms than to a model of their actual operation, which is what presumably was initially envisioned but would still have to be developed.

## Group-Level Derivations

A further general use presented by Coleman for this type of model concerns extensions in another direction: the derivation of group-level propositions from process models built on assumptions about relationships between individual-level variables. Coleman is interested in following through the implications of more readily observable individual-level processes (such as the different types of sanctioning, discussed as reward structures above) in order to determine and then examine their systemic consequences or parallels (Coleman, 1966, p. 168). One of the examples he gives is the group-level proposition "[political] consensus is a function of [political] activity," which is derived from a model with the individual-level assumption that "the more active one is on a given topic, the more he will convince his associates to believe as he does" (1964a, p. 248). As the proportion of active individuals in a group and, hence, the transition rates into alternative political-preference states increases, the relative proportion of groups in or near the state of neutrality (an even split) decreases. It is this deduction that the group-level proposition expresses (Coleman, 1964a, p. 250).

In itself this procedure is legitimate as long as one remains clear about the fact that the statements made and the conclusions arrived at concern analytical properties of the collectives in question, that is, features of the probability distributions of individuals over states (Lazarsfeld and Menzel, 1969, pp. 503f). The import of any further claims remains undecided, however, until it is demonstrated in what sense the emergent or derived group-level concepts (consensus, for example) can be used (and preferably also measured, at least indirectly) on the group level on their own.

## Questions of Measurement

Besides expounding the utility of the models in question as providing substitute procedures for direct aggregation, Coleman also puts forth a general claim as to the principal contribution they allegedly represent in the field of measurement. His process models embody a strategy, he asserts, for circumventing ("surmounting or by-passing") the problems posed in sociology by the difficulties normally encountered in attempts to apply the classical criteria for fundamental measurement as developed in physical science (Coleman, 1964a, p. viii). These difficulties usually arise when attempts are made to validate, by direct measurement of the properties or the behavior in question, the legitimacy of ratio-order linear operations on the values assigned to various manifestations of a variable, for example, cohesion. The strategy Coleman suggests to cope with this problem is to desist from attempting validation at the measurement stage and to postpone validation until a model's or a theory's deductions are tested against corresponding data. For measures formed, as in the models outlined above, by the superimposition of a counting process upon the nominal identification of alternative states, he argues, there can be no immediate validation for the comparison and combination operations implicitly carried through. As Coleman (1964a, p. 71) says:

> For neither the comparison operation nor the combination operation is there an empirical validation that the operation fulfills the necessary requirements. The operation is carried out by fiat, so to speak, by the investigator's counting, rather than by behavior of the objects themselves . . . . The important consequence of this . . . is that there *can* be no validation of the assignment of a measure in the measurement operation itself, since it is the investigator, rather than the behavior of the objects themselves, who establishes an equivalence between events and combines them by adding.

The only alternative, he continues, lies in considering the confirmation of predictions constructed out of such materials as proof of the latter's quality. As he says (1964a, p. 71): "The validation, in theories of this sort, lies in a very different place, in a comparison of the theory's deductions with the data to be predicted. That is, do the objects behave according to the predictions of a theory which establishes given equivalence classes, and combines them by counting?" In this type of approach to measurement validation, "the investigator postulates a particular assignment of numbers, and the postulate is tested only by test of the theory's deductions. If he has established equivalence classes in such a way that all elements identified as equivalent are in fact equivalent in those aspects of their behavior treated by the theory, then the theory will be confirmed; if not, the theory will be disconfirmed" (Coleman, 1964a, p. 72).

There seem to be a number of limitations, however, on the usefulness of this suggestion. In the first place its applicability seems to be limited to concepts of a type that already incorporate numbers of individuals (preferably in alternative states) as the mode of their formulation, that is, distribution phenomena. In the second place, one might in actual cases have to justify assuming that individuals (in different social positions, for example) represent equivalence classes in terms of the behavior effected and constituting the process. And finally, it seems doubtful whether the goodness-of-fit of predictions with data should simultaneously be burdened with demonstrating the validity both of measurements of a concept and of theoretical assumptions about its further relationships. Conceivably both could be invalid, and the combined deduced result still fit. In the more usual case, in which predictions based on initial conceptualizations do not fit, nonvalidated measurements only complicate the issue and render more difficult the decision at what point to try to introduce testable variants and improvements in the assumptions.

## Theory as a Goal

A final general claim that Coleman advances concerning his models is that they constitute the beginnings of a theory of social dynamics. He does not explicitly state this claim for the separate models, only for the conceptualization presented in them in general. In the preface (Coleman, 1964a, p. vii) he states: "This book aims to provide mathematical tools for conceptual elaboration in sociology . . . its principal aim is . . . to begin the development of a mathematical language which is equally at home with the empirical results of social research and the ideas of social theory." In Chapter 1 he goes on to say that mathematics is a language particularly suited for the representation of theory because of its power to express relations between abstract concepts in a theory and that it constitutes the ultimate natural language, so to speak, of a science that has come to recognize the formal structures inherent in its theories (1964a, pp. 8, 9, and 34). He points out that the models under discussion introduce such a mathematical language for the study of social and psychological processes and, ultimately, for the theory of social dynamics (1964a, p. viii).

There is no gainsaying that Coleman does present us with process models in which certain states of social systems are defined, identified, and deductions drawn about their further development (given certain assumptions) that lead to predictions (given the necessary parameter values and initial conditions) that can be and have (in examples) been tested, even with a certain degree of success. And to this extent they do contribute to a general knowledge of social dynamics. The question, however, is how far they carry us in the direction of a theory of this subject. For, there is one rather stringent limitation on the explanatory range that these models cover: almost all of them are restricted to dealing with the development of only *one* variable over time. This means that questions concerning relationships to other sociological concepts or variables are, for the most part, cut off, which runs counter even to Coleman's own statement (1964a, p. 7) of what is desirable in the way of theory: "if fruitful theory is to be developed, far more than this [the locating of relevant variables in an important area of behavior] is necessary. A logically consistent framework of variables [in the plural!] incorporating or explaining the empirically established relations is necessary."

It is of course legitimate to concentrate on one kind of phenomenon or analytical aspect at a time. But if such work is to contribute to theory, explication of its relationship to other aspects, phenomena, and generalizations should constitute a prime concern, perhaps even determine the approach to the particular topic. Determining the analytical structure and the over-time form of the development of a type of variable or phenomenon does constitute a generalization that simplifies matters once a phenomenon has been identified as such, but what leads does Coleman's work give us for such identification? It hardly seems satisfactory to leave this identification to the result of trial-and-error applications of various probabilistic models, as Coleman's formulations concerning the "sometimes-true" theories of social processes seem to suggest (1964a, pp. 516ff). Two-way transitions, limited group size, and contagion, it is true, are all conditions that can be looked for, but together they do not constitute anything like a guiding substantive principle that would unite and coordinate the representation and analysis of a wide range of phenomena, and the drawing of inferences about them.[7]

What seems to be lacking is a kind of relational analysis, that is, consideration of the relations between social actors and of the sets of conditions or forces that govern the general pattern of these relations in a society, that work to change the society, and that, presumably, also govern the particular combinations of conditions that Coleman's models formalize as assumptions, the over-time consequences of which they then extrapolate.[8] To some extent this deficiency may be due to the type of phenomenon Coleman has concentrated upon—distributions on dichotomous attributes. If individuals enter into the conceptualization

---

[7] On this function of substantive principles, see Toulmin (1960, Chapter 2).

[8] Relational analysis is a term Coleman uses to point out what traditional survey research overlooks—the relations between individuals (see Coleman, 1964a, p. 89, footnote 23; 1958).

only in terms of their contribution to aggregation phenomena of this type, then the interrelationships between them and the study of what contributes to the form of these interrelationships necessarily drops out of the picture. But perhaps this is the price to be paid for the advantages the counting procedure offers in respect to quantification. It does, however, restrict the theoretical character of the generalizations derived within the framework of this conceptualization.

Coleman introduces a distinction between explanatory and synthetic theorizing that should perhaps be reviewed for the bearing it has on the matter. The point of introducing the distinction seems to be the establishing of the latter kind of theorizing as a category to which his models belong. We shall review the specifications involved in the distinction, and shall consider how they apply to the work under discussion.

Synthetic theorizing, it seems, differs from explanatory theorizing in three respects. The first is the direction in which the relationship between postulates and deductions is initially set up and exploited. In explanatory theorizing explanations are sought for relationships known to hold empirically in terms of constructs that are developed to try to derive deductions that agree with as wide a range of phenomena as possible. In synthetic theorizing the postulates are taken as known, and their combination studied for the consequences that follow. The primary thrust of model building of the kind outlined in this chapter is in the latter category. But at least in the present case, the theoretical scope of synthetic theorizing is limited, as was pointed out above, by the rudimentary character of what the assumptions are about. To achieve generalizations of a wider scope, the explanatory type of probing might very well have to be resumed, with formal models as instruments.

The second is the observability of postulated processes or states. For synthetic theorizing the correspondence of the assumptions to observable behavior is thought to be direct; whereas explanatory theory often takes recourse to constructs or relationships that are only indirectly related to observables. Again, the assumptions made in Coleman's models directly concern verifiable relationships and, hence, place these models in the synthetic category. However, the question again arises as to what the direct relationship of the models to observability contributes to their theoretical character—apparently very little. In fact, Coleman does not favor qualitative empirical generalizations of the Homans-Simon type as postulates on which to base theorizing.[9] He prefers to see

[9] For example the statement: "The change in friendliness in a group is an increasing function of the amount of interaction . . . carried on in the group, and a decreasing function of the existing level of friendliness" (according to Coleman, 1964a, p. 47).

them as results against which the deductions of a theory should be tested (1964a, pp. 522–524).

The third is the peculiar synthesizing character of synthetic theorizing. Coleman asserts that the combination of postulates on the individual level, where behavior is observable, can lead to frameworks for larger systems of action and, thus, to deductions on the group level (1964a, pp. 37 and 41; also the previous section "Group-Level Derivations"). It seems rather doubtful, however, that the emergent syntheses can be attributed to specifically theoretical inference-drawing activity. For, in many cases, the emergent conclusions include the system character of the entity under discussion as an empirical assumption [for example, Coleman's example of Simon's formalization of Homans' propositions about groups (1964a, p. 48)]. In other cases, economic market models, for example, the set of general conditions constituting the market mechanism is presupposed as a theoretical assumption. Moreover, if this type of economic theory constitutes the paradigm for synthetic theorizing, then one would expect Coleman to concentrate on aspects of a central-exchange mechanism rather than on features of separate distributions. Finally, it is difficult to see any combining that synthetic theorizing is able to perform on the level of theoretical concepts, that explanatory theorizing cannot. A difference may exist in the handling of concrete phenomena, but this it seems represents a stage preliminary to the activity of abstracting, not to speak of theory proper.

Synthetic theorizing, that is, the exploration of what selected assumptions—confirmed or hypothetical—together imply, appears to constitute a *phase* of the activities normal theorizing encompasses rather than a separate type. The fact that postulates are set up and their joint consequences followed through does not in itself constitute theory; rather, it is the fact that such operations are guided by *questions* concerning substantive problems that bestows upon these activities their theoretical character. The compounding of various formal conditions can of course be analyzed for its implications, but from the point of view of sociological applications, this constitutes abstract modelling of possible representational structures rather than theory (Coleman, 1964a, p. 517). Any actual applications, however, are guided by an implicit definition of the overall phenomenon of interest and by at least a question, if not an expectation, concerning the relationship to be investigated. In fact, the analytical properties and propositions obtained for the group-level synthesis examples seem to serve to clarify initial assumptions and intuitions rather than to introduce significantly new results (see the section "Group-Level Derivations" above). There is, after all, nothing particularly counterintuitive about the conclusion that in groups with

politically active (and also influenceable) members, any existing dis-
proportions between alternative parties will tend to increase, and one or
the other party will tend to win out. Similarly, it seems groups in which
any concentration of members at either alternative position increases
the pressures to leave that position can naturally be expected to turn out
to be more balanced. The gain seems to lie not so much in the conclusions
per se but in the clarity and precision of the insights concerning how these
general states develop. At any rate, the hypothetical element in the question or expectation underlying "synthesizing" exploration implies explanatory theorizing in a general sense, although not necessarily of the
hypothetical-construct kind. It is upon the existence and the quality of
this problem-defining question that the theoretical character of related
activities depends—upon whether it unifies a search, upon its breadth
and generality, upon the clarity with which it is formulated and pursued,
and upon the depth to which diverse phenomena are intellectually organized. However, it seems Coleman's models do not satisfy the majority
of these criteria, especially the last one, to any great extent.

It is admittedly much easier to list desiderata as criteria that
theorizing should fulfill than to actually produce an exact representation
of a sociologically significant phenomenon. Our purpose is not to detract
from Coleman's achievements, which are considerable and which stand
on their own. It is a question, rather, of reducing the claims presented
with the models to a level that seems justifiable. The conclusion we draw
from the above review of the claims of Coleman's models upon the label
theory is that the models belong to the representational rather than the
theoretical type. A comparison with the functions that Berger et al.,
suggest as characteristic for the representational type of model indicates
that they accurately circumscribe Coleman's models (Berger et al.,
1962, pp. 56ff).

> (1) The model provides a precise description of the con-
> formity [or contagion] process. (2) The entire process can be
> specified in terms of a small number of underived quantities.
> (3) The model provides a means for exhibiting and systemati-
> cally studying the relation of various aspects of the process to
> each other. (4) The model provides a means for systematically
> studying experimental [and other] variations in the phe-
> nomena. (5) The model provides a means of generating the
> entire process.

The specifically differentiating function of a theoretical model, that of
providing a means of extending the theory to different types of related
phenomena, does not, however, apply (Berger et al., 1962, p. 98). In
other words, what the models presented above generalize, simplify, and

in themselves, unite are separate phenomena but not areas of social behavior. This then represents the principal limitation to be expected in their further development and use.

## REFERENCES

BAILEY, N. T. J.
1957 *The Mathematical Theory of Epidemics.* London: Charles Griffin.

BARTHOLOMEW, D. J.
1967 *Stochastic Models for Social Processes.* New York: Wiley.

BERGER, J., COHEN, B. R., SNELL, J. L., AND ZELDITCH, M.
1962 *Types of Formalizations in Small-Group Research.* Boston: Houghton Mifflin.

COLEMAN, J. S.
1969 "An expository analysis of some of Rashevsky's social behavior models." Pp. 105–165 in P. F. Lazarsfeld (Ed.), *Mathematical Thinking in the Social Sciences,* reissued 1969. New York: Russel and Russel.

1958 "Relational analysis: the study of social organization with survey methods." *Human Organization* 17.

1963 "Comment on 'On the concept of influence.'" *Public Opinion Quarterly* 27: 63–82.

1964a *Introduction to Mathematical Sociology.* Glencoe, Ill.: Free Press.

1964b *Models of Change and Response Uncertainty.* Englewood Cliffs, N.J.: Prentice-Hall.

1966 "Reward structures and the allocation of effort." Pp. 159–173 in P. F. Lazarsfeld and N. W. Henry (Eds.), *Readings in Mathematical Social Science.* Cambridge, Mass.: M.I.T. Press. Reprinted from J. Criswell and others (Eds.) *Mathematical Methods in Small Group Processes.* Stanford: Stanford University Press 1962.

1968 "The mathematical study of change." Pp. 428–478 in H. M. and A. B. Blalock (Eds.), *Methodology in Social Research.* New York: McGraw-Hill.

COLEMAN, J. S., KATZ, E., AND MENZEL, H.
1957 "The diffusion of an innovation among physicians." *Sociometry* 20: 253–270.

FARARO, T. J.
1969a "Stochastic processes." Pp. 245–260 in E. F. Borgatta

(Ed.), *Sociological Methodology: 1969*. San Francisco: Jossey-Bass.

1969b "The nature of mathematical sociology, a non-technical essay." *Social Research* 36: 75–92.

FELLER, W.

1949 "On the theory of stochastic processes, with particular reference to applications." Pp. 403–432 in J. Neyman (Ed.), *Berkeley Symposium on Mathematical Statistics and Probability: (1945–1946)*. Berkeley: University of California Press.

1968 *An Introduction to Probability Theory and its Applications*. (3rd ed.) Vol. 1. New York: Wiley.

KARLIN, S.

1966 *A First Course in Stochastic Processes*. New York: Academic Press.

LAZARSFELD, P. F. AND MENZEL, H.

1969 "On the relation between individual and collective properties." Pp. 499–516 in A. Etzioni (Ed.), *A Sociological Reader on Complex Organizations* (2nd ed.) New York: Holt, Rinehart, and Winston.

NORTHROP, F. S. C.

1967 *The Logic of the Sciences and the Humanities*. New York: Meridian Books.

TORGERSON, W. S.

1958 *Theory and Methods of Scaling*. New York: Wiley.

TOULMIN, S.

1960 *The Philosophy of Science, An Introduction*. New York: Harper and Row.

PART FOUR

ASSOCIATION AND
PREDICTION OF
VARIABLES

# 10

# INTEGRATED APPROACH TO
# MEASURING ASSOCIATION

*Robert K. Leik*

UNIVERSITY OF WASHINGTON

*Walter R. Gove*

VANDERBILT UNIVERSITY

In spite of the variety of measures of association available for data analysis, there is considerable difficulty in finding any consistent logic which can provide an integrated approach to association at all levels of measurement. Ideally, as data progress from nominal to ordinal to equal interval in mathematical character, association measures should simply incorporate the added properties into the format used at the lower levels. In this way ordinal measures of association would be the same as nominal measures with the fact of ordered data utilized. Interval measures would be the same as ordinal measures with the degree of ordered difference utilized. Such is hardly the case for current procedures.

This chapter will present an approach to measure association such that a single basic logic is used regardless of the measurement level of the variables being associated. The logic is adapted, as indicated above, to the types of measurement present in the independent and dependent variables so that a complete range of association measures is available. Fortunately, the approach requires little new at the interval-measurement level (dependent variable) and only modest modification of existing procedures for ordinal dependent variables. Equally fortunately, at the nominal level the new approach suggested is derived from techniques already in use, and the proposed measure can readily be compared to the more limited measures already known. In general, it is a superior procedure.

There are, in our view, two compelling reasons for attempting to integrate procedures for measuring association. First, with current methods there is considerable difficulty in determining the comparability of two different index values if the indexes are based on differing logic. Since current procedures do differ as measurement level differs, relating diverse results is often problematic. Second, there is considerable heuristic value in using a single approach. For those who do not teach statistics, this may appear to be relatively trivial; but for those recurringly faced with perplexed students asking how one knows to use $\lambda$, $\tau$, $\phi$, $C$, $T$, $\gamma$, $d_{yx}$, $r$, and so on, the question is not trivial.

The approach we propose has one further advantage; it is based on a comparison of pairs of cases (as is Goodman and Kruskal's (1954) $\gamma$). For students lacking in mathematical sophistication, it can be difficult to gain intuitive feel for a procedure which compares each case with an abstraction such as the mean or median. Comparison of pairs, however, carries the immediately clear notion of each person (case) comparing himself (being compared) with each other person. Carrying this idea throughout the range of measures provides both clarity and continuity.

The two basic approaches to association measures appear to be assessing departure from randomness and determining extent of predictive accuracy. Departure from randomness is characteristic of the chi-squared based measures, which typically suffer from normalizing procedures that admit no easy operational interpretation (for example, $\phi$ for large tables, $C$, and $T$). Measures which can be releated to prediction procedures, such as $\lambda$, $\gamma$, and its variations and various correlation forms ($r^2$, $\eta^2$, and so on), are useful if some clear basis for assessing degree of predictive accuracy is available. Costner (1965), building on the work of Goodman and Kruskal (1954) and Guttman (1941), has suggested a proportional reduction in error (PRE) form that consistently compares prediction error, when an independent variable is used optimally, with prediction error when the independent variable is ignored. Since the latter error assessment in reality concerns random prediction, it appears that PRE measures combine both the departure-from-randomness and the predictive-accuracy approaches.

Assuming PRE type measures, we still find diversity in basic logic in the manner in which prediction rules are specified. Correlation forms as well as $\lambda$ examine a value of $X$ and then predict an associated value of $Y$; whereas $\gamma$ requires we examine the direction of change in $X$ between a pair of observations and then predict the direction of change in $Y$. If a single logic is to underly the range of association measures to be used, either we need an ordinal measure based on case-by-case prediction or a generalized pair prediction for nominal and equal-interval levels of measurement. Elsewhere (Leik, 1966) a measure of association for ordinal dependent variables has been presented that provides a parallel to $\lambda$ and $\eta^2$ though it does not strictly involve case-by-case prediction. This chapter as already indicated, will demonstrate the applicability of a pair-prediction approach to all levels of measurement such that the relationship of nominal measures to ordinal measures to equal-interval or ratio measures is clear. The discussion will focus first on association of two nominal variables.

The notation used will be the same as that used in previous discussions of $\gamma$ variations (Somers, 1962; Leik and Gove, 1969). For our purposes it will be very useful to retain the distinction between concordant and discordant pairs, although obviously for nominal data such pairs may be grouped together.

$C$ = number of concordant pairs
$D$ = number of discordant pairs
$X_o$ = number of pairs tied on $X$ only
$Y_o$ = number of pairs tied on $Y$ only
$Z$ = number of pairs tied on both $X$ and $Y$
$N$ = number of cases

Clearly, the total number of pairs is $\frac{1}{2} N(N - 1)$, and

$$\tfrac{1}{2} N(N - 1) = C + D + X_o + Y_o + Z \tag{1}$$

For convenience, the following additional designations will be needed.

$X_T$ = number of pairs tied in the marginal distribution of $X$
$X_D$ = number of pairs different in the marginal distribution of $X$
$Y_T$ = number of pairs tied in the marginal distribution of $Y$
$Y_D$ = number of pairs different in the marginal distribution of $Y$

Parallel to equation (1) we have

$$\tfrac{1}{2} N(N - 1) = X_T + X_D = Y_T + Y_D \tag{2}$$

## PROPERTIES OF CONTINGENCY TABLES

A moment's reflection on equations (1) and (2) makes evident that there are a number of dependencies among the various types of pairs in a contingency table. To explore some of these relationships, consider first the marginal distribution of $X$. Of those pairs tied marginally ($X_T$), some will be in the same cell of the table, and all others will be in the same column (value of $X$) but not the same row (value of $Y$). Consequently,

$$X_T = Z + X_o \tag{3}$$

Similarly, those not tied in the marginal distribution of $X$ will show one of two conditions: different columns but the same row (tied on $Y$) or different columns and different rows (not tied on $Y$). The latter case includes all pairs which are concordantly arrayed and all pairs which are discordantly arrayed. Consequently,

$$X_D = C + D + Y_o \tag{4}$$

Adding equations (3) and (4) will produce

$$X_T + X_D = C + D + X_o + Y_o + Z$$

which follows from equations (1) and (2) as well.

Any two sets of values satisfying the above equations and coming from a table with fixed marginal distributions can differ only in specific ways. With fixed marginals, the values of $X_T$ and $X_D$ are constant, and from equation (3) we find

$$Z = X_T - X_o \tag{5}$$

and also, for any alternative set of values,

$$Z' = X_T - X'_o \tag{6}$$

Subtracting equation (6) from equation (5) leads to

$$Z - Z' = -(X_o - X'_o) \tag{7}$$

Equation (7) means, for fixed marginals, that any change in the number of pairs tied on both variables is exactly counterbalanced by an equivalent, negative change in the number tied only on $X$. The theoretical utility of this observation will be discussed after examining the $Y$ distribution.

Parallel to the foregoing, it can be shown that the following equations hold:

$$Y_T = Z + Y_o \tag{8}$$
$$Y_D = C + D + X_o \tag{9}$$
$$Z - Z' = -(Y_o - Y'_o) \tag{10}$$

Equation (10) indicates that changes in pairs tied on both variables are balanced by changes in those tied on $Y$ only. Together, equations (7) and (10) explicitly link $X_o$, $Y_o$, and $Z$ for rearrangement of any table. These may in turn be linked to $C$ and $D$ by equations (4) and (9). Specifically, from equation (4) it is evident that

$$Y_o = X_D - (C + D) \tag{11}$$

and, alternatively,

$$Y'_o = X_D - (C' + D') \tag{12}$$

Again, $X_D$ is constant due to fixed marginals, and equation (11) minus equation (12) produces

$$-(Y_o - Y'_o) = (C + D) - (C' + D') \tag{13}$$

The same procedure will provide the equivalent version of equation (13) using $-(X_0 - X'_o)$. All told, then,

$$Z - Z' = -(X_o - X'_o) = -(Y_o - Y'_o)$$
$$= (C + D) - (C' + D') \tag{14}$$

Equation (14) becomes particularly meaningful given two considerations. The first concerns the meaning of the types of pairs. The next portion of the chapter develops that meaning. The second consideration involves substituting for the primed values the expected numbers of pairs under the condition of independence or no association. Assuming the expected frequencies for independence, which are familiar from chi square, allows ready computation of expected values for $C$, $D$, $X_o$, $Y_o$, and $Z$. Although expected cell frequencies can be computed, and expected values for the pair frequencies found from these, there are direct solutions based on marginal frequencies. With subscripts $i$ and $j$ indicating row and column respectively, the solutions for independence are

$$Z' = \frac{1}{2N^2} \left( \sum_i N_i^2 \right) \left( \sum_j N_j^2 \right) - \frac{N}{2} \tag{15}$$

$$Y'_o = \frac{1}{2} \sum_i N_i^2 - \frac{N}{2} - Z' \tag{16}$$

$$X'_o = \frac{1}{2} \sum_j N_j^2 - \frac{N}{2} - Z' \tag{17}$$

$$C' = D' = \tfrac{1}{2}[\tfrac{1}{2} N(N - 1) - X'_o - Y'_o - Z'] \qquad (18)$$

These solutions are much simpler than those using expected cell frequencies. The assertion that $C' = D'$ becomes self-evident when we remember that independence is a condition producing $\gamma$ equal to zero, which implies that $C - D = 0$ or $C = D$.

### NOMINAL VARIABLES

Two approaches that derive from the logic of analysis of variance (and the related correlation ratio) will be used in developing an appropriate measure of association for nominal variables. These different ways of developing an index, as will be shown, lead to the same conclusion but emphasize different aspects of the idea of association.

Basic to analysis of variance is the division of total sum of squared deviations into deviations of individual cases around category means and the complementary deviations attributable to category means differing from the grand mean. Although deviations cannot be measured, and means cannot be computed for nominal data, it is appropriate to discuss dispersion within categories versus dispersion in the marginal distribution of the dependent variable. In terms applicable to pairs of cases in contingency tables, dispersion becomes a function of the number of pairs which are in different cells. This concept is familiar as the basis of the index of qualitative variation (IQV), although the latter is defined for a single distribution rather than a table.

Considering $Y$ as the dependent variable, marginal dispersion can be designated as $\text{IQV}_Y$ and computed in the usual manner. For $m$ categories of $Y$, it can be shown that

$$\text{IQV}_Y = \frac{m}{m - 1}\left(1 - \frac{1}{N^2} \sum_i N_i^2\right) \qquad (19)$$

A comparable ratio of actual to maximum pair differences within categories of the table can be designated $\text{IQV}_{YX}$, and it can be shown that

$$\text{IQV}_{YX} = \frac{m}{m - 1}\left(1 - \frac{1}{\sum_j N_j^2} \sum_{ij} N_{ij}^2\right) \qquad (20)$$

Constructing a PRE measure involves subtracting within dispersion, or error, from marginal dispersion, then dividing by marginal dispersion. Thus a PRE measure of association for nominal variables could be defined as

$$\frac{IQV_Y - IQV_{YX}}{IQV_Y}$$

Although a proof will not be presented here, it is demonstrable that the above measure is also the ratio $(X'_o - X_o)/X'_o$, which is interpretable as a PRE form if pairs tied on $X$ but not on $Y$ can be considered as errors in some prediction sense. In fact, the $X_o$ pairs are those actually different on $Y$ within categories of $X$, and the $X'_o$ pairs are those which would be different if $X$ and $Y$ were independent. Consequently, if the prediction rule were if $X$ does not change between the members of the pair, predict that $Y$ will not change, prediction would be for the $X_T$ pairs. All $X_o$ pairs would be errors, $X'_o$ would be the expected value of $X_o$, and the ratio would be a defensible measure of association.

The other approach to association is the complementary view of that just described. Implicit in the analysis of variance models is the idea that perfect association means no variability within categories of $X$. Translated into contingency-table terms, all pairs should be $Z$ pairs for perfect association, which means that a particular value of $X$ implies a particular value $Y$. From this point of view it is clear that the prediction rule would turn out the same as above and that the PRE ratio would again be $(X'_o - X_o)/X'_o$.

Note that the preceding discussion has involved predicting only for the $X_T$ pairs. Previous discussions of gamma-type measures have involved predicting only for the $X_D$ pairs. Although order (hence $\gamma$) is not at ssue here, it is relevant to inquire into the implications of predicting for all pairs.

Considering the $X_D$ pairs leads to a prediction rule complementing the one already stated. If $X$ changes between the members of the pair, we predict that $Y$ will change. For this rule errors will be those cases differing on $X$ but tied on $Y$, that is, $Y_o$, and correct prediction will be either concordant or discordant pairs, since direction is not definable for nominal variables. It is possible, then, to combine errors under the rule for $X_T$ pairs with errors under the rule for $X_D$ pairs. Because of peculiarities caused by marginal restraints on the relationship, a further adjustment of the index will eventually be desirable. The problem of marginal restraints will be examined after an index treating all pairs has been formed.

Combining both prediction rules, so that all pairs are considered, produces the following: For $X_T$ cases predict tied on $Y$ also.

$$\text{Correct prediction} = Z$$
$$\text{Error} = X_o$$
$$\text{Expected error under no association} = X'_o$$

For $X_D$ cases predict different on $Y$ also.

$$\text{Correct prediction} = C + D$$
$$\text{Error} = Y_o$$
$$\text{Expected error under no association} = Y'_o$$

A complete PRE measure will be of the following form:

$$\frac{(X'_o + Y'_o) - (X_o + Y_o)}{X'_o + Y'_o} = \frac{(X'_o - X_o) + (Y'_o - Y_o)}{X'_o + Y'_o} \qquad (21)$$

Note that this measure is symmetrical; either $X$ or $Y$ can be considered the independent variable. From previous discussion $X'_o - X_o = Y'_o - Y_o$, so that if $X'_o = Y'_o$, equation (21) reduces to the same ratio obtained above; $(X'_o - X_o)/X'_o$.

Under what conditions will $X'_o = Y'_o$? Examination of the equations for these values indicates that equality obtains only when the marginal distribution of $Y$ contains the same set of frequencies as does the marginal distribution of $X$. That is to say, for each $N_i$, there is an identical $N_j$. Such a condition is indeed unusual, and the problem it poses is a familiar one in the literature on association in contingency tables. If the number of rows does not equal the number of columns, or if they are equal but the distributions of the two variables differ (for example, in skew), then it is not possible to reach perfect association. Consequently, either $X_o$ or $Y_o$ could be zero while the other remained nonzero. The implication for a supposedly symmetrical measure would be that taking one variable as dependent could result in no within dispersion; whereas taking the other as dependent could result in some nonzero amount of within dispersion, a not very symmetrical situation. Equation (21) would be a kind of average of the two cases.

To aid in interpretation of a relationship, it would be preferable to avoid the above confusion by explicitly determining the number of pairs lost to marginal requirements of the table. Association can then be defined within those limits, enabling the index to reach unity if cases are as close to a perfect pattern as the marginal distributions will allow.

As noted before, any change in $X_o$ or $Y_o$ is directly offset by a reverse change in $Z$, making $Z(\max_N)$ coincide with $X_o(\min_N)$ and $Y_o(\min_N)$. The subscript $N$ indicates maxima and minima for nominal data. In general, the ordinal counterparts have different values. Letting $z = Z(\max_N) - Z$, $x = X_o - X_o(\min_N)$, and $y = Y_o - Y_o(\min_N)$, and defining $z'$, $x'$, and $y'$ as parallel deviations of expected frequencies from their maxima or minima, we note that $z = x = y$ and also that $z' = x' = y'$. An appropriate revision of equation (21) involves either substituting these deviations for their raw equivalents or computing a maximal value for the measure by using max and min values in the equation, and then dividing this maximum into the uncorrected value of the index. The former approach is illustrated below, but the latter is generally to be preferred in that both uncorrected and corrected values of the indexes will have interpretive value. It is easy to demonstrate that the two approaches lead to the same answer.

Parallel to Somers' index label $d_{yx}$ and the Leik-Gove variation $d'_{yx}$, we will retain the letter $d$ for the index and use subscript $N$ to indicate the relevance of $d$ to a nominal dependent variable case. Other subscripts that will be used with the other measurement levels are $O$ for ordinal and $I$ for interval. A superscript $C$ indicates correction for marginal limitations.

$$
\begin{aligned}
d_N^c &= \frac{(x' - x) + (y' - y)}{(x' + y')} \\
&= \frac{2(y' - y)}{2y'} \\
&= \frac{Y'_o - Y_o(\min_N) - [Y_o - Y_o(\min_N)]}{Y'_o - Y_o(\min_N)} \\
&= \frac{Y'_o - Y_o}{Y'_o - Y_o(\min_N)} \tag{22}
\end{aligned}
$$

As a consequence of considering marginal limitations, we find the measure becomes symmetrical for all tables and the denominator is reduced. Since the latter inflates the value of the expression, it should always be accompanied by a statement of the proportion of cases eliminated from consideration or, perferably, the proportion still being considered. The latter proportion is

$$
1 - \frac{2 \, [X_o(\min_N) + Y_o(\min_N)]}{N(N - 1)}
$$

A complete statement of the characteristics of a contingency table for nominal variables involves, therefore, the proportion of cases not subject to marginal restraints on association and the proportional reduction in prediction error among those cases, as represented by $d_N^c$.

Although the development of $d_N$ has been more discursive than formal, there is a simple way to formalize what has been presented. First, define $X_{ij} = f_N(X_i - X_j)$ and $Y_{ij} = f_N(Y_i - Y_j)$, where $f_N$ is a nominal-level function assigning a score of 0 if the two scores are the same and 1 if they differ. Second, predict $Y_{ij} = X_{ij}$ for all $ij$ pairs. Prediction error is therefore $E_{ij} = Y_{ij} - X_{ij}$, which takes on values of $+1$, $0$, or $-1$ only. Third, use the sum of squared error, both observed and expected under independence, as the error statements in the PRE format. These rules restate the ideas already presented and will produce the $d_N$ and $d_N^c$ formulas.

The remaining chore is to determine the value of $Z(\max_N)$, since it is easier to compute than is $X_o(\min_N)$. Maximum $Z$ occurs when as few cells as possible contain nonzero entries (maximal clustering of cases). This amounts to seeking those integers which are maximal common subsets of both the $X$ and $Y$ marginal frequencies. The following program describes the sequence of steps for determining the needed values. For convenience, we designate those values as members of the set $\{n_{ij}\}$. This set contains the same number of elements as there are cells in the table, though as many of these as possible have a value of zero.

We begin by listing the two marginal distributions, then follow these steps until reaching STOP.

STEP 1: Is any pair of frequencies, one from each set, identical? (a) If yes, enter that value in the set $\{n_{ij}\}$ and reduce those two frequencies to zero. Check for further identical pairs, one from each set; treat them in the same manner. (b) If no, go to step 2.

STEP 2: Find the largest remaining (nonzero) frequency in each set. Enter the smaller of these two values in the set $\{n_{ij}\}$, and subtract that value from each of those two largest frequencies. Go to step 3.

STEP 3: Have all frequencies been reduced to zero? (a) If yes, go to step 4. (b) If no, return to step 1.

STEP 4: Set all remaining values of $\{n_{ij}\}$ equal to zero. STOP.

Table 1

X

|   | | | | |
|---|---|---|---|---|
| | 15 | 5 | 0 | 20 |
| Y | 15 | 25 | 10 | 50 |
| | 0 | 10 | 20 | 30 |
| | 30 | 40 | 30 | 100 |

Using Table 1, composed of fictitious data, and following the procedure just stated, we find the distributions $X(30, 40, 30)$ and $Y(20, 50, 30)$.

STEP 1: Yes, 30 is common to both sets. Enter 30 in $\{n_{ij}\}$, and reduce the distributions to $X(0, 40, 30)$ and $Y(20, 50, 0)$. There are no further identical pairs.

STEP 2: The largest remaining frequencies are $X(40)$ and $Y(50)$. Of these, 40 is smaller. Enter 40 in $\{n_{ij}\}$, and reduce the distributions to $X(0, 0, 30)$ and $Y(20, 10, 0)$.

STEP 3: No.

STEP 1: No.

STEP 2: The largest remaining frequencies are $X(30)$ and $Y(20)$. Of these, 20 is smaller. Enter 20 in $\{n_{ij}\}$, and reduce the distributions to $X(0, 0, 10)$ and $Y(0, 10, 0)$.

STEP 3: No.

STEP 1: Yes, the remaining frequencies both equal 10. Enter 10 in $\{n_{ij}\}$, and reduce the distributions to $X(0, 0, 0)$ and $Y(0, 0, 0)$.

STEP 2: There are no nonzero remaining frequencies.

STEP 3: Yes.

STEP 4: The remaining five values of $\{n_{ij}\} = 0$.

The entire set, then, is $\{n_{ij}\} = (30, 40, 20, 10, 0, 0, 0, 0, 0)$. There *may* be alternative locations in the table for the nonzero entries, meaning that, for some tables, more than one arrangement can satisfy the conditions of $Z(\max_N)$, but these nine values must be in the table. It is then possible to compute

$$Z(\max_N) = \tfrac{1}{2} \left( \sum_{ij} n^2_{ij} - N \right)$$
$$= 1450 \text{ for Table 1} \qquad (23)$$

Equation (15) may be used to find that $Z' = 596$, and $Z$, computed directly from Table 1, is

$$Z = \tfrac{1}{2} \left( \sum_{ij} N^2_{ij} - N \right)$$
$$= 800$$

Thus, $Z - Z' = 204 = Y'_o - Y_o$, and $Z(\max) - Z' = Y'_o - Y_o(\min_N) = X'_o - X_o(\min_N)$. Consequently, $d^c_N = 204/854 = 0.239$ and the percentage of pairs free of marginal restraint is found to be 0.88.

The information obtained about Table 1 allows the statements that about 12 per cent of the pairs are restrained by marginal distributions of the variables and that of the remaining 88 per cent, about 24 per cent of prediction error that would have occurred under independence has been eliminated by use of $X$ to predict $Y$.

The most important advantage of stating both the proportion of pairs free of restraint and the value of $d^c_N$ for that proportion lies in the possibility of sorting out the causes of covariation or its absence. If a table showed a relatively small proportion of unrestrained pairs yet high predictability for that proportion, it is possible that a strong relationship exists intrinsically but is masked by factors which affect marginal distributions rather than joint distribution. Obviously, asking whether a relationship appears when conditions are favorable is quite different from asking whether conditions are favorable. The subsequent research engendered by these divergent questions would be just as different as the questions are.

## COMPARISON OF $d_N$ WITH OTHER MEASURES

It is appropriate and instructive to compare more systematically $d_N$ and some of the well-known nominal association indexes. Among the most commonly used indexes of association for nominal variables are those based on chi square, notably phi square, Tschuprow's $T$ and Cramér's $V$. These will be examined first.

Blalock (1960, p. 230) notes that "all measures based on chi square are somewhat arbitrary in nature, and their interpretation leaves a lot to be desired." Chi square itself is not bounded suitably in that both sample size and degrees of freedom are involved in its magnitude. As $\chi^2/N$, phi square represents a correction for the first problem. It meets no serious problem for binary variables, but with tables greater than $2 \times 2$, the limits of phi square again become problematic. Even for $2 \times 2$ tables skewed marginals will restrict the maximum value of phi square, and a correction for that restriction is available (Mueller and Schuessler, 1961; p. 256). The index $d_N$ also provides for marginal restraint correction, but what about the other problems of chi square?

Since the maximum value of $d_N$ is under consideration, compared to those of $T$ or $V$, it should be remembered that $d_N^c$ can always reach unity regardless of table size or sample size. The maximum for phi square is unity for a $2 \times 2$ table with appropriate marginals but may greatly exceed that value in larger tables. Both $T^2 = \phi^2/\sqrt{(r-1)(c-1)}$ and $V^2 = \phi^2/\min(r-1, c-1)$ attempt to correct for table size, where $r$ and $c$ represent the number of rows and columns respectively. Since $\phi^2 = \chi^2/N$, $T^2$ and $V^2 = \chi^2/N(m-1)$ for a square table of dimension $m$. It can be shown that perfect association in a square table with the $X$ marginals containing the same frequencies as the $Y$ marginals will produce a chi-square value of $N(m-1)$. Thus, under ideal conditions both $T^2$ and $V^2$ have maxima of one; but when those conditions are not met, the formulas do not continue to make appropriate adjustments.

Further analysis leads to the fact that when all marginals for a square table equal $N/m$, for example, when there is perfectly even distribution of cases over all rows and all columns of the table, $d_N = \chi^2/N(m-1)$ regardless of the degree of association present. Consequently, $d_N^c = d_N = T^2 = V^2$ for such special cases. When either or both variables depart from perfect rectangular distributions, and when the table is no longer square, $d_N$ is no longer a simple function of these other measures.

The above comments indicate that $d_N$ and $d_N^c$ agree with the traditional chi-square based measures under conditions which are ideal for those measures. Under less ideal circumstances, as Blalock has noted, these traditional measures are no longer clearly interpretable. In contrast, $d_N^c$ has a clear PRE interpretation under all marginal conditions provided it is used in conjunction with a statement of the proportion of cases that are marginally restricted. The use of a pair logic has thus enabled a general solution of the problems of sample size, table size, and marginal distributions within an operationally interpretable framework that uses all available information. Furthermore, because it is so clearly related to chi square, in that the same notion of departure from expectation under independence is common to both, an appropriate test of the null hypothesis is chi square itself.

Three other measures for nominal data warrant comment. The first, $Q$, is appropriate for $2 \times 2$ tables only. Its generalization to larger tables is $\gamma$ which relies on ordinal properties of the variables. Consequently, $d_N$ is more general than $Q$. It is also considerably more conservative, particularly in cases of extreme distributions.

Goodman and Kruskal's $\tau$ and $\lambda$ are both PRE measures of association which are appropriate for any size table and which are not subject to sample-size fluctuations. Both, however, have drawbacks which appear to make $d_N^c$ preferable. One of the difficulties with $\lambda$ is illustrated by the fact that $\lambda$ will equal zero whenever all categories of the independent variable have the same crude mode. With relatively few categories on the dependent variable and with considerable marginal skew on that variable it is likely that the modes will be the same even though the proportional distribution may differ. The impression from such a table is often that there is some association, and a chi-square test may well reveal significant nonindependence, yet $\lambda$ shows nothing. Goodman and Kruskal's $\tau$ is also fairly weak in some instances, apparently in part because it does not take into account marginal limitations. However, when the circumstances are ideal for either $\lambda$ or Goodman and Kruskal's $\tau$, these measures are quite powerful. This is especially true of $\lambda$. The variation in the power of $\lambda$ and Goodman and Kruskal's $\tau$ from table to table makes the use of these measures, at least for comparative purposes, somewhat questionable. In contrast, as far as we can ascertain, $d_N^c$ is a stable and relatively powerful index in all instances, and variation in $d_N$ from table to table would appear to be readily interpretable.

Given the assumption that an integrated approach is preferable, a second difficulty with $\lambda$ and Goodman and Kruskal's $\tau$ is the apparent limited generality of their logic. At the outset we stated that a logic would be developed which remained consistent throughout all levels of measurement. The pair logic fills that requirement, but we do not, at this time, see any way of generalizing the logic underlying $\tau$ and see only limited generalizability of the logic underlying $\lambda$. Consequently, in the interest of integrated statistical conceptualization, it would seem appropriate to choose the measure which is clearly related to ordinal and interval level procedures $(d_N^c)$.

## PAIR-BASED MEASURES FOR ORDINAL AND INTERVAL LEVELS

The use of pair logic for the other levels of measurement involves a straightforward addition of their higher mathematical properties. Rather than pairs being either the same or different (nominal case), they can take on a signed difference (ordinal case) or a signed interval difference (interval case). Ideally, the consideration of higher levels of measurement should cover, in turn, each of the various combinations of independent-variable and dependent-variable level. The development of $d_N$ concerned only nominal measurement for both variables. For practical use there is little reason to examine those cases in which the dependent variable is lower in measurement level than the independent variable because the underlying logic of prediction cannot use the added information in the independent variable. As a result we shall classify cases in terms of the dependent variable, with certain procedural variations dependent upon the independent variable. The cases are (1) nominal: dependent variable nominal, independent variable any level; (2) ordinal: dependent variable ordinal and (a) independent variable nominal, (b) independent variable ordinal or higher level; (3) interval: dependent variable interval or higher level and (a) independent variable nominal, (b) independent variable ordinal, (c) independent variable interval or higher level.

## ORDINAL DEPENDENT AND INDEPENDENT VARIABLES

The nominal case has already been discussed. It will be convenient at this time to bypass case 2a and consider the ordinal-ordinal type of problem. Earlier discussion should have made clear the close similarity between the logic of $d_N$ and the existing gamma variations, requiring only a distinction between concordant and discordant pairs among those differing on both $X$ and $Y$.

Consider the $X_D$ pairs, which consist of $C$, $D$, and $Y_o$ cases. Using the added power of ordinal data, we can restate the prediction rule for $X_D$ pairs as, if $X$ changes between the members of the pair, predict that $Y$

will change concordantly (disconcordantly). Clearly, all $C$ cases will be correct (for the concordant case), and all $D$ cases will be in error. Whether $Y_o$ cases should be considered error or not has been discussed at length both by Somers (1962) and by Leik and Gove (1969). Gamma treats $Y_o$ pairs as acceptable, Somers' $d_{yx}$ treats them as half right and half wrong, and Leik and Gove offer a most stringent version which treats all $Y_o$ pairs as errors. All forms are shown to be subsumed under a general formula, $(C - D)/(C + D + kY_o)$, where $0 \leq k \leq 2$ and the particular value of $k$ depends on the seriousness of $Y_o$ pairs in light of certain methodological and theoretical considerations (Leik and Gove, 1969).

Following this earlier work, we define all $D$ cases as errors. In addition, we let $Y_o$ pairs, which are in a sense lesser errors, be variably treated as errors by multiplying $Y_o$ by a constant $l$. This constant is specifically indicative of the seriousness of $Y_o$ cases and has a range of $0 \leq l \leq 1$. If $l = 1$, $Y_o$ cases are just as serious errors as are $D$ pairs, whereas a value of zero implies that the $Y_o$ cases are as acceptable as the $C$ pairs. Intermediate values of $l$ indicate intermediate seriousness of the $Y_o$ errors. The obvious values for $l$ are 0 (weak monotone), $\frac{1}{2}$ (as with Somers' $d_{yx}$), and 1 (strong monotone); for a more detailed discussion of the reasoning behind these and other possible values, see Leik and Gove (1969). The reason for using $l$ rather than $k$ is algebraic and will become evident shortly. Parallel to the development of $d_N$, we define an ordinal measure as follows:

$$d_0 = \frac{\text{error under independence} - \text{actual error}}{\text{error under independence}}$$

For the $X_D$ pairs only, the measure would take the form

$$d_0 = \frac{(D' + lY_o') - (D + lY_o)}{D' + lY_o'}$$

Since $D' = C'$, $D' = \frac{1}{2}(C' + D')$, so that

$$d_0 = \frac{\frac{1}{2}(C' + D') - D + l(Y_o' - Y_o)}{\frac{1}{2}(C' + D') + lY_o'}$$

Reference to equation (13) provides the fact that $C' + D' = (C + D) - (Y_o' - Y_o)$. With a little algebra (proof of this and other assertions is available on request), it can be demonstrated that

$$d_0 = \frac{(C - D) + (k - 1)(Y_o' - Y_o)}{(C + D + kY_o) + (k - 1)(Y_o' - Y_o)} \tag{24}$$

Thus the current measure is the same as the general form of the gamma measures except for the term added to both the numerator and the denominator. That term is the difference between expected and observed $Y_o$ cases times a factor related to the seriousness of that type of error. The question of the $X_T$ pairs will be examined after the current form is discussed in some detail.

The additional term in the numerator and denominator of $d_o$ is disconcerting if one assumes that such a measure ought to agree in algebraic form with the earlier gamma forms. After all, the development was the same, wasn't it? Actually there is one notable difference between the two. Following Costner (1965) in his discussion of the PRE basis for $\gamma$, we note that the expected number of errors would be computed as $\frac{1}{2}(C + D)$. This value assumes that, for the actual set of observed cases, one tried to predict the direction of change in $Y$ without using $X$, which restricts attention to only those cases which are not tied on either variable. Since the number of such cases equals $C + D$, and a 50–50 probability rule is used, $\frac{1}{2}(C + D)$ is a correct figure. It depends, though, on knowing the interior of the table.

In contrast, $d_0$ computes the expected errors based on what would occur under statistical independence. Thus, the marginal distributions of both variables, involving all cases, have been employed. No knowledge of the interior of the table is assumed. This approach is comparable to the use of marginal variance of $Y$ in interval data as the amount of error when not using $X$ to predict $Y$. Also, as has been shown, it is in keeping with the spirit of chi-square measures at the nominal level. In the formula for $d_0$, when $k = 1$, as with $d_{yx}$, the terms added to the numerator and denominator disappear, and $d_0 = d_{yx}$. When $k = 0$, as with $\gamma$, we see that the above formula will give a smaller value than $\gamma$ (subtracting a constant from a numerator and denominator of a ratio less than unity decreases its value). Based on the logic developed here, then, $\gamma$ overestimates the degree of relationship even when $Y_o$ (and $X_o$) pairs are treated as correct. This error is in general small. Similarly, when $k = 2$, it can be seen that $d'_{yx}$ gives a slight underestimate of the degree of association.

What about the pairs tied on $X$? The appropriate way to handle these pairs is to consider them correctly predicted if $Y$ does not change and incorrectly predicted if $Y$ does change, but incorrectly predicted to the same degree that the $Y_o$ pairs are called errors. Thus the $k$ factor will be needed for these pairs as well. Treating the entire set of cases formally leads to the following extension of the nominal case rules: First, define $X_{ij} = f_o(X_i - X_j)$ and $Y_{ij} = f_o(Y_i - Y_j)$, where $f_o$ is an ordinal level function assigning a score of 0 if the two scores are the same, $+1$ if the first is the greater, and $-1$ if the second is the greater. Second, predict $Y_{ij} = X_{ij}$ for all $ij$ pairs. Prediction error is therefore $E_{ij} = Y_{ij} - X_{ij}$, which takes on values of $+2, +1, 0, -1, -2$. Note that the $+1$ and $-1$ values represent all $X_o$ and $Y_o$ cases. The apparent metric of these scores, in violation of ordinal assumptions, will be eliminated if the values associated with the $X_o$ and $Y_o$ pairs are made intermediate between 0 and 2, leaving fixed scores representing only the two extreme discrepancies. Since these both indicate discordance, with the sign indicating only whether $X_{ij}$ or $Y_{ij}$ was larger, they should be equally distant from 0, or concordance. Step 3 provides this intermediate indeterminancy to the $X_o$ and $Y_o$ cases. Third, use the sum of squared errors, both observed and expected under independence, as the error statement in the PRE format except that a squared error of 1 (all $X_o$ and $Y_o$ cases) will be assigned a value of $k$. Thus squared errors take on values of 4, $k$, or 0, maintaining a truly ordinal character. These rules restate the ideas presented for the ordinal case, including indeterminancy of the $X_o$ and $Y_o$ pairs re the statistical hypothesis, and generate the following variation on equation (24).

$$d_0 = \frac{C - D + (k - 1)(Y'_o - Y_o)}{C + D + k\left(\frac{Y_o + X_o}{2}\right) + (k - 1)(Y'_o - Y_o)} \qquad (25)$$

The only difference here is that the $Y_o$ term of the denominator is replaced by a mean of $X_o$ and $Y_o$. The reason a similar adjustment does not appear in the last term is that $Y'_o - Y_o = \frac{1}{2}[(Y'_o - Y_o) + (X'_o - X_o)]$. For the data in Table 1, $X_o = 850$ whereas $Y_o = 1050$, which means that the value of $d_0$ would slightly increase over the form in equation (24). For some tables the equation may have slightly lower value than equation (24), but in general, they should be quite close in value. Note that like $\gamma$, but unlike $d_{yx}$, formula (25) defines $d_0$ as a symmetric measure in spite of being based on an asymmetric prediction logic. Because equation (25) is the most general form and fits precisely with the other measurement-level forms of the measures being developed here, we recommend its use over the admittedly similar forms now in the literature.

As was true for $d_N$, it is desirable to determine a maximum value for $d_0$ as fixed by marginal distributions. This value is readily found by using the appropriate maximum and minimum values in the place of observed values in equation (25). With algebraic manipulation and the identities established earlier in the chapter, it can be shown that the equation for $d$ (max) reduces to

$$d_0(\text{max}) = \frac{2\,C' + k[Y'_o - Y_o(\text{min})]}{2\,C' + k[(Y'_o + X'_o)/2]} \qquad (26)$$

Dividing $d_0(\text{max})$ into $d_0$ for any ordinal-ordinal table will provide the extent to which ordinal association has approached the limits imposed by the table's marginal distributions.

Computation of $d_0(\max)$ requires a value of $Y_o(\min)$ which has, as yet, no formula. As with earlier computations, it will be easiest for many tables to compute $Z(\max_o)$ first, find its difference from $Z$, and subtract that amount from $Y_o$ to obtain $Y_o(\min_o)$. The earlier form of $Z(\max_N)$ is no longer appropriate, though, because the maximizing criterion will now be $C - D$ (That is, maximal ordinal association) rather than $Z$ itself. In general $Z(\max_o)$ will be less than or equal to $Z(\max_N)$.

The following program will provide necessary cell frequencies for obtaining ordinal $Z(\max_o)$.

STEP 1: List the marginal frequencies for $X$ in their proper order (the inherent order of the variable). Do the same for $Y$. Set index $i$ equal to 1.

STEP 2: Set $n_i$ equal to the smaller of the first nonzero $X$ marginal and the first nonzero $Y$ marginal. Subtract $n_i$ from each of these two marginal frequencies. Set $i = i + 1$.

STEP 3: Are all marginals of both variables equal to zero? (a) If no, go to step 2. (b) If yes, set remaining $n_i = 0$. STOP

Note that the instructions require that all of the first marginal of each variable be used up before proceding to the next marginal, and so on. Having obtained the values of set $\{n_i\}$, we can compute $Z(\max_o)$ according to the earlier formula.

To illustrate the computations for $d_0$ and $d_0(\max)$, again refer to Table 1. The values of $Y_o' = 1254$ and $X_o' = 1054$ can be found as stated earlier. $Y_o = Y_o' - 204$, the value of $Z - Z'$ already computed. Similarly, $X_o = X_o' - 204$, and in the usual way for $\gamma$, it can be found that $C = 2075$ and $D = 175$. Letting $k = 1$ for the equivalent of the Somers variation provides

$$d_0 = \frac{2075 - 175 + 204}{2075 + 175 + (1050 + 850/2) + 204} = 0.62$$

As outlined above, $C'$ may be computed as 1023 and $Y_o(\min)$ as 400 so that

$$d_0(\max) = \frac{2046 + 854}{2046 + 1154} = 0.91$$

A marginally corrected value of $d_0$, designated $d_0^c$, is therefore, 0.62/ 0.91 = 0.68.

Incidentally, the value of Somers' $d_{yx}$ for Table 1 is very close to

$d_0$ that is ,0.58. Also, corrected $d_{yx}$ is exactly equal to $d_0^c$, a fact that can be demonstrated mathematically.

It is apparent from a comparison of the results of the more complex formulas generated by considering all pairs with the results of $\gamma$ and its simpler variations that the latter provide close numerical approximations of the former. This is particularly true for marginally corrected values. In the interest of ease, it might appear more convenient to use the simpler approximations for research, but to maintain the logic we have set forth as a basis for interpreting and teaching about ordinal association measures, we recommend use of $d_0$ and $d_0^c$.

## NOMINAL INDEPENDENT–ORDINAL DEPENDENT VARIABLES

Returning to case 2a, in which the independent variable is only nominal, requires a very simple adjustment in the computation of $d_0$. First, it should be noted that the only difference between ordinal and nominal independent variables is that the categories of the latter need not to be kept in any particular order. As an initial conception, the appropriate measure should be concerned with ordinal clustering of cases within categories of $X$ such that those categories have differing medians. This would be directly comparable to the correlation ratio for an interval-level dependent variable. However it should be recognized that, for the ordinal-ordinal case, the value of $d_0$ and the amount of ordinal clustering within categories of $X$ covary positively.

The ordinal-ordinal solution can be adapted to the nominal-ordinal problem by allowing columns ($X$ categories) to assume whatever order would maximize $d_0$ while requiring that rows ($Y$ categories) remain in fixed order. If a high value of $d_0$ can be obtained for some ordering of $X$, then there is appropriate evidence of a relationship between $X$ and $Y$ within the limits of the measurement levels of the variables. As an example, consider Table 2.

Table 2

$X$

|     | | | | |
|-----|------|------|------|------|
| | $\begin{bmatrix} 15 \\ 15 \\ 0 \end{bmatrix}$ | $\begin{matrix} 0 \\ 10 \\ 30 \end{matrix}$ | $\begin{matrix} 5 \\ 25 \\ 0 \end{bmatrix}$ | 20 50 30 |

$Y$ label is to the left of the matrix (middle row). Column totals below:

|  |  |  |
|------|------|------|
| 30 | 40 | 30 |

If $X$ is a nominal variable, then the computed value of $d_0 = 0.13$ (assuming $k = 1$) would not give a valid impression of nominal-ordinal association. Reordering the categories of $X$ by interchanging the last two columns of Table 2 provides a noteworthy $d_0 = 0.72$. If a corrected value is desired, it can be computed exactly as in the ordinal-ordinal case; obtain $d_0(\text{max})$ in the same manner, and divide it into the observed $d_0$. Since Table 2 has the same marginals as Table 1, the maxima are the same, making $d_0^c = 0.12/0.91 = 0.79$. This procedure provides a completely appropriate association measure for the nominal-ordinal case.

## INTERVAL-LEVEL DEPENDENT VARIABLE

It will be easy to extend the pair logic to the interval-level dependent variable cases, for all pairs, because that logic exactly recreates standard parametric procedures, such as product-moment correlation (interval-level independent variable), the correlation ratio (nominal-level independent variable), the Leik-Gove (1969) monotonic-association index for an ordinal independent variable, and whatever nonlinear forms might be desired. That this is so will not surprise those familiar with variance expressed in terms of pair differences. A brief review for linear $r$ will demonstrate the identity of results produced by the two approaches.

Exactly parallel to previous rules, define $X_{ij} = X_i - X_j$ and $Y_{ij} = Y_i - Y_j$. Predict $X_{ij} = bY_{ij}$, which really says $Y_i - Y_j = b(X_i - X_j)$ or, in terms appropriate to change in variables, $\Delta Y = b\Delta X$. This is a common alternative expression of linearity, which does not bother with the intercept in $Y = a + bX$. In fact, the pair difference, as noted for the nominal case, is intuitively simpler. It says that if two cases (individuals, and soon) differ on $X$, you can expect them to differ proportionately on $Y$. There is no need to be involved with the concept of error about a regression line unless regression per se is under discussion.

Error is then defined as the difference between prediction and observation, as before. It can be shown that the criterion of least-squared error (we have used squared error throughout, and least-squared error is a standard criterion) provides $b = \text{COV}(XY)/\text{VAR}(X)$ by the standard definitions of those functions. If there were independence between $X$ and $Y$, then $\text{COV}(XY) = 0$, making $b = 0$. The mean squared error for pairs, given independence, can then be shown to be proportional to $\text{VAR}(Y)$, which becomes the first term in the index numerator. Actual mean squared pair error can also be shown to be proportional to the usual error variance from linear regression and becomes the second term in the numerator. Since the proportionality is the same, and the $\text{VAR}(Y)$ term occurs also in the denominator, the linear pair case

$d_I =$

$$\frac{\dfrac{2}{N(N-1)}\displaystyle\sum_i\sum_{j>i}(Y_i-Y_j)^2 - \dfrac{2}{N(N-1)}\displaystyle\sum_i\sum_{j>i}[(Y_i-Y_j)-b(X_i-X_j)]^2}{[2/N(N-1)]\displaystyle\sum_i\sum_{j>i}(Y_i-Y_j)^2}$$

is equivalent to

$$d_I = \frac{\sigma^2 Y - \sigma^2 E}{\sigma^2 Y} = r^2$$

Parallel to the foregoing, we can show that a pair approach plus a least-squared error criterion will generate a variety of parametric procedures according to the form of the prediction equation. For example:

$$Y_i - Y_j \begin{cases} = 0 \text{ if } X_i = X_j \\ \neq 0 \text{ if } X_i \neq X_j \end{cases}$$

produces the correlation ratio, but this prediction is exactly the same rule that was stated for $d_N$ at the outset.

$$Y_i - Y_j \begin{cases} >0 \text{ if } X_i > X_j \\ <0 \text{ if } X_i < X_j \end{cases}$$

produces the Leik-Gove monotonic adaptation of the correlation ratio, but this prediction rule duplicates the rule for $d_0$, with the difference that interval procedures allow precise determination of intermediate errors.

What about marginal limitations on $d_I$? Although no extended discussion of the interval level forms will be undertaken, it is worth pointing out that $r^2$ is, in general, not able to reach unity, although the assumption of a joint normal distribution would allow $\rho = 1$ for the population. The limit on $r$ can be demonstrated as follows: For any set of $X$, $Y$ observations, place the $X$ values in, for example, descending order. Disregard which $Y$ goes with which $X$, and do the same for the $Y$ values. Now, compute $r^2$ as if the two highest values were paired, the two next highest, and so on. Unless the marginal distributions of $X$ and $Y$ contain identical (within linear transformation) values, $r^2$ will be short of unity, and clearly, this is the largest value it could obtain for these data. Again, it may be quite important, theoretically, to realize that a moderate value of $r^2$ may as readily be a consequence of whatever influences the marginal distributions of $X$ and $Y$ as it is evidence of only partially related variables. This issue has, typically, been ignored, perhaps in part due to the implications of an assumption of joint normality.

To illustrate marginal limits on $r$, let us consider the data in Table 3. Without checking marginal distributions, a researcher could readily compute $r = 0.69$, giving slightly under 50 per cent explained variance. Both distributions are skewed, however, and in opposite directions. Maximum $r$ for these data is 0.79. Consequently, observed $r$ is about 87 per cent of its maximum value, which means there is over 75 per cent of variance that could be explained (that is, that is free of marginal restriction) that is systematically related to $X$.

Table 3

| Original Distribution | | Ordered Distribution | |
| --- | --- | --- | --- |
| $X$ | $Y$ | $X$ | $Y$ |
| 2 | 5 | 10 | 10 |
| 5 | 10 | 7 | 9 |
| 1 | 6 | 5 | 9 |
| 3 | 8 | 4 | 8 |
| 1 | 1 | 3 | 8 |
| 2 | 8 | 2 | 7 |
| 10 | 9 | 2 | 6 |
| 4 | 7 | 1 | 5 |
| 7 | 9 | 1 | 3 |
| 1 | 3 | 1 | 1 |

## CONCLUSIONS

It has been our intention to demonstrate that a pair-based logic will generate PRE type association measures for whatever independent- and dependent-variable measurement levels are available. Furthermore, the measure is so generated that the nominal case is superior, though related, to existing measures, the ordinal cases are only slight variants of known procedures, and the interval-level cases duplicate standard parametric procedures. The strength of the approach, beyond the improved nominal case, lies in the consistency of its application throughout all cases. This is of value both for interpretation and comparison of results and for teaching purposes. The intuitive ease of comparing each case with each of the other cases should make all variations of the $d$ measures more easily understood by students first becoming acquainted with statistical operations. Finally, the systematic concern with marginal limitations on association should encourage a routine distinction between possible reasons for less-than-breathtaking amounts of association. We do not suggest that marginally corrected values be a cheap way of buying higher indexes so as to increase the probability of acceptance for publication, but they may provide easy leads for profitable future research and theory.

## REFERENCES

BLALOCK, H.
1960 *Social Statistics.* New York: McGraw-Hill.

COSTNER, H.
1965 "Criteria for measures of association." *American Sociological Review* 30: 341–353.

GOODMAN, L. AND KRUSKAL, W.
1954 "Measures of association for cross classifications." *Journal of the American Statistical Association* 49: 733–764.

GUTTMAN, L.
1941 "An outline of the statistical theory of prediction." Pp. 261–262 in P. Horst (Ed.), *The Prediction of Personal Adjustment.* New York: Social Science Research Council Bulletin 48.

LEIK, R.
1966 "A measure of association for ordinal variables." Paper read at the meeting of the American Sociological Association.

LEIK, R. AND GOVE, W.
1969 "The conception and measurement of asymmetric monotonic relationships in sociology." *American Journal of Sociology* 74: 696–709.

MUELLER, J. AND SCHUESSLER, K.
1961 *Statistical Reasoning in Sociology.* Boston: Houghton Mifflin.

SOMERS, R.
1962 "A new asymmetric measure of association for ordinal variables." *American Sociological Review* 27: 799–811.

## 11

# CONTINUITIES IN SOCIAL PREDICTION

*Karl Schuessler*

INDIANA UNIVERSITY

*Presented at the meet-
ings of the International Sociological Association, Varna, Bulgaria, September 18, 1970, as part of a session on measurement and prediction arranged
by H. M. Blalock, Jr.*

The general purpose of this chapter is to convey some notion
about prediction as a specialty in American sociology from 1920 to the
present. Our main question is whether, during this period, efforts at
prediction have been sequential and cumulative or whether they form
an irregular series without discernible continuity? Anticipating our
answer to this question, we shall discover that no line of work has been
doggedly pursued and that few, if any, matters, theoretical or methodological, have been settled by prediction research.

American sociologists have more or less taken for granted that
prediction is one of their main objectives. This assumption is rooted in

302

the writings of nineteenth-century European sociologists and was fostered in the United States by the writings of the philosophical pragmatists (for example, John Dewey) who maintained that the validity of social science inhered in the accuracy of its social predictions. The eruption of work on prediction in the 1920's was an expression of a tendency in American sociology present from the beginning and reflected the urge of sociologists to realize the promise of their discipline as a natural science.

The work itself has consisted of two somewhat different endeavors, forecasting the future and predicting an outcome under stated conditions. Some sociologists would regard this as no categorical difference but merely a distinction between scientific knowledge and the application of that knowledge for purposes of social planning and control. They would argue that scientific knowledge may exist even though no forecasts are made; just as forecasts may be made, and often are, in the absence of scientific knowledge. Nevertheless, because the term *prediction* is sometimes used synonymously with forecasting in sociological writing, it may not be amiss to distinguish between these two concepts at the outset.

## TERMINOLOGY

When we state beforehand what will happen at a certain time and place, we are making a forecast. In our daily lives each of us makes literally hundreds of forecasts, practically all of which are correct by reason of the orderly nature of social life. "The Seventh World Congress of Sociology will meet in Varna on September 15, 1970;" "His daughter will be married on June 15;" "The county fair will run from August 10 to 20;"—all are cases in point. Perhaps we should not dignify such announcements and speculations as social forecasts and should reserve that term for statements about events fraught with general social significance—wars, revolution, depressions, and so on. But, however we restrict the meaning of the term, a forecast is a preview of the future. Forecasts are tied to both the map and the calendar and are analogous to the farmer's almanac, which gives weather information, in advance, by date and place.

On the other hand, a prediction by definition gives the expected result under stated conditions and is bound by neither time nor place. If the stated conditions hold, the result will materialize. The statement that heads will appear 50 times in 100 on the average, given that both the coin and the tossing are intrinsically fair, is a prediction. Similarly, the $q$ values in a conventional life table constitute predictions for some well-defined population. The law of falling bodies permits us to calculate (predict) the duration of a body's fall from instant of release to instant of impact.

Predictions themselves may be classified according to whether they are based on events concurrent or sequential in time and whether stochastic disturbances (sampling and measurement error aside) are present or absent.

When two or more events in a system occur at the same instant, we may predict from the known events in that system to the unknown events; when two or more events occur in sequence over time, we may predict from antecedent events in the system, as they materialize, to later events in the chain. If we predict by Engel's law that the wealthy spend relatively more of their income on luxuries than the poor, we are predicting from one concurrent event to another; if we predict a person's occupational attainment from his school record, we are predicting from an antecedent to a subsequent event. In the latter example it is possible to arrange events in time; in the former case no such arrangement is possible, since the factor of time is ignored.

Although predictions are usually based on relations among variables, the limit of accuracy of predictions depends on whether the relations are deterministic or stochastic. To indicate that a relation is stochastic, it is conventional to write the prediction equation as follows (Wold, 1967, p. 9):

$$y = f(x) + e \tag{1}$$

where $e$ is the stochastic term. When $e$ tends to zero the prediction equation reduces to the form,

$$y = f(x) \tag{2}$$

or a deterministic relation.

Since predictions based on stochastic relations are necessarily less accurate than those based on deterministic relations, we might suppose that such predictions should be slighted by sociologists in favor of those whose potential accuracy is greater. But that conclusion is sociologically unrealistic, since many social actions are the result of both deterministic and stochastic factors. For example, the movement of a worker from one industry to another is affected by both determining and chance factors. We mention this as a counter to the opinion, promoted in the United States by the writings of Znaniecki, that the investigation of stochastic relations is less important than the investigation of deterministic relations.

## FORECASTING

The services of American sociologists as forecasters have never been in great demand, and today, forecasting is routinely carried on in only a few areas of sociology. The forecasts themselves have been based largely on recent social trends and take the form of either a quantitative estimate or literary description. Since all such forecasts, whether couched in numbers or words, have been derived from historical data, it is proper to ask whether the forecast of the sociologist differs from the conjecture of the professional historian. A brief answer is that the difference between them lies not in their empirical source but rather in their scope and method. Sociological forecasts are usually restricted to a well-defined variable which lends itself to measurement and statistical analysis and rest, to the degree possible, on sociological principles when these appear relevant to the problem in hand. The ensuing discussion aims to point up the distinctive features and problems of such forecasting as well as to reflect the development of forecasting as a specialty within American sociology.

### Population

Techniques for forecasting the population have evolved during the last one hundred years through the efforts of workers from several disciplines (Dorn, 1950). Sociologists not only contributed to the development of the population forecast but also helped to establish it as a regular feature of the U.S. Bureau of the Census. Their entry into this line of work may be marked by the publication of Whelpton's article in 1928, in which he suggested that population forecasts be based on separate estimates of births, deaths, and net immigration rather than on a mere extrapolation of a fitted growth curve. In devising his method, Whelpton was expressly reacting to the work of Pearl and Reed (1920), who had fitted a logistic of the form

$$y = \frac{1}{a + be^{-kt}} \tag{3}$$

Table 1
Projected Population (in millions) of the United States according to Pearl
and Reed (1920) and Whelpton (1928): 1920–2000

| Projection | 1920 | 1930 | 1940 | 1950 | 1960 | 1970 | 1980 | 1990 | 2000 |
|---|---|---|---|---|---|---|---|---|---|
| Pearl and Reed | 107 | 122 | 136 | 149 | 159 | 168 | 185 | 180 | 185 |
| Whelpton | | 124 | 138 | 152 | 163 | 171 | | | |
| Enumerated Population | 106 | 123 | 132 | 151 | 171 | 205 | | | |

to the United States population from 1790 to 1910 ($1/a$ is the ultimate population, $b$ is a constant of integration, and $k$ is the rate of increase per capita) and extrapolated that empirical curve into the future. Their forecasts are given in Table 1.

Whelpton suggested that a more accurate forecast might be made by adjusting the enumerated population at any moment by the anticipated number of births and deaths, and immigrants and emigrants. In symbolic form

$$P_t = P_0 + (B - D) + I \tag{4}$$

where $P_t$ = estimated population at time $t$, $P_0$ = present population, $B$ = births, $D$ = deaths, and $I$ = net immigration. Since each component of population change is calculated separately, this method has come to be known as the component method of forecasting. It is of historical interest that, despite Whelpton's claims for the superiority of his method, his forecasts were not much better than those given by Pearl and Reed's fitted logistic, as may be seen from Table 1.

However, the importance of these early efforts should be gauged not by their accuracy but rather by the developments both basic and applied to which they led. For example, forecasts of the United States population, periodically supplied by the Census Bureau, are based on a refinement of Whelpton's technique which takes into account cohort differences in fertility. The most recent such forecast is given in Table 2.

Table 2

Projected Population (in millions) of the United States according to the U.S. Bureau of the Census (1970): 1970–2020

| Year (July 1) | Series B[a] | Series C | Series D | Series E |
|---|---|---|---|---|
| Projections | | | | |
| 1970[b] | 205 | 205 | 205 | 205 |
| 1975 | 219 | 218 | 216 | 215 |
| 1980 | 237 | 232 | 228 | 226 |
| 1985 | 257 | 249 | 241 | 237 |
| 1990 | 277 | 266 | 255 | 248 |
| 1995 | 298 | 283 | 268 | 257 |
| 2000 | 321 | 301 | 281 | 266 |
| 2005 | 347 | 320 | 294 | 275 |
| 2010 | 376 | 341 | 307 | 284 |
| 2015 | 407 | 363 | 322 | 292 |
| 2020 | 440 | 386 | 336 | 299 |

[a] The four series use identical assumptions of mortality and immigration but differ in their assumptions about fertility.

[b] A preliminary estimate for July 1, 1970, is 205,394.

These official forecasts are instructive for the light they shed generally on the problem of social forecasts. First, the population forecast, in the light of its record, points to the hazard of assuming that relative frequencies of the past, and the causal forces they manifest, will maintain themselves for the period over which the forecast extends. To guard against this hazard, demographers sometimes refer to their extrapolations as projections rather than forecasts. A population projection is a statement of what would happen if a fixed schedule of births and deaths maintained itself over time, whereas a forecast is more a statement of what will actually happen and is, therefore, more of a gamble. However, in selecting the most probable projection from among several alternatives, as demographers sometimes do, one is making a forecast whether or not one calls it by that name.

Second, the population forecast is a reminder that estimates for the very near future (for example, next year) are no less useful than estimates for the distant future and that methods for arriving at short-term estimates are no less deserving of investigation. At least for the time being, sociologists might be advised to concentrate on short-term projections since the success of such efforts and the analyses on which they rest is probably a prerequisite to, if no guarantee of, successful long-term forecasting.

Third, population forecasts are reflexive in the sense that they may affect the events they forecast. For example, the fertility rate may reach a replacement level or lower owing in part to the anxiety aroused by the forecast of a population explosion. Population forecasts have in common with social forecasts generally a potential for throwing themselves into error by feedback.

Fourth, the population forecast entails an analysis of the past and in that analysis the process of growth (and decay) may be clarified. The attempt to forecast may produce a better explanation of social change which in turn may produce a better forecast. It is generally acknowledged that an improved understanding of cohort differences as they affect the fertility rate grew out of the effort to forecast the population. We mention the foregoing points, not as strengths or weaknesses of the population forecast but rather as problems present in practically all social forecasting.

## Election

As our second example, we take the election forecast and its methodology. An election forecast rests on a succession of sample polls taken during the period from nomination of candidates to election day. Based on the trend of these results, with allowance for sampling and measurement error, the percentage of the total vote for each candidate is estimated, and the probable winning candidate is named.

The election forecast, like the population forecast, was not the product of a single discipline but rather represented the efforts of diverse specialists—journalists, psychologists, political scientists, and so on. From the informal, casual straw vote, it gradually evolved during the 1930's into an objective and systematic technique for predicting the outcome at the polls. Sociologists, notably Stouffer and Lazarsfeld, contributed to its refinement as a method in general and as a set of procedures for obtaining unbiased data in particular. However, its complexities were not fully appreciated by its early practitioners, and their efforts were not always successful. This is borne out by Table 3 where actual and predicted figures for the United States presidential elections of 1936–1948 are shown.

The poor showing of the polls in 1948 was the object of an intensive inquiry, conducted under the auspices of the Social Science Research

Table 3

Actual Vote Cast and Final National Predictions of Presidential Vote by Crossley, Gallup, and Roper, 1936–1948

| | 1936 | 1940 | 1944 | 1948 |
|---|---|---|---|---|
| | Democratic percentage of total vote | | | |
| Actual vote | 60.2 | 54.7 | 53.4 | 49.4 |
| Crossley | 53.8 | b | | 44.8 |
| Gallup | 53.8 | | | |
| Roper | 61.7 | 55.2 | | 37.1 |
| | Errors of prediction in percentage points | | | |
| Crossley | −6.4 | | | −4.6 |
| Gallup | −6.4 | | | |
| Roper | +1.5 | +0.5 | | −12.3 |
| | Democratic percentage of two-party vote | | | |
| Actual vote | 62.2 | 55.0 | 53.8 | 49.8[a] |
| Crossley | 55.0 | b | 52.0 | |
| Gallup | 55.7 | 52.0 | 51.5[c] | 44.5[a] |
| Roper | | | 53.6 | |
| | Errors of prediction in percentage points | | | |
| Crossley | −7.2 | | −1.8 | |
| Gallup | −6.5 | −3.0 | −2.3[c] | −5.3 |
| Roper | | | −0.2 | |

[a] Figures for 1948 are Democratic percentage of four-party vote.

[b] No prediction for nation, no national poll taken.

[c] Estimated civilian vote—not quite comparable to Democratic percentage of two-party vote since the latter includes the soldier vote.

Source: Mosteller and others (1949).

Council. The final report (1949) stressed the importance of anticipating the distribution of actual voters and significant shifts in that distribution before the election. The difficulties of staying abreast of such shifts may be broached by comparing the election forecast with the population forecast in the following three respects: First, the population forecast is based on objective events of the past—births, deaths, and migration—while the election forecast is based on the stated intentions of people. Such statements may be quite unstable either because the respondent has not made up his mind or because he is reluctant to disclose his true feelings to the interviewer. Second, the population forecast is based on an enumeration and analysis of all events in the population, insofar as that is possible, while the election forecast, at least in practice, is based on a relatively small sample of respondents. Election forecasts must take into account sampling error as well as measurement error. Third, public opinion is subject to sudden shifts which may go undetected without continual monitoring, whereas population growth is presumably more stable and less given to abrupt change. An implication is that a sampling of opinion (whatever the topic) may have little predictive value for even the immediate future and may be highly misleading when used for that purpose. We draw this comparison not to downgrade the election forecast but rather to point up some of the special problems of the sample survey on which American sociologists heavily rely as a source of data.

## Social Change

During the last fifty years, American sociologists have devoted much thought and energy to the subject of social change (Moore, 1963). But, contrary to what one might expect, this work has not issued in a steady stream of forecasts about the future of American society. The work of Ogburn is something of an exception in its actual use of theory about the future of social organization in the United States. We cite it here because it stands virtually alone as a large-scale effort to forecast the pattern of activities in one sector of American society from changes occurring in another sector.

In explaining social change, Ogburn attached considerable importance to invention and discovery. He held that in the modern world inventions commonly come first and social effects later. By reason of this lag, it is possible, he argued, to anticipate the future and plan for its eventualities. In elaborating on this point, he wrote that not all parts of society change at the same rate and at the same time. Some move ahead, while others lag behind. Scientific discoveries and inventions produce change first in the economic organization. Next, change occurs in institutions such as the family, then church and the state.

Some time later come changes in social philosophy, manners, and morals.

Changes in social organization may thus be anticipated from an analysis of recent technological change. This possibility is implicit in a special project of the U.S. National Resources Committee (1937), for which Ogburn was mainly responsible, which undertook to forecast the impact of technological change in the United States; later he worked out in greater detail the social effects of aviation (Ogburn, Adams, and Gilfillan, 1946). The method of this latter study, which may be taken as representative, was to calculate the direction and strength of recent trends in aviation and to consider the effects of these developments on such major social institutions as the family and education. While the statistically fitted trend lines showed the rates of change over time, the forecasts themselves were limited largely to somewhat imprecise statements about the direction of change. By way of example, consider this selection of conclusions.

POPULATION: "Aviation . . . will tend to lessen the differential of density in population between widely separated . . . areas with differing degrees of population pressure" (p. 329).

FAMILY: "The influence of our passenger transportation is in line with the general trend of increasing separation of the members of the family from one another, especially through the travel of the husband" (p. 339).

EDUCATION: "As to the impact of aviation on the organized education of the schools, the most important changes will be those in the curricula, with scarcely a subject being untouched in some way" (p. 463).

OCEAN SHIPPING: "In the latter part of the first postwar decade, the steamships are expected to lose about fifty per cent of their first- and second-class passengers to the airlines. . . . In the second postwar decade, a large proportion of the remaining passengers are expected to be diverted to the airlines" (p. 497).

GOVERNMENT: "The development of aviation will reinforce the already existing trend to shift powers and functions from local to national centers" (p. 658).

INTERNATIONAL RELATIONS: "The natural influence of aviation . . . is to speed the evolution of states into still larger size" (p. 705).

We quote these conjectures, not to question their accuracy or ingenuity, but rather to call attention to the difficulties both in making forecasts and in evaluating them (Iklé, 1967). These difficulties are symptomatic of the problematical (to sociologists) nature of social change, problems in measuring social change, and the absence of dependable indicators of variables whose change is in question (Duncan,

1969a and 1969b). Together, these factors account for both the dearth of social forecasts and the lowly state of the art of social forecasting.

## Planning

Despite the promise of Ogburn's methodology, it has not caught on in American sociology and has more or less fallen into disuse. Today, few sociologists practice forecasting by trend analysis. When called upon, sociologists do make projections about the future, but these neither embody standard procedures nor are they phrased so as to be readily evaluated. They are often concerned with social ends and means—avoiding social calamity or attaining social goals (Miller and Roby, 1970). At the moment these conjectures, extrapolations, and speculations are something of a preoccupation of a growing number of social scientists, including sociologists, and for that reason are mentioned here.

Daniel Bell is perhaps the leading exponent of this specialty in sociology. He has been especially instrumental in maintaining a national dialogue among American social scientists on predicting the future and planning to meet its contingencies. (Kenneth Boulding (1964) represents a similar orientation in economics.) This effort of Bell and his coworkers finds expression in the 1967 summer issue of *Daedelus* which contains 35 essays on the possible shape of American society in the year 2000. Sociology is represented by Moynihan (1967) and Riesman (1967) (along with Bell (1967)), and their contributions will serve to illustrate the general method of these forecasts as well as substantive matters of special concern to sociologists. So that the overall purpose of this volume is not misrepresented, we quote from Bell's introductory article (1967, p. 641): "There do not exist today any reliable methods of prediction or forecasting (even in technology), but some spectacular predictions are often encouraged or demanded to enhance the game and attract attention. As is shown in these pages, the serious effort is devoted not to making predictions, but to the more complicated and subtle art of defining alternatives." Later on he iterates (1967, p. 646): "The problem of the future consists in defining one's priorities and making the necessary commitments. This is an intention of the Commission of the Year 2000."

As his subject for discussion, Moynihan takes the relationship of federal to local authorities. In the light of recent trends, he anticipates more federal funding of state and local authorities, more consolidating of schools, a proliferation of governmental forms, a continuing quest for community, a rediscovery of the free market, and a more accurate method of social accounting. Although these forecasts about eventualities for the "last third" are probably correct, no special training in sociology is required to make them. They are thoughts that would occur to practically all who are abreast of the times and reasonably familiar with recent social and political trends in this country. We make this point not to disparage the undertaking but rather to stress that the forecasts of American social scientists are frequently quite informal and nontechnical.

Riesman's (1967) essay supplies our second example. He takes as his point of departure Michael Young's thesis that in England, owing to the growing demand for optimal social efficiency, the principle of aristocracy is giving way to the principle of meritocracy. Riesman's comments "are principally an American embroidery on some of the themes" in Young's writing. In his essay, he notes the special pressures that a meritocracy will probably create in the United States and some of the resistance a meritocracy is likely to encounter. His views, like Moynihan's, embody no standard methodology and more nearly resemble the insights of an experienced physician than the technical forecasts of an applied scientist (for example, a meterologist). It is not our purpose to belittle these provocative and sometimes gloomy prophecies; rather we cite them as what sociologists sometimes do when they are called upon to make pronouncements about the future. These pronouncements usually differ very little from the conclusions of lawyers, economists, governmental officials, and others having an enlightened concern in public affairs.

## PREDICTION

The main focus of prediction in American sociology from 1920 to 1950 was personal adjustment in specific social situations (Schuessler, 1968a); recently (circa 1960) it has shifted to the theory of sociological prediction. While prediction has lost a substantive focus, it has gained a methodological perspective. The reaction of American sociologists to this trend has been mixed. Some argue that the emphasis on prediction in the abstract is misplaced, that the emphasis should be on the explanation of problematical effects; others argue that the concern with the formal structure of prediction will serve to refine the process of sociological explanation and its products. Realists find truth in both views.

### Personal Adjustment

A probabilistic estimate that a person will succeed (or fail) by a given criterion in a specific social undertaking is a prediction of personal adjustment (as the term is used here). Examples include the prediction that a person will succeed on parole, on the job, in marriage, in the army.

Much of this work, which flourished in the 1930's, appears to have had its roots in a tradition of concern among sociologists with social problems such as crime and divorce. The very first efforts in prediction (Hart, 1923; Burgess, 1929) sought to demonstrate that prisoners differed in their chances of success on parole and implied that convicts should be sentenced for indeterminate periods and should be released on parole when ready, however brief their stay in prison. The methodology of these studies was gradually extended by statistically minded criminologists to cover practically every phase of the criminal career, including, for example, the delinquency of adolescents and the infractions of prison inmates.

At about the same time, sociologists (along with psychologists) were exploring the possibility of predicting adjustment in marriage. This effort was probably a reaction to the apparently increasing instability of American marriage and the prospect of reversing that trend by improving on the technique of mate selection. The magnitude of this work collectively may be gauged by Kirkpatrick's (1947) assessment of the significance of 88 factors as predictors of marital success; that this line of endeavor failed to fulfill its initial promise is suggested by Bowerman's review (1963).

During World War II various branches of the military availed themselves of sociologists for whatever assistance they (as sociologists) might render. Among other services they were called upon to analyze and to predict the adjustment of soldiers under varying conditions of stress and their adjustment in civilian life after discharge from the armed forces. In their use of the actuary's method, these studies were essentially similar to the earlier studies on parole and marriage; and, like these forerunners, they were undertaken primarily to help make personnel decisions, for example, to guard against giving a soldier the wrong assignment. Examples (Star, 1950; Clausen, 1950) are contained in *Studies in Social Psychology in World War II*, which presents in four volumes the work of the Research Branch, Information and Education Division, War Department. These studies are worthy of note here for two reasons: (1) in their refinements, they register an increasing awareness of the problems of the actuary's approach to prediction; (2) in these same problems, they foreshadow the drift away from this approach during the next decade.

## Method

The method of predicting personal adjustment (at least in principle) is to regress a criterion of adjustment on a composite of $n$ predictor variables (regressors). In symbolic form

$$\hat{y} = b_1 x_1 + b_2 x_2 + \cdots + b_n x_n \tag{5}$$

where $\hat{y}$ is the predicted value, $x_i$ is the $i$th predictor (possibly a dummy variable), and $b_i$ is its weight (coefficient).[1] Once regression values have been calculated, it is possible to obtain the frequency of success (however defined) for persons with similar regression values. The regression analysis thus leads to a set of empirical frequencies, which, for purposes of prediction, are treated as probabilities, much as the frequencies of a life table.

Success is predicted for all persons whose probabilities of success exceed 0.50; otherwise, failure is predicted. By weighting the frequency of each prediction by its expected number of errors, we can calculate the number of errors for all cases. To determine the efficiency of the experience table, the number of errors made with benefit of table is compared with the number of errors made without benefit of table. This approach to efficiency was broached by Guttman in a relatively early paper (1941), subsequently applied by Ohlin and Duncan (1949) to prediction tables in criminology, analyzed as a measure of association by Goodman and Kruskal (1954), and recently, considered for its utility in social analysis by Costner (1965).

## Numerical Example

To illustrate this method and the difficulties it encounters, we briefly consider its use in parole prediction. For purposes of illustration,

Table 4
Frequency distribution of 1,000 parolees, by prediction score

| Prediction score[a] | Number of men in each class interval | Per cent violators on parole |
|---|---|---|
| 16–21 | 68 | 1.5 |
| 14–15 | 140 | 2.2 |
| 13 | 91 | 8.8 |
| 12 | 106 | 15.1 |
| 11 | 110 | 22.7 |
| 10 | 88 | 34.1 |
| 7–9 | 287 | 43.9 |
| 5–6 | 85 | 67.1 |
| 2–4 | 25 | 76.0 |

[a] Score for each parolee is the number of factors on which he scored above the group mean.

Source: Burgess (1928, p. 248).

---

[1] When the prediction system consists altogether of qualitative variables, we may replace equation (5) by a more suitable symbolic expression. For the use of nominal scales in prediction, see Stuckert, 1958; Gould and Schrag, 1962.

the pioneer work of Burgess (1928) will do very well. That investigation culminated in (among other things) a classification of 1,000 parolees according to their prediction scores and the rates of violation in each of nine subclasses. These rates are given in Table 4. (The prediction scores themselves, it should be noted, satisfy no statistical criterion of goodness-of-fit; they merely represent the number of factors favorable to success on parole. They are regression weights in the loosest sense of the term.)

By combining scores above and below 6 in Table 4, we get a 2 × 2 table (Table 5), which is convenient for analyzing the efficiency of the composite predictor variable. (Such a regrouping is possible

Table 5
Outcome

| Score | S | F | Total |
|-------|-----|-----|-------|
| 7–21 | 681 | 209 | 890 |
| 2–6 | 34 | 76 | 110 |
| Total | 715 | 285 | 1000 |

whenever the rates for successive class intervals form a regular progression from low to high.) The expectation (statistical) of a prediction error without benefit of the table is 0.285; the expectation with the table is 0.243. To measure the efficiency of the table, we calculate

$$\text{PRE} = \frac{0.285 - 0.243}{0.285}$$
$$= 0.15$$

Our conclusion is that the table has an efficiency of 15 per cent or that it leads to a 15 per cent reduction in prediction error.

When prediction from the joint table does not produce a substantial reduction in error, one may question whether the table was worth the trouble. That question was behind Ohlin and Duncan's aforementioned investigation (1949) into the efficiency of prediction in criminology. Their general conclusion, based on a comprehensive survey of published works, was that prediction in criminology was not very efficient. This negative conclusion, support for which accumulated during the 1950's, held equally for prediction in other substantive fields (for example, marriage and the family) with the result that the experience table lost some of its attraction as a research topic.

### Decision Theory

The loss in attraction is also attributable to the rise of decision theory, which stressed that selection for parole and the like should

take into account the utilities (social costs) of the various outcomes
as well as the efficiency of a given tabulation (Goodman, 1952; Schuessler, 1968b). To contrast these criteria, by way of example, let us assume
(unrealistically) that, by not releasing a violator, we save $300 and, that
by paroling a nonviolator, we save only $100. These payoffs (around
an arbitrary origin) may be tabulated as follows:

|         | Nonviolator | Violator  |
|---------|-------------|-----------|
| Release | $100.00     | $  0.00   |
| Detain  | 0.00        | 300.00    |

Let us further suppose that one parolee in three is a violator. Should we
release all or none? To minimize our prediction errors, we release all and
make one error in three; to maximize our savings, we detain all in accordance with this logic: we save $\frac{1}{3}$($300 \times 100$) = $10,000 for every
100 persons detained; whereas our saving for every 100 released is
$\frac{2}{3}$($100 \times 100$) = $6,665; therefore, we detain everyone. We thus see
that alternative criteria lead to opposing decisions. If our interest lies
solely in predictive efficiency, we parole all; if our interest lies solely
in minimizing cost or maximizing gain, we parole none.

The conflict between opposing criteria will be eased if we have
access to information about prisoners which permits them to be grouped
into subclasses with violation rates approaching zero or one. For example, if two out of three prisoners fall into class I with a violation rate of
0.125, as in Table 6, it will be advantageous to release all in that class
since the expected utility of that action for every 100 persons is
(0.875)($100 \times 100$) = $8,750, whereas the utility for detention is
(0.125)($300 \times 100$) = $3,750. On the other hand, we would detain all
in class II since the gain for every 100 cases is (0.75)($300 \times 100$) =
$22,500, as compared with (0.25)($100 \times 100$) = $2,500 for the decision
to release everyone. The savings for both subgroups would be $13,333,
which is larger by $3,333 than the expected savings of detaining all
without exception. An implication is that it will be worthwhile to sub-
classify prisoners, provided that sample information costs less than
$3,333 per 100 inmates.

Table 6

| Subclass | Frequency | Violation Rate |
|----------|-----------|----------------|
| I        | .67       | .125           |
| II       | .33       | .750           |
|          | 1.00      |                |

From the foregoing example, one should not conclude that decision theory has suffused the thought and work of contemporary American

sociologists—quite the contrary. With a few scattered exceptions, sociologists have made little use of this method. We mention it here as a development creating doubts about the actuary's experience table as an approach to sociological prediction.

Although the experience table is regularly used for selecting personnel by some public agencies, as a line of sociological research it has been slighted, if not ignored, in recent times. Therefore, it is proper to inquire into its benefits to the discipline. The answer is somewhat platitudinous—a keener appreciation of the obstacles to this line of endeavor. One major obstacle is the deficit of sociological theory which permits predictions to be drawn. In the absence of such theory, predictions are necessarily based on empirical regularities; but empirical correlations and the like, being subject to the accidents of local time and place, do not generally afford a secure basis for prediction. For example, the best weights for predicting a criterion variable in one period may be relatively useless for predicting the same criterion in a later period. The obvious solution is to base predictions on scientific laws which hold regardless of local conditions. But this is much easier said than done.

A second major obstacle is the relatively undeveloped state of sociological measurement (previously noted in another connection). In the absence of discriminating measures of known dependability, it is impossible to determine whether a weak result is a reflection of fact or the consequence of unreliable measurement. It is impossible, for example, to assess the force of anomie as a factor in suicide if reliable measures of anomie are unobtainable. We mention this point because of its implications for improving the efficiency of prediction tables. The obvious remedy is to devise better measures of sociological phenomena. But, like devising adequate theory, this is easier said than done. We note in passing that the problems of theory and measurement are present in every branch of sociology.

## Mathematical Models

Owing to their indifferent success, sociologists have not pressed their investigation into the prediction of personal adjustment, and few are engaged in this endeavor at the moment. Increasingly, their attention has been drawn to mathematical models (Coleman, 1964), which appear to have some promise for the prediction of social behavior. Although they have looked into a wide variety of models, their efforts have revolved largely around simultaneous equations and Markov-chain processes. Corresponding to this concentration, we limit our review to the utilization of these methods in sociology.

## Structural-Equation Model

Simultaneous-equation models have made their way into American sociology from economics and biology, although in somewhat different guises. Blalock (1969) has been largely responsible for bringing in the structural-equation models of econometrics; Duncan (1966) for bringing in the path models of genetic biology. However, our concern is not with the diffusion of this technique but rather with its potentiality for sociological prediction, as reflected in current studies. Before considering these studies, we give a little information about the method in general, extracted largely from Klein's (1968) essay on the theory of economic prediction.

If we start with a system of $m$ dependent variables ($y$'s), and $(n - m)$ predetermined variables ($x$'s), this method requires that the error term ($e_i$) for each dependent variable be written as a function of all $n$ variables. If we restrict ourselves to linear equations, as in this discussion, we obtain each error term as the sum of $n$ weighted variables. In the simple case of two dependent $y_1$ and $y_2$ and a single predetermined variable $x$ we have the model

$$-e_1 = b_{11}y_1 + b_{12}y_2 + a_1x$$
$$-e_2 = b_{21}y_1 + b_{22}y_2 + a_2x \tag{6}$$

Because equation (6) represents the structure of the system (as defined), it is said to be in structural form; because the coefficients on the variables are measures of properties of the structure, they have come to be known as structural coefficients.

The model may be simplified by setting some coefficients equal to zero. For example, if we set $b_{12} = 0$, we get

$$-e_1 = b_{11}y_1 + a_1x$$
$$-e_2 = b_{21}y_1 + b_{22}y_2 + a_2x \tag{7}$$

or a recursive system in which all relations are asymmetrical. Such a simplification may be dictated either by sociological theory or by the statistically unmanageable nature of a more general formulation (for example, one making provision for reciprocal influence). My impression is that the use of recursive models in sociology has been dictated more by practical statistical considerations than by incontrovertible sociological reasoning.

By manipulating the structural equations, we can express each dependent variable as a function of its error term and of the $(n - m)$

predetermined variables. In the case of equation (7), each variable would take the form of a sum of weighted parts as follows:

$$y_1 = \frac{a_1}{b_{11}}(x) + \frac{1}{b_{11}}(e_1)$$
$$y_2 = \frac{b_{21}}{b_{22}}(y_1) + \frac{a_2}{b_{22}}(x) + \frac{1}{b_{22}}(e_2)$$

(8)

Because coefficients on the right side of equation (8) have been reduced by the factor $1/b_{ii}$, the model is said to be in reduced form. The significance of reduced form for prediction is this: the general problem of prediction is to estimate the value of a given dependent variable from the known values of the predetermined variables. Since the equations in reduced form will yield such estimates without further operations, they are related most directly to the requirements of prediction (Klein, 1968, p. 18).

In their work American sociologists have generally framed their models in reduced form, although they have usually not had predictions in mind. Furthermore, they have generally restricted themselves to systems of linear, additive, and asymmetrical relations. This latter point is not made as a criticism but rather as an indication that at the moment sociologists are operating at a relatively elementary level in their use of simultaneous-equation models. As an example of this assessment, we cite two recent studies.

Our first case in point is Hodge and Treiman's (1968) study of individual differences in social participation (as defined). These investigators sought to determine, among other matters, whether differences in participation ($x_1$) among men in their sample could be explained by the individual's own occupation ($x_2$) and education ($x_3$) together with his father's social participation ($x_4$), occupation ($x_5$), and education ($x_6$). They took as their point of departure the following linear system; all variables in standard form at the start:

$$x_1 = p_{12}x_2 + p_{13}x_3 + p_{14}x_4 + p_{15}x_5 + p_{16}x_6 + p_{1u}u_1$$
$$x_2 = \qquad p_{23}x_3 + p_{24}x_4 + p_{25}x_5 + p_{26}x_6 + p_{2u}u_2$$
$$x_3 = \qquad\qquad p_{34}x_4 + p_{35}x_5 + p_{36}x_6 + p_{3u}u_3$$
$$x_4 = \qquad\qquad\qquad p_{45}x_5 + p_{46}x_6 + p_{4u}u_4$$

(9)

where $p_{ij}$ is the coefficient of the $i$th dependent variable on the $j$th predetermined variable and $u_i$ is the error term for the $i$th dependent variable. Since $p_{ij}$ measures the strength of the path from $j$ to $i$, it is referred to as a path coefficient.

For what seemed to them plausible sociological reasons, they set

$p_{15} = p_{16} = p_{24} = p_{34} = 0$ and, thereby, obtained the simpler model

$$
\begin{aligned}
x_1 &= p_{12}x_2 + p_{13}x_3 + p_{14}x_4 && + p_{1u}u_1 \\
x_2 &= \phantom{p_{12}x_2 +} p_{23}x_3 && + p_{25}x_5 + p_{26}x_6 + p_{2u}u_2 \\
x_3 &= && \phantom{+} p_{35}x_5 + p_{36}x_6 + p_{3u}u_3 \\
x_4 &= && \phantom{+} p_{45}x_5 + p_{46}x_6 + p_{4u}u_4
\end{aligned}
\tag{10}
$$

To estimate the path coefficients they had recourse to ordinary least squares, with results as shown in Table 7. Now it may be shown that these estimates are identical with standardized partial-regression coefficients, or beta weights. And by virtue of this identity, the mean of the squared estimates for each dependent variable is equal to the squared multiple correlation coefficient ($R^2$) of that variable and its regressors. Also, it may be shown that $1 - R^2 = p_{iu}^2$, or the squared path coefficient of the $i$th variable on its own disturbance term. Hence, to gauge the efficiency of specific estimates within a recursive system, it is necessary only to calculate $1 - p_{iu}^2 = R^2$.

Table 7

Estimated $p_{ij}(i < j)$ and $R^2$ for Hodge-Treiman Model

| Variable | 2 | 3 | 4 | 5 | 6 | $u$ | $p_{iu}^2$ | $1 - p_{iu}^2 = R^2$ |
|---|---|---|---|---|---|---|---|---|
| 1 | 0.13 | 0.19 | 0.29 | | | 0.91 | 0.82 | 0.18 |
| 2 | | 0.53 | | 0.06 | 0.04 | 0.82 | 0.68 | 0.32 |
| 3 | | | | 0.28 | 0.19 | 0.92 | 0.84 | 0.16 |
| 4 | | | | 0.15 | 0.22 | 0.95 | 0.89 | 0.11 |

Source: Hodge and Treiman (1968).

These calculations, given in the last two columns of Table 7, more or less speak for themselves. In no case do the predetermined variables reduce the criterion variance by more than one-third. All in all, estimates based on fitted path coefficients were 20 per cent more efficient than estimates based on the means of the variables themselves; that is, squared deviations from regression estimates were 20 per cent smaller than squared deviations from means. Nevertheless, the model, as it stands, may be a reasonably accurate representation of the social process giving rise to differences in social participation. These differences may be largely the product of a process in which determining factors are swamped by random factors. Exponents of path models and the like stress that the validity of a model does not depend on the magnitude of $R^2$ but rather on the assumption that all determining variables have been included in the system and their relations to the dependent variables correctly specified.

Sewell, Haller, and Portes' (1969) study of individual differences in educational and occupational attainment supplies our second example. Their recursive system consisted of eight variables—two predetermined ($x_7$ and $x_8$) and six endogenous (dependent)—whose relations they took to be linear, additive, and asymmetrical. For apparently sound reasons, they eliminated some of the possible direct links to arrive at the following specialized model:

$$
\begin{aligned}
x_1 &= p_{12}x_2 + p_{13}x_3 + p_{1u}u_1 \\
x_2 &= p_{24}x_4 + p_{25}x_5 + p_{2u}u_2 \\
x_3 &= p_{35}x_5 + p_{3u}u_2 \\
x_4 &= p_{45}x_5 + p_{4u}u_4 \\
x_5 &= p_{56}x_6 + p_{57}x_7 + p_{5u}u_5 \\
x_6 &= p_{68}x_8 + p_{6u}u_6
\end{aligned}
\tag{11}
$$

where $x_1$ = occupational attainment, $x_2$ = educational attainment, $x_3$ = occupational aspiration, $x_4$ = educational aspiration, $x_5$ = significant others' influence, $x_6$ = academic performance, $x_7$ = socioeconomic status, and $x_8$ = mental ability.

To test the validity of this model, they calculated every possible standardized partial regression coefficient for the fully recursive system and compared the observed and predicted values. These results are given in Table 8. From this table, it may be seen that their hypotheses are generally sustained. The authors' comment: "Each of the path coefficients for the causal lines hypothesized . . . is larger than those not hypothesized" (p. 88). Later, they state: "None of the unpredicted paths is very strong" (p. 88). They do take cognizance of $p_{46} = 0.18$, and $p_{26} = 0.17$ which were by hypothesis equal to zero and offer some possible substantive explanations.

Table 8

Estimated $p_{ij}(i < j)$ for All Possible Paths

| Variable | 2 | 3 | 4 | 5 | 6 | 7 | 8 |
|---|---|---|---|---|---|---|---|
| 1 | 0.38 | 0.19 | −0.10 | 0.11 | 0.06 | 0.00 | 0.04 |
| 2 | | 0.07 | 0.34 | 0.23 | 0.17 | 0.05 | 0.03 |
| 3 | | | | 0.42 | 0.12 | −0.02 | 0.16 |
| 4 | | | | 0.45 | 0.18 | 0.07 | 0.08 |
| 5 | | | | | 0.39 | 0.21 | 0.13 |
| 6 | | | | | | 0.01 | 0.62 |

Source: Sewell, Haller, and Portes (1969).

However, our interest lies not in the evidential value of the findings but rather in their value for purposes of estimating educational and occupational attainment. Upon calculating $1 - p_{iu}^2$, which may be taken as a measure of the efficiency of fitted constants, we get the results in Table 9.

Table 9

| Variable | $p_{iu}$ | $1 - p_{iu}^2 = R^2$ |
|----------|----------|----------------------|
| 1        | 0.81     | 0.34                 |
| 2        | 0.71     | 0.50                 |

These results are consistent with what was said before, namely: the use of path models does not necessarily lead to a significant reduction in prediction error.

This conclusion is deserving of elaboration since it may be misunderstood. The purpose of a prediction model, by definition, is to make predictions. However, the validity of such a model should not be judged by its predictive efficiency, since that efficiency will depend on the relative force of the determining factors in the system. If their force relative to the stochastic term is negligible, predictive efficiency (as measured by $R^2$) will tend to zero even though the model is a valid representation of the process in question. On the other hand, when the stochastic terms tend to zero, efficiency ($R^2$) may be high even though the specifications of the model are poorly drawn. An indeterminate system will necessarily yield low predictive efficiency, however valid the modeling; whereas the efficiency of a determinate system may be high, even though the system is incorrectly specified.

## Markov-Chain Models

The current interest of American sociologists in the Markov-chain process, including its potential for prediction, was probably kindled by its suggestive applications in psychology and economics. In fact, much of their recent work is directly or indirectly related to Blumen, Kogan, and McCarthy's (1955) attempt to determine whether the movement of workers among industries from one quarter (three months) to the next might be represented by a Markov-chain process. Their general procedure was to ascertain the fraction of workers moving from one industry to another, from one quarter to the next. They interpreted these fractions as "probabilities in the sense that if a worker is selected at random from among those employed in 1 in the first of two quarters, the probability is $p_{11}$ that he is employed in 1 in the second quarter, and so on" (p. 51). Together, these probabilities constitute a stochastic matrix, by reason that all entries are nonnegative and all row sums are equal to one.

By raising the matrix of transition probabilities to some power $k$, we can determine the probability of a worker staying or moving to some other category after $k$ quarters (on the assumption that worker mobility is a Markov-chain process). In their analysis Blumen, Kogan, and McCarthy (1955) calculated the probability of one's being in a given industry after twelve consecutive quarters (since they had figures for that many quarters). By comparing expected (calculated) frequencies with those observed, they were able to test the possibility that worker mobility conformed to a Markov process. Because this initial fitting was not very good, they divided their sample of workers into stayers (those never moving) and movers and repeated the exercise on these two subclasses.

Our concern is not with the details of these findings but rather with the suggestive value they seemed to hold for sociologists. They carried the implication that social mobility on the level of the person is a process which lends itself to representation by a probability process. Understandably, this possibility has been pursued mainly by statistically minded sociologists with a substantive interest in social mobility (Goodman, 1962). It seems fair to say that their contributions thus far have been mainly along methodological lines and that the potential of this approach—except perhaps in the field of demography—has not been convincingly demonstrated by empirical materials. To exemplify this line of endeavor and the complications it faces, we comment briefly on recent papers by McGinnis (1968) and McFarland (1970), whose contributions are closely related although not strictly complementary.

McGinnis accepts the idea that mobility between social statuses is a stochastic process but rejects the simple Markov chain as unrealistic. He comments (1968, p. 716): "people are not necessarily homogeneous in their tendencies to be mobile even though they may be in a common location at a particular time. A number of sources made it seem equally plausible that movement out of a status position . . . is constrained chiefly by one's ties to that position. Moreover, the strength of those ties normally should be expected to grow with the passage of time."

To take into account the effect of "cumulative inertia" (the tendency to become tied down), McGinnis suggests that probabilities of moving be conditional on both status and duration within status. In brief, probabilities are permitted to vary within statuses as well as between them. Since the model assumes that probabilities change over time, it becomes necessary to calculate probabilities within each status for longer or shorter intervals. And from such calculations one may approximate the functional relationship between the transition probabilities and duration in status, and from this mathematical function one may go on to estimate the rate of change in these probabilities at any instant. In its essentials this is the technique proposed by McGinnis and his associates. As of this writing, it has not been applied to large bodies of actual data, and the problems it will encounter in practice are unknown. The mobility of American scientists is currently under study by McGinnis and his coworkers (located at Cornell University), and this undertaking may yield data to test both the practical limitations of the technique and the validity of the model itself.

As our second example, we cite McFarland's (1970) recent paper, partly because of its continuity with the work of McGinnis (which itself is a continuation of earlier efforts) and partly because it brings out the issues which unite and divide this circle of investigators. Mc-Farland does not question the finding that the rate of mobility in a cohort declines over time but does question whether persons within the same status are homogeneous in their transition probabilities, as in the cumulative-inertia model. As an alternative, he advances the hypothesis that a population, heterogeneous in its transition probabilities, could experience a decline in mobility rates over time, notwithstanding that individuals in their own probabilities are constant over time (the assumption of stationarity).

Whatever the validity of this counter claim, it does reflect recent efforts to formulate probability process models without the restrictions that transition probabilities be constant over time, a given move be affected only by one's present state, and persons within states be homogeneous in their probabilities. Since one or more of these assumptions may be at odds with the sociological process, it is understandable that exponents of this method have moved toward sociologically less naive alternatives.

## Concluding Remark

The modelling of social process, whether by probability chain or linear equations, has not produced much in the way of predictive knowledge, and judging from its results to date, one might suppose that its prospects of doing that are not very bright. There is truth to this skepticism if one means that modelling will yield predictive knowledge next month or next year. But its long-run prospects may be better. The modelling of social structure and process, particularly by means of structural equations, requires that the lines of influence among the elements (variables) comprising a system be precisely specified and that the magnitude of these effects be identified and measured. Although these requirements may be no more than a version of the principle that hypotheses be exactly stated and conclusively tested, they are less easily disregarded when made explicit. If the methods of sociometrics—equivalent by definition to those of econometrics—reach their goal of specifying and identifying all of the factors producing a given effect, then an emphasis on those methods should facilitate the attainment of predictive knowledge in the long run. Of course, if the social process by nature is intractable to measurement, or if sociologists are insufficiently clever to measure it, then the prospects of sociometrics for yielding predictive knowledge are dim.

## EPILOGUE

The foregoing account more or less supplies its own answer to our starting question: There has been no unbroken chain of efforts in the field of sociological prediction during the last 50 years. In fact, one gets the opposite impression that efforts were somewhat episodic and, at times, no more than faddish. One may ask whether this negative conclusion holds only for our sample of materials and whether it might be dispelled by a comprehensive review and analysis of the literature. My view on this is that the materials included herein are quite representative and that an exhaustive content analysis would not change the conclusion of little or no continuity in prediction work.

At this juncture, it is therefore proper to raise the question: Why has there been the lack of continuity? The general answer to that question lies in the uncertainty of American sociologists over their goals and priorities. American sociologists have been torn between physics and history as models for their subject. Those taking physics as their model tend to concentrate on scientific laws and prediction; those taking history as their model tend to concentrate on recent social and political movements and their implications for social planning. Although there is no intrinsic connection between one's conception of sociology and one's method, those conceiving of sociology as a natural science tend to emphasize mathematical methods, while those conceiving of sociology as history tend to rely on more traditional methods of historical study.

Now if it were possible to separate sociologists into circles according to whether their emphasis was on scientific laws and prediction or on social history and forecasting, one could survey the progress of each circle and pass judgment on its progress. But matters are not that simple. Not only do sociologists differ among themselves about priorities, but also they differ within themselves from time to time. The same person may declare at one time that the utility of his research for purposes of planning the future is irrelevant and later argue that such utility is its principal justification.

To complicate matters, much work carried on in the name of prediction is essentially prognostic in nature and only loosely related to the search for predictive knowledge. For example, the parole prediction table is sometimes used clinically to make a prognosis (favorable or unfavorable) of recidivism for the individual convict; still, as in this chapter that table is commonly cited as an example of sociological prediction. On the other hand, social forecasts are sometimes drawn from general propositions which purport to afford a universal basis for prediction. Ogburn's forecast of the social effects of aviation rests in the last analysis on his laws of social change which to his mind held irrespective of time or place.

In alluding to the diversity of effort among and within sociologists, our aim is not to suggest (presumptuously) that in the past sociologists should have arranged their work schedules differently but rather to account for the lack of continuity in the field of prediction. Until such time as sociologists are less uncertain as regards their objectives, we may anticipate a continuation of this state of affairs. The recent attack on social mobility by various methods carries promise, and, if sustained over a period of time, may yield a reliable basis for prediction.

## REFERENCES

BELL, DANIEL
    1967    "The year 2000—the trajectory of an idea." *Daedalus* (Summer): 639–651.
BLALOCK, H. M., JR.
    1969    *Theory Construction*. Englewood Cliffs, N.J.: Prentice-Hall.
BLUMEN, I., KOGAN, M., AND MCCARTHY, P.
    1955    *The Industrial Mobility of Labor as a Probability Process*. New York: Cornell University Press.
BOULDING, K.
    1964    *The Meaning of the Twentieth Century*. New York: Harper & Row.
BOWERMAN, C. E.
    1964    "Prediction Studies." Pp. 215–246 in H. T. Christensen (Ed.), *Handbook of Marriage and the Family*. Chicago: Rand McNally.
BURGESS, E. W.
    1928    "Factors determining success or failure on parole." Pp. 203–249 in Illinois Committee on Indeterminate-sentence Law and Parole. *The Workings of the Indeterminate-sentence Law and the Parole System in Illinois*. Springfield, Ill.: Division of Pardons and Paroles.
CLAUSEN, J. A.
    1950    "Studies of the postwar plans of soldiers: A problem in prediction." Pp. 568–708 in S. A. Stouffer and others

(Eds.), *Measurement and Prediction: Studies in Social Psychology in World War II*. Vol. 4. Princeton, N.J.: Princeton University Press.

COLEMAN, J. S.

1964 *Introduction to Mathematical Sociology*. Glencoe, Ill.: The Free Press.

COSTNER, H.

1965 "Criteria for measures of association." *American Sociological Review* 30: 341–353.

DORN, H. F.

1950 "Pitfalls in population forecasts and projections." *Journal of the American Statistical Association* 45: 311–334.

DUNCAN, O. D.

1966 "Path analysis: Sociological examples." *American Journal of Sociology* 72: 1–16.

1969a "Social forecasting: The state of the art." *The Public Interest*, Number 17, 88–118.

1969b *Toward Social Reporting: Next Steps*. New York: Russell Sage Foundation.

GOODMAN, L.

1952 "Generalizing the problem of prediction." *American Sociological Review* 17: 609–612.

1962 "Statistical methods for analyzing processes of change." *American Journal of Sociology* 68: 57–78.

GOODMAN, L. AND KRUSKAL, W. F.

1954 "Measures of association for cross-classification." *Journal of the American Statistical Association* 49: 732–763.

GOULD, L., AND SCHRAG, C.

1962 "Theory construction and prediction in juvenile delinquency," *Proceedings of the American Statistical Association* 68–73.

GUTTMAN, L.

1941 "Mathematical and tabulation techniques." Pp. 251–364 in P. Horst and others (Eds.), *The Prediction of Personal Adjustment*. New York: Committee on Social Adjustment, Social Science Research Council.

HART, H.

1923 "Predicting parole success." *Journal of Criminal Law and Criminology*, 14: 405–414.

HODGE, R. W. AND TREIMAN, D. J.

1968 "Social participation and social status." *American Sociological Review* 33: 722–739.

IKLÉ, F. C.

1967 "Can social predictions be evaluated?" *Daedalus* (Summer): 733–758.

KIRKPATRICK, C.

1947 *What Science Says about Happiness in Marriage*. Minneapolis: Burgess Publishing Co.

KLEIN, L. R.

1968 *An Essay on the Theory of Economic Prediction*. Helsinki: Jahnsson Foundation.

MCGINNIS, R.

1968 "A stochastic model of social mobility." *American Sociological Review* 33: 712–721.

MCFARLAND, D. D.

1970 "Intragenerational social mobility as a Markov process." *American Sociological Review* 35: 463–476.

MILLER, S. M. AND ROBY, P. A.

1970 *The Future of Inequality*. New York: Basic Books.

MOORE, W. E.

1963 *Social Change*. Englewood Cliffs, N.J.: Prentice-Hall.

MOSTELLER, F., AND OTHERS

1949 *The Pre-Election Polls of 1948*. New York: Social Science Research Council.

MOYNIHAN, DANIEL P.

1967 "The relationship of federal to local authorities." *Daedalus* (Summer): 801–808.

OGBURN, W. F., ADAMS, J. L., AND GILFILLAN, S. C.

1946 *The Social Effects of Aviation*. Boston: Houghton Mifflin.

OHLIN, L. E. AND DUNCAN, O. D.

1949 "The efficiency of prediction in criminology." *American Journal of Sociology* 54: 441–451.

PEARL, R. AND REED, L. J.

1920 "On the rate of growth of the population of the United States since 1790 and its mathematical representation." *Proceedings of the National Academy of Science* 6: 275–288.

RIESMAN, DAVID

1967 "Notes on meritocracy." *Daedalus* (Summer): 897–908.

SCHUESSLER, K. F.

1968a "Prediction," *International Encyclopedia of the Social Sciences* 12: 418–423.

1968b "Notes on sociology and the Bayesian approach." Paper read before meeting of Southern Sociological Society at New Orleans.

SEWELL, W. H., HALLER, A. O., AND PORTES, A.

1969 "The educational and early occupational attainment process." *American Sociological Review* 34: 82–92.

STAR, S.

1950 "The screening of psychoneurotics in the army." Pp. 486–567 in S. A. Stouffer and others (Eds.), *Measurement and Prediction: Studies in Social Psychology in World War II*. Vol. 4. Princeton, N.J.: Princeton University Press.

STUCKERT, R. P.

1958 "A configurational approach to prediction." *Sociometry* 21: 235–237.

U.S. BUREAU OF THE CENSUS

1970 "Projections of the population of the United States by age and sex: 1970–2020." *Current Population Reports*, Series P-25, No. 448, Washington, D.C.

U.S. NATIONAL RESOURCES COMMITTEE

1937 *Technological Trends and National Policy*. Washington: Government Printing Office.

WHELPTON, P. K.

1928 "Population in the United States, 1925–1975." *American Journal of Sociology* 34: 253–270.

WOLD, H. O.

1967 "Forecasting and scientific method." Pp. 1–65 in *Forecasting on a Scientific Basis*. Lisbon: Gulbenkian Foundation.

# NAME INDEX

331

# SUBJECT INDEX

## A

Autocorrelated errors, 142

## C

Canonical correlation, 106, 112–114
Coding, 60–78 passim
Comparative statics, 191–192
Computer simulation, 189
Confirmatory factor analysis, 84, 90
Correlation ratio, 149, 284, 298

## D

Dependence analysis, 81
Detection theory, 34–58 passim
Discriminal distribution, 37, 39, 42–43, 47, 49, 54
Discriminal processes, 37, 39, 53
Dummy-variable analysis, 131–132, 149, 155–156, 159, 169, 314
Dynamic model, 191, 222, 225, 227–229

## E

Effect-proportional recalibration, 148, 165–169
Endogenous variables, 151, 192–197, 202, 212–213
Exogenous variables, 151, 156, 192–193, 212
Explanatory theorizing, 271–273

## F

Factor analysis, 91, 93, 95, 99, 100n, 119. *See also* Confirmatory factor analysis, Second-order factor analytic model
Feedback, 148. *See also* Nonrecursive model
Forecasting, 305–307, 309. *See also* Prediction

## G

General linear model, 112

335